LSAT Hacks

Explanations for 10 Actual, Official LSAT Preptests, Volume V

LSATs 62-71

Volume II: Preptests 67-71

Graeme Blake

ISBN 13: 978-1-927997-05-5
ISBN 10: 1-927997-05-4

Testimonials

Self-study is my preferred way to prep, but I often felt myself missing a few questions each test. Especially for Logic Games, I wanted to see those key inferences which I just couldn't seem to spot on my own. That's where *LSAT Hacks* came in. These solutions have been a tremendous help for my prep, and in training myself to think the way an experienced test taker would.

- Spencer B.

Graeme paraphrases the question in plain terms, and walks through each step in obtaining the right answer in a very logical way. This book uses the same techniques as other guides, but its so much more consistent and concise! By the time you read through all the tests, you've gradually developed your eye for the questions. Using this book is a great way to test your mastery of techniques!

- Sara L.

Graeme's explanations have the most logical and understandable layout I've seen in an LSAT prep book. The explanations are straightforward and easy to understand, to the point where they make you smack your forehead and say 'of course!

- Michelle V.

"Graeme is someone who clearly demonstrates not only LSAT mastery, but the ability to explain it in a compelling manner. This book is an excellent addition to whatever arsenal you're amassing to tackle the LSAT."

- J.Y. Ping, 7Sage LSAT,
www.7Sage.com

I did not go through every single answer but rather used the explanations to see if they could explain why my answer was wrong and the other correct. I thought the breakdown of "Type", "Conclusion", "Reasoning" and "Analysis" was extremely useful in simplifying the question. As for quality of the explanations I'd give them a 10 out of 10.

- Christian F.

LSAT PrepTests come with answer keys, but it isn't sufficient to know whether or not you picked the credited choice to any given question. The key to making significant gains on this test is understanding the logic underlying the questions.

This is where Graeme's explanations really shine. You may wonder whether your reasoning for a specific question is sound. For the particularly challenging questions, you may be at a complete loss as to how they should be approached.

Having these questions explained by Graeme who scored a 177 on the test is akin to hiring an elite tutor at a fraction of the price. These straightforward explanations will help you improve your performance and, more fundamentally, enhance your overall grasp of the test content.

- Morley Tatro, Cambridge LSAT,
www.cambridgelsat.com

Through his conversational tone, helpful introductions, and general recommendations and tips, Graeme Blake has created an enormously helpful companion volume to *The Next Ten Actual Official LSATs*. He strikes a nice balance between providing the clarity and basic explanation of the questions that is needed for a beginner and describing the more complicated techniques that are necessary for a more advanced student.

Even though the subject matter can be quite dry, Graeme succeeds in making his explanations fun and lighthearted. This is crucial: studying for the LSAT is a daunting and arduous task. By injecting some humor and keeping a casual tone, the painful process of mastering the LSAT becomes a little less painful.

When you use *LSAT Hacks* in your studying, you will feel like you have a fun and knowledgeable tutor guiding you along the way.

- Law Schuelke, LSAT Tutor,
www.lawLSAT.com

Graeme's explanations are clear, concise and extremely helpful. They've seriously helped me increase my understanding of the LSAT material!

- **Jason H.**

Graeme's book brings a different view to demystifying the LSAT. The book not only explains the right and wrong answers, but teaches you how to read the reading comprehension and the logical reasoning questions. His technique to set up the games rule by rule help me not making any fatal mistakes in the set up. The strategies he teaches can be useful for someone starting as much as for someone wanting to perfect his strategies. Without his help my LSAT score would have been average, he brought my understanding of the LSAT and my score to a higher level even if english is not my mother tongue.

- **Patrick Du.**

This book is a must buy for any who are looking to pass or improve their LSAT, I highly recommend it.

- **Patrick Da.**

This book was really useful to help me understand the questions that I had more difficulty on. When I was not sure as to why the answer to a certain question was that one, the explanations helped me understand where and why I missed the right answer in the first place. I recommend this book to anyone who would like to better understand the mistakes they make.

- **Pamela G.**

Graeme's book is filled with thoughtful and helpful suggestions on how to strategize for the LSAT test. It is well-organized and provides concise explanations and is definitely a good companion for LSAT preparation.

- **Lydia L.**

The explanations are amazing, great job. I can hear your voice in my head as I read through the text.

- **Shawn M.**

LSAT Hacks, especially the logic games sections, was extremely helpful to my LSAT preparation.

The one downside to self study is that sometimes we do not know why we got a question wrong and thus find it hard to move forward. Graeme's book fixes that; it offers explanations and allows you to see where you went wrong. This is an extremely helpful tool and I'd recommend it to anybody that's looking for an additional study supplement.

- **Joseph C.**

Regardless of how well you're scoring on the LSAT, this book is very helpful. I used it for LR and RC. It breaks down and analyzes each question without the distraction of classification and complicated methods you'll find in some strategy books. Instead of using step-by-step procedures for each question, the analyses focus on using basic critical thinking skills and common sense that point your intuition in the right direction. Even for questions you're getting right, it still helps reinforce the correct thought process. A must-have companion for reviewing prep tests.

- **Christine Y.**

Take a thorough mastery of the test, an easygoing demeanor, and a genuine desire to help, and you've got a solid resource for fine-tuning your approach when you're tirelessly plowing through test after test. Written from the perspective of a test-taker, this book should help guide your entire thought process for each question, start to finish.

- **Yoni Stratievsky, Harvard Ready,** www.harvardready.com

This LSAT guide is the best tool I could have when preparing for the LSAT. Not only does Graeme do a great job of explaining the sections as a whole, he also offers brilliant explanations for each question. He takes the time to explain why an answer is wrong, which is far more helpful when trying to form a studying pattern.

- **Amelia F.**

Explanations for 10 Actual, Official LSAT Preptests
Volume II: Preptests 67-71

Table Of Contents

Preptest 69

Preptest 70

Introduction

The LSAT is a hard test.

The only people who take the LSAT are smart people who did well in University. The LSAT takes the very best students, and forces them to compete.

If the test's difficulty shocked you, this is why. The LSAT is a test designed to be hard for smart people.

That's the bad news. But there's hope. The LSAT is a *standardized* test. It has patterns. It can be learned.

To get better, you have to review your mistakes. Many students write tests and move on, without fully understanding their mistakes.

This is understandable. The LSAC doesn't publish official explanations for most tests. It's hard to be sure why you were wrong.

That's where this book comes in. It's a companion for LSAT Preptests 62-71. This volume covers 67-71.

This book lets you see where you went wrong. It has a full walk through of each question and of every answer choice. You can use this book to fix your mistakes, and make sure you understand *everything*.

By getting this book, you've shown that you're serious about beating this test. I sincerely hope it helps you get the score you want.

There are a few things that I'd like to highlight.

Logical Reasoning: It can be hard to identify conclusions in LR. You don't get feedback on whether you identified the conclusion correctly.

This book gives you that feedback. I've identified the conclusion and the reasoning for each argument. Try to find these on your own beforehand, and make sure they match mine.

Logic Games: Do the game on your own before looking at my explanation. You can't think about a game unless you're familiar with the rules. Once you read my explanations, draw my diagrams yourself on a sheet of paper. You'll understand them much better by recopying them.

Reading Comprehension: You should form a mental map of the passage. This helps you locate details quickly. Make a 1-2 line summary of each paragraph (it can be a mental summary).

I've written my own summaries for each passage. They show the minimum amount of information that you should know after reading a passage, without looking back.

I've included line references in my explanations. You do not need to check these each time. They're only there in case you aren't sure where something is.

Do these three things, and you can answer most Reading Comprehension questions with ease.:

1. Know the point of the passage.
2. Understand the passage, in broad terms. Reread anything you don't understand.
3. Know where to find details. That's the point of the paragraph summaries. I usually do mine in my head, and they're shorter than what I've written.

Review This Book

Before we start, I'd like to ask you a favor. I'm an independent LSAT instructor. I don't have a marketing budget.

But I do my best to make good guides to the LSAT. If you agree, I would love it if you took two minutes to write a review on amazon.com

People judge a book by its reviews. So if you like this guide you can help others discover it. I'd be very grateful.

Good luck!

Graeme

p.s. I'm a real person, and I want to know how the LSAT goes and what you think of this book. Send me an email at graeme@lsathacks.com!

p.p.s. For more books, check out the further reading section at the back. I'm also offering a free half hour LSAT lesson if you fill out a survey.

How To Use This Book

The word "Hacks" in the title is meant in the sense used by the tech world and Lifehacker: "solving a problem" or "finding a better way".

The LSAT can be beaten, but you need a good method. My goal is for you to use this book to understand your mistakes and master the LSAT.

This book is *not* a replacement for practicing LSAT questions on your own.

You have to try the questions by yourself first. When you review, try to see why you were wrong *before* you look at my explanations.

Active review will teach you to fix your own mistakes. The explanations are there for when you have difficulty solving on a question on your own or when you want another perspective on a question.

When you *do* use the explanations, have the question on hand. These explanations are not meant to be read alone. You should use them to help you think about the questions more deeply.

Most of the logical reasoning explanations are pretty straightforward. Necessary assumption questions are often an exception, so I want to give you some guidance to help you interpret the explanations.

The easiest way to test the right answer on a necessary assumption question is to "negate" it.

You negate a statement by making it false, in the slightest possible way. For example, the negation of "The Yankees will win all their games" is "The Yankees will *not* win all their games (they will lose at least one)."

You *don't* have to say that the Yankees will lose *every* game. That goes too far.

If the negation of an answer choice proves the conclusion wrong, then that answer is *necessary* to the argument, and it's the correct answer.

Often, I negate the answer choices when explaining necessary assumption questions, so just keep in mind why they're negated.

Logic games also deserve special mention.

Diagramming is a special symbolic language that you have to get comfortable with to succeed.

If you just *look* at my diagrams without making them yourself, you may find it hard to follow along. You can only learn a language by using it yourself.

So you will learn *much* more if you draw the diagrams on your own. Once you've seen how I do a setup, try to do it again by yourself.

With constant practice, you *will* get better at diagramming, and soon it will come naturally.

But you must try on your own. Draw the diagrams.

Note that when you draw your own diagrams, you don't have to copy every detail from mine. For example, I often leave off the numbers when I do linear games. I've included them in the book, because they make it easier for you to follow along.

But under timed conditions, I leave out many details so that I can draw diagrams faster. If you practice making drawings with fewer details, they become just as easy to understand.

Keep diagrams as minimal as possible.

If you simply don't *like* the way I draw a certain rule type, then you can substitute in your own style of diagram. Lots of people succeed using different styles of drawing.

Just make sure your replacement is easy to draw consistently, and that the logical effect is the same. I've chosen these diagrams because they are clear, they're easy to draw, and they *keep you from forgetting rules*.

I've included line references to justify Reading Comprehension Answers. Use these only in case you're unsure about an explanation. You don't have to go back to the passage for every line reference.

Short Guide to Logical Reasoning

LR Question Types

Must be True: The correct answer is true.

Most Strongly Supported: The correct answer is probably true.

Strengthen/Weaken: The answer is correct if it even slightly strengthens/weakens the argument.

Parallel Reasoning: The correct answer will mirror the argument's structure exactly. It is often useful to diagram these questions (but not always).

Sufficient Assumption: The correct answer will prove the conclusion. It's often useful to diagram sufficient assumption questions. For example:

The conclusion is: A ➝ D

There is a gap between premises and conclusion:

A   B ➝ C ➝ D   **missing link:** A ➝ B or B̶ ➝ A̶

A ➝ B ➝ C   D   **missing link:** C ➝ D or D̶ ➝ C̶

A ➝ B   C ➝ D   **missing link:** B ➝ C or C̶ ➝ B̶

The right answer will provide the missing link.

Necessary Assumption: The correct answer will be essential to the argument's conclusion. Use the negation technique: If the correct answer is false (negated), then the argument falls apart.
The negation of hot is "not hot" rather than cold.

Point at Issue: Point at Issue questions require two things. **1.** The two speakers must express an opinion on something. **2.** They must disagree about it.

Flawed Reasoning: The correct answer will be a description of a reasoning error made in the argument. It will often be worded very abstractly.

Practice understanding the answers, right and wrong. Flawed Reasoning answers are very abstract, but they all mean something. Think of examples to make them concrete and easier to understand.

Basic Logic

Take the phrase: "All cats have tails."

"Cats" is the sufficient condition. Knowing that something is a cat is "sufficient" for us to say that it has a tail. "Tails" is a necessary condition, because you can't be a cat without a tail. You can draw this sentence as C ➝ T

The **contrapositive** is a correct logical deduction, and reads "anything without a tail is not a cat." You can draw this as T̶ ➝ C̶. Notice that the terms are reversed, and negated.

Incorrect Reversal: "Anything with a tail is a cat." This is a common logical error on the LSAT.

T ➝ C   (Wrong! Dogs have tails and aren't cats.)

Incorrect Negation: "If it is not a cat, it doesn't have a tail." This is another common error.

C̶ ➝ T̶ (Wrong! Dogs aren't cats, but have tails.)

General Advice: Always remember what you are looking for on each question. The correct answer on a strengthen question would be incorrect on a weaken question.

Watch out for subtle shifts in emphasis between the stimulus and the incorrect answer choices. An example would be the difference between "how things are" and "how things should be."

Justify your answers. If you're tempted to choose an answer choice that says something like the sentence below, then be sure you can fill in the blank:

Answer Choice Says: "The politician attacked his opponents' characters",

Fill In The Blank: "The politician said _____ about his opponents' characters."

If you cannot say what the attack was, you can't pick that answer. This applies to many things. You must be able to show that the stimulus supports your idea.

A Few Logic Games Tips

Rule 1: When following along with my explanations....draw the diagrams yourself, too!

This book will be much more useful if you try the games by yourself first. You must think through games on your own, and no book will do that for you. You must have your mind in a game to solve it.

Use the explanations when you find a game you can't understand on your own, or when you want to know how to solve a game more efficiently.

Some of the solutions may seem impossible to get on your own. It's a matter of practice. When you learn how to solve one game efficiently, solving other games becomes easier too.

Try to do the following when you solve games:

Work With What Is Definite: Focus on what must be true. Don't figure out every possibility.

Draw Your Deductions: Unsuccessful students often make the same deductions as successful students. But the unsuccessful students forget their deductions, 15 seconds later! I watch this happen.

Draw your deductions, or you'll forget them. Don't be arrogant and think this doesn't happen to you. It would happen to *me* if I didn't draw my deductions.

Draw Clear Diagrams: Many students waste time looking back and forth between confusing pictures. They've done everything right, but can't figure out their own drawings!

You should be able to figure out your drawings 3 weeks later. If you can't, then they aren't clear enough. I'm serious: look back at your old drawings. Can you understand them? If not, you need a more consistent, cleaner system.

Draw Local Rules: When a question gives you a new rule (a local rule), draw it. Then look for deductions by combining the new rule with your existing rules. Then double-check what you're being asked and see if your deduction is the right answer. This works 90% of the time for local rule questions. And it's fast.

If you don't think you have time to draw diagrams for each question, practice drawing them faster. It's a learnable skill, and it pays off.

Try To Eliminate a Few Easy Answer Choices First: You'll see examples in the explanations that show how certain deductions will quickly get rid of 1-3 answer choices on many questions. This saves time for harder answer choices and it frees up mental space.

You don't have to try the answer choices in order, without thinking about them first.

Split Games Into Two Scenarios When Appropriate: If a rule only allows something to be one of two ways (e.g. F is in 1 or 7), then draw two diagrams: one with F in 1, and one with F in 7. This leads to extra deductions surprisingly often. And it always makes the game easier to visualize.

Combine Rules To Make Deductions: Look for variables that appear in multiple rules. These can often be combined. Sometimes there are no deductions, but it's a crime not to look for them.

Reread The Rules: Once you've made your diagram, reread the rules. This lets you catch any mistakes, which are fatal. It doesn't take very long, and it helps you get more familiar with the rules.

Draw Rules Directly On The Diagram: Mental space is limited. Three rules are much harder to remember than two. When possible, draw rules on the diagram so you don't have to remember them.

Memorize Your Rules: You should memorize every rule you can't draw on the diagram. It doesn't take long, you'll go faster, and you'll make fewer mistakes. Try it, it's not that hard.

If you spend 30 seconds doing this, you'll often save a minute by going through the game faster.

You should also make a numbered list of rules that aren't on the diagram, in case you need to check them.

Preptest 67
Section I - Reading Comprehension
Passage 1 - Lorenzo Tucker
Question 1-7

Paragraph Summaries

1. Lorenzo Tucker played an important role in the development of African American film and theatre.
2. The author researched Tucker by doing library research and examining Tucker's films. Most importantly, the author interviewed Tucker before he died.
3. When writing a biography, it is useful to listen to what the person says, but also you must be skeptical.
4. How the author used and verified Tucker's oral evidence.

Analysis

This is an unusual passage. From the first paragraph, you might expect to learn something about Tucker and his art.

But the rest of the passage mainly discusses the author's research methods. The most important element is oral testimony and whether it can be trusted.

The author is writing a biography of Tucker. They have used all the usual materials, but also conducted extensive interviews with Tucker. The author takes pains to tell us that they have verified Tucker's oral testimony as much as possible, and included only relevant information.

The tone of this article is scholarly. This seems to be an introduction to a longer piece in an academic journal, or a scholarly biography. It is normal for academics to describe their research methods before they present the results of their research.

The scholar is making an argument. They want to prove that their research methods are appropriate.

This is not a particularly difficult passage, except for the final question. As such, my analysis section is short. There's not much else to say.

Question 1

s

DISCUSSION: The main point of the passage was to explain how the scholar researched Tucker's life, and to justify those methods.

A must be true question must first be true, and then describe the whole passage. You can first eliminate any answers that are simply false.

A. Not even true. This says that Tucker is important because of *how* the author researched him. Nonsense. Tucker is important for his contributions, not because of how the author researched him.
B. **CORRECT.** This covers everything: the importance of Tucker, the author's methods, and the end result - a new study. Of course, it would have been a better answer if it also described how the author argues his methods are appropriate.
C. This only describes the second part of the first paragraph. It's one of the reasons the author wanted to study Tucker.
D. This mainly describes the third paragraph.
E. Actually, the first paragraph says that historians had ignored Tucker entirely.

Question 2

DISCUSSION: The best way to answer this question is simply to finish reading the sentence that mentioned memorabilia.

Tucker's collection has given us insight into a significant part of US entertainment history.

And since the author is studying Tucker, we can assume this memorabilia was a useful source.

————————————

A. CORRECT. The author's purpose in writing this passage is to describe the sources he used. Tucker's collection is one of the sources.

B. *What* general claim about scholarly data gathering? The author doesn't even mention scholarly methods in the first paragraph.

C. The author justifies reliance on Tucker's oral testimony in paragraphs 3 and 4. The memorabilia is actually a reason the author doesn't have to *exclusively* rely on oral testimony.

D. Tucker's memorabilia were from film and theatre. They were *professional* memorabilia.

E. Actually, Tucker's collection is unusual. If everyone kept collections like that then there Tucker's collection would not have shed new light on anything (lines 17-18).

Question 3

DISCUSSION: See lines 37-43. The author thinks we should be skeptical of someone's own description of their story - even though it provides valuable information.

————————————

A. CORRECT. This is true because the author of the book can't be sure of remembering everything correctly, and they have an incentive to paint themselves in a favorable light.

B. The scientist is publishing their own personal opinions. Those aren't usually on public record.

C. The third and fourth paragraphs describe how scholars can use oral testimony and personal opinions in scholarly works. The author doesn't say this is a rare type of evidence.

D. The author never makes a distinction between entertainment and science. The author is giving guidelines for scholarship in general.

E. Lines 37-43 contradict this. Scholars must *always* verify personal evidence before accepting it.

Question 4

DISCUSSION: The author is introducing their own text. They've done extensive research on Tucker - this passage describes their research methods as a prelude to presenting the research itself.

The first paragraph describes Tucker's importance. An interesting man in his own right, he also collected much evidence about an important part of US entertainment history.

Lines 1-3 and 16-18 show that Tucker and early 20th century African-American film and theatre have not been well studied. The author's biography attempts to fix this.

A. The author is an academic, he's very concerned about research methods. If anything, the author would argue that the material is appropriate for an academic publisher but not a popular publisher.
B. Paragraphs 3 and 4 show that the author hasn't developed any new methods. The author uses standard methods to assess Tucker's oral testimony.
C. **CORRECT.** See the explanation above, and the first paragraph. The author's study is groundbreaking. Few have studied Tucker or the period of entertainment history he took part in.
D. It's not clear why the author would say this. They are providing a history of Tucker's life and role, so the biography will include this information, at least. The author never says how we should interpret the study.
E. This misses the point. The study is about Tucker, and also his collection. It's not a general guide to identifying trinkets.

Question 5

DISCUSSION: The first paragraph explains why the author is studying Tucker. The rest of the passage justifies the author's methods.

A. This is an incredibly vague answer. The author is making a study of Tucker. He doesn't have a grand plan to correct intellectual traditions.
B. Oral testimony isn't an alternative method of historical investigation. It's implied that other scholars have used it (lines 35-36).
C. The author hasn't told us what's in his biography of Tucker. He's only mentioned why it's important, and how he gathered evidence.
D. Lines 1-3 say that Tucker hasn't really been studied. So there are no previously held historical views to revise.
E. **CORRECT.** The first paragraph explains the author's subject matter. The other paragraphs justify his use of oral testimony.

Question 6

DISCUSSION: On this type of question, if you can't find the answer in the passage, it's not correct.

The wrong answers often use relevant terms in the wrong context, to mislead you. Or the wrong answers use terms from the passage, but go beyond what we know.

————————————

A. The author never mentions critics.
B. *Tucker* collected memorabilia. We don't know if Tucker's fellow performers collected any.
C. The author mentioned watching some of Tucker's films (lines 25-26), but he never mentioned scripts.
D. CORRECT. See lines 26-29. The author interviewed some of Tucker's fellow performers.
E. Line 10 mentions that Tucker was in an actor's union, but we're never told anything about union records.

Question 7

DISCUSSION: For an inference question, identify 1-2 answers you think are correct, then look to justify them using the passage.

If you find this takes too long, then practice doing it faster when reviewing. You can learn to find the relevant section of the passage in less than 10 seconds, usually faster.

————————————

A. Lines 1-3 and 16-18 make clear that this is an area of history that isn't well studied. It doesn't sound like any of these films are well known.
B. There's no evidence that the scholar ever worked with Tucker.
C. The author says that Tucker has not been studied in the mainstream (lines 1-3). But the author doesn't say they expect their study of Tucker will be ignored. It would be odd to write a biography if you were pessimistic about it's reception.
D. CORRECT. Tucker acted in 20 films (line 5). Lines 24-26 show that the author examined Tucker's 10 remaining films. 10/20 is not a preponderance, which requires at least a majority of the films be studied. It also doesn't sound like author gave the films much study: he 'also examined' the films. They were secondary evidence. Lines 29-32 show that the interviews were the main source of evidence.
E. The author never says what rhetorical structure he uses in his study. He just describes the evidence he's gathered.

Passage 2 - Personal Ethnography
Question 8-14

Paragraph Summaries

1. *Nisa* tells three stories about the !Kung. It goes against the usual anonymous style of ethnography, by telling a woman's story and involving the ethnographer in the story.
2. *Nisa* shows the complexity of living in a 'simple' society. Western views of 'simple' societies are often inaccurate.
3. *Nisa* uses the perspective of a !Kung woman to address issues faced by all women.
4. *Nisa* is a dialogue between the subject and the ethnographer.

Analysis

This passage is a fairly neutral description of Shostak's book *Nisa*. The main point seems to be that the book is different from traditional ethnography.

It is clear that the author of the passage approves of *Nisa*. Lines 41-43 show that most ethnographic literature does not deal *appropriately* with women's stories. Lines 25-34 show that *Nisa* gives an *accurate* view of the difficulties of !Kung society. Small adjectives are extremely important on LSAT reading comprehension. If the author says *Nisa* is accurate, you can take that to mean "I think *Nisa* is the most spectacular book I've read this year and should be a classic of ethnography".

Nisa is groundbreaking for several reasons. First, *Nisa* shows both an individual woman's perspective, and a society's perspective. Most ethnographic literature only views the society.

Second, the third paragraph makes clear that Nisa's experience as a !Kung woman tells us about women in general. Most ethnography ignores women's views on women (lines 41-43).

Finally, the fourth paragraph tells us that Shostak inserts her own story into *Nisa*. This runs counter to traditional ethnography, but it's an important truth:

both Shostak and Nisa are people. As Shostak learns about Nisa, she must inevitably become a part of Nisa's life for a time. *Nisa* is the story of this collaboration.

The final paragraph also mentions that Shostak employs the convention of narrative. Narrative just means storytelling. Our lives are not stories with beginnings, middles and conclusions. Yet that's how we write books.

Nisa both uses this convention, and breaks from it slightly. Lines 54-57 show that the story is indirectly told through dialogue.

Question 8

DISCUSSION: The passage mentioned a few ways that Shostak's ethnography differed from traditional ethnography.

Your job is to find an answer choice that mentions one of those ways, and then confirm it using specific lines from the passage.

A. The !Kung are the only group mentioned.
B. Shostak does study individuals' experiences. But she seems to be studying Nisa *within* the cultural context of Nisa's group. She doesn't view Nisa apart from the !Kung.
C. Same as B. Shostak tells Nisa's story along with the story of the !Kung. They are intertwined.
D. We're not told whether Shostak used empirical data (evidence) in her study or whether she made many general hypotheses about the !Kung. *Nisa* mainly seems to be the story of one !Kung woman's life.
E. CORRECT. See lines 4-7. Shostak is not following ethnographic convention: ethnography focusses on anonymous, general statements. Shostak is instead focussing on the personal story of Nisa.

Question 9

DISCUSSION: See lines 40-43. The author is shocked that ethnographic literature ignores women's stories about women.

'Salutary' means 'good', but you don't need to know that to see that the author approves of Shostak's approach to women's stories about women.

A. Quite the opposite. The author likes the fact that Shostak has focussed on women's views of women.
B. We only know Shostak discusses women's views of women. As far as we know, most ethnographers ignore this perspective.
C. CORRECT. This paraphrases lines 40-43.
D. The ethnographic studies might use some information available from those interviews. What the studies do not do is present the information from the point of view of women's views about women.
E. Actually, most ethnographic literature ignores individual experience entirely (lines 5-6). This answer is false, and is irrelevant to presenting women's views about women.

Question 10

DISCUSSION: Paragraph 2 shows described the 'received' attitudes we in the West have about traditional societies.

We tend to see only the good, and ignore the bad. So if we are happy observing a 'simple' society, we think that society is good.

The question asks for an example of these attitudes. Received attitudes are ideas that oversimplify !Kung society and prevent us from seeing the bad parts.

————————————

A. 'Charm' is a positive attribute, but it's not necessarily delusional to view a people as charming. Someone might say 'The !Kung have considerable charm, but their society has many problems'.

B. The question wants an *example* of received attitudes. This is just something that's true. Watching the !Kung makes us happy *because* we hold received attitudes about the !Kung. the fact that we're happy is not an example of received attitudes.

C. **CORRECT.** We think that seminomadic societies are simple. So we see the good parts and ignore the bad parts. This is exactly the type of received attitude described in lines 19-25.

D. This is just a fact. And it's a negative fact, so it goes against the false, idealistic ideas Westerners have about the !Kung.

E. This doesn't sound like wishy-washy idealism about a 'simple' society. It may or may not be true, but it doesn't match the received attitudes of Westerners.

Question 11

DISCUSSION: The third paragraph mentions that Nisa's experience tells us about women in general.

The passage doesn't tell us *how* Nisa's experience lets us learn about women in general. It's not obvious that the issues faces by a !Kung woman are faced by all women.

Since we're working with a blank slate, almost any answer could work. When that happens, just keep your mind open for something that would achieve the goal of informing us about women.

————————————

A. Sympathy with someone is not the same thing as being similar to them.

B. This has very complex wording. It means describing someone's experience, and using that experience to gain insight. It only mentions using that insight to study issues in non-Western society. We don't know if this will help us study 'women in general'. Also, the fact that this answer mentions men shows us that it's off track.

C. The feminists are applauding the use of the dialogue technique, not Shostak's work itself. We don't know if the feminists think Nisa teaches us about all women. Also, it's not clear if these feminists are a relevant authority.

D. **CORRECT.** This shows that Nisa's experiences are relevant outside of her own culture. So it might be true that her experiences are relevant for women in all cultures.

E. This only shows that Nisa's experiences are relevant to !Kung women in. We want to know if Nisa's experiences are relevant to women in all cultures.

Question 12

DISCUSSION: You have to read around line 50 for context. The passage describes the 'potent convention' in the lines that follow.

Our lives do not arrange themselves into stories with recognizable shapes. That's Shostak's literary convention - the idea that lives can be described as stories.

―――――――――――

A. The word revelation doesn't even occur in the passage, let alone near line 50.
B. *What* dramatic emphasis? This has nothing to do with what's discussed in lines 47-53.
C. Shostak doesn't compare Nisa to anyone else.
D. Line 10 mentions that Nisa's story is a metaphor for women's experience, but this is far from line 50 and there's no mention of poetry.
E. **CORRECT.** Shostak's describes Nisa's life as though she were a character in a novel. See lines 51-53.

Question 13

DISCUSSION: Shostak uses the example of one woman to make claims about that woman's culture and about women in general. See lines 6-13.

Shostak also includes herself and her relations with Nisa as a subject of study. See lines 13-15.

―――――――――――

A. **CORRECT.** This is like lines 13-15. The director involves himself in the story just like Shostak involved herself in Nisa's story.
B. This book is just a fraud. Shostak didn't lie in her biography of Nisa. She indicated which parts were autobiography.
C. We don't know that Shostak included the day to day details of Nisa's life. We only know Nisa gave Shostak an autobiography of her life. Nisa might not have concerned herself with every little detail.
D. This would be Shostak giving an autobiography. *Nisa* was a biography of another woman. Shostak only describes herself to the extent that she interacts with Nisa.
E. Shostak only used one life: Nisa's. She did not use the experiences of a broad group of people.

Question 14

DISCUSSION: The sentence starts at line 51. Our lives can't properly be told as stories.

Nisa's quote is intended to illustrate this. Few stories go like that. No one wants to read a novel about how people live somewhere and eat food. There's no plot.

But that is how we live our lives. So our conceptions of stories and our actual lives don't match.

A. Nisa doesn't seem to attach any special importance to the details in her story.

B. **CORRECT.** Exactly. There's no plot or story to what Nisa tells us. But it's an accurate description of her life. This quote is an example of how our lives don't fit into the conventions of stories.

C. There's nothing unpleasant in what the quote describes. This answer is trying to make you think of the second part of the second paragraph.

D. There's no story in what Nisa describes. Where's the plot? Where are the characters?

E. Nisa is just telling details. Shostak isn't involved in the narrative in this short excerpt.

Passage 3 - Invasive Species (Comparative)
Question 15-19

Paragraph Summaries

Passage A

1. Conservationists now realize that invasive species can invade even healthy ecosystems.
2. The everglades look healthy, but Australian invasive trees are disturbing ecosystems in the everglades. Australia itself also has problems with invasive plants.

Passage B

1. Invasive species can increase ecosystem diversity.
2. Invasive species transform ecosystems, rather than damaging them.
3. Most invasive species are pretty harmless. The main issue is what kind of nature we'd like to be surrounded by.

Analysis

The two passages have very different philosophies. The author of the first passage clearly believes that invasive species are harmful, and that the changes they bring to ecosystems are bad.

The author of the second passage views invasive species as a mild positive force. Generally, they add to ecosystems rather than destroying them.

They both agree that invasive species can change ecosystems. They disagree on whether we should worry about invasive species.

Elton is not central to Passage A. He's just mentioned to provide an example of an opinion the author disagrees with. Elton thought that only weak ecosystems were threatened by invasive species. The author of passage A argues that all ecosystems are at risk. The second paragraph of passage A is just an example supporting this claim.

The author of passage B thinks that invasive species make ecosystems *different,* but not worse, in most cases. Species counts may even go up. An invaded ecosystem may be less useful to humans, but that doesn't necessarily make it worse or under attack.

Question 15

DISCUSSION: You need to find something mentioned in both passages. Many wrong answers talk about things that only one passage mentions.

A. Only passage A deals with this.
B. Passage A seems to assume that all invasive species are by definition bad.
C. Passage B doesn't even seem to think a protective approach is needed.
D. **CORRECT.** Passage A argues the ecosystems are weakened. Passage B argues that they simply change.
E. We're never told how invasive species arrive in new habitats, in either passage.

Question 16

DISCUSSION: You should be able to find specific lines in passage A that justify the answer. If you just go on gut feeling, you'll risk making a mistake.

If it takes a while for you to find lines, work on making a better mental map of the passage before starting the questions, and practice finding line references when you review.

A. Line 10 says that ecologists recognize that ecosystems are threatened. They recognize the ecological risks. They aren't concerned with the economic impact of this destruction, or any other economic impacts.
B. Passage A doesn't say what defines an ecosystem.
C. Passage A doesn't mention extinctions. They just say that ecosystems will be 'weakened'.
D. A nonsense answer. We're not told what people believed before Elton. His theory is the earliest belief we're told about.
E. **CORRECT.** See lines 8-10. Passage A says that ecologists realize that even healthy ecosystems are threatened. Passage B doesn't say what ecologists think of Elton's view.

Question 17

DISCUSSION: The author of Passage A claims that the Everglades are not natural because of invasive forest species.

The author of Passage B would claim that the Everglades are just changing into a different ecosystem, but that this has nothing to do with weather they are 'natural'. Nature includes change.

A. The author of passage B doesn't agree that habitats can be 'disturbed'.
B. Passage A has a pretty consistent definition of nature: ecosystems as they evolved before invasive species.
C. The line in question says 'wild and natural'. Passage A implies that the two words mean the same thing. Passage B doesn't say any different.
D. Unconventional means unusual. But a lot of people would agree with the definition of nature given in passage A.
E. **CORRECT.** The ideal of nature in passage A is an ecosystem undisturbed by invasive species. Passage B thinks that physical nature is more important. Even if an ecosystem has been changed by an invasive species, it is still physical nature.

Question 18

DISCUSSION: Passage B's point is that change in an ecosystem isn't necessarily bad, even if the change comes from outside influences.

A. This isn't it. In this case, there is an actual loss: you have one less piece of clothing. Yet ecosystems often have more species when species invade.

B. **CORRECT.** This is pretty similar. An outside influence produces change, but the change isn't necessarily bad.

C. Passage B didn't say that invasive species produce 'progress' or that species invasion is necessary. Passage B just claimed invasion isn't necessarily *bad*.

D. This is very narrow. It's like saying that ecosystems can never change from within. Passage B's point was just that outside change isn't necessarily bad.

E. This would be like saying that humans can produce species invasion but species invasion also happens on it's own. That's not what passage B was talking about.

Question 19

DISCUSSION: Passage A was concerned with the effects of invasive species. It told us that ecologists are worried that all habitats are vulnerable.

Passage B presented an argument for why Passage A's concern was unfounded. Invasive species are not dangerous (though that doesn't necessarily mean we should encourage them).

A. Neither passage discussed the causes of invasive species.

B. Passage A questioned an *old* assumption about invasive species (Elton's), not a common assumption. Passage B didn't confirm Elton's assumption - it said invasive species were not a threat at all.

C. Passage B's point was that invasive species aren't bad. They didn't say they were good. If invasive species were good, then we should encourage *more* species invasions. But passage B didn't recommend that. Also, passage A didn't show that *everyone* though invasive species were bad. They just said ecologists think so.

D. **CORRECT.** Passage A warns about the dangers of invasive species; it describes the beliefs of ecologists. Passage B argues that the ecologists have an incorrect definition of nature, and that invasive species are not harmful. Note that 'not harmful' isn't the same thing as 'good'.

E. Passage A doesn't say what we should do. Passage B does more than 'raise questions' about Passage A's argument: Passage B disagrees completely.

Passage 4 - Sovereign Omnipotence
Question 20-27

Paragraph Summaries

1. Introduction to paradox of sovereign omnipotence.
2. Omnipotence can cause problems for sovereigns.
3. It is in a sovereign's interest to limit their own power. For example, by limiting their power to cancel loans. This can help them get loans in the first place.
4. England and France needed capital to expand their empires. But their sovereigns couldn't commit to paying loans back, and so lenders charged them higher rates of interest.
5. The English Crown got lower interest rates after the Glorious Revolution. Parliament controlled the King's money. Parliament represented commercial interests that valued property.
6. Actually, the Glorious Revolution simply transferred omnipotence from the King to Parliament.

Analysis

First, vocabulary. Sovereign means King, Queen, Emperor or Empress or monarch. These are all words for the ruler of a country.

Sovereigns want to pay low interest rates. But they have a problem. They can cancel loans whenever they want, and throw the bankers in jail if they feel like it. Yay, no more debt!

But....throw your lenders in jail, and no one will lend to you, unless you pay very high rates of interest to compensate for the risk of losing money and going to prison.

Sovereigns couldn't limit their power. So they couldn't promise not to ruin lenders, and so sovereigns were stuck paying high rates of interest. The bankers were rightfully afraid that the sovereigns might cancel the loans.

After the revolution, Parliament had power over money, and interest rates dropped.

The final paragraph points out that now it is Parliament that has unlimited power. The paradox of omnipotence still exists.

So why did Parliament pay lower interest rates even though they were omnipotent? Lines 42-44 show that Parliament was full of merchants who respected property rights.

So there were philosophical reasons that lenders could trust Parliament not to cancel loans. This was why interest rates fell, even though the paradox of omnipotence still applied to Parliament.

It's helpful to know a bit about loans. You make your profit on a loan by charging interest. But if the debtor doesn't pay back the loan, then you lose a lot of money.

So if you're certain that someone will pay back a loan, then you can charge a low interest rate and still be sure of a profit. If you think that someone might not pay back the loan, then you have to charge a higher interest rate to compensate for the risk.

Question 20

DISCUSSION: A main point answer must be true, and cover the entire passage. You can first eliminate any answers that are not true.

The main point is to describe the problem of omnipotence, using the examples of the English and French Kings, and the English Parliament.

———————————

A. **CORRECT.** This is pretty good. Most of the passage describes the problems faced by Kings. The final paragraph shows that Parliament (a different constitutional arrangement) still faced the same problem.
B. The paradox of omnipotence is anything but abstract. It applies directly to sovereigns and parliaments. An analogue would be something different but similar.
C. This only describes the 5th paragraph. It ignores the problems of omnipotence, and the fact that Parliament now has those problems.
D. This is false. Paragraph 5 shows that the problem *was* solved for English monarchs. This answer also ignores much of the passage.
E. This only describes the first paragraph. The rest of the passage discussed the practical problems of sovereignty, not logical contradictions.

Question 21

DISCUSSION: Wealthy subjects are mentioned in lines 35-37. Lenders gave wealthy subjects interest rates that were lower than those lenders gave to monarchs.

This was because sovereigns could cancel debts whenever they pleased. Wealthy subjects couldn't cancel debts, so lenders thought they were more likely to pay back loans.

———————————

A. What do creditors care about imperial expansion? They just want someone to pay back their loans.
B. This is something that creditors might believe about sovereigns, not wealthy subjects. If a sovereign cancels a debt, then they owe less money, but they lose credibility if they want new loans.
C. This describes Parliament after the Glorious Revolution (lines 42-45).
D. The *only* thing we know about wealthy subjects is that they paid lower interest rates. We don't know what they thought about omnipotence.
E. **CORRECT.** This is why lenders gave them lower interest rates. They believed that wealthy subjects would be more likely to pay back their loans, because they couldn't cancel the debt.

Question 22

DISCUSSION: See lines 42-45 and lines 57-64.

Parliament still had sovereign omnipotence. They could cancel loans if they wanted. But because Parliament represented commercial interests, they could be trusted not to cancel loans.

So as long as lenders believed that Parliament represented commerce, lenders could give Parliament lower interest rates.

———————

A. The point of the paradox is that it doesn't matter if the Sovereign is aware of it (that includes Parliament). A sovereign can't legally limit their own power, even if they want to.
B. **CORRECT.** If Parliament represents commercial interests, then they would not cancel loans even if they have the power to do so. They value property rights (lines 42-45).
C. This is irrelevant. Parliament has to pay back loans whether or not there was a recent election.
D. Why should creditors care about the number of laws? They only care whether Parliament is likely to pay back loans.
E. This seems a bit relevant. But as long as Parliament is committed to paying back loans, it shouldn't matter whether borrowing has increased a bit. Also, the total amount of debt is more relevant than whether borrowing has increased recently.

Question 23

DISCUSSION: The last paragraph says that Parliament still has omnipotence. The constitutional change in England didn't get rid of the problem - it just transferred it from King to Parliament.

———————

A. The last paragraph didn't mention practical consequences. And actually, the transfer of omnipotence to Parliament did solve the practical problem of high interest rates, even if the theoretical problem of omnipotence remains.
B. **CORRECT.** The cause is omnipotence. The effects are high interest rates. Transferring power to Parliament got rid of the high interest rates, but the underlying cause (omnipotence) still exists.
C. The passage didn't say how to solve the problem of sovereignty. It's implied that it *can't* be solved.
D. It *was* better for power to rest with Parliament. But that's not because Parliament was elected. Rather, it's because Parliament represented commercial interests (lines 42-45). The same effect could be achieved with an unelected body that represented those interests.
E. This wouldn't solve the problem. There's no way to explicitly specify that a sovereign power is not omnipotent. The problem just gets transferred. In any case, the passage never mentions explicitly defining powers. England's constitution is unwritten. (lines 60-61).

Question 24

DISCUSSION: The fourth paragraph covers the practical problems of sovereign immunity.

_____

A. **CORRECT.** Read the fourth paragraph. Sovereigns wanted to expand their empires (lines 24-26), but because they had unlimited power they were charged high interest rates (lines 34-37).

B. The passage never mentions monarchs passing laws.

C. We only know that it was easier for subjects to borrow money (lines 35-35). We don't know if it had only become easier in the 17th century.

D. Actually, the monarchs borrowed less than they would have liked (or at higher rates) precisely because they had unlimited power.

E. The point of the passage is that monarchs *couldn't* commit to respecting property rights, because they had unlimited power.

Question 25

DISCUSSION: The need for capital shows why monarchs wanted loans. It means that omnipotence was a very real problem for sovereigns, because they paid higher interest rates on their loans.

_____

A. Actually, this proves that it would be in the sovereign's interest to limit their ability to cancel debts. Then they could get lower interest rates.

B. Creditors didn't have a low opinion of sovereigns because they wanted money. Rather, creditors distrusted sovereigns because they could refuse to pay debts.

C. The fact that monarchs *needed* capital is actually a weakness in their real world power. It doesn't help show their unlimited legal power.

D. **CORRECT.** Exactly. If sovereigns didn't need loans, then high interest rates wouldn't have been a problem for them. But these lines show that sovereigns needed loans quite badly, and their omnipotence meant they could only get loans at high interest rates.

E. We're never given actual examples of sovereigns breaking their commitments to pay debts.

Question 26

DISCUSSION: The final paragraph shows that no one can restrict Parliament's power. So if Parliament joins the organization, then they also have the power to leave.

———————————

A. We have no idea what creditors think of this international body. It might be an international banking organization that encourages loan payment.

B. Same as A. Lenders might like this body, or they might not. We don't know whether joining will affect Parliament's willingness to repay debts.

C. **CORRECT.** See lines 61-63. Parliament can do anything it wants, including withdrawing from the international body. There is no way for Parliament to limit it's own power to withdraw.

D. Same as A and B. We have no idea what commercial interests think of this international body.

E. Parliament already has unlimited power. See the last paragraph.

Question 27

DISCUSSION: See lines 52-53. In the last paragraph, the author disagrees with the scholars. The author thinks the scholars have ignored the fact that Parliament has unlimited power now.

———————————

A. The author agrees with this; that's why lenders gave Parliament lower interest rates.

B. North and Weingast might still think that the problem of omnipotence applies to the world's remaining absolute sovereigns (or dictators).

C. Both the author and the scholars agree on this point.

D. Everyone agrees on this. It's in the fourth paragraph.

E. **CORRECT.** In the final paragraph, the author argues that this problem hasn't been solved, because Parliament is now omnipotent. Lines 52-53 show that the scholars disagree with the author on this point.

Section II - Logical Reasoning

Question 1

QUESTION TYPE: Weaken

CONCLUSION: The Johnsons should plant peach trees, rather than apricot trees.

REASONING: Peach trees cost less, and grow fruit earlier than apricot trees do.

ANALYSIS: This argument has a classic flaw: it's given us some advantages for peach trees, and pretended that this means that we know peach trees are better.

We don't know that. There could also be *disadvantages* to peach trees that make them a lousy purchase. Perhaps they attract many pests.

There could also be other advantages to apricot trees that make them an even better choice. Maybe they require no upkeep.

––––––––––––––––––

A. **CORRECT.** If apricots sell at a higher price, then it might make sense to plant apricot trees instead of peach trees.
B. This is a *disadvantage* for apricots, and supports planting peaches.
C. This tells us that both trees are equal in this respect. It doesn't help us choose apricots.
D. The most tempting wrong answer. But we already knew that peaches and apricots are equally popular in this area. And, this answer doesn't tell us that the market for apricots has grown *faster* than the market for peaches.
E. This is a fact about the past. It doesn't say what farmers should do in the future. Peach production could have declined for innocent reasons that don't affect the future.

Question 2

QUESTION TYPE: Paradox

FACTS: A type of camel experienced population decline because it lived in a weapons testing ground. Now that the testing is done, the camels are dying even faster.

ANALYSIS: You have to explain why camels are dying faster, even though bombs aren't falling on them.

There are many ways humans kill camels: we hunt them, we clear their land for farming, we build buildings in their habitat, etc.

The bombs would have prevented us from harming camels. If bombs fall in an area, humans stay away.

This is a good example of how real world knowledge can be used appropriately to speed you up. If you grew up near an army base, you may know their training grounds often double as nature reserves.

Most of the wrong answers talk about dangers that existed when the range was in operation. We only care about dangers that arose when the range was *shut down*.

––––––––––––––––––

A. **CORRECT.** This helps explain the paradox. Now that the testing range is safe, poachers can come kill the camels.
B. This doesn't explain why camels kept dying in the years *after* the testing was complete. This is just a useless fact about the past.
C. This shows that there is still *some* danger, but it doesn't explain why the danger increased.
D. This is like B. It talks about the years the testing range was in operation. We only care about the years *after* the range was shut down.
E. Same as B and D. This is information about the years the range was in operation. It can't tell us much about dangers after the range was shut down.

Question 3

QUESTION TYPE: Strengthen

CONCLUSION: You should read fewer books and spend more time on them, rather than reading many books quickly.

REASONING: You read books for pleasure in order to broaden your understanding, rather than to acquire information. This makes you like a tourist, and tourists benefit from visiting fewer places, for more time.

ANALYSIS: This is an argument by analogy. The author wants to show that the conclusion is correct because reading is like tourism.

There's a problem. The author hasn't proven that his tourist analogy is correct. We don't know that you learn more by spending more time in a place.

It's possible you learn the most about a place in the first couple of days, and you can maximize learning by quickly moving from place to place. The right answer shows that you do in fact learn the most by staying in one area.

I didn't figure this question out until I skimmed the answers. I noticed they all talked about tourists. So I reread the analogy and only then noticed that the argument hadn't proven it's point.

——————————

A. That's nice. This doesn't tell us whether tourists learn more if they linger.
B. CORRECT. This tells us that tourists will maximize learning only if they linger.
C. So? This mixes the two situations. The author didn't propose learning about places by reading about them. They mentioned tourists who *visit* places - tourism was an analogy.
D. This doesn't tell us whether tourists learn more by staying longer.
E. This doesn't tell us what is the best way to learn while traveling.

Question 4

QUESTION TYPE: Paradox - Exception

FACTS: Modular furniture is more expensive than normal furniture. Modular furniture allows you to buy furniture by parts.

ANALYSIS: You're not given much information about modular furniture. There's no way to prephrase every wrong answer.

So before answering this type of question, just take a moment to open your mind to possible reasons modular furniture could be more expensive.

——————————

A. Mass production of regular furniture can lower costs.
B. CORRECT. This doesn't distinguish between normal sofas and modular sofas.
C. Fashionable, trendy furniture will cost more.
D. If you can't ever get a discount on modular furniture, that will raise the average price you have to pay.
E. If modular sofas are bigger, then more materials will be required to build them. Extra materials cost more. Maybe this is true for other modular furniture as well.

Question 5

QUESTION TYPE: Complete The Argument

CONCLUSION: The argument will likely finish by saying that testosterone may help prevent Alzheimer's.

REASONING: Testosterone lowers levels of a certain protein linked to Alzheimer's, and testosterone also helps prevent brain injuries. Brain injuries are linked to Alzheimer's.

ANALYSIS: Testosterone helps prevent two likely causes of Alzheimer's. Therefore testosterone probably helps prevent Alzheimer's as well.

A. Way too strong. Just because injury can lead to Alzheimer's doesn't mean that it *will*. Otherwise just about everyone would have Alzheimer's.
B. Nonsense. The stimulus clearly said that injuries can also affect the likelihood of developing Alzheimer's.
C. This gets things backwards. We know low testosterone may increase risk of Alzheimer's, but that doesn't mean Alzheimer's will lower testosterone. That's reversing cause and effect.
D. This is silly. It means I could hit you on the head with a hammer, but you'd be fine as long as you didn't have Alzheimer's.
E. **CORRECT.** This is well supported. Lower testosterone increases risk of brain injury and increases levels of beta-amyloid. Both are risk factors for Alzheimer's.

Question 6

QUESTION TYPE: Necessary Assumption

CONCLUSION: It is unwise to pay senior staff in stock options, because it increases the wage gap.

REASONING: Employees with only a fixed salary won't benefit from stock options. Anything that undermines morale is bad.

ANALYSIS: Necessary assumption questions are often easier than they look. You just have to find where the argument skipped a step.

We know that anything that damages morale is bad. Great. But the argument doesn't show that wage gaps or stock options damage morale.

Oops. So we have no way of knowing stock options are bad.

The conclusion is very specific. It says that low morale is the reason that stock options reduce profits. Any answer that doesn't help link stock options to low morale is wrong.

A. **CORRECT.** This tells us that wage gaps lower morale. We know that anything bad for morale reduces profitability. This gives us a reason to believe that wage gaps are bad.
B. Who cares? If reductions in morale usually come from natural disasters or incompetence (for example), that doesn't tell us whether stock options are a good idea or a bad idea.
C. This is just correlation. It doesn't tell us that the stock options cause low profits.
D. This doesn't help link a wage gap to low morale. The argument said low morale was the reason profit sharing would hurt profits.
E. This talks about sharing profits with employees, which is a different issue. The argument's point is that you shouldn't increase a wage gap by giving senior executives a share of profits.

Question 7

QUESTION TYPE: Most Strongly Supported

FACTS:

1. Antibiotics keep animals healthy and improve meat production.
2. Scientists recommend stopping the use of antibiotics. This practice may decrease the effectiveness of antibiotics in humans.
3. If animals produce less meat, then some farmers will go out of business.

ANALYSIS: We know that antibiotics help yields, and that if yields go down, some farmers will go out of business.

We don't know that antibiotics will be banned. Society might not listen to scientists.

But if we do listen to scientists, some farmers will go out of business.

A. This is only true if we take scientists' advice and stop giving antibiotics to animals. We don't do everything scientists say.
B. The stimulus is vague on this point. Antibiotic use in animals *may* make antibiotics *less* effective. They might still work to a lesser degree.
C. Meat yields might drop for some other reason. Plague of locusts, perhaps?
D. Close, but we don't know exactly how antibiotics increase meat yields. It might not be because they increase animals' health.
E. **CORRECT.** This has to be true. Meat yields will drop if antibiotic use is phased out, unless farmers find some other way of keeping yields up.

Question 8

QUESTION TYPE: Principle

RULE: Public officials shouldn't even appear to use their influence to benefit from public contracts.

APPLICATION: The mayor tried to get the city to award a contract to one of the mayor's relatives.

ANALYSIS: The application *seems* correct. The mayor helped his family - that appears corrupt.

But the rule is pretty specify: officials are prohibited from appearing to help *themselves*. You have to take things very literally on the LSAT. The mayor's relative is not the mayor.

You need to prove that the mayor appeared to help *himself.*

The first three answers are all the same. They help show that the rule is a good rule, but they don't help us show that the mayor was benefitting himself.

A. This helps justify the guideline, but it doesn't show that the mayor violated the rule.
B. Same as A.
C. Same as A and B.
D. Excessive risk? That's not mentioned. The rule says the mayor shouldn't appear to benefit himself. It doesn't matter whether he places city interests at risk.
E. **CORRECT.** This states what seems obvious. If you help your family, you're effectively helping yourself, which is banned by the rule.

Question 9

QUESTION TYPE: Flawed Reasoning

CONCLUSION: Sarah must use the pool at least sometimes.

REASONING: Sarah has a membership, and *only* members can use the pool.

ANALYSIS: Classic error. This argument confuses a necessary condition for a sufficient condition. If you got this wrong, repeat this question later. This error will show up elsewhere. Here's the premise:

Can use pool → Member

Sarah is a member. But just because Sarah *can* use the pool doesn't mean she *will*. I'll use an analogy. You could surely scrape enough money together to visit Guyana. Flights are cheap - why not go to Central America? You *could*.

But, you probably won't fly to Guyana. Just because you can do something (i.e. you meet the necessary conditions), doesn't mean you will.

The right answer is hard to understand. That doesn't give you an excuse to skip it. Instead, break it down part by part until you reach a section you understand. Then expand out from there.

————————

A. The stimulus doesn't mention enforcement.
B. **CORRECT.** This is hard to understand, but it means the author mistook a necessary condition for a sufficient condition.
   Truth is required for the conclusion = necessary
   Truth ensures the conclusion = sufficient
C. The stimulus didn't mention alternatives. This is a different mistake. It's like saying: 'Obama and Romney are the only two candidates for president, so one of them will be elected.' I didn't exclude alternatives, such as one of them resigning and being replaced.
D. There's no group mentioned. Sarah *definitely* has the attribute of 'having a membership'.
E. This is code for 'circular reasoning'. The argument isn't circular. Instead, it mistakes necessary for sufficient.

Question 10

QUESTION TYPE: Point At Issue

ARGUMENTS: Annie says that administrators caused the library's woes, and a tax on students should be used to pay to fix the problem.

Matilda doesn't think the students should pay.

ANALYSIS: With point at issue questions, you must find something that both speakers talk about, and disagree on.

Annie and Matilda agree there is a problem, and that the administration is to blame. They disagree on whether students should pay.

————————

A. Both agree that administrators are to blame.
B. Neither Annie nor Matilda talks about how fast the problem could be solved. Matilda doesn't even mention a solution.
C. Matilda doesn't mention benefits. She just says students shouldn't pay anything.
D. **CORRECT.** Yes. The students aren't responsible. Annie says they should nonetheless pay a fee to fix things, while Matilda disagrees.
E. Annie doesn't say whether there are alternatives to student fees.

Question 11

QUESTION TYPE: Most Strongly Supported

FACTS: Some diamonds formed in a certain way. This could only have happened if the earth's atmosphere didn't have much oxygen.

ANALYSIS: Don't let this question's scientific language fool you. It's very straightforward. I intentionally simplified it in my summary.

The diamonds formed due to a chemical reaction. The reaction couldn't have happened if there was much oxygen in the atmosphere.

O → R̶ (evidence)
R → Ө (contrapositive)

Therefore, since the reaction did happen, there wasn't much oxygen in the atmosphere.

A. We have no clue when most diamonds of this type were formed. Maybe most were formed 1.5 billion years ago. The atmosphere might have stayed low oxygen for quite a while.
B. We have no idea how the chemical reactions worked. But since they couldn't have happened if there was much oxygen, they probably didn't involve oxygen.
C. CORRECT. See the last sentence . If the atmosphere had contained oxygen, then the reactions wouldn't have happened and the diamonds wouldn't have formed.
D. Read the second sentence. These diamonds have a *higher than normal* concentration of sulfur-33. That doesn't mean modern diamonds have *none*.
E. Not quite. The stimulus is talking about the formation of diamonds *high in sulfur-33*. We have no idea how normal diamonds form.

Question 12

QUESTION TYPE: Method of Reasoning

FACTS: When the patient took herbal tea, neither the original dose nor double the dose worked.

When the patient stopped taking herbal tea, the original dose was ineffective but double the original dose worked.

ANALYSIS: This is a very tricky question. It's important to have a firm grasp on what happened.

The medicine was effective, but only at double the initial dose, and only when the patient didn't drink herbal tea.

So the doctor proved two things: The herbal tea interfered, and the original dose wasn't enough.

The question stem asks about the *second* set of experiments. These proved that herbal tea wasn't the only problem.

A. The doctor didn't say the drink was unhealthy. He just said thought that it interfered with the medicine. It might have other, beneficial effects.
B. The opposite of this is true. The medicine only worked when the patient stopped drinking the beverage. The beverage almost certainly contributed to the medicine's initial ineffectiveness.
C. This is really tempting. But D is a better choice. First, the beverage wasn't wholly responsible for the failure of the *prescribed* medication (the initial dosage). The initial dosage failed even when the patient stopped taking the drink.

So while the beverage seems to have contributed to the failure, we can't say that it's *responsible*. It's possible the failure was 90% dosage problems and 10% beverage side effects.
D. CORRECT. This is true. Even without the beverage, the original prescribed dosage didn't work. So inadequate dosage was also a cause.
E. No other medication is mentioned, and the original medication worked once the dosage was increased.

Question 13

QUESTION TYPE: Flawed Reasoning

CONCLUSION: Papercrete is likely promising for large scale construction.

REASONING: Builders who use papercrete regularly for small scale projects think that it will work well for large scale projects. These builders are familiar with papercrete.

Most builders disagree, but they don't work regularly with papercrete.

ANALYSIS: This is a tricky question. The argument *implies* that those who work with papercrete know papercrete the best. After all, they know papercrete's properties.

But maybe the other builders also understand papercrete. They don't use it because they know it is a terrible material for large scale projects.

The argument doesn't say that large scale builders *don't* know about papercrete. Papercrete could be a cheap material that works well for small projects but fails during large projects.

––––––––––

A. Tempting. But read carefully - we're not told that papercrete actually is 'promising for small scale construction'. It's possible that the small scale builders are idiots who use papercrete despite its flaws.
B. The argument was more than an appeal to uninformed popular opinion. The author implied that small scale builders had special expertise which would let us trust their opinion.
C. Promising is used in the same sense both times: material that would likely be useful.
D. We have no idea who is most familiar with papercrete. The passage doesn't say what large scale builders know about it.
E. **CORRECT.** It's possible that large scale builders are *very* familiar with papercrete, and because they know what it's like, they realize that it would be disastrous for large scale projects.

Question 14

QUESTION TYPE: Necessary assumption

CONCLUSION: None of the plays written last year will be popular centuries from now.

REASONING: None of the plays written last year will be performed centuries from now.

Only plays that skillfully explore human nature will continue to be performed, and the plays written last year don't skillfully explore human nature.

ANALYSIS: Necessary assumption questions often pretend that two different things are the same things.

I've read Hamlet. But I've never seen it performed. A play can be popular with readers even if no one *performs* it anymore. (though Hamlet is performed, of course)

The argument assumes that being performed is a necessary condition for a play to be popular.

––––––––––

A. **CORRECT.** Exactly. If plays can be popular even if they aren't performed, then the argument hasn't proven anything.
B. The conclusion wasn't about whether plays deserve critical acclaim. This is a red herring.
C. It doesn't matter whether the drama critic has personally read or seen all the plays. They only need evidence that none of the plays explored human nature very well. They could have got this evidence from reading reviews.
D. Critical acclaim is not relevant. Acclaim is neither necessary nor sufficient for a play to be performed or popular.
E. That's nice. But none of the plays performed last year skillfully examined human nature, so it's hard to see how this is relevant.

Question 15

QUESTION TYPE: Principle

CONCLUSION: Medicals researchers shouldn't keep their research confidential.

REASONING: Humans might suffer if researchers keep research confidential.

ANALYSIS: You can't assume *any* moral principles on the LSAT. Even something as obvious as: 'it is a bad thing for humans to suffer needlessly'.

Pretend you're a space alien. You can assume facts are true, such as 'humans breathe oxygen'. But you can't assume anything about what is right or wrong.

Many modern principle-justify questions simply ask you to assume the moral principle that already 'feels' right.

————————————

A. Too narrow. This doesn't cover behavior that only 'might' cause humans to suffer. The stimulus doesn't say that withholding info always causes suffering.
B. That's nice. But this is just a conditional statement - it doesn't tell us anything about the world. It's like saying 'if I had a billion dollars, I'd be rich'. That statement doesn't help pay my electricity bill, and this statement doesn't justify the stimulus.
C. **CORRECT.** Here we go. It's definitely possible that withholding info causes suffering. This principle tells us that it's wrong to allow that possibility.
D. This is useless. Maybe researchers also have a moral obligation not to share company info. This principle says researchers must obey all obligations.
E. This tells us what would be wrong for a *company* to withhold information. The stimulus is about what *researchers* should do.

Question 16

QUESTION TYPE: Point At Issue

ARGUMENTS: Marife says the movie was bad because it violated mystery movie conventions.

Nguyen says the conventions don't matter, since the main point of the movie was to show the relationship between the detective and the assistant.

ANALYSIS: For point at issue questions, find something the authors have an opinion about, and disagree on.

Marife thinks the movie was bad and that the mystery movie standards were important. Nguyen thinks the standards weren't the main point. Nguyen doesn't say whether the movie is good.

————————————

A. Very tempting trap answer. But Nguyen doesn't say whether the movie is good or bad.
B. Marife doesn't say whether the relationship was important. She just thinks that not following murder mystery conventions was unforgivable.
C. **CORRECT.** A bit tricky. Nguyen says that the murder shouldn't be taken to define the film. This is another way of saying that the movie shouldn't be classified as a murder mystery. Marife clearly believes the movie *was* a failed attempt at a murder mystery.
D. Neither person talks about universal criteria necessary for *every* murder mystery. Marife might think that mysteries only need 5 of 7 characteristics, for example.
E. No one mentions this. This is playing on outside assumptions that good mysteries allow viewers to solve the murder.

Question 17

QUESTION TYPE: Weaken

CONCLUSION: 'First Teacher' programs should be expanded.

REASONING: Some educational programs teach parents to be their child's 'First Teacher'. These children do better in school.

ANALYSIS: There could be selection bias. Who participates in these experimental education programs?

If only wealthy, educated parents enroll their children in experimental programs, then those children could be succeeding because of their background rather than the programs.

The right answer gives another alternate explanation: The parents in the program tended to be teachers. It makes sense that teachers did a good job teaching their children.

A. Who cares what children enjoy? The stimulus is only concerned with their school performance.
B. **CORRECT.** If your mother is a teacher, she will literally be your 'First Teacher'. It's possible the program only worked because the parents have educational experience. Maybe most parents couldn't achieve success withe the program because they don't know how to teach.
C. Who cares what parents think? The stimulus is about whether the program *works,* not whether it is popular.
D. The argument didn't hinge on cost. And precise estimates aren't always needed. Suppose you'd be willing to spend up to $10 million on this program. If we knew the cost would be somewhere between $1-$2 million, then there'd be no problem funding the program even though the costs aren't precise.
E. 'Some' is a very useless word on strengthen questions. This could mean that 2 out of 100,000 children didn't succeed. That's to be expected.

Question 18

QUESTION TYPE: Principle

CONCLUSION: We should ban anarchist novels if they would harm society.

REASONING: Anarchist novels have a couple of things wrong with them.

ANALYSIS: This argument is missing a step. We know anarchist novels might cause problems. That doesn't necessarily mean we should ban them.

For example, maybe it's wrong to ban books, no matter what's wrong with it. That's actually a principle in many societies, including ours (for the most part).

To support the argument, we need to show that it's permissible to ban books.

A. This tells you when *not* to ban books. We want to show that we *can* ban anarchist books.
B. Very tempting. But, this shows that we can ban books if *banning them* does more 'good than harm'. The stimulus says we can ban books if *the books* do more 'harm than good'. Those are different things.
C. This gives us a necessary condition for banning a book ('only if'). We need a sufficient condition.
D. **CORRECT.** This works. Anarchist novels have two objectionable characteristics. So this shows that it's permissible to ban them.
E. Same as C.

Question 19

QUESTION TYPE: Parallel Reasoning

CONCLUSION: The Gilman survey must have been funded by private corporations.

REASONING: All ResearchTech projects were funded by the government or private corporations. The Gilman survey was a ResearchTech project, and it wasn't funded by the government.

ANALYSIS: This is a good argument. It says everything that falls into a certain category is either A or B. Since this particular thing is in the category and isn't option A, it must be option B.

All the answer choices use the same language. On this type of question, it's extra important you understand the argument's structure, since that's the only way to distinguish answer choices.

———————————

A. Bad argument. This doesn't say that legal restriction are *only* paternalistic or designed to protect civil liberties.
B. **CORRECT.** Ordinance 304 is in the group of laws that are either paternalistic or protect civil liberties. Since it isn't paternalistic, it must protect civil liberties.
C. Close, but we're not told whether Ordinance 304 is a legal restriction on consumer purchases.
D. This argument correctly proves that Ordinance 304 is a legal restriction on consumer purchases. But this argument doesn't say which of the two alternatives it is.
E. This is a bad argument. It's possible the mayor used Ordinance 304 for a purpose he shouldn't have used it for.

Question 20

QUESTION TYPE: Role in Argument

CONCLUSION: Life on Earth may have started when a Martian meteorite carried microbes to Earth.

REASONING: Earth used to be sterile. Mars could have had life at that time. Many meteorites from Mars bombarded Earth.

ANALYSIS: I couldn't prephrase this one. I scanned the answers and saw there were two questions:

1. Was there justification for saying that there could have been life on Mars?
2. Was life on Mars necessary, sufficient or neither for the argument's conclusion?

The justification for the claim is that Mars wasn't sterilized. Mars could have had life.

This is a necessary condition for the argument. Mars couldn't send life unless Mars *had* life. But it's not sufficient. Just because you have life doesn't mean you would send it.

———————————

A. There is *some* justification. We know Mars wasn't sterilized by asteroid bombardment. That's not proof that Mars did have life, but it's evidence Mars could have had life. The second half of this answer is right.
B. This has the same problem as A, and the second half is wrong too. Even if Mars could have had life, that doesn't ensure that a meteorite would have carried it to Earth.
C. **CORRECT.** The justification is that Mars was not sterilized by bombardment. The fact that Mars could have had life is necessary. Otherwise how could Mars have sent life to Earth?
D. The first part is a bit strong. The language in C ('some justification') is better. The argument didn't prove this point very well. Second, the conclusion is not justified. The fact that Mars might have had life doesn't establish that the life could have reached Earth.
E. Wrong. The possibility of life on Mars is definitely required for the argument's conclusion. If there were no life on Mars, how could Mars have sent life to Earth?

Question 21

QUESTION TYPE: Flawed Reasoning

CONCLUSION: Gardeners without a use for homegrown honey will tend to have gardens that don't have excellent pollination.

REASONING: You need bees for excellent pollination. If you install a beehive, you will definitely have bees. But you probably won't have a beehive unless you have a use for homegrown honey.

ANALYSIS: This is like saying that if you install an $8,000 water filtration system, you'll definitely have drinking water. So if you don't install such a system, you'll die of thirst.

A beehive is sufficient for excellent pollination. It's not necessary. I had plenty of bees and pollination in my backyard even though my parents didn't establish a beehive.

A. There may be other advantages to beehives, but it simply isn't economical unless the gardener needs honey.
B. The sufficient-necessary mixup is about whether bees will be present, not whether pollination will occur. Bees are a necessary condition for pollination, that's very clear.
C. The argument doesn't say that a lack of pollination will lead to a lack of fruits and vegetables. The conclusion is not about fruits and vegetables.
D. **CORRECT.** Beehives are a sufficient condition for bees. But they aren't necessary. There are lots of bees in areas without beekeepers.
E. The argument didn't say that beehives always lead to excellent pollination. The author just said that bees are a necessary condition for excellent pollination, and that beehives make sure that a garden will have bees.

Question 22

QUESTION TYPE: Role in Argument

CONCLUSION: It's misguided to praise a poem for its truth.

REASONING: Most common beliefs are true. Poetic excellence must be something rare, not common.

ANALYSIS: This is a tricky question because the final sentence uses the word 'must' which is often used in conclusions. But the final sentence is not a conclusion. In this case, the word 'must' just indicates a necessary condition. Whatever quality is praiseworthy in poems is necessarily rare.

To find the conclusion, ask yourself if a statement is supported by the other statements, or instead supports other statements. A conclusion is supported, and doesn't support other statements.

The statement in question is a premise supporting the conclusion. The main idea is that it's wrong ('misguided') to think that truth contributes to aesthetics. Claiming that an idea is 'wrong' is usually an indication of the main conclusion.

A. The conclusion must be supported by the other statements. But the second sentence doesn't support the final sentence. Instead, the final sentence supports the second sentence.
B. **CORRECT.** The other premise is the second to last sentence. Together they show that people are praising poems for something that is common, not rare. Common things aren't a basis for poetic excellence. This supports the conclusion that praise for poetic truth is misguided.
C. The statement isn't good enough on its own. We need the help of the second to last sentence which tells us that truth isn't rare.
D. 'Background information' is usually data, such as 'most poems use truth'. This statement is a rule about what must be praiseworthy, and it's definitely relevant.
E. The argument doesn't say why commonplace elements of poems aren't praiseworthy.

Question 23

QUESTION TYPE: Flawed Parallel Reasoning

CONCLUSION: Some members of the mayor's staff are suspects.

REASONING: The suspects are former treasury employees, and some members of the mayor's staff are treasury employees.

ANALYSIS: I'll make a parallel argument. 'The suspects are from New York State, and some members of the staff are from New York State.'

That argument obviously doesn't let us prove that some of the suspects are on staff. Millions of people live in New York State.

Back to the argument. There could be 3,000 former treasury employees, 10 of them are suspects, and 5 of the 3,000 are on staff. There's no reason the suspects and staff must overlap, it's a big group.

It's helpful to draw the structure. I've bolded the term in common:

Suspect → **Treasury**

Mayor's Office   SOME   **Treasury**

You can't connect a 'some' statement with the necessary condition of an 'all' statement. You *can* connect with the sufficient condition, but that's another story.

_____

A. This has two 'some' statements. The argument had an 'all statement'. Apart from that, this makes the same flaw. But B is a better choice.
B. **CORRECT.** This has an all statement, and a some statement that connects with the necessary condition. We don't know if the groups overlap.
C. This is a bad argument. It's like saying: all dogs are pets, all cats are pets, therefore some dogs are cats. But it's not the same flaw.
D. This is a bad argument (supermarkets never sell *all* types of food), but it's a different error.
E. The conclusion here is an 'all' statement'. The stimulus concluded with a 'some' statement.

Question 24

QUESTION TYPE: Complete the Argument

CONCLUSION: The type of wood Stradivarius used helped account for the quality of his instruments.

REASONING: We have evidence that the wood in Stradivarius' region was special, and we have no evidence of other causes for the quality of his works.

ANALYSIS: LR questions often get easier near the end. This question is straightforward. The only evidence we have is that special wood may have accounted for the quality of Stradivarius' instruments.

All the wrong answers say things that could be true, or must be false, or have a logical relationship to the stimulus.

You're not looking for a 'could be true' relationship. You want something that completes the argument. The first sentence tells us the purpose of the argument: we must find out why Stradivarius made good violins. The wood is the only solution mentioned.

_____

A. This is contradicted by the first sentence.
B. Irrelevant. The argument is trying to find out why Stradivarius violins are superior. (It's of course possible other violin makers used the wood, but that they couldn't make equally good violins.)
C. This is likely true (see the first sentence). But it doesn't make sense. The argument aims to discover why Stradivarius made better violins.
D. **CORRECT.** This is likely. The third sentence says that the wood Stradivarius worked with had special acoustic properties.
E. Who knows? This is a complete non-sequitur. It doesn't complete the argument. We need something that explains why the violins are special.

Question 25

QUESTION TYPE: Principle

RULE: Accuse someone of plagiarism only if you think they purposely presented someone else's ideas as their own.

APPLICATION: The professor shouldn't accuse Walters of plagiarism.

ANALYSIS: You're not given any facts in this question. Just a conclusion: don't accuse Walters of plagiarism.

The principle gives us a necessary conditions for accusing someone of plagiarism. Only accuse if you think someone did it on purpose.

If the professor is missing this necessary condition, then he shouldn't accuse. Missing the necessary condition is the same thing as the statement's contrapositive.

The contrapositive is: if you don't know whether someone plagiarized on purpose, don't accuse them.

Accuse → Believe purposefully present as own

~~Believe purposefully present as own → Accuse~~

The right answer has to be about the professor's *belief*.

_____

A. The professor might still believe Walters plagiarized even if the evidence isn't completely compelling.
B. This doesn't deal with what the professor believes.
C. **CORRECT.** This deals with the professor's beliefs. Since the professor doesn't think Walters is guilty, he shouldn't accuse him of plagiarism.
D. This is like asking a criminal whether they are guilty. Who cares what Walters thinks?
E. This tells us what the professor *will* do. It doesn't tell us what he *should* do.

Section III - Logic Games
Game 1 - Student Speeches
Questions 1-5

Setup

This is a grouping game, with two sets of variables. The students are grouped into making speeches on friendship and liberty. You also must assign majors to each of the students.

I read this setup a few times before drawing anything, as there were many variables to consider. If a game confuses you, it's worth taking your time to decide on the best way to draw it. A diagram you draw while confused is a bad diagram.

I decided it was best to represent the two groups of speeches horizontally. Friendship has two slots because of the first rule:

```
F  ___  ___
    G    H

L  ___  ___  ___
```

I also added in the second rule: G and H are the majors of the students making friendship speeches. The order doesn't matter, since this is not an ordering game.

Next, it's easy to add rules 3 and 4. I've drawn M floating above F, because we don't know which major M is.

Rule four says R makes a liberty speech. Again, order doesn't matter, so I put R directly in the first spot of L..

```
       M
F  ___  ___
    G    H

L   R   ___  ___
    Ǵ
```

The fifth rule says R isn't a Geology major, so I added that too.

Lastly, P is not a Geology major, and N *is* a Geology major.

$$P \neq G$$

$$N = G$$

I didn't include the part about R from rule 5, as I already drew that directly on the diagram.
O has no rules.

We can list majors for the other two spaces. Remember that there are two geology majors, two history major and one journalism major.

So liberty needs one G, one H and one J:

```
       M
F  ___  ___
    G    H

L   R   ___  ___
    Ǵ    G   H/J
   J/H
```

R can only be J/H since they can't be G. G and H/J fill the other spots.

This game *seems* pretty open ended. However, the last rule is actually pretty restrictive. (The rule about N and P)

N can only be a geology major. If she speaks on friendship, she forces M to be a history major.

Likewise, P can't be a geology major. If P speaks on friendship, M must be a geology major.

Many of the questions use local rules to restrict where N, P and M can go.

43

Main Diagram

F M
 $\overline{G}$ $\overline{H}$

L R
 $\overline{\cancel{G}}$ $\overline{G}$ $\overline{H/J}$
 J/H

(1) P ≠ G

(2) N = G

(3) O is random

Question 1

For list questions, apply the rules one by one to eliminate answers.

This question is a bit different, because we can't use the first four rules. They deal with the groups, friendship and liberty. This question is about majors.

The fifth rule eliminates **D.** P can't be a geology major.

The sixth rule eliminates **E.** N has to be a geology major, not a history major.

Another rule is in the setup paragraph: there are two geology majors, two history majors and one journalism major.

A is wrong because it has two journalism majors.

B is wrong because it has three history majors.

C is **CORRECT.**

Question 2

For this question, P speaks on friendship. Whenever a question gives you a new rule, think how it affects or is affected by existing rules.

P can't be a geology major, and M always speaks on friendship. So that means M must be the geology major, and P is the history major.

```
F   M    P
    ─    ─
    G    H
L   R    __    __
    ─          ─
    Ø     G   H/J
   J/H
```

N has to speak on geology, so she takes that spot in the liberty speeches. I put O in the only spot left.

```
F   M    P
    ─    ─
    G    H
L   R    N     O
    ─    ─     ─
    Ø    G    H/J
   J/H
```

As you can see, the only points of uncertainty are R and O. They can each major in journalism or history.

This disproves **A, B, C,** and **E.**

D is CORRECT.

Question 3

First, fill in the local rule. O speaks on friendship and majors in geology. Since M always speaks on friendship, that means M must major in history.

```
F   O    M
    ─    ─
    G    H
L   R    __    __
    ─          ─
    Ø    G    H/J
   J/H
```

N and P are left and they will have to speak on liberty. N is a geology major (rule 6).

P and R can major in either journalism or history:

```
F   O    M
    ─    ─
    G    H
L   R    N     P
    ─    ─     ─
    Ø    G    H/J
   J/H
```

And that's all we know. **A** is **CORRECT.** M must be a history major.

So we solved a bit more than we needed too, but it's good practice to get all the deductions you can if they flow naturally. You never know which one will be the right answer.

Question 4

N is a geology major. So if she speaks on friendship, M must be a history major, because M always speaks on friendship:

```
F  N    M
   ─    ─
   G    H
L  R    __    __
   ─         G   H/J
   Ø
   J/H
```

O is a geology major because P and R can't be.

```
F  N    M
   ─    ─
   G    H
L  R    O     __
   ─    ─    H/J
   Ø    G
   J/H
```

However, we didn't need to go that far. **A** is **CORRECT**. M can't be a geology major, so **A** must be false.

Question 5

All the answers on this question list two things happening. That should tell you that *both* things need to have a big effect for an answer to be correct.

In several wrong answers, only one of the two elements has an effect. That's not enough to force R to be a journalism major.

For instance, **D** and **E** are wrong. We already knew that M speaks on friendship, so half of these answers add no information.

A makes M a geology major. That has little automatic effect on the setup. It just makes N a geology major in liberty. There are two history major spots left, so P can fill one without forcing R to be a journalism major.

The first part of **B** is good. If O is a geology major, then O and N fill both geology major spots. This forces M to be a history major:

```
F  O/N   M
   ─     ─
   G     H
L  R     N/O   __
   ─     ─    H/J
   Ø     G
   J/H
```

But, the second part of this answer just repeats this deduction. It says M is a history major. We already knew that, based on the first part. This answer doesn't force R to be a journalism major.

C is **CORRECT**. Let's extend the diagram I made for B. If P is a history major, then they must be in L. This forces R to take the journalism major:

```
F  O/N   M
   ─     ─
   G     H
L  R     N/O   P
   ─     ─     ─
   Ø     G     H
   J
```

Game 2 - Seven Professors
Questions 6-12

Setup

This looks like a simple linear/sequencing game, but it's a bit complex due to the fourth and sixth rules.

The first three rules are straightforward ordering rules, though they can't be combined:

$$P - W$$
$$T - S$$
$$V - Z$$

The fourth rule combines with the second rule. It says S can be 3rd at the latest.

So, S can only be 2nd or third since T goes before S. I prefer to make two scenarios, one with S in third and one with S in second.

This allows you to make separate deductions for each diagram, and it takes two rules out of your head and puts them directly on the diagram.

I drew the 5th rule directly on the diagram as well (Y is not last).

Instead of making two scenarios, you could draw 'not S' under spaces 4-7. Which option you go with is a personal choice, pick whichever feels more natural.

This rule about S going third at latest is one that you should internalize though. It's the rule most students forget, and the reason they don't make deductions. I keep space in my head to memorize one crucial rule for every game, and things go faster and much smoother.

The final rule is complicated. If Y is before Z, then P is first:

$$Y - V \rightarrow P_1$$

Here's the contrapositive:

(The V-Z rule fits well on the contrapositive, so I included it as a reminder.)

Note in the second scenario, P can't be first, so this contrapositive applies.

47

Main Diagram

T
___ ___ ___ ___ ___ ___ ___
1   2   3   4   5   6   7
     S   Y̶

T   S
___ ___ ___ ___ ___ ___ ___
1   2   3   4   5   6   7
                               Y̶

(1)   P—W

(2)   T—S

(3)   V—Z

(4)   Y—V $\longrightarrow$ P$_1$

(5)   P̶$_1$ $\longrightarrow$ V $\diagdown$ Y (above) Z (below)

Question 6

For a list question, go through the rules one by one to eliminate answers.

The first rule eliminates **C.** P must be before W.

The fourth rule eliminates **A.** S can't be later than third.

The fifth rule eliminates **D.** Y can't be seventh.

The sixth rule eliminates **E.** Since Y is before V, P should have been 1st.

B is CORRECT.

48

Question 7

S can't lecture first, because T goes before S. So **A** is wrong.

B is **CORRECT.** This scenario shows one possibility that obeys all the rules.

V	T	S	P	W	Y	Z
1	2	3	4	5	6	7

W can't lecture first, because P comes before W. So **C** is wrong.

D is wrong. Y can't lecture first, because of the sixth rule. Here it is again:

$$Y - V \longrightarrow P_1$$

If Y is first, they are before V. So then P must be first, not Y.

E is wrong because V must be before Z.

Question 8

E is **CORRECT.** W can't give the second lecture.

The first three spaces are very limited. We already have to put T-S there. And P goes before W.

So if we put W second, then P goes first and there are four lectures for the first three spaces: T-S, P-W

None of the other answers force two variables into the first three spots. Those letters only have lectures that come *after,* not before.

Question 9

First, draw the local rule: Z is fourth and S is second. I've added in the rule that T goes before S:

$$\underset{1}{T} \quad \underset{2}{S} \quad \underset{3}{\_} \quad \underset{4}{Z} \quad \underset{5}{\_} \quad \underset{6}{\_} \quad \underset{7}{\_}$$

Then, ask yourself what other rules apply. Rule 3 says V goes before Z, so they must go 3rd.

That leaves P-W and Y to go after Z:

$$\underset{1}{T} \quad \underset{2}{S} \quad \underset{3}{V} \quad \underset{4}{Z} \quad \underset{5}{\_} \quad \overset{P-W,Y}{\underset{6}{\_}} \quad \underset{7}{\_}$$

Answers **B-E** don't work based on this scenario. They all violate a rule.

A is **CORRECT.** P could be sixth, as shown by this scenario. It's one possibility that works based on the diagram above:

$$\underset{1}{T} \quad \underset{2}{S} \quad \underset{3}{V} \quad \underset{4}{Z} \quad \underset{5}{Y} \quad \underset{6}{\boxed{P}} \quad \underset{7}{W}$$

Question 10

E is **CORRECT.** V can't go seventh because of the third rule. Z must go after V.

Question 11

First, draw the local rule:

$$\underset{1}{T} \quad \underset{2}{\_} \quad \underset{3}{\_} \quad \underset{4}{Y} \quad \underset{5}{\_} \quad \underset{6}{\_} \quad \underset{7}{\_}$$

Then ask yourself what other rules apply. V must go before Y, because P isn't first. That's rule 6. So V goes 2nd or 3rd.

And S must be 3rd at the latest. That's rule 4. So V and S fill the 2nd and 3rd slots, in either order.

$$\underset{1}{T} \quad \overset{V,S}{\underset{2}{\_}} \quad \underset{3}{\_} \quad \underset{4}{Y} \quad \underset{5}{\_} \quad \overset{P-W,Z}{\underset{6}{\_}} \quad \underset{7}{\_}$$

P-W and Z will fill the slots after Y.

C is **CORRECT.** V now has the same restriction as S, they are interchangeable in this scenario.

All the other answers are possible. The final three variables are very flexible, as long as P is before W.

(I've departed from the two scenarios for this diagram, because it seemed clearer. Always feel free to modify a setup if it doesn't make sense in context)

Question 12

Place Z fourth, and then ask what other rules apply. T-S must be third at the latest (2nd and 4th rules) and V must be before Z (3rd rule).

$$\underset{1}{\underline{\quad}} \quad \underset{2}{\underline{\quad}} \quad \underset{3}{\underline{\quad}} \quad \underset{4}{\underline{Z}} \quad \underset{5}{\underline{\quad}} \quad \underset{6}{\underline{\quad}} \quad \underset{7}{\underline{\quad}}$$

T — S, V   Y, P — W

7 ✗

P-W and Y fill the remaining spots after Z. The only restriction is that Y can't go last.

(As in question 11, I've departed from the two scenarios for this diagram.)

A and **C** are wrong because P-W must be after Z in this case.

B is wrong because W must come after P.

D is wrong because Y must come after Z in this case.

E is **CORRECT,** as shown by this scenario:

$$\underset{1}{\underline{T}} \quad \underset{2}{\underline{S}} \quad \underset{3}{\underline{V}} \quad \underset{4}{\underline{Z}} \quad \underset{5}{\underline{P}} \quad \underset{6}{\boxed{Y}} \quad \underset{7}{\underline{W}}$$

7 ✗

51

Game 3 - Toy Aisles
Questions 13-17

Setup

This is a grouping game with sequencing elements. I found it easiest to represent vertically. You can draw it horizontally if you prefer. These things are just a matter of taste.

1 ___
2 ___
3 ___

The first rule:

R $\longrightarrow$ F or M

The second and third rules:

F   S
/ \ /
M   P

The fourth rule:

[SH] or   H
           I
           S

The fourth rule is harder to draw. H can be before S OR in the same group as S. That's why you can't just attach this to the diagram I drew with F, S, M, P.

Since it's a hard rule to draw, I prefer to just memorize it. I try to keep space in my head for at least one rule to memorize. It makes things go much smoother.

Try it, it's easier than you think to memorize rules. Just take 20-30 second pre-game to load them into your head and repeat them mentally.

There are no deductions to make in this game (apart from combining rules 2 and 3). Instead, you'll have to know the rules well and apply them quickly.

If you can't memorize the rules, then at least make a list like I've drawn in the main diagram section below, and refer to it for each question.

Rules 2 and 3 present the main limit in this game. There are only three groups, and many questions artificially block off one group. That means that F-M&P or S-P will be split between the remaining groups.

Main Diagram

1 ___
2 ___
3 ___

① R $\longrightarrow$ F or M

②   F   S
         / \ /
         M   P

③ [SH] or   H
              I
              S

Question 13

H blocks off the first group. The second rule says F goes ahead of M and P. So That means that F goes 2nd and M and P go third.

The third rule says S goes ahead of P, so S is also second.

```
1  H |
2  F    S
3  M    P
```

That's all we know. R can go in either group, their rules are satisfied either way.

D is CORRECT.

Question 14

P blocks off the third group. That means that F has to go first and M has to go second (second rule):

```
1  F
2  M
3  P |
```

This is a routine deduction. When a question gives you a local rule, you should run through your main rules and see which of them are affected.

That's all we can deduce for this question. Fortunately, it answers the question.

A is CORRECT.

Question 15

This is an unusual question. You may have felt paralyzed at first. There seem to be many possibilities, it's hard to figure out what *must* be true.

Here's the trick. The question tells you that S *must* be in the same aisle as one other variable. So *all* you have to do is make a scenario that obeys the rules.

Whoever you place S with is the variable they *must* be beside, because *any* scenario would place S with that same variable.

This question has given you prior knowledge that S can only be with one person on this question. That's rare on logic games.

Here's the first scenario I tried. I put F second, and MP third (rule 2):

```
1  __   __
2  F    __
3  M    P
```

Then I put R with F (rule 1)

```
1  __   __
2  F    R
3  M    P
```

Then I put HS first (rules 3 and 4)

```
1  H    S
2  F    R
3  M    P
```

This diagram obeys every rule. **B is CORRECT.**

53

Question 16

This question tests your understanding of how the rules interact.

The possibilities in the answers are: H, M, R, and S

You could try drawing all of them. But it's best to decide which are hard to place in the middle.

If you're unsure about these explanations, try drawing the diagrams yourself, and including the rules that apply. For example, place S in them middle, and put H above S.

Ok, let's talk about those four letters. R and S are easy to include in the middle. R can go anywhere as long as it is with F or M.

S has to be above P and at the same level or below H, so the middle is a natural place for S.

Likewise, M only has to be below F, so the middle is a normal place for M.

H is difficult to place in the middle. If H does go in the middle, they must go with S.

Why? Rule 4 says S must go below H or be in the same group. S can't go third because rule 3 says S is before P.

So is H is middle, then S has no option but to go with H.

A is **CORRECT.** For the reasons above, H and M can't be the only ones together in the middle. H has to go with S if H is in the middle.

Question 17

As with all other local rules, you must check which of the rules relates to S.

S comes before P, so P is last (rule 3):

```
1 ___
2  S |
3  P
   ___
```

F comes before P (rule 2), so F comes first. There is no space in group two; the question says S is the only one there.

```
1  F
   ___
2  S |
   ___
3  P    M
   ___  ___
```

F comes before M (rule 2) so M goes in group three.

H must go first, due to rule three. There is no space for H to go with S in group two, due to this question's restrictions.

```
1  F    H
   ___  ___
2  S |
   ___
3  P    M
   ___  ___
```

R can go either first or third. Either order meets the conditions of the first rule.

E is CORRECT.

Game 4 - Zones
Questions 18-23

Setup

If you found this game very hard, don't worry: you're not alone. This game truly confused many LSAT students.

I've thought about it, and decided it's mainly a problem of language. Zones, subzones? What the hell are those?!

Well, here are the three zones:

$$\underline{\quad}\ \ \underline{\quad}\ \ \underline{\quad}$$
$$\ \ 1\qquad 2\qquad 3$$

That's not so complicated. They're really just the places you out variables. That's something you've seen on *dozens* of other games.

'Subzones' are just the variables. Here's an example of the zones with some subzones filled in:

$$\begin{array}{ccc} I & & \\ I & H & R \\ \hline 1 & 2 & 3 \end{array}$$

There are no limits to the number of subzones you can put in a zone, except those limits which we'll see in the rules.

I won't be using zones/subzones again for the rest of the walkthrough. I feel they make this game unnecessarily complicated. The Zones are just groups! And the subzones are just normal letter you put in groups. I'll call them variables.

In some ways, this game has few restrictions. There are *no* rules that force you to place any variables in the diagram. A completely blank diagram is acceptable!

All the answers depend on catching violations of the game's four listed rules, and the restriction that you can have at most three of R, H or I.

The first rule is simple. R can't go first.

$$\underline{\quad}\ \ \underline{\quad}\ \ \underline{\quad}$$
$$\ \ 1\qquad 2\qquad 3$$
$$\ \cancel{R}$$

The rest of the rules are a bit unique. There's no standard way to draw them, so you can just make up whatever drawing works best.

I often use the word 'max' in these situations. The specific form you choose doesn't matter, as long as the rules are clear. Standard diagrams are only important for rule types that repeat.

Here are rules 2-4, as I drew them:

H max 2

H $\longrightarrow$ 1R max

I $\longrightarrow$ $\cancel{H}$ and $\cancel{3R}$

Here are the contrapositives of rule 3 and 4. I don't normally draw these when doing games myself, but if you haven't yet mastered seeing contrapositives in your head, you should draw contrapositives for rules.

$+1R \longrightarrow \cancel{H}$

H or 3R $\longrightarrow \cancel{I}$

That's it. There's no way to make deductions. Instead, you should make a clear list of the rules, and commit them to memory if possible.

Main Diagram

$$\frac{\quad}{\underset{\cancel{R}}{1}} \quad \frac{\quad}{2} \quad \frac{\quad}{3}$$

(1) H max 2

(2) H $\longrightarrow$ 1R max
    +1R $\longrightarrow$ $\cancel{H}$

(3) I $\longrightarrow$ $\cancel{H}$ and $\cancel{3R}$
    H or 3R $\longrightarrow$ $\cancel{I}$

(If you're comfortable with contrapositives, you only have to draw the first half of 2 and 3.)

Question 18

For list questions, use the rules to eliminate answers one at a time.

The third rule eliminates **A.** H can't go with more than 1R.

The fourth rule eliminates **B.** H and I can't go together.

The first rule eliminates **C.** R can't go in group 1.

The second rule eliminates **D.** There can only be max 2H in a group.

E is CORRECT.

Question 19

There's no obvious answer for a must be false question that has no local rule.

Don't get bogged down considering each answer. You should read through them all first, and start with the 1-2 answers that seem most restricted.

Answers **A-C** violate no rules. They were unlikely candidates to be correct, since they use small quantities.

D and **E** are most likely, as they have four variables.

E is fine though. Only rule 4 restricts retail and industrial going together: you can't have 3R with any I's. 2R is fine though. You could even have 3I and 2R in the same group.

D is **CORRECT,** because of rules 2 and 3.

rule 2: We can have at most 2H in a group.

rule 3: When there is H, we can only have 1R.

There are no I's in this answer choice. Since we're stuck with only H and R, we can have three of them at most: 2H and 1R.

Question 20

Approach this question with the mindset that you want to put as many variables in as you can.

Unless a rule tells you *not* to put in a variable, you can put it in.

H and R don't mix very well (rules 1 and 2). And rule 4 says H's and I's can't mix at all.

So R and I are the best candidates.

Rule 4 says that you can have at most 2R in a group that has I. We can include 3I, as you can always do that unless a question says otherwise.

So you can have 2R and 3I = 5

D is **CORRECT.**

Question 21

There aren't many possibilities when we have all nine variables included.

Remember, R can't go in group 1 (first rule).

We also can't have three houses together. But we can't put three houses across all three groups, because H's and I's can't mix.

So we need to put 2H and 1H in two groups. We'd better put at least some of them in group 1, because having H in a group restricts R (rule 3).

R is already blocked from group 1, so putting H there adds no further restriction.

I'm going to build a diagram with 2H in group 1 for now:

```
 H
 H      H
___    ___    ___
 1      2      3
 R̸
```

Since I's can't go with H's, we have to put all 3I in group 3.

```
                I
 H              I
 H      H       I
___    ___    ___
 1      2      3
 R̸
```

We can put at most 2R with the 3I (rule 4), and at most 1R with any of the H (rule 3).

R can't go in group 1. So we end up with this diagram:

```
                R
                R
                I
 H      R       I
 H      H       I
___    ___    ___
 1      2      3
 R̸
```

The only possible alternative would be to put 2H in group 2 rather than group 1:

```
                R
                R
        R       I
        H       I
 H      H       I
___    ___    ___
 1      2      3
 R̸
```

So the answer will involve H and how we place them.

B is **CORRECT.** 2H could go in group 2.

Question 22

Having an I in each group restricts things quite heavily.

First, there are no H in this scenario. H's and I's can't go together (rule 4). This eliminates **B**.

Second, there can be at most 2R in any group in this scenario. I's and 3R can't go together (rule 4). This eliminates **E**.

Third, this means that the only variables left to place are 3R, split between groups two and three. There are a total of six variables in this question, at most.

Here's our base scenario:

```
    I       I       I
  ____    ____    ____
   1       2       3
   R̸
```

A is CORRECT. Here's how it looks:

```
            R
            R       R
    I       I       I
  ____    ____    ____
   1       2       3
   R̸
```

C is wrong because R can't go in group one. So there's no way to put anything there apart from the single I we already have.

D is wrong because there are only 3R left to place in those two groups. We have a max of five variables to put in groups 2 and 3.

Question 23

This question says we use 3R, and there is an H in group 2.

The H in group 2 restricts where we can place our three R. We can put at most 1R there (rule 3)

And we can't place R in group 1 (rule 1). So either we place 1R in group 2 and 2R in group 3, or we place all 3R in group 3:

```
            R       R
            H       R
  ____    ____    ____
   1       2       3
   R̸
```

```
                    R
                    R
            H       R
  ____    ____    ____
   1       2       3
   R̸
```

Remember that we don't *have* to place other letters. We don't have to place any I's, for example.

We *could* place I's, but we don't have to. This is not a game where every variable has to be used, or where every group must be filled.

There's nothing stopping us from putting 2H in group 1. **A is CORRECT.**

B is wrong because no I's can go in group 2, since H is there (rule 4)

C is wrong because there can only be 1R in group 2, since H is there (rule 3)

D is wrong because we're including 3R, and R can't go in group 1. So there's no way to put 1R in both groups 2 and 3. One group has an odd number.

E is wrong because if H were in group 3, then we could only have 1R there. We wouldn't have space to put 3R.

Section IV - Logical Reasoning

Question 1

QUESTION TYPE: Identify The Conclusion

CONCLUSION: The conclusion will likely be that wealth increases carbon dioxide emissions.

REASONING: Money lets us buy things that emit carbon, and countries with recessions emit less carbon.

ANALYSIS: Identify The Conclusion questions are good practice for LR. You should be able to identify the conclusion in *all* arguments. A couple of tips:

- Look for a sentence that is supported by all the others.
- Often, the first sentence is the conclusion.

In this argument, the second and third sentences give reasons that the first sentence is true.

_____

A. This is just a fact about carbon dioxide. You could have removed it and the argument would be the same.
B. CORRECT. This rephrases the first sentence.
C. This is evidence that supports the conclusion: wealth leads to carbon emissions.
D. Same as C.
E. This is just a fact mentioned in the second sentence. It supports the conclusion.

Question 2

QUESTION TYPE: Necessary Assumption

CONCLUSION: The clean city campaign has been a success.

REASONING: There is less trash on the streets than when the campaign started.

ANALYSIS: The argument hasn't shown that the campaign *caused* the decrease in trash. Trash might have declined for some other reason.

_____

A. CORRECT. The negation of this answer is that the trash *was* already declining at the same rate before the campaign started. That means the campaign had no effect.
B. It doesn't matter what the critics *believe*. We only care about what actually happened. The critics' beliefs could be wrong.
C. This could mean that other campaigns were miserable failures, and this campaign was only mildly successful.
D. This affects the spokesman's character. We don't care about that. We only care if his argument is correct.
E. This doesn't matter. If the campaign was really successful the first week and sort of successful the rest of the time, it would still be an overall success.

Question 3

QUESTION TYPE: Paradox

FACTS: Eating sugar raises blood sugar. But people who eat lots of sugar have low blood sugar.

ANALYSIS: Don't be scared by the scientific language. You're just trying to solve a paradox. Sugar raises blood sugar, but in large amounts it reduces it. So sugar must have some other effect that reduces blood sugar.

You don't have to know what metabolized means. You just need to figure out that metabolized and unmetabolized are opposites.

Answer C says insulin metabolizes sugar, reducing the amount of unmetabolized sugar in the blood. And eating sugar raises insulin.

A. This doesn't tell us whether overweight people eat sugar, or why their blood sugar levels are low.
B. This tells us about the kinds of food that have sugar, but it doesn't tell us about their effect.
C. **CORRECT.** Insulin could overcompensate and reduce blood sugar below its normal levels.
D. This would *increase* blood sugar levels.
E. This tells us how sugar is metabolized, but not why blood sugar levels are low if you eat a lot of sugar.

Question 4

QUESTION TYPE: Strengthen

CONCLUSION: Consumers often benefit when companies get a government monopoly.

REASONING: If a company has a monopoly, it doesn't have to spend money on advertising. It can instead invest in research and other things that benefit consumers.

ANALYSIS: Corporations *might* spend their savings on research. Or....they might spend it on whiskey. Mmm, whiskey.

We can strengthen this argument by showing that corporations actually do spend their savings on things that benefit consumers.

A. This tells us that research helps, but it doesn't tell us that corporations actually *do* spend money on research.
B. This shows a necessary condition for benefits, but it doesn't tell us that corporations actually do spend money on things that benefit consumers.
C. **CORRECT.** Here we go. This shows that consumers tend to benefit from monopolies.
D. Great. But this doesn't tell us that a monopoly will increase research spending.
E. This doesn't tell us how the company spends the money. They might waste it.

Question 5

QUESTION TYPE: Most Strongly Supported

FACTS: The skins have decayed from heat and humidity. New fluorescent lights produce less heat than the old tungsten lights, while producing just as much light.

ANALYSIS: It's likely that with fluorescent lights, skins will still be damaged, but less damaged. Humidity is the same, but fortunately there will be less heat.

A. **CORRECT.** Probable. Switching to fluorescent lights should reduce heat, and heat was one of the causes of the skins' deterioration.
B. Who knows? Fluorescent lamps still produce some heat, so multiple fluorescent lamps could still damage the skins.
C. We don't know how many old and new displays there are.
D. The stimulus doesn't say whether humidity will improve. As far as we know it's constant.
E. We have no idea what humidity levels were in the past, or what they are now.

Question 6

QUESTION TYPE: Weaken

CONCLUSION: The number of species on Earth is not declining.

REASONING: New species emerge at the same rate as in past centuries. The rate of extinction hasn't increased since 1970.

ANALYSIS: The conclusion is that the number of species is not declining. That depends on two things:

1. How many new species are emerging?
2. How many species are dying?

It's possible that even in past centuries there weren't enough new species to replace those going extinct.

That would mean that in 1970 the extinction rate was much higher than the new species rate, and the number of species was declining.

A. **CORRECT.** This is not a strong answer, as it only address one year, 1970. But it does *slightly* weaken the argument. It shows us that there are not enough new species to replace all the species going extinct.

  The conclusion only said that the number of species is not declining. So by showing that the number of species declined last year, this weakens the argument.
B. The argument was talking about the entire planet. Individual regions don't matter - they're part of the planet.
C. The argument was talking about the rate of extinction, not the total. We could have many new species even if most species that existed are extinct - the Earth has been around a long time.
D. The argument was about rates of extinction. That's a question of fact. Public opinion is irrelevant.
E. This gives us hope that scientist can prevent some extinctions. It doesn't tell us how many extinctions are happening.

Question 7

QUESTION TYPE: Principle

CONCLUSION: MacArthur should not have published his book.

REASONING: MacArthur's diet would damage people's health, since it doesn't include many fruits and vegetables.

ANALYSIS: With principle-justify questions, you have to find a moral principle that shows the actions in question were wrong. The conclusion is very specific. Publishing the book was wrong.

You can't assume any moral principles on the LSAT. Maybe, for example, it's always ok to publish books. Or maybe it's ok to damage people's health if you help them lose weight.

Many of the wrong answers tell us when we *should* publish, or they talk about what people following a diet should do.

That's irrelevant. We want to prove that McArthur should not publish his book.

———————

A. This goes too far. We don't know that MacArthur's diet would *seriously* damage anyone's health.
B. This tells us whether to follow a diet. The argument was whether you should *publish a book*.
C. This tells us when to publish. We need a rule telling us when *not* to publish.
D. This is the wrong issue. MacArthur knew that his book would help people meet their goal of weight loss. The question is: is it ok to help people lose weight if it hurts their health?
E. CORRECT. MacArthur ought to have known that his advice would harm people's health. According to this, he shouldn't have published.

Question 8

QUESTION TYPE: Principle

PRINCIPLE: Don't do something if it mostly hurts the poor.

APPLICATION: The law shouldn't pass. Rock salt can corrode cars, though modern cars are more protected.

ANALYSIS: You need to find some way that this law hurts the poor. Maybe the poor have cars that are much more likely to be corroded.

———————

A. This doesn't help. The new law wouldn't affect the poor, since they don't own cars.
B. Tempting. But rock salt is just a small part of road maintenance. And using rock salt might actually lower overall maintenance costs.
C. This means cars are harder to buy, but it doesn't mean the poor are more likely to be hurt.
D. CORRECT. Older vehicles are more likely to be corroded by rock salt, and the poor are more likely to buy older cars. This shows that the new law will cause more harm to the poor.
E. This is the opposite of what you need. It shows the poor are less affected by rock salt - they don't use salted roads as often.

Question 9

QUESTION TYPE: Flawed Reasoning

CONCLUSION: Many residents don't remember asking their doctor about severe headaches.

REASONING: 35 people reported asking doctors, but doctors reported 105 visits.

ANALYSIS: There are many other possible reasons why the numbers don't match.

- Maybe people saw their doctor more than once.
- Maybe doctors' records are inaccurate.
- Maybe people lied and didn't want to admit they suffer from headaches.

The right answer uses the first reason.

Watch out - questions often pretend that two things are the same when they're not. The first number is the number of *people* who reported visits. The second number is the number of *visits*. People aren't visits.

Most of the wrong answers only make sense if you completely misunderstand the situation. For any question, if you're confused by the situation in the stimulus, reread it. Wrong answers are always designed to further confuse.

_____

A. Read the first sentence. The study surveyed *all* residents. That's the best possible sample.
B. This would make the situation even stranger. The dilemma is that doctors reported 105 visits from residents, while only 35 people went to see their doctor. If some of those people went outside Groverhill, then there's an even bigger gap.
C. CORRECT. If some residents saw their doctors multiple times about headaches, then that could explain the discrepancy.
D. The argument didn't make this claim. It just said there was a discrepancy between the number of residents who saw their doctor and the number of visits.
E. Who cares about people who didn't see their doctor? The argument is talking about people who *did* go see their doctor.

Question 10

QUESTION TYPE: Weaken

CONCLUSION: Corporate executives are public officials.

REASONING: Corporate executives determine lots of important things in free market economies.

ANALYSIS: Terrible argument. It introduces the term 'public official' out of the blue. I have no idea what public officials do, or what are necessary conditions for being a public official.

Sure, corporate executives have an important job. But they may fail to meet some requirements of being a public official.

_____

A. This strengthens the argument somewhat. Executives are doing the same work that public officials do in other countries.
B. CORRECT. This weakens the argument. The main work of executive is not the work of a public official.
C. So? I'm sure business executives often get paid the same as some sports stars, but that doesn't make business executives athletes.
D. This shows that executives aren't omnipotent. It doesn't tell us whether they are public officials.
E. Democrats and Republicans often cooperate, but that doesn't mean they're the same.

Question 11

QUESTION TYPE: Necessary Assumption

CONCLUSION: Sci-Fi has created an unproductive dissatisfaction with the way the world is.

REASONING: Sci-Fi has created an *appetite* for interstellar space exploration. But technology won't let us explore space. Any gap between *expectations* and reality create discontent.

ANALYSIS: You may have an appetite for millions of dollars and being a Supreme Court justice. That doesn't mean you *expect* those things to happen.

This argument assumes that once you have an appetite for space exploration, you expect it. But just because you like something doesn't mean you assume it will happen.

On necessary assumption questions, look for a gap where a new term is introduced, or whether a link between two terms is merely implied, rather than stated.

A. CORRECT. This is it. If you can have an appetite for space exploration but not *expect* it, then Sci-Fi might not make you discontented.

B. A nonsense answer that strings together terms from the stimulus. It doesn't matter if appetites for exploration are the *only* way that Sci-Fi created discontent.

C. The argument only concerns itself with the appetite for space travel. That in itself may be enough to create discontent.

D. It doesn't matter what most people think. The negation of this answer is 'not most' - half or less. That could mean 49%, which is an insignificant difference.
As long as *some* people expect we can travel to the stars, they could become discontented. The argument didn't specify 'most'.

E. A nonsense answer that uses relevant terms. Read carefully. This answer talks about what would happen *if* we had more advanced technology. It's an irrelevant hypothetical. The argument talked about sci-fi's actual effect in the real world.

Question 12

QUESTION TYPE: Method of Reasoning

CONCLUSION: Lack of medical knowledge can't explain why doctors are getting fooled by medical fraudsters.

REASONING: Doctors have plenty of medical knowledge.

ANALYSIS: The argument shows one situation where lack of medical knowledge is a problem. Then it shows that doctors aren't vulnerable, because they have medical knowledge.

A. Read the second to last sentence. Doctors *are* vulnerable, they often fall for scams.

B. The argument isn't arguing against any hypothesis.

C. Read the last sentence. The argument says doctors *do* have much medical knowledge.

D. CORRECT. 'Disanalogous' just means different. Doctors and regular people are different in that doctors have much medical knowledge.

E. The argument said that the explanation (lack of knowledge) should *not* be accepted in the case of doctors.

Question 13

QUESTION TYPE: Sufficient Assumption

CONCLUSION: Managers should act in the best interest of shareholders.

REASONING: Managers should act in the way that shareholders would want them to act.

ANALYSIS: In sufficient assumption questions, you have to close the gap between evidence and conclusion. Look at the conclusion and reasoning above.

They talk about two different things: what shareholders want, and the best interests of shareholders.

It may seem like a stretch, but you can't assume that shareholders want what's in their best interest. Maybe they're irrational, or they don't realize what's in their best interest.

You can prove the argument correct by showing that shareholders *do* want what's in their best interest.

A. This only affects whether managers can fulfill that obligation. It doesn't tell us whether they *have* that obligation.
B. **CORRECT.** This connects the premise to the conclusion.
C. It doesn't matter which obligation is most important, as long as managers do have an obligation to shareholders.
D. This uses the word 'best' in a different sense. The stimulus talked about serving shareholders' best interests (helping shareholders). This answer talks about *who* can best serve shareholders. That refers to who can help them the most.
E. This doesn't tell us that managers should act in shareholders' best interests. It just makes it easier to do so.

Question 14

QUESTION TYPE: Flawed Reasoning

CONCLUSION: Tagar is wrong.

REASONING: Swiderski and Terrada disagree with Tagar.

ANALYSIS: You don't need to know anything about bacteria to answer this question. The science is just there to scare you.

The argument is simple. The author says that Tagar is wrong because some other scientists disagree with him. It's a silly argument. The author hasn't shown why we should believe those other scientists. Maybe *they* are wrong and Tagar is right.

A. The argument doesn't say how long those scientists have held their views. Why would it matter? People are allowed to change their minds.
B. **CORRECT.** Maybe Tagar is a more credible expert, and we should believe him.
C. The argument didn't say that the two scientists were right because they *outnumber* Tagar.
D. Swiderski and Terrada agree with each other. There's no contradiction.
E. This is silly. The author clearly believes that Tagar's opinion is less justified (i.e. he's wrong)

66

Question 15

QUESTION TYPE: Most Strongly Supported

FACTS:

1. Any good garden compost can help with soil drainage and fertility.
2. The best compost is dark brown, and 40-60% organic matter.
3. Compost with a strong smell of ammonia shouldn't be used for soil drainage and fertility. Its organic matter hasn't decomposed.

ANALYSIS: You can draw this question, though it's not crucial. The first sentence gives us a conditional statement, and so does the third.

Good compost → Drainage (1st sentence)
~~Drainage~~ → ~~Good compost~~ (contrapositive)
Ammonia → ~~Drainage~~ (3rd sentence)

Ammonia → ~~Drainage~~ → ~~Good compost~~

(I left out fertility to simplify this. It's just an extra word that doesn't affect the logic)

So, any compost that smells of ammonia is not good compost. This is because ammonia compost can't be used for drainage, and all good composts can be used for drainage.

A. We have no idea why compost with higher than 80% organic matter is not the best. It might not have anything to do with decomposition.
B. 40% organic compost is best, but other compost might still be *helpful*.
C. There are other reasons compost could be bad. If I laced 50% organic compost with salt, it would be terrible compost, since salt kills plants.
D. This goes too far. The last sentence tells us that organic matter needs to be *sufficiently* decomposed. But maybe it shouldn't be *completely* decomposed.
E. **CORRECT.** This combines the first and third facts. All good compost can be used for drainage, and ammonia compost can't be used for drainage. So ammonia compost isn't good.

Question 16

QUESTION TYPE: Necessary Assumption

CONCLUSION: The department won't get an award unless it gets more funding from non-profit sources.

REASONING: The department won't get an award unless it gets more funding for basic scientific research.

ANALYSIS: I simplified the reasoning above so you can more easily spot the gap. This is *almost* a good argument.

The professor has shown that his department needs more funding for basic science. What the professor *hasn't* shown is that that funding must come from non-profit sources.

There's no reason corporations couldn't fund basic science. The professor has to assume that they won't.

Several wrong answers talk about what will happen *if* the department succeeds. We don't care about that. We only care about *whether* the department can succeed without additional non-profit funding.

A. The professor didn't say that his department was guaranteed success if they get funding. He just said that the department would fail without basic science funding. It's a *necessary* condition.
B. This would be a nice side effect, but it doesn't matter what would happen if the department succeeds. The professor's argument is about whether the department *could* succeed.
C. The professor didn't say the department had to give up it's corporate funding. He just argued the department needed outside funding as well.
D. **CORRECT.** Exactly. The professor has to assume that corporations won't provide additional basic science funding. If corporations did provide extra funding, then the department *wouldn't* need more outside funds.
E. We don't care whether the corporations benefit. We only care if they *believe* they ought to increase basic science funding. Belief and fact are two different things.

Question 17

QUESTION TYPE: Must Be True

FACTS:

1. Stores that distribute coupons often have higher average prices, even after coupon discounts.
2. Stores that use coupons raise their average prices to pay for the high costs of issuing coupons.

ANALYSIS: Some stores use coupons as bait. You can get savings on a *few* items by using coupons. But all other items are more expensive.

So you're lured into the store by the promise of paying $2 less for pizza. You *do* save on pizza, but then you pay more for milk, bread and beef if you buy those items without coupons.

That's because the store's average prices are higher, to make up for the cost of printing coupons. It's hard to say whether coupon users save money overall. They might only buy discounted items, and buy everything else at cheaper stores. However, if a consumer doesn't use coupons at these stores, they will pay more at this store.

A. This sounds tempting. But maybe most consumers who use coupons are smart about it, and shop for non-couponed items at another store. They will save money on couponed items.
B. **CORRECT.** The final sentence shows that this is true. Stores pass expenses on to consumer. How do they do this? By raising the average price in their store. By the way, it's perfectly acceptable for 'certain products' to mean 'most products'. We wouldn't normally say that, but it's accurate.
C. We don't know. There are many factors that affects profits. Stores might introduce coupons *because* profits are low.
D. We're told *nothing* about non-coupon stores, except that they have lower average prices. They might still pass on some costs.
E. The stimulus says that prices will be higher on *average*. That doesn't mean that every single item is higher priced. Coupon items could be reasonably priced, even without coupons. Then other items would be priced far above average, making the overall average increase fairly small.

Question 18

QUESTION TYPE: Necessary Assumption

CONCLUSION: Birth order has no lasting effect on personality. It just affects how others perceive your personality.

REASONING: Birth order studies that rely on others' impressions show that birth order has an impact. Birth order studies that use regular personality tests don't show an impact.

ANALYSIS: The conclusion makes a valid distinction between how your personality is and how others see your personality. Fact and perception are different things.

However, the author hasn't proven their argument. They're assuming that all the studies are valid. But we don't know anything about these studies. Maybe all the studies that use standard personality tests are flawed.

A. **CORRECT.** If this isn't true, then standard personality tests are *completely* useless for studying birth order effects. They couldn't detect any effects. So the studies cited in the stimulus would be worthless.
B. This makes no difference. If you behave differently around your family, then that's just part of your personality, and it can be studied.
C. This is irrelevant. We only care if birth order affects perceptions. It doesn't matter if those perceptions change over time. It makes sense that they would, since your personality changes over time.
D. The conclusion says that birth order has no *lasting* effect on personality. So it doesn't matter if there is an effect in childhood, as long as that effect disappears before adulthood.
E. We don't care if perceptions are accurate. We only care if these perceptions (accurate or not) are *affected* by birth order.

Question 19

QUESTION TYPE: Parallel Reasoning

CONCLUSION: The jury must have returned a verdict.

REASONING: ~~Verdict~~ → Media Trucks, ~~Media Trucks~~ → Verdict

'There are no media trucks.'

ANALYSIS: This is a good argument. It gives a conditional statement as evidence, and one fact ('there are no media trucks').

This fact is used with the contrapositive of the conditional statement to draw a conclusion.

Some answers have good arguments, but they don't use the contrapositive. You should always pick the answer that most mirrors the stimulus.

A. This is a bad argument. It incorrectly assumes that negating the sufficient condition negates the necessary conditions. There could be other reasons that tourism is low.
   H → ~~T~~
   'There will be no hurricane.'
B. **CORRECT.** This argument combines a fact with the contrapositive of the conditional statement.
   H → A, A → H
   'Peter did not rent an apartment'
C. This is almost a good argument, but we don't know whether Renate always keeps her promises. Also, this argument doesn't use the contrapositive. It just uses the conditional statement as it is.
   ~~W~~ → D (Renate promised this)
   'Linus' car isn't working'
D. From the way this is phrased, it's actually not clear that 'last week' includes 'last night'. It might mean every day of the week leading up to last night.
   In any case, this argument doesn't use the contrapositive. It just uses the conditional statement as is.
E. This isn't a good argument. Maybe Manuela is the only person who could solve the problem.

Question 20

QUESTION TYPE: Complete the Argument

CONCLUSION: The argument will probably say that politicians try to convince voters that they will meet their already existing needs.

REASONING: Sales people don't try to change customers' needs. Instead they convince them that a product will meet their existing needs. Politicians are like salespeople.

ANALYSIS: Many complete the arguments use analogies. To answer these questions, think about the logic of the first situation, then apply that logic to the second.

Salespeople aren't trying to change customers' preferences. So politicians aren't trying to change voters' preferences. Instead politicians want to convince people that they offer what voters are looking for.

A. The argument never mentions political opponents or rival salespeople.
B. Same as A.
C. This is what politicians do *not* do. They do not try to change voters' preferences. Instead, they try to convince voters that their policies match those preferences.
D. Voters don't care if politicians are *interested* in the same issues as them. They care whether politicians *agree* with voters on those issues, and whether politicians will make policies that voters support.
E. **CORRECT.** Exactly. Salespeople convince customers that products match their needs, and politicians convince voters that they will enact the voter's preferred policies.

69

Question 21

QUESTION TYPE: Flawed Reasoning

CONCLUSION: My neighbor is wrong to say that my pesticides are spreading to her land in runoff water.

REASONING: My pesticides are harmless, and I don't spray them directly on my neighbor's land.

ANALYSIS: The farmer completely ignores the neighbor's argument. The neighbor says the pesticides are coming to her land via runoff water.

The farmer says the pesticides are safe. But the neighbor's complaint wasn't about safety. It was about the fact that pesticides were reaching her land.

To prove the neighbor wrong, the farmer would have to show that his pesticides weren't reaching his neighbor's land via runoff water.

It is true that the farmer hasn't proved his claim about the safety of organic pesticides (Answer choice A). But this would only be relevant if the neighbor's main complaint had been about safety.

―――――――――――――――

A. See the explanation above. The neighbor's claim was that the pesticides had reached her land, not that the pesticides were unsafe.
B. The neighbor never said that the farmer directly sprays pesticides on her land. That's the only thing the farmer was careful to avoid.
C. **CORRECT.** The farmer *completely* ignores the neighbor's claim about runoff water.
D. The farmer doesn't have to prove why the pesticides are on his neighbor's land. He just has to prove that it's not his fault.
E. The evidence about safety is actually irrelevant, because the neighbor's claim was that the pesticides had travelled to her land. She didn't say whether the pesticides were unsafe.

Question 22

QUESTION TYPE: Role in Argument

CONCLUSION: The disagreement isn't about the word 'art'.

REASONING: The second group agrees that some paintings are not art and should be ignored.

ANALYSIS: This is a bad argument. The two groups disagree on whether some paintings are art.

Just because they both agree that *some* painting are not art, that doesn't mean they agree 100% on what the word 'art' means.

The first group might have a definition of art that excludes 70% of paintings, while the second group only excludes 20% of paintings. There would agree that certain paintings aren't art, but their definitions are different.

The argument cites the statement in question to attempt to prove that both groups agree about the meaning of the word art.

―――――――――――――――

A. The main point of disagreement is whether post-impressionist paintings are art. The two groups *agree* that some other paintings are not art.
B. Complicated nonsense. The argument hasn't given any other evidence that the two groups agree on the definition of art. And this evidence is hardly a commonly accepted reason for concluding that the two groups do agree. I doubt enough people care about these groups for us to describe beliefs about them as 'common'.
C. The argument doesn't say whether the groups are correct that certain paintings aren't art. They just claim that the two groups agree with each other.
D. We have no idea if the dispute is only about aesthetic concerns. This is a nonsense answers designed to sound important.
E. **CORRECT.** Both groups accept that some paintings aren't art. The argument uses this to conclude (incorrectly) that both groups agree what art is.

Question 23

QUESTION TYPE: Paradox

PARADOX: Plankton have declined 10%, and three fish species have started dying. Scientists think these two things are connected.

ANALYSIS: The correct answer must explain both situations and show that they are related.

The best explanation would provide a common cause for both phenomena, or provide a cause for one decline and show that it causes the other decline.

The right answer shows that a bacteria is attacking both the plankton and the fish.

_____

A. The decline in population is *recent*. Waste dumping couldn't explain the deaths if it's been going on for a while.
B. CORRECT. This new bacteria could account for the recent deaths in both plankton and fish, as it attacks both species. This answer shows that the phenomena are related.
C. This explains the slight decline in plankton population. It doesn't explain the *massive* drop in fish populations.
D. This doesn't explain the massive drop in fish populations, it just shows that plankton are contributing.
E. This is very broad. The decline in populations is pretty specific: one type of plankton and three types of fish. The stimulus said other species in the ecosystem are unaffected.

Question 24

QUESTION TYPE: Weaken

CONCLUSION: One of Laroque's students made the painting.

REASONING: The painting was either made by Laroque or one of his students. The painting has a pigment that has never been found in Laroque's paintings before.

ANALYSIS: This is a classic error. The argument tells us something about one group (Laroque), and then implies that the argument has given us information about another group (Laroque's students).

We don't know anything about Laroque's students' paintings. Maybe *they* didn't have the pigment either.

In that case we'd be back to square one - we have no idea whether Laroque made the painting, or whether his students did. Neither of them used the pigment.

You can't choose between two possibilities unless you have information about *both* of them.

_____

A. This slightly strengthens the idea that one of Laroque's students made the painting. They all used a similar style.
B. This explains why we're confused about the painting. It doesn't show that Laroque painted it.
C. CORRECT. This shows we know nothing about the painting. Orpiment has never been found in Laroque's paintings OR in paintings made by his students. So we have no evidence which one of the two groups painted this painting.
D. It doesn't matter whether Laroque's students are important. They could still have made the painting.
E. This might explain why Laroque didn't use orpiment, and why his students would have used it. If anything, it strengthens the argument.

Question 25

QUESTION TYPE: Flawed Parallel Reasoning

CONCLUSION: Dentists agree that brushing with Blizzard is the most effective way to fight cavities.

REASONING: Five out of five dentists agreed that the tartar control in Blizzard is the best tartar control available in a toothpaste.

ANALYSIS: Five dentists is much too small a sample to make a conclusion about the entire dental profession.

There are also flaws with the evidence. Maybe tartar control is useful, but not the most important thing in fighting cavities. It could be that other elements of toothbrushes are more important. Or maybe flossing is also more important.

A. This does go from ten voters to all voters. But this argument goes from Gomez being popular to Gomez having the best policies. Those are unrelated: popularity doesn't make policy. Tartar control is at least related to cavities.

B. This makes a conclusion about *some* voters. You can eliminate it instantly - the stimulus made a conclusion about the *entire* dental profession. Though the rest of this answer is nearly identical to the right answer.

C. Same as B. This says voters 'generally' believe. But we want a conclusion about all voters. Also, this argument sampled many voters, while the stimulus only sampled five dentists.

D. CORRECT. This repeats both major errors. It goes from a small sample to all of 'the nation's voters'. Secondly, it only considers one factor: Gomez's policies. Good policies are helpful, but there are other factors that might not make Gomez best for the nation. Maybe he's corrupt, or can't work well with other politicians.

E. In the stimulus, we were told that the tartar formula is better than all others. Here, the voters just say that Gomez would 'help' the nation. That's not the same as being more helpful than any other candidate.

Preptest 68
Section I - Reading Comprehension
Passage 1 - Corridos
Questions 1-7

Paragraph Summaries

1. The history, features, and function of corridos.
2. Only conventional figures of speech and imagery are used in corridos.
3. Discussion of conventional, repeated lines in corridos.

Analysis

This passage is a straightforward discussion of the history and features of corridos. The author is not making an argument. Rather they are describing corridos for us, based on accepted facts.

Corridos are simple, unembellished narratives that tell stories of the US-Mexico border region using elements and conventions familiar to their listeners.

You should know what each paragraph talks about. The questions mostly test you on details. For this type of passage, you'll do well if you understood everything and can locate facts quickly.

If you read it and still felt confused about what Corridos are, then you should reread the passage. Rereading will help you understand better, and actually speed you up when you do the questions.

Question 1

DISCUSSION: The main point must be true, and cover the purpose of the entire passage.

It's usually easiest to first eliminate answers that are not true.

Here, the purpose is to describe the history, role and characteristics of corridos.

A. This isn't even true. Line 20 says that corridos help reaffirm the cohesiveness of border communities, but we don't know if corridos are the main indicator of cohesiveness.
B. Not even true. The passage doesn't say why we know corridos have their roots in Spain's ballad tradition.
C. Way too specific. Cortez is only used as an example to explain corridos. Corridos themselves are the focus of the passage.
D. This ignores the history of corridos, and the passage's descriptions of how they use imagery and convention.
E. **CORRECT.** Close enough. This doesn't mention the use of imagery, but it covers the first and third paragraphs and comes close to summing up the passage.

Question 2

DISCUSSION: You can't prephrase this type of question. Instead, skim the answers and identify 1-2 that you find most likely to be correct. Then look for confirmation in the passage. There will almost always be a few lines that prove the right answer with 100% certainty.

If you can't find the specific lines that support the right answer, then practice doing this on review. You should be able to do it very quickly.

_____

A. This is never mentioned. Line 23 says corridos *don't* use embellishments.
B. Line 24 says figures of speech are rare.
C. CORRECT. This is mentioned in line 42.
D. Rhyme is mentioned in line 50, but we're not told if it is complex.
E. The word 'English' *never* appears in the passage.

Question 3

DISCUSSION: The tone of the passage is neutral, and fairly scholarly. It seems to be describing settled fact, so this passage likely comes from a textbook than the subject of an academic paper.

The correct answer mentions a book of song forms, which is appropriate.

_____

A. It's unlikely that a tourist brochure would focus on nothing but the history of song. A brochure would describe historical sights, and use less complex language.
B. This passage is about the music of the American-Mexican border area, not Spain.
C. Newspaper editorials are *arguments*. This passage is not an argument.
D. There is not *one* famous native mentioned in this passage.
E. CORRECT. This works. The passage is neutral and simply gives a brief description of corridos. That would fit well into a book describing a variety of song forms.

Question 4

DISCUSSION: Metaphors are mentioned in the second paragraph. You should look there to confirm.

A metaphor uses one thing to describe something else. So if I say that the cattle stampede passed by lightly as a mist, then 'mist' is the metaphor, not stampede.

(Technically that's a simile, not a metaphor, since I used 'as'. I don't care)

———————————

A. Line 35 mentions cattle drives, but as a fact, not as a metaphorical comparison.
B. **CORRECT.** Line 32 mentions mist as a metaphor for a small fight.
C. Line 45 mentions a cypress tree, but it's an actual tree, not a metaphorical tree.
D. Line 30 mentions a fight, but that's the fact. Mist is used as a metaphor to describe the fight.
E. Line 34 mentions stampedes. They are a fact, nor a metaphor.

Question 5

DISCUSSION: Look at the start of the paragraph. It says that corridos are direct. The passage then says that metaphors are used *rarely*.

The lack of metaphors is mentioned to emphasize that corridos use direct language.

———————————

A. **CORRECT.** See the explanation above. The lack of metaphor helps show that corridos use direct language.
B. This is nonsense. There is no commonplace assertion that corridos use narratives. Further, corridos *are* narratives.
C. Corridos are direct. They generally avoid poetic language.
D. Actually, corridos aren't that old. The oldest surviving corrido is only 150 years old.
E. The article mentions variants of the corrido of Cortez in line 43. The passage doesn't say that they all have a metaphor in common.

Question 6

DISCUSSION: For this type of question, pick the 1-2 answers that seem most likely, then look to the passage to find support.

There will usually be a specific line to support the correct answer. If you don't support your answers using the passage, you will make mistakes.

_____

A. We're never told how often this particular corrido was sung.
B. Line 11 says that the oldest complete corrido is from 150 years ago. Apart from that, we have no idea how many corridos survived or how many are complete.
C. **CORRECT.** Lines 45-47 indicate that some corrido lines are a set convention, i.e. they don't change from corrido to corrido.
D. Lines 47-48 say that some lines in the despedida are variable.
E. We have no evidence that the corrido de kiansis was composed by someone from another reason. We're told *nothing* about the author.

Question 7

DISCUSSION: For this type of question, pick the 1-2 answers that seem most likely, then look to the passage to find support.

There will usually be a specific line to support the correct answer. If you don't support your answers using the passage, you will make mistakes.

_____

A. The second paragraph makes clear that corrido writers avoided metaphor because corridos were a very direct form of narrative.
B. We're told *nothing* about other ballads. They may also be familiar to local audiences.
C. Corridos descended from spanish ballads, but that doesn't mean they use the same imagery. It sounds like corridos use imagery from their local area.
D. Rhyme is only mentioned in line 50. Freedom from the constraints of rhyme is never mentioned.
E. **CORRECT.** Corridos share many elements: They're from the border region (line 9), they're direct (lines 21-23), they use local imagery (lines 18-20). Even without a despedida we could probably identify them.

Passage 2 - Secondary Substances in Plants
Questions 8-14

Paragraph Summaries

1. Primary substances are found in all plants. The secondary substances that plants have varies, but the same substances are found in related plants. Secondary substances cause tastes and smells.
2. New secondary substances may be kept by natural selection if they attract helpful insects or repel predator insects.
3. Plants and predatory insects are locked in an arms race. Insects specialize in their methods to overcome plant defenses. This reduces number of types of plants insects can eat.

Analysis

This passage is a neutral description of plant evolution and how insects guide the selection of secondary characteristics. It is not an argument.

If you have trouble with scientific passages, you should realize the *concepts* are not that complicated.

It's the *language* that's difficult. Scientific terms hide simple ideas. *Don't* read through quickly.

Instead, slow down and reread. I promise this material is within your capacity to understand. Spend a bit more time reading the passage, and you'll be able to do the questions *much* faster.

I normally don't recommend outside reading for RC. But if you still have trouble with science passages, I recommend reading *Science* magazine or *Nature*. They're scientific journals. Reading these will help get you comfortable with scientific language.

This is a detail oriented passage. The questions can be answered by finding specific lines in the passage. You *can* get faster at this. On review, practice finding lines that support or eliminate answers.

Question 8

DISCUSSION: The correct answer for main point questions must be true, and it must cover the whole passage.

You can first eliminate answers that aren't true, then eliminate those that are incomplete.

———————————

A. This ignores evolution, which was a major part of paragraphs 2 and 3.
B. This isn't even true. Evolution has narrowed the range of plants that insects can eat, true. But we're not told that plants have fewer secondary substances. It sounds like they have *more* secondary substances, for protection against a wide variety of insects.
C. **CORRECT.** This covers the evolutionary process (paragraphs 2 and 3) as well as plants' tastes and smells (paragraphs 1).
D. This ignores the evolutionary *interaction* mentioned in paragraph 3. Answer C is better. Plants influence insect evolution as well.
E. This ignores the first paragraph, and also does a poor job of describing the final two paragraphs. It isn't just the mutation of secondary substances that's led to the competition. It was the fact that some of them were defensive.

Question 9

DISCUSSION: Insect adaptations are mentioned in the third paragraph. The best approach is to select an answer that seems likely, then check for confirmation there.

A. CORRECT. Line 44 mentions this.

B. Leaf and flower structures aren't mentioned as being indicators of plant defenses. Only flavors and odors (line 49) are mentioned as being signs of defenses.

C. This is amusing. Insects could reproduce more and try to overwhelm plant defenses with an army of vast numbers. Sadly, this wasn't mentioned.

D. Pollination is *helpful* to plants. Plants don't try to form defenses against pollinating plants. The defenses are against insects *eating* plants.

E. The passage *never* mentions different parts of plants.

Question 10

DISCUSSION: Primary substances are only mentioned in part of the first paragraph. They're mentioned to provide contrast with secondary substances. This information clarified what secondary substances are and are not.

A. We're told that primary substances are required for plant growth (line 7), but we're not told *how* they help growth.

B. CORRECT. By mentioning primary substances, the passage clarified what secondary substances are *not*.

C. No. The distinction is between selecting characteristics that help pollination, and selecting characteristics that defend against predators. That's all done with secondary substances. We're not told whether insects have a role in selecting primary characteristics.

D. The *secondary* substances have 'a multitudinous array of chemical' (line 9). We have no idea which chemicals are in primary substances. Maybe it's just a few.

E. Plants use *secondary* substances to adapt, not primary substances. See paragraph 2.

Question 11

DISCUSSION: For an inference question, you should attempt to justify your answer using the passage. There are always specific lines that will allow this.

––––––––––––––

A. **CORRECT.** Lines 8-11 say that secondary substances have no direct role in plant growth or metabolism. But paragraphs 2-3 explain how secondary substances protect against or attract insects.

B. Lines 54-56 suggest the opposite: insects eat only a narrow range of plants.

C. Lines 50-51 show that insects use taste and smell to identify plants they can eat. We don't know if insects can use any other methods.

D. The passage never mentions anything like this. It's unclear why toxic substances would have survived in few species if they helped protect against insects.

E. The passage never mentions if plants have toxic defenses apart from secondary substances.

Question 12

DISCUSSION: Primary substances are the main parts of a plant. They allow plants to grow and use energy.

Secondary substances assist this process by keeping the plant alive. Secondary substances are not strictly necessary to plant survival, they just *help* plants survive.

––––––––––––––

A. The generators aren't a good analogy. Hospitals only use them in case of emergency, while secondary substances are always used.

B. **CORRECT.** This is the best analogy, though it's far from perfect. Primary substances are what allow the plants to function. A plant would be at great risk from predators without secondary substances, but it *could* function. And secondary substances do provide distinctive looks and useful functions, just like paint and taillights on cars.

C. It sounds like both components are necessary in this analogy. Secondary substances are not necessary, they're just useful.

D. This just describes two parts of train brakes. There's no analogy to secondary characteristics, which are the less necessary part of plants.

E. The storage analogy has no relation to plants.

Question 13

DISCUSSION: On most strongly supported questions, look for lines in the passage that support your answer.

Many wrong answers use elements from the passage out of context to confuse you.

A. **CORRECT.** Lines 20-21 says secondary substances continue to appear, due to genetic mutations.
B. Lines 15-16 say that secondary substances give plants their taste and smell. It's possible a single secondary substance could fulfil both rules, the passage never says this can't happen.
C. This simply isn't mentioned in the passage. If you chose this, you must learn to support your answer in the passage before choosing it. With practice, you'll be able to locate relevant lines quickly.
D. Lines 10-12 say only a few secondary substances occur in each species. So the variety is small. However, we don't know if any species only has *one* secondary substance. Maybe all plants have at least 2-3.
E. The word regulator is *never* mentioned in the passage. This is a nonsense answer. Secondary substances protect plants, but they don't assist in primary substances role, as far as we know.

Question 14

DISCUSSION: As with the other questions on this passage, the best approach is to choose 1-2 answers that seem likely, then find lines in the passage to support that answer.

If you can't find lines to support an answer, it's almost certainly wrong.

A. The author never mentions the number of insects. A small number of deadly insects might have a bigger impact than a large number of harmless insects.
B. Absolute nonsense. We're not told whether plants benefitted from evolution. Plants *changed*. It's impossible to say whether they're better or worse, that depends on the situation.
C. The passage never mentions how many species are in a family or how many plant families exist.
D. **CORRECT.** Secondary substances appear due to *mutations*. (Lines 19-21). Paragraphs 2-3 describe how insects have influenced which secondary substances plants keep.
E. Lines 48-50 mention that insects can circumvent plant defenses, but those lines don't mention *how* insects do this.

Passage 3 - Two Economic Theories
Questions 15-22

Paragraph Summaries

1. Warsh found a contradiction in economic theory.
2. Smith discussed efficiency gains from increased size (the pin factory), and also discussed how the invisible hand guides marketplaces.
3. Efficiency gains from size hurt free markets, which require many participants.
4. Economists assumed diminishing returns, because the math was pretty.
5. Better math has allowed economists to model the 'underground river' of the pin factory

Analysis

This is a technical discussion of economic theory. There are things you don't have to know. The most important thing is to have a clear sense of what 'pin factory' and 'invisible hand' refer to.

The main ideas are the pin factory and the invisible hand. In a pin factory, the factory became more efficient when the it grew and workers specialized. Bigger → more efficient. I.e. a small factory produces iPads for $600, a giant one produces them for $100. This can lead to monopoly.

The invisible hand describes the idea of a marketplace. People act out of self-interest and produce public benefit. For example, businesses compete to offer low prices in order to win customers. They don't offer low prices out of the goodness of their hearts, but the effect is the same.

If businesses grow large and efficient, then there will be fewer businesses. This reduces the competition necessary for the invisible hand.

So the pin factory and the invisible hand are conflicting forces. This doesn't mean the *ideas* are wrong. It just means the two things work against each other in the real world.

Lastly, economists ignored the pin factory until they could describe it mathematically.

Question 15

DISCUSSION: The correct answer for main point questions must be true, and it must cover the whole passage.

You can first eliminate answers that aren't true, then eliminate those that are incomplete.

––––––––––––––

A. This isn't even true. Paragraph 4 says economists assumed diminishing returns.
B. This isn't true. *Lack* of rigor prevented the pin factory from being accepted. Rigor is a *necessary* condition. But it's not sufficient. There are probably other reasons the invisible hand was accepted.
C. This only describes the last paragraph.
D. This only describes the second part of the second paragraph.
E. **CORRECT.** This isn't a satisfying answer, but it does directly summarize paragraphs 4 and 5. Paragraphs 1-3 were a lead up to those paragraphs. They showed there was a conflict. Paragraph 4 explained why the conflict had been ignored. Paragraph 5 implies the conflict will now have to be addressed, because economists are considering the pin factory.

Question 16

DISCUSSION: The author agrees that increasing returns exist (lines 50-51). He claims that economists ignored increasing returns not because the idea was wrong, but because the math was hard.

A. The author never says the pin factory idea is wrong.
B. The author agrees that increasing returns exist (lines 50-51). There is a conflict between the pin factory and the invisible hand, but the author accepts both ideas as true descriptions of competing processes.
C. The 'curiosity' here refers to the idea that the pin factory ought to be accepted as a true economic idea - the author has no doubts on that point. They accept the pin factory as a accurate metaphor.
D. Why would the author repeatedly mention the pin factory if he felt indifferent about the idea?
E. **CORRECT.** See lines 50-51. The author agrees that increasing returns occur in many industries. The author speaks positively of the pin factory idea throughout the passage, and never says it is wrong.

Question 17

DISCUSSION: When a question mentions a specific paragraph, you should quickly reread/skim that paragraph and decide on the purpose of the paragraph, *before* reading the answers.

This will take a bit more time, but it will let you answer the question much faster.

The fourth paragraph shows that the pin factory idea was not rejected because it was wrong. Rather it was because the math was hard.

A. Nonsense. There is no theory that attempts to resolve the tension between the pin factory and the invisible hand. This definitely isn't mentioned in the fourth paragraph.
B. **CORRECT.** Close enough. It was mathematically difficult to model the pin factory, and that is why the idea was ignored.
C. Nonsense. The word intuition isn't even mentioned in the passage, let alone the fourth paragraph.
D. The third paragraph mentions the tensions between the two assumptions. But no paragraphs mention the tensions between modeling the two different assumptions.
E. There's no argument against an economic assumption given anywhere in the passage. The author accepts both the pin factory and invisible hand as true, without questioning them.

Question 18

DISCUSSION: Make sure you understand what 'underground river' means.

Economists were always aware of the pin factory. They understood that increasing returns to scale existed.

But they couldn't model increasing returns. So while economics was influenced by the pin factory, it was a hidden, 'underground' influence.

The fifth paragraphs shows that better math allowed economists to model the pin factory.

A. Actually, the scientific aspirations of economics were what *blocked* economists from taking the pin factory idea seriously. See lines 41-47.
B. Warsh's book just describes the conflicting ideas in Smith's book. Better mathematical modeling was what allowed the pin factory to be taken seriously. See the final paragraph.
C. CORRECT. See lines 53-59. The new mathematical methods allowed economists to model the pin factory.
D. The tendency of industries towards monopoly is an *effect* of the pin factory. The passage never mentioned an increase in this tendency. It was better math that allowed the pin factory to be modeled.
E. Economists didn't lower their standards. Instead they created a better model. See lines 53-59.

Question 19

DISCUSSION: Railroads are an example of an industry with increasing returns to scale, i.e. the pin factory idea.

The example shows that economists were aware that increasing returns existed. They just didn't pay much attention to increasing returns because they couldn't model them.

A. There's no ambiguity in the invisible hand. It's perfectly clear. And, railroads referred to the pin factory idea, not the invisible hand.
B. We have no idea why the pin factory was hard to model.
C. Railroads are just an example of increasing returns. The passage doesn't say that such industries are becoming more common.
D. CORRECT. Yes. The pin factory model is a better description of railroads. They don't follow the invisible hand model, because railroads tend towards monopoly.
E. Increasing returns often lead to *monopoly,* not competition. See lines 25-26.

Question 20

DISCUSSION: Increasing returns means that the bigger your business gets, the more efficient it is. This creates a natural monopoly - the biggest business is the most profitable.

The pin factory model says that specialization allows increasing returns to scale.

Many of the wrong answers involve an industry getting more efficient, but not bigger.

A. The publishing house has gotten *smaller*. It seems more efficient, but a company has to get *bigger* to get returns to scale.
B. **CORRECT.** Specialization has allowed the beehive to grow and specialize further, becoming more efficient in the process. This is exactly the pin factory model.
C. The school hasn't gotten bigger - there are no returns to scale here.
D. The lobster industry has gotten more efficient, but not bigger.
E. Here the colony did not get more efficient as it grew. In fact, it gets less efficient, because two anthills can keep more ants than a single hill. For increasing returns to scale, a single large anthill should have been more effective.

Question 21

DISCUSSION: To solve this question, you should find the line in the passage that states the answer. If you're slow at doing this, then practice doing it on review. You can learn to find specific lines very quickly - but it's a skill you need to train.

A. Paragraph two just says that specialization is one way to increase returns to scale. It doesn't have to be the only way.
B. The passage didn't say whether economics succeeded in being scientific. And the passage implies that most economic models *do* have mathematical rigor.
C. **CORRECT.** See lines 38-40.
D. Lines 24-26 actually say that the pin factory tends to produce monopoly.
E. The first paragraph shows that Warsh emphasized this contradiction. However, Adam Smith may have been aware of it too. The passage never says whether or not Smith understood the contradiction.

Question 22

DISCUSSION: We're told that increased size allows specialization, which offers increasing returns to scale.

This allows monopoly, because bigger businesses become more efficient and can outcompete smaller businesses.

We need to show a reason why that won't happen. Maybe there are problems to scale as well.

A. This just shows that there could be multiple local monopolies. Lines 24-26 just said there's a tendency towards monopoly, not that increasing returns always lead to absolute power for one company.

B. Who cares what workers get paid? We care about market control by a company.

C. This says nothing about specialization. We have no idea why these businesses dominate their industry. Might have nothing to do with returns to scale.

D. This doesn't prove that returns to scale won't happen. They just vary across industries.

E. CORRECT. This shows that some costs increase as workers specialize. It decreases returns to scale.

Passage 4 - Overinclusive Laws (comparative)
Questions 23-27

Paragraph Summaries

Passage A

1. Police have the power to nullify laws by not enforcing those laws.
2. General laws always punish more than they intend to. If you try to make laws very specific, then you will produce loopholes. Police can avoid the problem of over-general laws by using discretionary non-enforcement.
3. If the law enforcement agency does a poor job of discretionary non-enforcement, the legislature can scold them.

Passage B

1. The city will cut water to a few high income neighborhoods. This will encourage people to pay their water bills.
2. Why doesn't the city just attach a lien to the properties? They'll get money if the house is sold.
3. A loophole prevents the city from attaching liens to houses. It would be better to change the law than to cut off water.

Analysis

On dual passages, you must think about the relation between the two passages.

The first passage is theoretical. The second passage is practical - it's an example of how laws should be changed to be more general.

Discretionary non-enforcement is the idea of having a general law, but not enforcing it when enforcement goes against the spirit of the law.

For example, it is against the law to speed. But, suppose a man is driving his pregnant wife to the hospital so she can have her baby. We would not want to prosecute speeding in that case, driving fast is justified.

If we tried to make an exception for every special case, the law would get complicated. Loopholes would appear. For example, if the law said 'speeding is wrong, unless a pregnant woman is on the way to the hospital', then you might allow speeding if a woman is five months pregnant and going to the hospital for a blood test.

So it's better to have a general law, but allow the police to decide when it doesn't make sense to apply the law.

In the second paragraph, the city did not use a general law. They prevented the city from using a lien except for a tax.

This creates the undesirable situation where the city must shut off water. It would have been better if the city could apply liens for all fees, but only for fees that are like taxes.

Question 23

DISCUSSION: The question asks for a word that is 'explicitly' mentioned.

That means you actually have to *find* the word, in both passages. This is a scanning question.

A. Neither passage mentions this.
B. Only line 54 mentions this.
C. **CORRECT.** See lines 25 and 56.
D. Only passage A mentions this (line 12).
E. Only passage A mentions this (lines 6 and 15).

Question 24

DISCUSSION: For this passage, there is no line that says water shutoffs have never been tried before. But it's implied. Otherwise the author would have mention how they worked in the past.

Normally if a controversy has been going on for a while, then reports will mention the history.

_____

A. We know that over 200,000 customers were late (line 37), but we don't know the total number of customers.
B. High income neighborhoods are being targeted only because they won't be hurt as much. See lines 45-47.
C. The passage says it is better to target high income neighborhoods than low income neighborhoods. But the author may still think its bad to target either group.
D. **CORRECT.** It's implied that this is the first time water has been shut off, e.g. lines 60-61. Otherwise the passage would have made reference to whether water shutoffs had worked in the past.
E. Line 59 does recommend changing the law. But the change could also be to allow liens for fees, and not just taxes.

Question 25

DISCUSSION: If you read the area around line 42, you'll see that some houses are being 'selectively' chosen as an example for the others.

That's closest to answer D, 'discretionary'. Discretion means you have a choice. Officials are choosing which houses they cut water to.

Remember that you have to read the relevant section of passage A to get the meaning of the word in the answer choice. Several of these words have multiple definitions.

_____

A. In this case, particularly means 'thoroughly'.
B. In this case, probability means 'likelihood'
C. In this case, alternative means another option.
D. **CORRECT.** Discretionary means that officials have a choice in who to prosecute, just as officials have a choice in whose water they shut off.
E. Capricious means a sudden change in mood or behavior. In the case of enforcement, it would mean random enforcement, rather than rational discretionary enforcement.

Question 26

DISCUSSION: The plan is to shut off water to some houses. It would be better to apply a lien, but an over-specific law prevents this.

The author of passage A would agree that this is a case where a more general law would have been helpful.

A. I don't see why the author would have an opinion on when the plan ought to be put in place.

B. CORRECT. I think anyone would agree that it wouldn't be nice to turn off water to 231,000 just because they were a bit late on their bill. The author of passage A would probably say this wouldn't be the legislature's intent.

C. The author of passage A would probably say the only reasonable response is to change the law to allow leans for water fees.

D. The author would probably agree, though he's given no opinion on liens. But this course of action isn't an option. The only plan that would allow this would involve changing the law.

E. The author of passage A is against specific laws.

Question 27

DISCUSSION: See lines 32-35. Legislative oversight is a protection against capricious enforcement. The legislature wants to make sure enforcement sticks to the intent of the law (line 35).

A. This is just common sense. Cities won't enforce the law beyond their capacity to do so.

B. Following the legislature's intent is the opposite of capricious enforcement. Lines 32-35 show that the legislature is watching to *prevent* capricious enforcement.

C. Enforcing based on damage is a decent idea. Capricious enforcement, on the other hand, is *bad*. The legislature is watching to make sure it doesn't happen.

D. This is close. Capricious enforcement ignores the intent of the law (line 35). But we don't know why police officers ignore the intent of the law. They might understand the difference between intent and letter of the law, but enforce capriciously for other reasons. Maybe they're mean?

E. CORRECT. See line 35 and the explanation above.

Section II - Logical Reasoning

Question 1

QUESTION TYPE: Must Be True

FACTS: Mice are kept in small cages. That's not healthy or normal. Mice aren't as useful for research if we keep them in a non-normal environment.

ANALYSIS: You can connect the premises.

Small cages → ~~Normal~~ → ~~Useful~~

Keeping mice in small cages makes them less useful for research.

Normally on a test I'd draw that with letters, not words, but the words make it clearer for a book.

_____

A. We're not told whether there will be any changes.
B. We have no idea what's appropriate. It might be appropriate to use mice even if they're not kept in normal conditions. Or maybe it's always wrong to experiment on mice.
C. **CORRECT.** You get this from combining the premises. The non-normal conditions in the cages make the mice less useful for research.
D. We're not told anything about how scientists develop new techniques.
E. We aren't told anything about other mice.

Question 2

QUESTION TYPE: Argument Evaluation

CONCLUSION: Country F is dumping shrimp.

REASONING: Dumping is when you sell for less than the cost of production. Producers from country F are selling for less than the cost of production in country G.

ANALYSIS: The argument doesn't say what cost of production means. Country F could have a different production cost than country G.

It's possible that producers from country F are selling for more than the production cost in country F. In that case, it's unclear whether they are dumping.

This is a rare question type.

_____

A. **CORRECT.** If Country F's producers are selling above the cost of production in their country, they may not be dumping.
B. Who cares whether dumping is harmful or not? The argument is trying to conclude that dumping happened, not whether it is good or bad.
C. This talks about selling for a different price in different countries. That's not dumping. Dumping is selling below production cost.
D. We don't care if shrimp producers make money. We only care whether they are dumping, which is selling below production cost.
E. This doesn't matter. As long as the price is below production cost, it's dumping. Doesn't matter whether it's one cent or a thousand dollars.

Question 3

QUESTION TYPE: Paradox

FACTS: Venus and Earth both have to expel heat. Earth does it with volcanos and fissures. Venus doesn't have those things.

ANALYSIS: The only real possibility is that Venus has some other way to expel heat. On this type of question, just keep your mind open and consider whether the answer would give Venus a way to expel heat.

_____

A. That's nice, but solid rocks won't help Venus expel heat.
B. **CORRECT.** This shows that Venus doesn't need openings in its surface. The surface is slender enough to allow heat to escape.
C. Same as A. This may be interesting information, but it doesn't tell us how the heat escapes.
D. Surface movement is irrelevant unless it creates fissures that allow heat to escape.
E. This is just a fact. Is the atmosphere warm because heat is escaping? If so, _how_ is heat escaping Venus' core?

Question 4

QUESTION TYPE: Weaken

CONCLUSION: Managers shouldn't donate company funds.

REASONING: Managers don't own company funds. The money belongs to the owners.

ANALYSIS: The author hasn't said what owners think of these donations. Maybe it was their idea.

_____

A. If someone is taking care of my money, I'd prefer for all of it to be returned, not just a part of it.
B. **CORRECT.** This shows that the owners know about the donations and approve. The managers aren't stealing.
C. Donating to charity doesn't excuse theft.
D. This is just a fact about how charities _spend_ money. It doesn't show that it's ok for managers to donate money.
E. This is just a fact about how charities get donations. It doesn't tell us whether managers are right to donate.

Question 5

QUESTION TYPE: Principle

PRINCIPLE: Only enforce this law against people who threaten wild animal populations.

APPLICATION: We shouldn't prosecute snake charmers who violate the law by capturing wild snakes.

ANALYSIS: The principle says not to enforce the law if violators aren't causing much harm. So snake charmers must not be doing much to harm snake populations. Snakes' survival isn't at risk.

————————————

A. CORRECT. This shows that snake charmers are pretty harmless. They aren't threatening wild snake populations. There are too few snake charmers for them to make a dent in the snake population.

B. This doesn't tell us that we shouldn't prosecute. It only tells us we might have to prosecute better.

C. Awareness of the law doesn't matter. We want to know whether snake charmers cause harm.

D. Maybe snake populations are less threatened because of strict enforcement of the law. This doesn't tell us not to prosecute snake charmers.

E. This tells us *why* snake charmers break the law. It doesn't mean we should let them off the hook.

Question 6

QUESTION TYPE: Paradox

FACTS: Films profit if more people see them. So movie executives want to get many people to see their movies. TV executives aren't as concerned with getting many people to see their shows.

ANALYSIS: It must be the case that TV shows makes profits some other way.

————————————

A. Irrelevant fluff. You can only watch one movie or TV show at a time, so total audience size is just the number of people watching. Doesn't matter whether they are repeaters.

B. Who cares about movie theatre owners. The stimulus is about the profits of movie and TV executives. They don't own theatres.

C. This is about costs. The stimulus was talking about revenues.

D. CORRECT. This explains it. The money comes from sponsors, because people pay to watch TV. And sponsors care about audience quality, not audience quantity.

E. This felt tempting to me. But it's actually a strange answer. We're talking about all TV shows, not 'the most popular shows'. And why does it matter whether people pay to watch TV? That doesn't explain why executives don't want more people to watch their shows.

Question 7

QUESTION TYPE: Flawed Reasoning

CONCLUSION: The claims are false.

REASONING: No scientific study supports the claims.

ANALYSIS: Absence of evidence is not evidence of absence. An idea isn't wrong just because it hasn't yet been proven correct.

The claims about ginseng could be true even though we don't yet have any evidence to support them.

A. This refers to an ad hominem argument. An example would be 'the claims about ginseng are wrong because marketers are scum.'
B. **CORRECT.** Exactly. Things are true or false, whether or not we believe it. Gravity was always true even when we hadn't discovered it.
C. Irrelevant. There's no sample mentioned. The argument is talking about all ginseng. A unrepresentative sample would be a few ginseng plants out of the millions that exist.
D. It doesn't matter whether people enjoy the tea. The conclusion referred to the claims about stress.
E. Tempting. But the conclusion wasn't about whether the tea reduced stress. It was about whether *ginseng* reduced stress.

Question 8

QUESTION TYPE: Most Strongly Supported

FACTS:
1. Scientists think that microbes eat organic molecules in shale.
2. This takes oxygen out of the atmosphere and adds carbon dioxide.
3. Evidence says carbon dioxide increases global warming.
4. Scientists think the microbes reproduce faster at high temperatures.

ANALYSIS: I couldn't do much to summarize this stimulus. There are four facts. Think about how they work together. It's helpful to use real world knowledge of global warming to think through this.

The question stem asks what will happen *if* the conjectures are true. If the statements are true, then microbes cause global warming *and* are caused by global warming since microbes reproduce faster with higher temperature.

A. We have no idea how many sediments and organic molecules there are. Maybe there are more than enough to last for decades.
B. Umm....all animals produce carbon dioxide, when we breath. We have no evidence that animals reproduce faster with temperature.
C. **CORRECT.** This seems likely. Global warming will increase the activity of the microbes, and the microbes will release carbon dioxide and increase global warming.
D. The stimulus was three sentences. There's no reason to believe that was enough space to tell us everything about the microbes. They might affect other gases as well.
E. We know the microbes produce carbon dioxide. We have no idea how much they produce.

Question 9

QUESTION TYPE: Parallel Reasoning

CONCLUSION: We shouldn't recommend that everyone eat fish.

REASONING: It's healthier to eat fish. But if everyone eats fish, then fish would go extinct and no one could eat fish.

ANALYSIS: On parallel reasoning questions, look for structure.

Here, the structure is that we shouldn't that recommend everyone do something, because then that thing would be destroyed. No one could do it.

A. The conclusion is the same, but the reasons are different. There's no vitamin E shortage.
B. The conclusion is different. This should have said that we should avoid high cigarette taxes because they will destroy smoking.
C. **CORRECT.** Here we go. Something is good for individuals, but if everyone did it, then no one could.
D. The conclusion is different. The conclusion has to say that not everyone should do something.
E. Totally wrong. This just says there is uncertainty about what to do. The stimulus had a clear recommendation.

Question 10

QUESTION TYPE: Most Strongly Supported

FACTS:
1. If you're allergic to cats, you're actually allergic to proteins in their skin and saliva.
2. Different people are allergic to different proteins.
3. Every cat can cause allergic reactions.
4. Many cats only cause allergic reactions in some allergic people, but not all allergic people.

ANALYSIS: This question has a lot of details, making it seem more complicated than it is.

We know that cats don't produce the same reactions. Since skin and saliva proteins cause reactions, that means that skin and saliva proteins probably differ between cats.

A. 'Any' is a sufficient condition indicator. This says *everyone* is allergic to some cats. Nonsense.
B. This made me laugh. There could definitely be some horrible cat that causes reactions in everybody. It could have every terrible protein.
C. **CORRECT.** This seems likely. Otherwise all cats would cause the same people to have allergic reactions.
D. The stimulus doesn't mention intensity.
E. Why would this be true? We might be able to analyze the proteins and determine which cats would cause reactions in certain people.

Question 11

QUESTION TYPE: Role in Argument

CONCLUSION: We shouldn't think that people won't be fooled by maps, even though they aren't often fooled by words.

REASONING: People are taught to beware language, but people aren't taught to beware maps.

ANALYSIS: This is an argument by analogy. We might think that people won't be fooled by maps, because they aren't fooled by language.

The statement in question tells us that there is an explanation for why people won't be fooled by words, but there is no explanation for why people won't be fooled by maps.

A. The statement in question isn't an analogy. It's *part* of an analogy.
B. Nonsense. It's evidence. The claim about map education even comes *after* the claim in question. It can't be drawn from it.
C. **CORRECT.** Yes. The distinction is that people are taught to be cautious with words, but not taught to be cautious with maps.
D. No, the first sentence has this support.
E. The conclusion is the second sentence. It's indicated by the 'should not'. Any sentence with 'should' is generally a conclusion.

Question 12

QUESTION TYPE: Flawed Reasoning

CONCLUSION: The critique is without merit.

REASONING: The doctor probably has personal reasons to claim the drug is safe.

ANALYSIS: Personal bias doesn't make an argument wrong. You should never attack the person making an argument. You should attack their reasons.

The doctor might be right, even if he benefits from his opinions.

A. It doesn't matter whether the critique was broad. The conclusion refers only to the claims about the drug.
B. The argument what degree of a connection to a company means they can't be trusted. The doctor is *employed* by the company. That's a pretty close connection.
C. Why would the *author* be biased against the drug? The argument didn't ignore this possibility. The author argued that the doctor was biased against the drug.
D. **CORRECT.** It's possible the doctor had good reasons to argue the drug is safe. Personal benefit doesn't automatically make you wrong.
E. Nonsense that uses relevant terms to sound plausible. This just says he might have been wrong for reasons other than personal bias. But we want to prove the doctor was *right*.

94

Question 13

QUESTION TYPE: Strengthen

CONCLUSION: Sales will exceed expectations.

REASONING: Sales meet expectations, and rentals exceed expectations. Renters get a discount. The game is addictive and people want to complete it. Rentals are for a couple of days.

ANALYSIS: We need to know how long it takes to complete the game. If you can do it in two days, then renters won't need to buy the game.

If it takes longer than two days, then renters will get hooked and want to buy.

_____

A. It doesn't matter where you buy as long as you do buy the game.
B. CORRECT. This shows that a rental doesn't give you enough time. Renters will get hooked, want to complete the game, and buy it.
C. That's nice. I'm sure the publisher will make good profits. It doesn't tell us whether sales will exceed expectations.
D. It doesn't matter how long you play the game, as long as you buy it.
E. This would _weaken_ the argument. You don't need to buy the game if you get it from a friend.

Question 14

QUESTION TYPE: Evaluate The Argument

CONCLUSION: If an inspector finds a cocker spaniel near Flynn Heights, then the dog probably belongs to someone in Flynn Heights.

REASONING: Most cocker spaniels are registered to addresses in Flynn Heights.

ANALYSIS: Many LSAT questions present two things that seem the same, but actually aren't.

Here, the two things are 'dogs registered in Flynn Heights' and 'dogs that live in Flynn Heights'.

Maybe not all dogs are registered. The correct answer hints that residents of Flynn heights are more likely to register their dogs.

If that's true, then maybe most dogs live outside of Flynn Heights, and registrations are misleading. There could be millions of unregistered cocker spaniels in other neighborhoods.

_____

A. Who cares about other dogs? This is totally irrelevant. The argument would be exactly the same even if there were _no_ other dogs in the city apart from cocker spaniels.
B. Same as A.
C. This doesn't tell us anything about cocker spaniels. Also, it doesn't really matter where officers find cocker spaniels. It could be they don't spend much time in Flynn Heights and therefore don't find many dogs there.
D. This could explain why more cocker spaniels are registered, but it doesn't help us evaluate the argument.
E. CORRECT. If residents are more likely to license their dogs, then maybe there _aren't_ more cocker spaniels living in Flynn Heights. You can assume that license means the same thing as registration. Common sense applies to the LSAT.

Question 15

QUESTION TYPE: Necessary Assumption

CONCLUSION: Genetics lets us associate certain facial expressions with distinct emotions.

REASONING: Humans across cultures can associate certain facial expressions with distinct emotions.

ANALYSIS: This is a bad argument. It did correctly shown that humans are all able to match facial expressions to emotions.

But then the argument concludes that genetics are responsible. That's *possible*, but not certain. Genetics aren't responsible for everything.

A. If an actor looks sad, everyone will recognize the emotion. It doesn't matter whether the actor actually feels sad. This is irrelevant.
B. Same as A. This refers to the emotions people feel. That doesn't matter. We only care about the emotions people *recognize* in others' expressions.
C. This would weaken the argument. The author says that behaviors common across cultures are genetically influenced.
D. **CORRECT.** The negation is 'behaviors common across cultures probably aren't genetically predisposed'. That definitely hurts the argument.
E. This doesn't matter. The main point is that people from different cultures all recognized the same emotions.

Question 16

QUESTION TYPE: Principle - Strengthen

CONCLUSION: The excuse is unacceptable.

REASONING: The defendant was charged with not complying with national codes, rather than local codes. He pleaded ignorance of which code applied.

ANALYSIS: The judge implies that ignorance of the law would have been an excuse if the code had been local. You need to find a reason why that would have been ok, or why violating national codes is inexcusable.

The right answer shows that anything in national codes is also in local codes. So the defendant was aware he was breaking the law no matter which code applied. I'll explain with an example.

Suppose that Hawaii has it's own criminal code. The only new law is that you can't wear funny hats. Every other federal law is also a crime.

You're on a small island. Not sure if it's part of hawaii or the mainland US.

You can't be sure if you're allowed to wear a funny hat. You don't know which code applies.

You can be sure murder is wrong. That's true whichever code applies.

A. If the codes don't overlap, then they're different. But this doesn't tell us what makes national codes worse to violate.
B. So? Presumably there are still penalties for violating both types of code. This doesn't say that it's ok to violate local codes.
C. **CORRECT.** Since the defendant violated national codes, then he also violated the local code. So his excuse that he didn't know which code applied is irrelevant. Both codes prohibited his behavior.
D. This hurts the judge's argument, since the judge said non-compliance with a local code due to ignorance might have been ok.
E. This doesn't tell us that it's ok to violate any laws.

Question 17

QUESTION TYPE: Identify The Conclusion

CONCLUSION: We should have bought the tree last summer.

REASONING: The tree would have had a better chance to survive, for various reasons.

ANALYSIS: Any sentence with 'should' or 'would' is highly likely to be the conclusion of an argument.

The argument is saying that, for the reasons listed, it *would* have been better to buy the tree last summer.

Keep in mind that the first sentence is often the conclusion. You're looking for a sentence supported by all the other premises.

––––––––––––––––––

A. CORRECT. See the explanation above.
B. This is just evidence that we should have bought the tree last summer.
C. Same as B.
D. Same as B.
E. Same as B.

Question 18

QUESTION TYPE: Must Be True

FACTS:
1. Delegates → Party Member
2. Delegates SOME government official
3. Government Official → Speaker

ANALYSIS: We know that all delegates are party members. And some delegates are officials.

Let's say that in fact, 5 delegates are officials. Those 5 officials are also party members, because *all* delegates are party members.

This reasoning works for all 'some' statements. If a sufficient condition is part of a some statement, you can replace it with the necessary condition.

Here's a diagram that shows both conclusions we can make from the facts in the argument. Notice that I am replacing the sufficient condition in the some statement with the necessary condition:

D → PM + D Some GO = PM Some GO
GO → S + GO Some D = S Some D

I think you're better off working towards an intuitive understanding of 'some' statements.

- Some statements are reversible.
- You can make a deduction when part of a some statement is also a sufficient condition
- You cannot make a deduction when part of a some statement is also a necessary condition

So "Cat → Tail, Cats Some Black" lets you conclude "some things with a tail are black"
"Cat → Tail, Tails Some monkeys" does not let you conclude that some cats are monkeys.

––––––––––––––––––

A. This gets the first fact backwards.
B. This is possible, but it doesn't have to be true.
C. CORRECT. Some delegates are government officials, and all officials are speakers.
D. This gets the third fact backwards.
E. We only know that some government officials are party members.

Question 19

QUESTION TYPE: Identify The Conclusion

CONCLUSION: AI won't produce true intelligence unless it radically changes focus.

REASONING: Right now AI only focusses on computation and ignores emotional and non-cognitive intelligence.

ANALYSIS: This says that unless AI changes focus, it will just make 'intelligent' machines that lack even basic emotional intelligence.

The first sentence is often the conclusion if there are no conclusion indicator words. In this argument, all the other sentences support the first sentence.

A. This is true, and it supports the first sentence, which is the conclusion. Because the current focus has this effect, AI won't produce true intelligence unless it changes focus.
B. **CORRECT.** This paraphrases the first sentence. Every other sentence supports this conclusion.
C. Totally irrelevant. We have no idea what AI's objectives are.
D. We have no idea which is more important. We just know that true intelligence requires both.
E. This is true, and it supports the conclusion. AI won't produce true intelligence unless it changes.

Question 20

QUESTION TYPE: Flawed Reasoning

CONCLUSION: Parents probably aren't right about the shows' educational value, assuming the psychologists are correct.

REASONING: Parents judge educational value based on how much they like the shows.

ANALYSIS: This is almost a good argument. The conclusion is hypothetical: it describes what would be true *if* the psychologists were correct.

But, the conclusion didn't show that the parents disagree with the psychologists. It's possible they agree on which shows are the best, even if they formed their opinions for different reasons.

In that case, both the psychologists and parents would be right.

A. There is no sample. This argument refers to all parents. An example of a sample would be 'we looked at 1,000 parents, and therefore we know what *all* parents think'.
B. The argument isn't about what shows children will enjoy. It's about what shows children will find educational.
C. The conclusion is about whether the shows are educational. The argument isn't about what shows children should watch.
D. **CORRECT.** Parents and psychologists might agree, even if they use different methods to judge educational value.
E. The argument didn't say this. It implied that parents *aren't* good judges, but that doesn't mean that psychologists are the *only* good judges. It's possible that school teachers are also good judges of a program's educational value, for example.

Question 21

QUESTION TYPE: Point At Issue

ARGUMENTS: Justine argues that Pellman settled because it thought it would lose the court case.

Simon argues that Pellman might have settled to avoid legal fees. They might have thought they would win, but that winning would be expensive.

ANALYSIS: Simon makes a good point. Whether or not Pellman would win, a court case would cost a lot of money. So the fact that they settled doesn't tell us whether they thought they would win.

Simon and Justine disagree about whether the fact that Pellman settled indicates whether Pellman thought it would win or lose.

_____

A. Neither of them says whether Pellman would likely have lost. Justine just says Pellman *believed* it would lose. They might have had a false belief.
B. Same as A. We have no idea if Justine thinks Pellman's beliefs were accurate.
C. Justine doesn't even mention cost-effectiveness.
D. Same as C. Justine doesn't mention legal fees.
E. **CORRECT.** Justine believes this. Simon argues that Pellman might have settled to avoid legal fees, even if they thought they would win.

Question 22

QUESTION TYPE: Role in Argument

CONCLUSION: It is unjustified to say that science has proven there is no correlation between astrological signs and personality types.

REASONING: Science doesn't have a good definition of personality types, so it can't disprove a correlation between personality types and anything else.

ANALYSIS: This question hinges on a technical understanding of argument structure. Intermediate conclusions are statements supported by evidence and used to support the main conclusion.

Here's an argument that uses an intermediate conclusion:

1. The house is 100 degrees (int. conclusion)
2. Because it's in the sun (premise)
3. Therefore the house is uncomfortably warm (main conclusion)

Statement two is a premise. It supports statement one, which is an intermediate conclusion. Statement 1 supports the main conclusion.

A claim → leads to intermediate conclusion → which supports a final conclusion

In this question, a *general* claim about the scientific understanding of personality is used to support a *particular* claim that science can't disprove astrology. General claims are different from particular claims.

_____

A. No. This describes the statement that science doesn't have a precise definition of personality.
B. **CORRECT.** It's an intermediate conclusion. One premise supports it, and it supports the main conclusion. See the explanation above.
C. The first sentence is the overall conclusion.
D. No. The argument only discredits the position in the first part of the first sentence.
E. Actually, this claim is a general claim that helps prove the specific instance in the first sentence.

Question 23

QUESTION TYPE: Sufficient Assumption

CONCLUSION: Tolstoy is wrong to say that if we knew enough then we wouldn't believe in free will.

REASONING: We can sometimes blame people for their actions, but only when we know a lot about their actions.

ANALYSIS: Let's review what the stimulus tells you:

1. You *can* judge people.
2. You can only judge people if you know a lot about their actions
3. Tolstoy says that if you know a lot about actions, you won't believe in free will.

Judge → Know a lot → No free will

That chain is Tolstoy's idea. We need to prove it wrong. You're allowed to use intuition. Most people would find it strange to judge people who have no free will.

If judgement requires free will, then Tolstoy is wrong, because the stimulus says we *can* judge people. This is answer C. Here's the diagram for C (Judging now has two necessary conditions):

Judge → Know a lot AND Free will → Tolstoy wrong

Tolstoy is wrong because he said knowledge about actions always leads to lack of belief in free will.

_____

A. This doesn't help show that Tolstoy is wrong. We *are* judging people. If Tolstoy is right, we are in fact judging them for things beyond their control. This answer only shows we *shouldn't* do that.
B. The question doesn't talk about whether someone is responsible for an act. It's about whether we *believe* they are responsible.
C. **CORRECT.** See the explanation above.
D. The stimulus doesn't talk about the degree of judgement we're able to make. Irrelevant.
E. This incorrectly negates Tolstoy's premise. It doesn't help show that Tolstoy's claim is wrong.

Question 24

QUESTION TYPE: Flawed Reasoning

CONCLUSION: Crying reduces emotional stress.

REASONING: Stress produces hormones. Crying removes those hormones.

ANALYSIS: This is a causation-correlation error. Stress produces hormones. That doesn't mean hormones *cause* stress.

Hormones may just be a side effect. In that case, removing them would be useless.

_____

A. A nonsense answer. The argument *didn't* prove that crying reduces emotional stress, so it's useless to argue about how it reduces stress.
B. This describes a sufficient-necessary error. That's a different error. (We don't know that the hormones are required for stress by the way. It's possible stress still occurs even if hormones are artificially blocked)
C. This answer says that two things might both influence each other. That's a valid point in general, but it doesn't apply to this argument. There's no two-way influence that we know of.
D. A different error. All the elements are clearly separated in this stimulus.
E. **CORRECT.** The argument assumes that hormones cause stress, because the body produces them when we are stressed. But it could be that they're just a byproduct, and removing them has no effect.

Question 25

QUESTION TYPE: Flawed Parallel Reasoning

CONCLUSION: If a feeder doesn't have a cover, it won't attract many birds.

REASONING: Squirrels keep birds from eating. Squirrels eat at a feeder *only if* it has no cover.

ANALYSIS: This argument makes a sufficient-necessary error. It's *possible* for squirrels to eat from a feeder if it lacks a cover. But you don't know if squirrels *will* eat from a feeder. Lack of a cover was just a necessary condition, not a sufficient condition.

C̶ → B̶ is the conclusion
S → C̶ AND B̶ is the evidence

These statements don't match up. The conclusion incorrectly links two necessary conditions (C̶ and B̶) that don't have a relationship.

It's important you see this structure before looking at the answers. They all use the same words, so structure is the only difference.

––––––––––––––––

A. This is a bad argument, it ignores other reasons that tires can wear out. But it has a different structure from the stimulus. It uses 'likely', which doesn't make a conditional statement.
B. **CORRECT.**
   C̶P̶ → W is the conclusion
   PL → W AND C̶P̶ is the evidence.
   This argument has exactly the same structure as the stimulus. Two necessary conditions (W and C̶P̶) for low pressure are incorrectly linked. Don't worry that 'wear out' is not negated - differences like that are not relevant to argument structure.
C. This argument introduces a moral principle, with the word 'should'. The stimulus only talked about facts, not morals. This also doesn't repeat the necessary condition error made in the stimulus.
D. This is a good argument. Neglect → Too low → Wear out.
E. This argument shows there are two possible causes of tire wear. Then it incorrectly says one cause is irrelevant because it's not the only cause. This is not the error made in the stimulus.

Question 26

QUESTION TYPE: Method of Reasoning

ARGUMENTS: Sarah says that fishermen should be allowed to keep accidental catches, to prevent waste.

Amar says this would give fishermen an incentive to make more 'accidental' catches.

ANALYSIS: Amar makes a good point. If fishermen could keep fish they catch by accident, then some would purposely catch more illegal fish.

If an inspector caught them, they could claim they caught the fish 'accidentally'. It would be hard to prove they caught the fish on purpose.

––––––––––––––––

A. Amar only thinks the recommendation would lead to bad results. He definitely agrees it could be implemented.
B. Amar uses the term 'accident' in a different sense, but he doesn't accuse Sarah of doing so.
C. Amar's argument *weakens* Sarah's case, by showing that fishermen might abuse the system.
D. **CORRECT.** The negative consequence is that Sarah's rule would encourage fishermen to cheat.
E. Amar doesn't mention the past.

Section III - Logical Reasoning

Question 1

QUESTION TYPE: Principle - Strengthen

CONCLUSION: We should continue restoring, despite the risks of acids.

REASONING: We can't see the paintings as they were originally painted.

ANALYSIS: On a principle question, you need an idea to help you decide which course of action is correct.

So you need something that tells you that the benefits of seeing the original paintings outweigh the risks of acid.

You also need a *sufficient* condition, something that says you should restore. Many wrong answers present necessary conditions for restoration.

A. This completely ignores everything the director said. It doesn't mention acid, or the fact that we can't see the paintings.
B. The director doesn't mention aesthetic value. We don't know if this is an important consideration.
C. **CORRECT.** This tells us that it's ok to risk acid damage, because restoration will allow us to appreciate the paintings in their original form.
D. The director didn't mention money, and he didn't say how many people would be able to see the restored painting.
E. This is a fact about the painting. It doesn't tell us whether to restore it.

Question 2

QUESTION TYPE: Most Strongly Supported

FACTS:
1. White footed mice thrive in fragmented forests.
2. Mice transfer Lyme disease to humans, via deer ticks.

ANALYSIS: This information suggests that forest fragmentation helps spread lyme disease to humans.

A. Not necessarily. The mice might be common in regular forests, and *even more* common in fragmented forests.
B. We only know this is true for white-footed mice. It might not be true for other animals.
C. We don't know. At least some species do better in fragmented forests, such as white-footed mice.
D. **CORRECT.** Specifically, efforts to stop forest fragmentation might reduce the spread Lyme disease.
E. We know white-footed mice reach their highest concentration in fragmented forests. But deer ticks might thrive even better in another environment, even if they still *exist* in fragmented forests.

Question 3

QUESTION TYPE: Flawed Reasoning

CONCLUSION: Bike lanes won't make bicyclists safer.

REASONING: Most bike accidents happen on roads with bike lanes.

ANALYSIS: This argument ignores that bicyclists are more likely to be on roads with bike lanes.

It's like arguing that crosswalks are useless, because most pedestrian accidents happen at crosswalks. That's only true because most pedestrians cross at crosswalks. They're still a safe place to cross.

It's a confusion between numbers and likelihood - this is a common LSAT error. Most bike accidents happen on roads with bike lanes, but a bicyclist is less *likely* to have an accident if there is a bike lane.

———————

A. Seriousness of injury is relevant, but this answer suggests that injuries are as serious with bike lanes. It should have said *less* serious.
B. **CORRECT.** Yes. It makes sense that most bicyclists would travel where there are bike lanes.
C. The author didn't even mention a road alteration that would enhance the safety of cyclists.
D. The author doesn't distinguish any roads as being safe. He just makes a blanket statements about all roads with bike lanes.
E. This is a different error. It's like saying: 'we have no evidence that diet soda is dangerous, therefore it's safe.'

Question 4

QUESTION TYPE: Must be True

FACTS:
1. There are now stricter environmental regulations, thanks to public outcry.
2. Cities that had very polluted air 30 years ago have less air pollution.
3. This reduction in air pollution wouldn't have happened without the regulations.

ANALYSIS: We know that air quality in polluted cities improved. This was thanks to the regulations, and those happened due to public protest.

So public protest allowed the reduction in pollution.

The diagram for this question is sort of strange. The statements are more about cause and effect than conditional rules. I couldn't make an A → B → C diagram, but nonetheless I'm very confident that we can conclude the correct answer.

My rule is that I don't diagram if it is a lot of effort to make them. Diagrams are just a tool to solve some questions, they're not the main goal.

———————

A. We only know about the cities that had the worst air pollution *30 years ago*. We don't know anything about the most polluted cities today.
B. We only know that this is true for the cities that had bad air pollution 30 years ago. Some less polluted cities may have become more polluted.
C. We have no idea who complained about air quality.
D. Tempting, but it could be that *all* cities improved their air quality by a similar amount. Also notice that this answer mentions all pollution, while the stimulus focussed on air pollution.
E. **CORRECT.** Public outcry led to the regulations, and the improvement in air quality wouldn't have been possible without the regulations.

Question 5

QUESTION TYPE: Flawed Reasoning

CONCLUSION: Music sharing services aren't to blame.

REASONING: The services deprive musicians of royalties, but recording studios take too large a cut of revenues.

ANALYSIS: This is a common argument in favor of file sharing, but it's not a good one.

If record companies take too much money, then that's a problem. But it's a different problem from file-sharing.

If a musician is entitled to $100,000 in royalties and file sharing takes away $10,000, then file sharing is to blame for that loss, whether or not the original $100,000 was a fair figure.

It's possible that both file sharing AND record companies deserve blame for taking money from musicians.

————————————

A. CORRECT. Yes. It's possible for two separate parties to be blameworthy.
B. This is like saying that cocaine is ok because lots of people do it. It's a different bad argument.
C. This describes an ad hominem flaw. The editorialist didn't attack anyone's character.
D. This is like saying that there is no asteroid coming to hit earth, because then we would all die. It's a different bad argument.
E. This is like saying that someone is a criminal because they drink water. Drinking water is a necessary condition for being criminal (and for staying alive), but it is very far from sufficient. It's a different bad argument.

Question 6

QUESTION TYPE: Paradox

PARADOX: Some doctors tell cancer patients not to take vitamin C, even though vitamin C has beneficial effects.

ANALYSIS: The doctors are telling cancer patients to *stop* taking vitamin C. This suggests there is harm from taking it.

Three of the wrong answers just show that vitamin C doesn't help. That doesn't resolve the paradox. Only answer choice A explains why vitamin C is *harmful* to cancer patients.

————————————

A. CORRECT. This shows that vitamin C helps cancer cells survive treatment. That's bad.
B. This just shows that vitamin C has no benefit. It doesn't show that it's *harmful* and that patients should stop taking it.
C. Same as B.
D. This adds to the paradox. Vitamin C can improve health, so why not take it? This advice recommends being in the best of health.
E. Same as B and C.

Question 7

QUESTION TYPE: Strengthen

CONCLUSION: Lichens can replace expensive pollution monitoring equipment.

REASONING: Lichens can detect copper as well as expensive equipment can detect it.

ANALYSIS: This is a very bad argument. We track many types of pollution. Copper is just one type.

We need to know if lichen can track other types of pollution as well as it tracks copper.

_____

A. This tells us where to install devices. It doesn't tell us if lichen works.
B. This tells us copper is part of the problem. It doesn't tell us whether lichen works for other types of pollution.
C. This doesn't tell us whether lichen can detect pollution apart from copper.
D. This tells us lichens are easy to grow, but it doesn't say whether they work.
E. **CORRECT.** This suggests that lichens will track all types of pollutants, not just copper.

Question 8

QUESTION TYPE: Identify the Conclusion

CONCLUSION: There is little evidence that birds have an innate homing sense.

REASONING: Birds may simply navigate via landmarks, as humans do. We don't say that humans have an innate homing sense.

ANALYSIS: Words such as 'however' are important, they indicate contrast. Authors use 'however' to express their opinion.

In this case the author believes there is little evidence that birds have an innate homing sense. They justify this conclusion with a theory about landmarks.

Homing sense is different from using landmarks. A homing sense would allow you to get home even if you were left in an unfamiliar area.

_____

A. We don't even know if this is true. Birds _might_ have an innate homing sense. It's just that the evidence is inconclusive.
B. **CORRECT.** This comes right after 'however', which often indicates a conclusion and always indicates the author's opinion. The rest of the argument supports this statement.
C. This is evidence to support the statement that we don't have much evidence that birds have an innate homing sense.
D. A nonsense answer. The argument suggests it is indeed possible that birds use landmarks. We don't know if this is an innate ability or not. The word 'innate' was used by the author to refer to a homing sense, not landmark navigation.
E. The author doesn't even say whether humans have an innate sense of direction. He just says that our ability to use landmarks doesn't prove we have such a sense of direction.

Question 9

QUESTION TYPE: Weaken

CONCLUSION: We have no evidence that 'ecological' detergents are greener than regular detergents.

REASONING: *All* laundry detergents have surfectants (including 'ecological' detergents), which are harmful.

We don't know what effect the other ingredients in detergents have on the environment.

ANALYSIS: This is a bad argument. We don't know what the ingredients in ecological detergents do.

We can only conclude that we know nothing. But the argument goes too far and concludes that the ecological detergents are as harmful, even though we have no evidence.

The right answer weakens the argument by a different method. It shows that while 'ecological' detergents have surfectants, they have *less*.

Many of the wrong answers don't distinguish between ecological and non-ecological detergents. To weaken the argument, you must show an advantage for ecological detergents or a disadvantage for non-ecological detergents.

———————————

A. CORRECT. This shows that ecological detergents cause less known harm than regular detergents. They have smaller quantities of a known pollutant.
B. This is a point in favor of regular detergents. It doesn't help us weaken the argument.
C. This tells us that detergents vary in their environmental harm, but it doesn't help us show that ecological detergents are less safe. We need more specific information.
D. That's bad news....but this answer choice doesn't distinguish between ecological and non-ecological detergents. Maybe they're all bad.
E. This raises the harm done by ecological detergent. If it had said *smaller* amounts of ecological detergent, then this would be correct.

Question 10

QUESTION TYPE: Most Strongly Supported

FACTS:
1. Officials want to eliminate pike, which could harm the local ecosystem.
2. Officials won't introduce a predator or drain the lake.
3. Poison has already been tried. It made residents mad.

ANALYSIS: Stick to what you know. Some of the answers *could* be true, but only answer C is supported by the stimulus.

It makes sense. If the poison had eliminated the pike, then the officials wouldn't need to consider other options.

———————————

A. We have no idea why officials ruled out draining the lake. Maybe it would have annoyed residents but caused no economic harm.
B. We don't know. It's possible officials tried poison on another occasion.
C. CORRECT. This is almost certainly true. Otherwise officials wouldn't still be considering options to eliminate the pike.
D. We can't read the officials' minds. We have no idea what they were thinking four years ago.
E. This could explain why officials want to eliminate the pike. But it doesn't have to be true. Maybe the officials just want to protect the ecosystem from damage.

Question 11

QUESTION TYPE: Identify the Conclusion

CONCLUSION: Personal conflicts are not inevitable.

REASONING: Personal conflicts only occur because people are irrational. We overemphasize evidence that other people are bad.

ANALYSIS: Anytime an author gives their opinion, they are usually expressing the main conclusion as well.

The first sentence shows the conclusion. The author disagrees with the assumption that personal conflicts are inevitable.

———————————

A. This is what the author disagrees with.
B. This is an example of how people are irrational.
C. This is true, but it's just an example of how people are irrational and how *that* causes personal conflicts. The main point is that conflicts wouldn't be inevitable if people weren't irrational.
D. **CORRECT.** This is in the first sentence. The author disagrees with the assumption that conflicts are inevitable.
E. This is an example of an irrational belief.

Question 12

QUESTION TYPE: Principle - Strengthen

CONCLUSION: Dried parsley shouldn't be used in cooking.

REASONING: Dried parsley isn't as tasty or healthy as fresh parsley.

ANALYSIS: This is a good argument for using fresh parsley rather than dried parsley. But the conclusion says that dried parsley should *never* be used in cooking.

That doesn't make sense. Maybe dried parsley should be used if there is no fresh parsley available.

To support the conclusion, you need a reason that you shouldn't use dried parsley in cooking, ever.

———————————

A. This doesn't tell us not to use dried parsley even if there is no fresh parsley available.
B. **CORRECT.** This does it. Dried parsley is *not* the tastiest ingredient, so it should never be used.
C. This doesn't help us conclude that dried parsley should never be used in cooking. It's just a general statement about ingredients we already know shouldn't be used.
D. We know fresh parsley is *more* tasty. But that doesn't mean that dried parsley is completely lacking in taste. Something can still taste good even if another food tastes better.
E. We already knew dried parsley is inferior. It doesn't matter if this is true of other foods as well.

Question 13

QUESTION TYPE: Most Strongly Supported

FACTS:

1. The bigger the seal population, the smaller the individual seals.
2. Seal size did not vary over an 800 year period when Natives hunted the seals.

ANALYSIS: By combining the two facts, you can say it's likely that the seal population was stable for those 800 years. Otherwise the seals would have varied in size.

———————

A. We know nothing about the Native peoples, apart from the fact that they hunted seals. We can't say anything about *how* they hunted.
B. *Nothing* in the stimulus mentions the health of the seals. We have no idea whether a larger seal is healthier or not.
C. We're not told *anything* about what the seals were like prior to the 800 year period.
D. We're not told anything Native hunting practices. Maybe they limited their hunt, or maybe there were enough seals that they didn't have to.
E. **CORRECT.** This is true. If the seal population had been reduced than the seals' bodies would have been larger.

Question 14

QUESTION TYPE: Paradox

PARADOX: The city has too much garbage; it will cause environmental damage.

Recycling could reduce the amount of garbage, but increase the environmental damage.

ANALYSIS: Normally we would expect recycling to reduce pollution. There are many possibilities.

Maybe people will produce more garbage if they can recycle. Maybe recycling plants produce pollution. Maybe the recycling program costs so much money that other pollution reduction efforts must be stopped.

On paradox questions it can help to prephrase, but it's best to just open your mind to new possibilities that would explain how recycling would make pollution worse. The right answer is often surprising.

———————

A. If the recycling vehicles cause *less* pollution, then that doesn't help explain why the recycling program will cause damage.
B. **CORRECT.** This could mean that recycling would reduce pollution by 10%, for example, but that recycling would block other projects that would have reduced pollution by 40%. So recycling hurt the effort to reduce pollution by preventing more useful projects.
C. This explains why there is a garbage and pollution problem. It doesn't explain why recycling will make the pollution problem worse.
D. This sounds like it would reduce pollution. We need an answer that shows how recycling will increase pollution.
E. This shows that recycling will encourage people to consume less. That should *help* reduce pollution.

Question 15

QUESTION TYPE: Sufficient Assumption

CONCLUSION: People who know Ellsworth will not be surprised that he's offended by accusations that he has been unethical.

REASONING: Ellsworth is self-righteous and says his generation is less greedy.

ANALYSIS: The conclusion is that no one who knows Ellsworth will be surprised.

The evidence is that Ellsworth is self-righteous, and has been accused of wrongdoing.

You need to join the two. Answer choice E does this. You get:

Self righteous → Easily Offended

So if you know Ellsworth is self-righteous, then you won't be surprised that he's easily offended as well. It's a necessary condition.

The other answers are irrelevant nonsense designed to sound relevant.

_____

A. This doesn't help. If Ellsworth's friends though he was unethical, then they might be surprised that he took offense at the (true) accusations.
B. Was Ellsworth offended by the previous accusations as well? This doesn't help show that no one was surprised.
C. This might mean that Ellsworth is a hypocrite, but it doesn't explain why no one is surprised that he is offended.
D. Just because someone is innocent doesn't mean they will get offended.
E. **CORRECT.** Everyone knows that Ellsworth is self-righteous. This tells us that everyone would therefore expect him to be easily offended.

Question 16

QUESTION TYPE: Flawed Reasoning

CONCLUSION: Declining voter turnout is caused by a belief that politicians can't solve our problems.

REASONING: People think that important problems can only be solved by attitude change AND people believe government can't make this change → declining voter turnout.

And it's true that voters think politicians can't solve our most important problems.

ANALYSIS: There are two problems with this argument.

1. We're told voters think that politicians can't solve our problems. This isn't the same as the sufficient condition in the premise, which was belief that problems can only be solved by attitude change. We don't know *why* people think that government can't solve our problems, it could be for another reason, e.g. corruption.
2. The conclusion says that declining voter turnout is *entirely* caused by the belief. But even if something is a cause, that doesn't prove it's the only cause. There can be multiple sufficient causes of a phenomenon that each contribute.

_____

A. **CORRECT.** Maybe it's also true that fewer people are voting because the internet is too distracting. Who knows? There can be multiple causes for the same phenomenon.
B. The argument was about what people *believe* to be true. It's not about what is *actually* true. Belief and truth are two different things.
C. I can hardly make sense of this one. It says that the argument claims problems can be solved if people decide the argument's premise is wrong. That's irrelevant. The argument didn't even say if this belief was blocking progress. The author just said it reduces voter turnout, which is different.
D. The argument *never* said people are dissatisfied with politicians. Maybe *no one* can solve the problems. In that case there's no reason to blame the politicians. They could be doing their best.
E. The argument never said whether the decline in voter turnout has any negative consequences.

Question 17

QUESTION TYPE: Strengthen

CONCLUSION: The geophysicist thinks there is a natural pattern to asteroid strikes.

REASONING: Asteroid strikes in the late cretaceous caused a halo-like pattern across the northern hemisphere.

ANALYSIS: We can't say that the asteroid strikes are organized just because the asteroids followed a halo-like pattern. Randomness can also produce patterns.

You need evidence that shows the halo wasn't an accident. Answer D does that by showing that the earth forced the asteroids into certain orbits. An object's orbit determines where it will land. This is basic physics, you're allowed to use this kind of knowledge.

Many wrong answer focus on the extinctions, or on the *effects* of the asteroid strikes. We only care whether they followed a pattern.

———————————

A. This explains how the asteroids caused extinctions. It doesn't show that the asteroid strikes followed a pattern.
B. This shows that asteroids could affect continental drift. It doesn't show that they followed an organized pattern.
C. This large cluster of asteroids could be random. This answer doesn't show the asteroid strikes followed an organized plan.
D. CORRECT. This shows that the earth controlled the locations of the asteroid strikes. If an asteroid follows a specific orbit, then it will strike in a pre-determined place. (basic physics, you're allowed to use this)
E. This shows that the asteroid strikes were unusual. It doesn't show they were planned.

Question 18

QUESTION TYPE: Necessary Assumption

CONCLUSION: Most employees will have more than a half hour commute.

REASONING: Most employees can't afford housing within a half hour drive of the new location.

ANALYSIS: You can't prephrase every question. On a question like this it's best just to quickly consider ways that employees could still have a shorter commute.

I thought maybe employees could rent apartments, or the company could subsidize housing.

The right answer gave a different reason, a pay raise. Just keep your mind open to anything that would allow employees to afford housing once the company moves.

———————————

A. This is irrelevant. We only care what happens once the company moves.
B. We don't care why the company is moving. We only care about the effects.
C. We don't care what people think. We only care about the effect the move will have on employees' commutes.
D. Same as A.
E. CORRECT. If the employees have more money after the move, then maybe they will be able to afford housing in Ocean View.

Question 19

QUESTION TYPE: Complete the Argument

CONCLUSION: The early stages of education are most important.

REASONING: Education is like painting. You build on what's been done before. In painting, the early layers are most important.

ANALYSIS: The argument is making an analogy between painting and education.

In painting, the early coats are most important. So it's logical for the argument to claim that education is the same: the early parts are most important.

Many wrong answers mention things that were *never* mentioned in the argument. This is no good for an analogy. You need to find something that was said about painting.

A. We have no idea what is effective in education. Maybe being undemanding is a terrible idea!
B. 'Fundamentals' is not necessarily the same thing as the early stages of education. Also, this answer talks about specific subjects, while the argument referred to education in general.
C. The argument doesn't talk about revising methods in painting, so there's no reason it would mention revising methods in education.
D. The argument never mentions painting being rewarding, so there's no reason it would mention education being rewarding.
E. **CORRECT.** The early coats of paint are most important, so it makes sense that the early levels of education are most important.

Question 20

QUESTION TYPE: Method of Reasoning

CONCLUSION: There are low odds that humans will colonize the universe.

REASONING: If we colonized, most humans would be alive during the era of space colonization. We are not alive during this era, so it's unlikely it will ever happen.

ANALYSIS: The author is attempting to make a probabilistic argument. The author's error is that he hasn't taken a random sample out of all humans that ever existed. He's only looking at our time.

Imagine if you could survey all of human history and ask 1000 people at random from different times: 'does space colonization exist?'. If they all say 'no', then it's likely it never existed.

This method doesn't work if you only survey your own time. It could just be that colonization hasn't happened yet.

In terms of formal procedure, the argument says space colonization will never occur because a something that would probably accompany space colonization (a population explosion) hasn't occurred yet.

A. Tempting, but the argument isn't as simple as this. An example of this reasoning would be 'He hasn't arrived, therefore he never will'.
B. This is a different error. To choose this answer you would have to be able to specify which premise was contradicted and why.
C. This statement is *way* to broad. The argument is talking about space colonization, not all situations.
D. **CORRECT.** The event that is likely is 'we are alive during the era of colonization'. The given event is 'space colonization'.
E. This isn't necessarily an error. For example, I'm confident in predicting that humans will still be breathing oxygen in 500 years.

Question 21

QUESTION TYPE: Flawed Reasoning

CONCLUSION: It isn't true that the president's speech was inappropriate, unless we have independent confirmation that the speech was inflammatory.

REASONING: Riley claimed that the speech was inappropriate because it was inflammatory. But we shouldn't believe Riley when he says the speech was inflammatory.

ANALYSIS: A complex argument. First, Riley introduces a conditional statement.

Inflammatory → Inappropriate

The author doesn't dispute this claim. But the conclusion makes a mistaken negation. It says that the speech is not inappropriate because it is not inflammatory.

I̶n̶f̶l̶a̶m̶m̶a̶t̶o̶r̶y̶ → I̶n̶a̶p̶p̶r̶o̶p̶r̶i̶a̶t̶e̶ (conclusion)

This is a bad technique. There could be other reasons the speech was inappropriate, even if it wasn't inflammatory. You can have a sufficient condition without a necessary condition.

_____

A. **CORRECT.** Yes. Maybe the speech was inappropriate because it was factually incorrect, even if it wasn't inflammatory.
B. On the LSAT, it's almost never a flaw to make a conditional statement, such as 'Inflammatory → Inappropriate'.
C. The author didn't favor the president because of his standing as president. The author just said Riley's evidence is unreliable because of Riley's interest in the matter.
D. We don't know whether Riley has anything to gain. It could be that nobody wins in this dispute.
E. Even if you're well founded in hatred, that could still bias your judgment.

Question 22

QUESTION TYPE: Parallel Reasoning

CONCLUSION: We should play more popular music.

REASONING: We can either play more popular music or go out of business. We shouldn't go out of business.

ANALYSIS: This argument presents two possibilities and argues that one is unacceptable. Therefore we should choose the other.

This isn't technically a good argument. It could be that both possibilities are unacceptable, and one is less unacceptable than others.

But it's a pretty good argument, because it's implied that playing popular music is less unacceptable.

Parallel reasoning questions are long. Several of the answers are structurally different from the stimulus. You can eliminate those first. Anything with three elements or more than two choices is out.

_____

A. We don't know if cost is the greatest concern. This isn't as clear cut as the stimulus.
B. **CORRECT.** This argument chooses one possibility by showing that another is unacceptable. It repeats the error from the stimulus: the argument hasn't shown that we can make curtains fast enough. Maybe neither option is acceptable. However, it's implied that curtain can be made faster.
C. This makes a different flaw. It's possible that curtains could provide privacy, but valences could be used at the same time for other benefits. The structure is different, the stimulus didn't say we could choose both options.
D. This is a complex argument. That alone should tell you that it's incorrect. The stimulus had a simple structure.
E. This introduces far too many elements to parallel the stimulus.

Question 23

QUESTION TYPE: Necessary Assumption

CONCLUSION: The painting is not a genuine Cassett. It is a forgery.

REASONING: Many elements are similar to Cassett paintings. But the brush style is different from any work known to be Cassett's.

ANALYSIS: We're not told whether any other Cassett paintings have unique elements. If other Cassett paintings have unique elements then it's not clear why a unique brush style implies forgery.

_____

A. Who cares? It's only important that it's *possible* for a forger to use those materials. It doesn't have to be easy.
B. **CORRECT.** If other Cassett paintings have unique brush styles, then why does it matter that this painting has a unique brush style?
C. It doesn't matter whether subject matter is unique to Cassett, as long as the subject matter is consistent with the subject matter used in Cassett's paintings.
D. It only matters that brush style *is* a characteristic feature. It doesn't have to be the *most* characteristic feature.
E. This could explain why the forger failed, but it doesn't matter. It only matters whether the brush style is indeed different from Cassett's.

Question 24

QUESTION TYPE: Flawed Parallel Reasoning

CONCLUSION: One Bedroom → ~~Fireplace~~

REASONING: Balcony → Fireplace
Balcony → ~~One Bedroom~~

ANALYSIS: This argument mixed up necessary and sufficient conditions. Having a balcony is *sufficient* to have a fireplace, but it isn't necessary. There can be apartments with fireplaces and no balconies.

It's possible that *every* apartment has a fireplace.

Structurally, the argument takes both necessary conditions and combines them, incorrectly.

Note that the translation for 'No politician is honest' is P → ~~H~~. You negate the necessary condition.

_____

A. Fish → Fur - Conclusion
Cat → Fur
Cat → ~~Fish~~

This is a strange argument, but it doesn't mix up sufficient and necessary. Note that the necessary conditions weren't combined in the same way. Neither is negated in this conclusion.
B. Rule this out right away; it uses a 'some'.
C. **CORRECT.** Dog → ~~Fur~~ - Conclusion
Cat → Fur
Cat → ~~Dog~~

This mistakenly assumes that Cat is necessary for Fur, because Cat is sufficient. Note also that the two necessary conditions have been used to make a statement.
D. Cat → Fish - Conclusion
Cat → ~~Dog~~
Dog → ~~Fish~~

Nonsense, but no sufficient-necessary error.
E. Fish → ~~Dog~~ - Conclusion
Dog → Mammal
Fish → ~~Mammal~~

This is a good argument!

Question 25

QUESTION TYPE: Point At Issue

ARGUMENTS: Alissa says we should keep funding the museum because it's interactive.

Greta says we should keep funding children's TV, because it reaches a wider audience.

ANALYSIS: Alissa and Greta are debating what to do *if* the mayor is correct.

Alissa says we should stop funding TV. Greta says we should stop funding the museum. That's all.

Some questions are actually pretty simple. You might have avoided the right answer here because it seemed too straightforward. That's never a reason to avoid an answer choice.

A. This is the mayor's claim, we don't know what they think about this. They're arguing about what we should do *if* the mayor is correct.
B. Neither of them debate the truth of the mayor's claim.
C. **CORRECT.** Alissa says we should stop funding television. Greta says we should instead stop funding the museum.
D. Greta agrees. Alissa doesn't say whether she thinks TV reaches more children.
E. Greta might agree that the museum provides a better experience. She just said that TV reaches more children.

Section IV - Logic Games
Game 1 - Seven Houses
Questions 1-5

Setup

This is a straightforward linear game, only slightly complicated by the addition of morning, afternoon and evening groups. Here's how you can draw the groups separated:

I drew M, A, and E on this diagram just to make it clear. But I don't actually think you need to include those on your diagram.

You know intuitively that morning is first, afternoon second, evening last. So the two separator lines are enough to divide the groups. I'm leaving out M, A, E on the other diagrams.

You can draw the first and second rules directly onto the diagram:

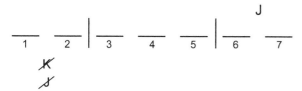

I put J above evening to show that J goes in one of those two spaces. It doesn't matter which one.

I also placed a 'not J' underneath morning, to remind myself that J can't go there. Likewise, K is not in the morning.

Next, K - L - M must go in that order:

K — L — M

This affects our main diagram. K goes in the afternoon, at the earliest, because K can't go in the morning (rule 2). Since L and M come after K, that means they also can't go in the morning:

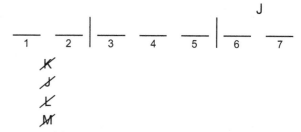

You could stop there, but there's more to deduce. This is a fairly restricted game. First, let's identify the random variables, those with no rules:

J K L M (N O P)

N, O and P have no rules. These are also the only variables that can go in the morning.

This is an important deduction. Two out of three of N, O and P must be in the morning. **If one of N, O and P is not in the morning, then the other two are.**

K and L are also quite restricted. They can only go in the afternoon. Why? Let's try putting them as near to the end as we can.

Remember that M comes after L:

N	O	P	K	L	M	J
1	2	3	4	5	6	7
M				A	E	
K̶						J
J̶						
L̶						
M̶						

There's no space for K or L to be shown in the evening, because J and M fill up the evening. J is always there, and M always comes after K and L.

So here's the full diagram:

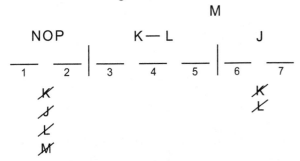

NOP are above the morning as a reminder that two of them go there. J is above evening because it must go there.

K-L are in the afternoon, so I placed them above that space.

M is somewhere after K - L. It could be in the afternoon or evening, so I put it between the two groups.

There's no need to draw M there, but I find it helpful to be able to visualize all 7 variables above the main diagram, roughly where they must be place. It's easy to waste time forgetting which letters are left.

It's very important to try to get the NOP and K-L deductions before moving on. Most of the questions test whether you understood that only NOP can go in the morning, and that KL can't go in the evening.

You don't have to repeat the full diagram on all questions. I'm repeating the full diagram in my explanations only because (I hope) it makes these explanations clearer.

But you should draw simpler diagrams on local rule question. Here is how I would actually draw the scenario I drew two diagrams above, if I were doing it in pencil for a question:

N	O	P	K	L	M	J

My main diagram has all the deductions, and I'll refer back to that when building a local scenario. Do not draw in your main diagram, make new diagrams for each question that requires them.

Main Diagram

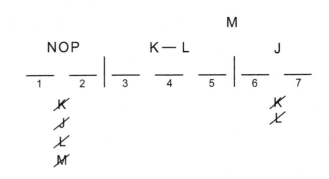

These last two diagrams are somewhat superfluous, but it's sometimes useful to include them to remember why you made the deductions that are on your diagram.

The circle around NOP shows that they have no rules. (though as we saw in the setup, two of them must go in the morning)

K — L — M

J K L M (N O P)

Question 1

For list questions, you should run through the rules one by one and eliminate wrong answers.

The first rule eliminates **E**. J has to be shown in the evening.

The second rule eliminates **A**. K can't be shown in the morning.

The third rule eliminates **B** and **D**. K-L-M must go in that order.

C is **CORRECT.**

Question 2

A is **CORRECT.**

J and K can't be shown beside each other because J goes in the evening, and K must go before L and M.

Here's the closest J and K can get to each other:

$$\underset{1}{\underline{\text{N}}} \quad \underset{2}{\underline{\text{O}}} \; \Big| \; \underset{3}{\underline{\text{P}}} \quad \underset{4}{\underline{\text{K}}} \quad \underset{5}{\underline{\text{L}}} \; \Big| \; \underset{6}{\underline{\text{M}}} \quad \underset{7}{\underline{\text{J}}}$$

The diagram also proves that M *can* go beside J.

C, D and **E** were not likely candidates, because they include P and O, which are random variables. P and O can go practically anywhere.

Question 3

Here's the main diagram again:

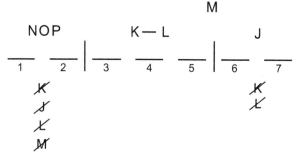

A is wrong because K *cannot* be shown in the evening.

B is **CORRECT.** Both K and L can only go in the afternoon.

This is because K can't go in the morning, and L goes after K. L can't go in the evening, because M goes after L. There's only space for M and J in the evening.

C is wrong, because L *cannot* go in the evening.

D is wrong because M *cannot* be shown in the morning. M must be shown after K, and K cannot be shown in the morning.

E could be true, but it doesn't have to be. Here's a scenario where M goes in the evening:

$$\underset{1}{\underline{\text{N}}} \quad \underset{2}{\underline{\text{O}}} \; \Big| \; \underset{3}{\underline{\text{P}}} \quad \underset{4}{\underline{\text{K}}} \quad \underset{5}{\underline{\text{L}}} \; \Big| \; \underset{6}{\underline{\text{M}}} \quad \underset{7}{\underline{\text{J}}}$$

Question 4

A and **B** are wrong because neither K nor L can go in the evening. K and L have to go before M. There's only space for J and M in the evening.

C is **CORRECT.** P is a random variable, so there is no reason it can't be shown after J. Here's a diagram that shows one way it could work:

D and **E** may seem tempting, because they use random variables. The problem is that they each use *two* random variables.

We saw in the setup that N, O and P are the *only* houses that can be shown in the morning. So two of them *must* be shown in the morning.

So two of these variables can't go after M or after K, because then there would only be one left to go in the morning.

Question 5

There is only one thing you know about N, O, and P: two of them have to be in the morning.

When a question introduces a local rule, you can assume it has an impact on the main diagram.

Here, P is shown in the afternoon. That means that only N and O are left to go in the morning. They *both* must go in the morning.

E is **CORRECT.**

Here's a diagram of the local rule. Note that NO are interchangeable:

P, K-L must be in the afternoon. M and J must be in the evening, since M goes after K - L.

Apart from that, the order doesn't matter.

A is wrong because M can always be shown 7th.

B is wrong because P could be shown 3rd, before K.

C is wrong because O could be shown first instead. O and N are reversible for this question.

D is wrong because M has to be shown in the evening. P, and K - L fill the afternoon.

Game 2 - Five Witnesses
Questions 6-10

Setup

This is a grouping game. It's easiest to draw vertically.

Note: The variables are F, G, H, Iturbe and J. I'm going to use Iturbe's full name because calling him 'I' makes for some weird sentences.

If you're ever unsure how to draw a game, look to the first question. *Usually,* the way things are set up in the first question is also the best way to draw the game, though there are some exceptions.

M ____

T ____

W ____

That's the basic template.

The first rule is that F and G don't testify on the same day. You can't show that on the diagram. Here's how you should draw it:

FG (crossed out in box)

The other rules can all be shown on the diagram.

H̶ M ____

T ____ ____ |

W _I_

I placed Iturbe directly on Wednesday. I filled in a blank spot for Monday, since the final rule says at least one person testifies then.

I drew two lines for Tuesday, thanks to rule 3. The vertical line shows that no more than two people testify.

The final thing you should do is identify the random variables. In this case, J has no rules. You can represent random variables with a circle:

(J)

The F/G rule is important. There are only three groups in this game: M, T, W. Some questions artificially fill one group. The means F and G are split between the remaining groups.

It's also important to think about the total number of spaces. There are only five, and Tuesday always has two people who testify.

Monday always has one person, and Wednesday always has Iturbe. That leaves just one more spot. So either two people will testify Monday, or two people will testify Wednesday.

Main Diagram

H̶ M ____

T ____ ____ |

W _I_

FG (crossed out in box)

(J)

Question 6

For list questions, you should run through the rules one by one to eliminate answers.

Unusually, the first rule eliminates no answers.

The second rule eliminates **A, B** and **C**. Iturbe has to testify Wednesday.

The third rule eliminates **E**. There must be two witnesses testifying on Tuesday.

That leaves only **D**, which violates none of the other rules. **D** is **CORRECT.**

Question 7

You're not given much guidance on this question. It's a cannot be true, and there is no local rule.

The best strategy is to quickly scan through all five answers, and identify those that seem most likely to violate rules. You should consider which variables are most restricted.

A and **B** are not good candidates. F's only restriction is that F can't go with G. Neither of these rules seem likely to place F with G.

The other three answers involve enough variables that they *might* break rules. It's often best to make quick sketches that prove a scenario *can* happen.

This scenario proves **C** can work:

```
H̸ M  F
   T  G   H |
   W  I   J
```

This scenario proves **D** can work:

```
H̸ M  G   |
   T  F   J |
   W  I   H |
```

If you have trouble seeing that these diagrams are correct, then it's possible you don't have a strong grasp of the rules.

You should know the rules like that back of your hand - spend some time learning them before you start the questions. This will speed you up and allow you to make correct diagrams quickly and effortlessly.

E is **CORRECT.** If you put two people on Monday, and Jackson testifies Tuesday then the diagram looks like this:

```
H̸ M  ___  ___ |
   T  J   ___ |
   W  I   |
```

F and G have to go on different days. That leaves one place open on Monday. H is the only variable left, but H can't go there, because H can't testify Monday.

```
H̸ M  F/G  ___ | H ?
   T  J   G/F |
   W  I   |
```

Question 8

You should always draw local diagrams when a question gives you a new rule.

Here, Iturbe and J testify Wednesday. That means only 1 person testifies Monday.

```
H̶ M ___ |

T ___ ___ |

W  I   J  |
```

F and G are split between Monday and Tuesday, because they cannot testify on the same day.

```
H̶ M  F/G |

T  G/F ___ |

W  I    J  |
```

That leaves H to go on Tuesday. Everything is settled.

```
H̶ M  F/G |

T  G/F  H  |

W  I    J  |
```

A and B are wrong because G and F are interchangeable. They could each go on either day.

C is **CORRECT.** If there are two witnesses on each of Tuesday and Wednesday, then there is only one left for Monday.

D is wrong, for the same reason C is right.

E is wrong for the same reason A and B are wrong. G could go on Tuesday with H, but G could also testify Monday.

Question 9

If J is the only witness on Monday, then that means two witnesses testify Wednesday. Tuesday always has exactly two witnesses.

```
H̶ M  J

T  ___  ___ |

W  I    ___ |
```

There are only two groups open now. Since F and G can't testify on the same day, one will testify Tuesday and one will testify Wednesday.

```
H̶ M  J

T  F/G    H  |

W  I     G/F |
```

H goes Tuesday, because that's the only open space left.

B is **CORRECT.**

All the wrong answers involve F and G. They can't be correct answers for a must be true question, because F and G are interchangeable.

Question 10

F and H can only testify together on Tuesday.

They can't testify Monday because H can't testify Monday (rule 4)

They also can't go Wednesday. Then there would be three people on Wednesday, because Iturbe always testifies Wednesday.

That leaves only G and J to testify on Monday and Tuesday. That's not enough, since one person must testify Monday (rule 5) and two people testify Tuesday (rule 3).

So if they testify together, F and H testify on Tuesday:

H̶ M ____

T _F_ _H_

W _I_ ____

That's really all we know. At this point, rather than think about all the possibilities, it's better to just look at the answers and see if you've already solved the question.

D is **CORRECT.** H has to testify Wednesday.

The other answers either can't be true, or could be true but don't have to be true.

Game 3 - Service Targets
Questions 11-16

Setup

This is a complex game. I'm going to use a few symbols that are unique to this game. To make these clear, I'm going to give you a math refresher.

This is a greater-than sign. It means that what comes on the left (or first) is bigger than what comes after.

$$>$$

For example, 6 is bigger than 5

$$6 > 5$$

This next sign is a greater-than-or-equal sign. It means that what comes first is the same size as what comes second, or it's bigger.

$$\geq$$

For example, 7 is greater or equal than 7 (it's equal) and 8 is greater or equal than 7:

$$7 \geq 7$$

$$8 \geq 7$$

6 would not work, because 6 is smaller than 7.

If you're not familiar with these symbols, you should get comfortable with them. They're occasionally useful in logic games.

So, there are three clients, and two different targets for each client: a voicemail target and a website target.

The clients are the base of the diagram. I represented them horizontally, though you could just as easily represent them vertically. That difference rarely matters.

This game is a little tough to wrap your head around. Service target are just numbers that get written in this diagram. So if T's website target is 3, then you would write in in like this:

The rules restrict what numbers we can set the targets to. The first rule says that clients can't have website targets that are longer than their voicemail targets.

This means that the voicemail targets are *greater than or equal to* the website targets. Which is why I showed you the greater than or equal to mathematical symbol. Here's how I represented that on the diagram:

This is a non-standard game. I've never seen a game that required this type of symbol before (arrow + greater-than). So the exact symbol you use isn't that important. You should only worry about perfecting symbols when a rule occurs in many games.

I'm going to draw the third rule next. S's website target is shorter than T's. This means T's is *greater than*. This is *not* the same symbol from the first rule, since the two targets can't be equal.

$$\geq \Big\lgroup \quad \begin{matrix} V & \underline{\quad} & \underline{\quad} & \underline{\not{1}} \\[4pt] W & \underline{\quad} & \underline{\quad} & \underline{\quad} \\ & I & S & T \\ & & \not{3} & \not{1} \end{matrix}$$

(arrow from T to S, labeled >)

Since the arrow goes from T to S, that means that T is bigger, since it is at the start of the arrow.

This a *bit* ambiguous, because the greater than side is facing S. I found this way clearer, but feel free to reverse it in your own diagram if you prefer.

Now, I'll explain the not rules I drew on the diagram. T's website target can't be 1, because then it couldn't be bigger than S's website target. Likewise, S's website target can't be 3.

Since T's website target can't be 1, that means T's voicemail target also can't be 1. The voicemail target has to be bigger or equal to the website target.

If S's website target is 2, then T's website target has to be 3. T's voicemail target also has to be 3, since it has to be larger or equal.

S restricts T. If S's website target is 1, then T's website target can be 2 or 3.

Now, the second rule. Image's voicemail target is shorter than the other two clients' targets. The targets can only be 1, 2 or 3.

That means Image's voicemail target can only be 1 or 2 days. If Image's target were 3, then the other targets couldn't be bigger.

Whenever there are only two possibilities, it's good to draw them both and see what happens.

(technically, there are also only two possibilities for S's website target. I'm splitting on Image's voicemail target because this leads to more restrictions. The voicemail target also restricts the website target)

In the first scenario, Image's voicemail target is 1 day. This means Image's website target is also 1 day, since is has to be smaller or equal than the voicemail target.

$$\geq \Big\lgroup \quad \begin{matrix} V & \underline{1} & \underline{\not{1}} & \underline{\not{1}} \\[4pt] W & \underline{1} & \underline{\quad} & \underline{\quad} \\ & I & S & T \\ & & \not{3} & \not{1} \end{matrix}$$

(arrow from T to S, labeled >)

S and T's voicemail targets can't be 1, because they have to be larger than Image's website target.

That's all we can deduce for the first scenario. For the second scenario, Image's voicemail target is 2.

That means S and T's voicemail targets are 3, because the second rule says their voicemail targets are bigger than Image's.

$$\geq \Big\lgroup \quad \begin{matrix} V & \underline{2} & \underline{3} & \underline{\not{3}} \\[4pt] W & \underline{\quad} & \underline{\quad} & \underline{\quad} \\ & I & S & T \\ & \not{3} & \not{3} & \not{1} \end{matrix}$$

(arrow from T to S, labeled >)

Image's website target can't be 3, because the website target must be smaller or equal to the voicemail target.

That's all we can deduce for this diagram. Still, making this deduction upfront simplifies things.

Main Diagram

```
≥ ⌐  V  1     X̶    X̶
   └  W  1     ___   ___
         I      S     T
               2̶     X̶
                 ⤸ >
```

```
≥ ⌐  V  2     3     3
   └         X̶
      W  ___   ___   ___
         I      S     T
         2̶    2̶    X̶
                 ⤸ >
```

Rules

1. Voicemail is at least as big as website
2. Image's voicemail target is smaller than S and T's voicemail targets.
3. S's website target is smaller than T's website target.

Most problems in this game come from forgetting one of these three rules. Try to memorize them, it's easier than it seems. As a back-up, make a clear list you can refer to quickly.

NOTE: Even I find website and voicemail incredibly confusing on this game. It's easy to mix them up.

If you don't understand something, there's a good chance you've mixed them up. Keep that possibility in mind as you read the explanations.

Question 11

If the first question is *not* a list question, then that is a strong sign that you should have made deductions before trying the questions. This is not a list question.

In the setup, I made two scenarios. The second scenario had two voicemail targets that were 3. So that scenario isn't allowed on this question. Here's the first scenario instead:

```
≥ ⌐  V  1     X̶    X̶
   └  W  1     ___   ___
         I      S     T
               2̶     X̶
                 ⤸ >
```

Since no voicemail target can be 3 on this question, there is only one option for S and T's voicemail targets. They have to be bigger than Image's voicemail target, so they must both be 2.

```
≥ ⌐  V  1     2     2
   └         X̶
      W  1     ___   ___
         I      S     T
               2̶     X̶
                 ⤸ >
```

There's only one rule left to apply. T's website target is bigger than S's website target. There is only one possibility:

```
≥ ⌐  V  1     2     2
   └         X̶
      W  1     1     2
         I      S     T
               2̶     X̶
                 ⤸ >
```

T's website target can't be 3, because the website target has to be smaller than the voicemail target.

B is **CORRECT.**

Question 12

This question restricts the possibilities for T's website target. It now can't be 3, because it has to be smaller than the voicemail target (instead of smaller or equal).

T's website target also can't be 1, because rule 2 says T's website target has to be bigger than S's website target.

So this is the only possibility. T's website target is 2, and their voicemail target is 3. S's website target is 1:

At this point, you could try to see if anything else has to be true....but that looks complicated.

When you make a deduction, it's better to scan the answers and see if you already solved the question.

In fact, this diagram does solve the question! **E** is **CORRECT.**

Question 13

There are only two scenarios for Image. In the first scenario, the voicemail and website targets for Image were both 1.

That doesn't work for this question. The voicemail target can't be 1, because then it would be smaller than the website target (rule 1)

So we must be in the second scenario from the setup. I added in this question's rule that Image's website target is 2:

As with the last question, at this point you should simply scan the answers and see if the diagram solves the question.

It does. **A** is **CORRECT.**

Question 14

This is the only question that mixes website targets and voicemail targets.

Let's review what we know about S's voicemail target.

It is *shorter* than T's website target (for this question).

It is *longer* than Image's voicemail target. (rule 2)

That means S's voicemail target is 2, since it's in the middle of the other two. Here's the diagram:

```
        V   1      2      3
≥  ⌐                       ⌡
   ⌐    W   1             3
            |      S      T
                   2      1
                    ⌣
                     >
```

Image's voicemail target is 1, due to rule 1. Website targets must be smaller or equal to voicemail targets.

Likewise, T's voicemail target is 3, due to the same rule.

The question is asking which slot can have a target of 2 days. The diagram proves that **A, B, D** and **E** are wrong.

C is CORRECT. S's website target can be 2 or 1, both of which are smaller than T's website target.

Question 15

Bigger numbers are more restricted, as many rules say that certain targets must be smaller than other targets.

A is wrong because both Image and S could have 1 day website targets. It's easy to make website targets small.

B is wrong. This scenario proves it.

```
        V   1      2      2
≥  ⌐                       ⌡
   ⌐    W   1      1      2
            |      S      T
                   2      1
                    ⌣
                     >
```

C and **D** are wrong. This scenario proves it.

```
        V   2      3      3
≥  ⌐                       ⌡
   ⌐    W   2      2      3
            |      S      T
            2      2      1
                    ⌣
                     >
```

E is CORRECT. Image's website target can never be three, because Image's voicemail target has to be at least as big, and rule 2 says Image's voicemail target cannot be 3.

S's website target can never be 3, because it must be smaller than than T's website target.

So only T's website target can potentially be 3.

Question 16

It *sounds* like there are many possibilities for this question. But actually, there aren't. If you get frozen, the easiest way to make progress is to just *try* drawing something, and you'll see they're quite restricted.

T's website target has to be bigger than S's. Since we can't use 2, the only possibility is 3 and 1.

We can also say that Image's website target is 1, since it can never be 3 and now it can't be 2.

Lastly, T's voicemail target is 3, since the voicemail target has to be at least as big as the website target (rule 1)

If you look through the answers, you'll see that they're all contradicted by the diagram, except one.

C is CORRECT. T's voicemail target could be 3, S;s could be 2, and Image's could be 1. The question only says that *website* targets can't be 2.

Game 4 - Editing Articles
Questions 17-23

Setup

This is the hardest LSAT logic games I've ever seen. Don't feel bad if you didn't do well. I had 15 minutes left, and still managed to get three questions wrong. That *never* happens to me.

On my second attempt, I got everything right, but still felt stressed and confused. I worked on it with students a few times, and still didn't feel like I had found the secret to the game. Again, that is not typical for me.

It turns out, there is no secret to this game. There are a few tricks to make things faster, but no magic bullet.

To make sure it wasn't my own blind spot, I checked other explanations and spoke to other tutors. No doubt about it: this is a hard, hard, game, and there no missing key that will make it easy.

The game actually looks straightforward. There are no major deductions to be made in the setup. Let's see what we can determine.

First, the groups are unusually important in this game, because no article from f or n can be edited beside another from the same group.

F : G,H,J

N : Q,R,S

W : Y

Note that the letters are in alphabetical order. You should try to memorize GHJ and QRS. You can also draw them separately as a reminder:

I'm going to do the second rule last. You should always read the rules before drawing: sometimes the best order to draw them in differs from the order they are presented in.

The third rules places S earlier than Y:

S—Y

The final rules places J, G, R in that order:

J—G—R

Now we can look at the second rule. It has an interesting effect. If S is earlier than Q, then Q is third.

So S could go 1st or 2nd....except, S and Q are in the same group. S can't go in 2, because then it would be beside Q. So S has to be 1st if it is before Q.

S		Q				
1	2	3	4	5	6	7
	R̶					
	G̶					

R and G can't go in 2, because they have to go after J. There are no other deductions, but keep this scenario in mind. It fills up easier than the alternative, which is useful for could be true questions.

If Q is *not* in third, then Q has to be before S and we get this chain of deductions:

$\cancel{3}$ → Q—S—Y

There's nothing we can do to combine these rules. The most important part of this game is the interaction between the ordering rules (Q - S - Y and J - G - R) and the blocks that can't go together (QSR, JGH)

In particular, QS can't go together, and JG can't go together. This restriction often forces the ordering rule to be placed in only 1-2 ways.

Main Diagram

This main diagram is unusual in that there is *nothing* we can place on it. (you could place a not rule for R and G in spot 1, but I chose not to)

1	2	3	4	5	6	7

F : G,H,J

N : Q,R,S

W : Y

Remember that G, H and J, can't go beside each other. Neither can Q, R and S. You can draw that separately like this:

Here's rule 2 combined with rule 3:

$\varnothing_3 \longrightarrow Q - S - Y$

$J - G - R$

Scenario where S - Q

S		Q				
1	2	3	4	5	6	7
	R̸					
	G̸					

Question 17

For list questions, the best approach is to go through the rules one at a time. Apply a rule to each answer choice and see what you can eliminate, then repeat.

The first rule eliminates **B.** G and H have the same topic, so the can't be beside each other.

The second rule eliminates **A.** S is before Q, and Q is fourth. S can only be before Q is Q is third.

The third rule eliminates **D.** S has to be before Y.

The fourth rule eliminates **E.** The correct order is J-G-R. This answer choice has G before J.

C is **CORRECT.** It violates no rules.

Question 18

This is a local rule question. Before you look at the answers, you must try drawing it.

It's helpful to think of what other rules involve Y. Rule 3 says that S has to be before Y. I'm going to make two drawings that use this, one with S-Q and one with Q-S.

If we put S before Q, then Q is in 3 (rule 2)

S		Q	Y			
1	2	3	4	5	6	7

If we put Q before S, then S goes in 3, and Q goes in 1. This is because S has to be before Y, and S and Q can't be beside each other (rule 1).

Q		S	Y			
1	2	3	4	5	6	7

We have not yet deduced anything that has to be true in both scenarios, so let's keep going. The other major, restrictive rule, is the order J - G - R.

There is no space for this after Y. J and G can't go beside each other (rule 1), so we need to put J before Y.

Q	J	S	Y			
1	2	3	4	5	6	7

S	J	Q	Y			
1	2	3	4	5	6	7

This diagram solves the question. **A is CORRECT.** J must be second in both scenarios.

In case you were curious, there's only one order for the remaining variables. G, R and H are left. G has to go before R, and G can't be beside H, so the order must be GRH in both scenarios.

Question 19

This question tests whether you recognized that putting S first and Q third is an easy way to build a scenario.

$$\frac{S}{1} \quad \frac{}{2} \quad \frac{Q}{3} \quad \frac{G}{4} \quad \frac{}{5} \quad \frac{}{6} \quad \frac{}{7}$$

H can't go fifth, thanks to rule 1.

J has to go second, thanks to rule 4.

$$\frac{S}{1} \quad \frac{J}{2} \quad \frac{Q}{3} \quad \frac{G}{4} \quad \frac{}{5} \quad \frac{}{6} \quad \frac{}{7}$$

We have H, Y and R left to place. Any combination is fine, as long as you don't put H in fifth.

This is a Could Be True question, so you should see if this scenario answers the question.

It does! Y can go sixth, so **E** is **CORRECT.**

$$\frac{S}{1} \quad \frac{J}{2} \quad \frac{Q}{3} \quad \frac{G}{4} \quad \frac{R}{5} \quad \frac{Y}{6} \quad \frac{H}{7}$$

Normally I recommend disproving all the other answers. However, since this is a very hard, time consuming game, I would just move on at this point and hope I hadn't made a mistake.

That's if you were doing the game in a timed setting. Since this book is a guide, I'll show you how to disprove the other answers. No need to read these unless you were stuck on one of the answers.

A is wrong because H can't go beside G.

For **B,** here's my attempt to put J first.

$$\frac{J}{1} \quad \frac{}{2} \quad \frac{}{3} \quad \frac{G}{4} \quad \frac{}{5} \quad \frac{R}{6} \quad \frac{}{7}$$
$$Q\!-\!S\!-\!Y$$

We still have to place Q - S - Y, and H and R.

S can't go beside Q, so S - Y must go after G.

$$\frac{J}{1} \quad \frac{}{2} \quad \frac{}{3} \quad \frac{G}{4} \quad \frac{S}{5} \quad \frac{Y}{6} \quad \frac{R}{7}$$

We still have to place H and Q. H is a problem. H can't go beside J or G. This diagram doesn't work.

So J *has* to be second, and **B** is wrong.

This also proves **C** is wrong. Q can't go second, because J has to be second.

D is wrong. Here's what happens if you try to put S fifth:

$$\frac{Q}{1} \quad \frac{J}{2} \quad \frac{}{3} \quad \frac{G}{4} \quad \frac{S}{5} \quad \frac{Y}{6} \quad \frac{}{7}$$

We still have R and H left to place. R has to go in seventh, after G. That leaves only spot 3 for H. This doesn't work, because H can't be beside J or G.

Question 20

Open-ended Could Be True questions are tricky. Refresh yourself on the rules, then see what you can eliminate.

In particular, remember that QSR and JGH can't be beside each other (rule 1).

A is wrong. Rule four says J is before G. If G is second, then the only space to put J before G is in 1. Then J and G would be beside each other, which isn't allowed.

As for **B** - there's no obvious reason why H can't be in second. There are no rules specific to H. In a timed section, that means you should skip **B** and try to eliminate other answers.

C is wrong. S can't go second. Q is the problem. If we put Q before S in space 1, then S and Q would be beside each other which violates rule 1.

If Q is after S, then Q has to be in 3 (rule 2). But then Q would still be beside S.

D is wrong. If R is third, then we need to put J-G-R in 1, 2, and 3. JG can't be beside each other (rule 1).

E is wrong. If Y is third, we run into problems placing Q and S.

If you put Q before S, then you get QSY in 1, 2 and 3. That doesn't work because QS can't be beside each other. (rule 1).

If you put Q after S, then Q would have to be third (rule 2). That doesn't work, because Y is third for this answer choice.

B is **CORRECT.** This scenario proves it can work.

Q	H	S	J	Y	G	R
1	2	3	4	5	6	7

Question 21

For a local rule question, you should start by drawing the new rule and making deductions:

		J				
1	2	3	4	5	6	7
	G̶		G̶			
	H̶		H̶			

G has to go after J, and R goes after G. You need two spots, and there are only three open spaces for GR - 5, 6 and 7. There are two possibilities:

		J		G	R	
1	2	3	4	5	6	7
	G̶		G̶			
	H̶		H̶			

		J			G	R
1	2	3	4	5	6	7
	G̶		G̶			
	H̶		H̶			

Next, you need to place Q-S-Y. Q is before S, since Q isn't third (rule 2).

QS can't both go before J, because they can't be beside each other. So Q goes before J, and S - Y go after.

Notice that there are four spaces after J, and now they're filled by S-Y and G-R. Also note that S can't go beside R.

Q		J	S	G		R,Y
1	2	3	4	5	6	7
		H̶	H̶			

Q		J	S	Y	G	R
1	2	3	4	5	6	7
		H̶	H̶			

S is forced to go in 4, so that it is not beside R and it is before Y.

132

Next, we have only Q and H left to place. H can't go beside J, so H is in 1 and Q is in 2.

H	Q	J	S	G	R,Y	
1	2	3	4	5	6	7

H	Q	J	S	Y	G	R
1	2	3	4	5	6	7

Now you just have to look at the answers and see which one is possible in one of these two diagrams.

E is **CORRECT.** All the other answers don't work.

Question 22

For this question it's easiest to use past scenarios.

Question 17 shows that S can be third. **B** is wrong.

The scenario from question 18 shows that S can be first. **A** is wrong.

Question 21 shows that S can be fourth. **C** is wrong.

We're left with **D** and **E**.

Now you just have to see whether you can put S fifth, or sixth. It turns out that you *cannot* put S fifth. **D** is **CORRECT.**

If you try to put S fifth, it ends up beside R. That's not allowed, since they're in the same group:

J	Q	G	R	S	Y	H
1	2	3	4	5	6	7

These diagrams show that S can be sixth. First we'll put in S-Y. R and Q can't go fifth, because of the first rule.

					S	Y
1	2	3	4	5	6	7

Next, add in J-G-R. J and G can't go beside each other, and R can't go on four, so this only fits in one place:

J		G	R		S	Y
1	2	3	4	5	6	7

Finally, Q can only go second, leaving H to go in sixth. Everything works, so **E** is wrong.

J	Q	G	R	H	S	Y
1	2	3	4	5	6	7

133

Question 23

For this question, it can help to look to previous diagrams.

For example, the correct answer on number 17 has H on 4, which is answer choice **A.**

That diagram has Q and S in 1 and 3. You can easily switch those without affecting anything:

S	J	Q	H	Y	G	R
1	2	3	4	5	6	7

So **A** is wrong. This also eliminates answer **D,** since R is seventh in this diagram.

B puts H on 6. This isn't very limiting. For example, this diagram shows that both S/Q and R/Y are interchangeable when H is on 6. **B** is wrong.

	S,Q				R,Y	
	J		G		H	
1	2	3	4	5	6	7

C puts R on 4. We saw this in question 22. It's actually quite restrictive, because J-G must be before R and can't be beside each other.

J		G	R			
1	2	3	4	5	6	7

Next, you have to add in Q-S-Y. Q and S can't be beside each other, or R, so there's only one way to place them:

J	Q	G	R		S	Y
1	2	3	4	5	6	7

Finally, H goes in spot 5:

J	Q	G	R	H	S	Y
1	2	3	4	5	6	7

C is CORRECT.

This diagram shows that **E** is wrong. If Y is fifth, then J/H are interchangeable.

		J,H				
S		Q		Y	G	R
1	2	3	4	5	6	7

S/Q are interchangeable as well, though I haven't drawn that.

Preptest 69
Section I - Logical Reasoning

Question 1

QUESTION TYPE: Strengthen

CONCLUSION: Officers can drink in moderation when they're undercover in nightclubs.

REASONING: It's useful for police to be able to work undercover in nightclubs.

ANALYSIS: Your first thought might have been: of *course* police have to drink in night clubs. Otherwise they'd seem strange.

Well, go with that thought. It's the basis for the right answer. More and more, LSAT questions require you to use intuition and outside knowledge.

You can't use outside knowledge to *prove* anything, but you can use it to form guesses.

We need an answer that shows that drinking in nightclubs offers a benefit. Only a benefit would allow the department to relax their rules.

————————————

A. Experience isn't an excuse for breaking the rules. This doesn't tell us why we should let these experienced officers drink.
B. **CORRECT.** If this were true, then police officers couldn't effectively go undercover in night clubs unless they drank.
C. Great, there are more nightclub operations. This doesn't tell us why drinking is necessary during those operations.
D. It doesn't matter what police officers think. They could be wrong. Also, to justify drinking in nightclubs, we need to show it has a *benefit*. This answer just says it doesn't cause problems.
E. This is just a fact about public awareness. It doesn't tell us whether police officers are right to drink in nightclubs.

Question 2

QUESTION TYPE: Agreement

ARGUMENTS: Jake says people should use antibacterial products. They kill common bacteria.

Karolinka says that people shouldn't use these products. The products create anti-biotic resistant strains of bacteria.

ANALYSIS: Both of them agree that the products kill some bacteria.

I got this question wrong. I thought it asked what Jake and Karolinka *disagree* about. Oops. There are two 'agreement' questions on this test. Agreement questions used to be quite rare. Watch out for them on future tests.

————————————

A. **CORRECT.** Jake and Karolinka both say the products kill some bacteria.
B. Neither of them mentions dirt.
C. Only Karolinka mentions this.
D. Neither of them mentions whether common bacteria are a health concern.
E. Jake says people should use anti-bacterial products. Karolinka disagrees. The question asked what they *agreed* about.

Question 3

QUESTION TYPE: Flawed Reasoning

CONCLUSION: Galactose causes cancer, if you have more of it than you can process.

REASONING: There are two groups, one with cancer and one without it. Each group ate a similar amount of Yogurt, which has galactose. The cancer group didn't have enough enzyme to process galactose.

ANALYSIS: This question makes a causation-correlation error. The fact that two things happen together doesn't mean one causes the other.

The group already had cancer. Maybe their cancer lowered their production of the enzyme. Then cancer would be the cause of galactose malabsorption, and not the reverse.

Or maybe a third factor causes both cancer and the reduction in the enzyme.

———————

A. This sounds tempting, but it's not necessary. Read carefully. It asks whether:

   1. *Everyone's* diet
   2. was *exactly* the same
   3. in *all* other respects

   No medical study meets this standard. It's impossible. People's diets are very different. A study can still tell us something, even if not every variable is controlled with perfect accuracy.
B. The argument is just making a claim about galactose. It doesn't have to make practical recommendations to improve people's lives.
C. The argument doesn't have to describe every possible cause of cancer. There are thousands of causes. The argument didn't say that galactose is the *only* cause of cancer.
D. CORRECT. If cancer causes low enzyme levels, then galactose malabsorption is an effect of cancer, not a cause.
E. The groups were presumably somewhat large. If one person in a group lacked the enzyme, that shouldn't affect the overall study.

Question 4

QUESTION TYPE: Necessary Assumption

CONCLUSION: Our company pollutes more than other companies our size do.

REASONING: Our company, and four other companies, release 60% of pollutants.

ANALYSIS: You, Warren Buffet, Bill Gates, and Mark Zuckerberg are together worth $100 billion dollars. You must be rich, right?

This is a whole to part flaw. This argument tells us about a group, then makes a claim about one member of the group. But individual members of a group don't always have the same properties the group as a whole has.

It could be that the other four companies release 59.8% of pollutants, and the employee's company only releases 0.2%.

———————

A. This is just an ad hominem attack. You can never reject an argument because of who someone is, or because of what they believe.
B. The employee is arguing that his company produces a lot of pollution. So his argument would be *stronger* if this answer isn't true. If processing *did* produce chemicals, his company would produce *even more* pollution.
C. The conclusion is only about this group of small chemical companies. Large companies are irrelevant.
D. CORRECT. If the four other companies account for 59.8% of pollution, then the employee's company would only produce a small amount of pollution.
E. The conclusion is that the employee's company produces more pollution than 'most' small chemical companies. So it doesn't matter if a few of the other 25 companies produce larger amounts of pollution. The rest would produce small amounts. There's only 40% of the pollution to go amongst those 25 companies.

Question 5

QUESTION TYPE: Argument Evaluation

CONCLUSION: Decaf coffee damages connective tissues.

REASONING: The decaf group had worse connective tissues than the caffeinated group.

ANALYSIS: There was no control group in this study. One group drank decaf, the other caffeinated coffee. A control group would drink no coffee at all.

It's possible that decaf damages connective tissues. It's also possible that decaf does no damage, and caffeinated coffee *helps* connective tissues. That could also account for the gap.

The wrong answers all talk about the population in general. We only care about these two groups. Each group drank three cups per day.

It doesn't matter what other coffee drinkers do - they weren't part of the group.

———————————

A. This doesn't matter. We don't know if exercise helps or hurts joints. We also don't know whether this specific group of decaf drinkers exercised. We care about this particular group, not decaf drinkers in general.
B. We don't care what people do in general. We only care about these two groups. They each drank three cups per day.
C. **CORRECT.** This is very relevant. If caffeine slows connective tissue degeneration, they maybe coffee *helped* the group that drank it. The decaf group didn't hurt themselves, they just didn't help themselves by drinking caffeine.
D. Same as A and B. We only care about these two groups, not coffee drinkers in general.
E. Same as all the other wrong answers. We only care about the two groups, not the general population.

Question 6

QUESTION TYPE: Principle

CONCLUSION: The agency classified the figurines as collector's items.

REASONING: The agency noted that the figurines were marketed as collector's items.

ANALYSIS: Principle-Justify questions are often pretty straightforward.

We have a conclusion, and a reason for the conclusion. We just have to say that the reason for the conclusion was proper.

Usually a principle does this by saying that the actions in question are 'good,' or by using the word 'should'.

The stimulus is just facts and actions. A principle adds moral judgment that shows the actions were correct.

So in this case, the agency 'should' classify toys based on how they're marketed.

———————————

A. **CORRECT.** The figurines were marketed as collector's items. This tells us to therefore classify them as collector's items.
B. This tells us what the company should do. We want to know what the *agency* should do.
C. We want to *justify* the agent's decision to classify the products as collector's items. But this gives us a reason *not* to classify things as collector's items.
D. The inspector gave the items a higher tariff by classifying them as collector's items. So this goes against his decision.
E. Same as B. This tells the company what to do. We want to tell the agency what to do.

Question 7

QUESTION TYPE: Necessary Assumption

CONCLUSION: If the customer's claim is correct, the store owes a refund.

REASONING: The customer says they handled the film properly. The film and camera worked.

ANALYSIS: Unusual. A necessary assumption question that uses linked conditional reasoning. Usually you shouldn't diagram necessary assumption questions.

We have these facts:

1. Customer says handled correctly (C)
2. Camera not defective (C̶D̶)
3. Film not defective (F̶D̶)
4. not processed correctly → refund (P̶C̶ → R)

If the store didn't process the film correctly, they owe the customer a refund. But the evidence doesn't lead to improper processing. I'm going to draw the evidence on the left and the conclusion on the right:

C and C̶D̶ and F̶D̶   P̶C̶ → R

The author wrongly assumes they're connected. To fix the argument, add an arrow connecting left and right. Here's the missing premise:

C and C̶D̶ and F̶D̶ → P̶C̶

If P̶C̶, then we can conclude 'R'. Unusually, this answer is sufficient and necessary.

A. We're must prove the store owed a refund. This says what happens *if* they owed one. Not helpful.
B. **CORRECT.** This links the premises to the conclusion. This has to be true for the argument's reasoning to work. Oddly, it's also a sufficient assumption.
C. The pictures weren't taken with a defective camera, so this tells us nothing.
D. The author talks about what happens if the client handled the film correctly. This is irrelevant.
E. Same as D. This question is about what happens if the claim *is* correct.

Question 8

QUESTION TYPE: Principle - Parallel

CONCLUSION: You shouldn't try to get rid of all weeds.

REASONING: Weeds hurt gardens. But the last few weeds take a lot of effort to remove and don't cause much damage.

ANALYSIS: This is a pretty reasonable argument.

Many of the wrong answers say that completely removing something would be bad. That's not parallel.

It *would* help your garden to remove the other weeds. But it's just not worth the effort.

A. This says that having some personality defects is useful. Weeds never help gardens.
B. This says a radical change will hurt you. But weeding a garden only helps a garden. The issue was that it was too much work to remove the final weeds.
C. **CORRECT.** This is exactly parallel. Each imperfection does make us worse. But, it's not worth the effort to get rid of the small, final ones.
D. This says you can't remove all imperfections. In the stimulus, you could remove all weeds. The problem was that it wasn't worth it.
E. This says removing some imperfections can cause problems. Removing weeds never harmed a garden.

Question 9

QUESTION TYPE: Identify The Conclusion

CONCLUSION: Taxing junk food would help public health.

REASONING: Junk food causes problems. Taxing junk food would encourage people to eat other food.

ANALYSIS: The doctor is arguing that taxing junk food would help public health. It's the first sentence.

The rest of the argument gives reasons that taxing junk food would improve public health.

A. **CORRECT.** This is the first sentence. The first sentence is often the conclusion.
B. This is evidence that supports the first sentence.
C. This is evidence that supports the first sentence.
D. This isn't even directly in the argument. It's a restatement of answer C.
E. The doctor doesn't say if junk food *should* be taxed. He just said that taxing it would improve public health. There might be other reasons not to tax it.

Question 10

QUESTION TYPE: Most Strongly Supported

FACTS: Nahcolite formed in salty lates during the Eocene. Labs tests show that nahcolite can only form in salt water where there is 1,125 PPM CO_2.

ANALYSIS: Since lab results show that nahcolite formed in salt water during the Eocene, it's probable that there was 1,125 PPM CO_2 during the Eocene.

This is a 'most strongly supported' and not a 'must be true' because it's possible the lab results are wrong.

A. We have no reason to think that CO_2 was lower for most of the 50 million years since the Eocene.
B. We have no reason to believe CO_2 levels changed *during* the Eocene.
C. We have no information about lakes in general. We just know that *some* salty lakes had nahcolite.
D. **CORRECT.** This is probably true, because nahcolite needs 1,125 PPM to form in salty lakes.
E. We don't know much about nahcolite. Maybe it forms easily in non-salty lakes, no matter what CO_2 levels are. We have no reason to believe Nahcolite only formed in the Eocene.

139

Question 11

QUESTION TYPE: Role in Argument

CONCLUSION: Something is very wrong with the educational system.

REASONING: Students either don't know any poets from Shakespeare's era, or they don't understand the word 'contemporaneous'.

ANALYSIS: The editor thinks the school system is not doing a good job. His evidence is that 60% of students picked a 20th century poet when asked to name a poet from Shakespeare's time.

The editor doesn't know what this evidence means, exactly. The students could be ignorant of poets, or perhaps they don't understand words.

Either way, it's evidence that something is wrong.

_____

A. Not necessarily. It's possible that the students understood the history of poetry, but didn't know what the word contemporaneous means.
B. The question wasn't ambiguous. Students were asked to name a poet from Shakespeare's time. It was perhaps a hard question, but it was clear.
C. The editor's conclusion is about the education system, not research results in general.
D. Same as C. The editor makes a specific conclusion about the education system. He's not talking about research results in general.
E. **CORRECT.** If the education system were doing its job, then students would know poets from Shakespeare's time, and they would understand the word 'contemporaneous'.

Question 12

QUESTION TYPE: Most Strongly Supported

FACTS:

1. Apologize → say it to person you wronged AND make apology for wronging them
2. Apologize sincerely → acknowledge wrong AND not repeat wrong
3. Sincerely accept → acknowledge wrong AND no grudge

ANALYSIS: I've drawn the facts as conditional diagrams. You can't really connect them together, beyond what I already did.

One important point is that this question talks about sincerely giving an apology, and sincerely accepting an apology.

They're different things, but related in that they're sincere. They also both require acknowledging a wrong was done. The right answer checks if you noticed this overlap.

So while this seems like a diagramming question, you can't really solve it with traditional diagramming connections. Fewer modern LR questions test your diagramming skills.

_____

A. A sincere apology only requires that you *intend* not to repeat the act. It's possible to intend not to do something and then later fail to keep your intention.
B. There are only two conditions for sincerely accepting an apology: acknowledge the wrong and vow not to hold a grudge.
C. The first sentence gives *necessary* conditions for apologizing. The stimulus never gives us any sufficient conditions. Only a sufficient condition would let us say we *should* apologize.
D. The stimulus doesn't say anything this. There are necessary conditions for offering an apology, but being sure that the apology will be accepted is not one of those conditions.
E. **CORRECT.** This is true. The necessary conditions for offering an apology and accepting an apology both include acknowledging a wrong.

Question 13

QUESTION TYPE: Strengthen

CONCLUSION: The implements went into the well during 375 A.D. at the earliest.

REASONING: There were coins beneath the implements. Some of the coins were from 375 A.D.

ANALYSIS: This sounds like a good argument. You have to use your real world knowledge of coins to see the flaw.

Coins are tiny. They fall all kinds of places. Maybe the implements were there in 200 A.D. and the more recent coins fell past them.

Attack these arguments as if they're obviously wrong. Try to find any hole. Real world knowledge is a great way to get *ideas* (but only ideas) for why an argument might be flawed.

A. It doesn't matter how long a coin remained in use after it was made. The date a coin was created is mentioned because it indicates the earliest date the coin could have been in the well.
B. **CORRECT.** This shows that the coins did not get below the implements by falling through accidentally. It sounds like the coins were there first.
C. Who cares what the coins were worth? We're trying to figure out when they were placed in the well, not what we could sell them for.
D. We already knew someone put the implements in the well. Knowing the circumstances doesn't change anything.
E. If the jewelry was *above* the implements, this information would weaken the argument.

As it is, the jewelry's age doesn't change anything. Maybe someone put the jewels (family heirlooms) in at the same time as the coins. The jewels are at the bottom of the pile so it makes sense that they are older.

Question 14

QUESTION TYPE: Flawed Parallel Reasoning

CONCLUSION: The investigators don't know that the fire was caused by either campers or lighting.

(i.e. The investigators can't rule out all other causes)

REASONING: The investigators don't know the fire was caused by campers. They also don't know whether the fire was caused by lighting.

ANALYSIS: It took me a few readings to see what this argument was saying. I'll use an analogy.

Suppose three people go into a room, A, B, and C. I hear a scream, open the door, and C is dead. Only A or B could have killed C.

It's true that I don't know A killed him, and I don't that know B killed him. But I do know that *one of* A or B killed him.

Maybe the investigators ruled out all other causes, apart from fire or lightning. So they know one of the two is the cause, they just don't know which one.

A. **CORRECT.** If Sada and Brown are the only two candidates, then Kim would have good reason to believe that one of the two will win the election.
B. This is a bad argument, but it's a different flaw. It's like saying "we have no proof that he got rich by business success, or by magic. So one theory is as likely as the other".
C. We can't say most are from out of town, since it could mostly be non-engineers who are from away. But this is not the same error as the stimulus. The stimulus didn't even use 'most' statements.
D. You can't ever combine two some statements. While this is an error, it's different from the error in the stimulus. The stimulus didn't use any some statements.
E. This is a different error. It's like saying "Obama can win, and Romney can win, therefore they can both win together". Obviously, only one person can be elected president.

Question 15

QUESTION TYPE: Paradox

PARADOX: We planted trees to attract birds. The birds eat mosquitos, but there are more mosquitos than ever.

ANALYSIS: Mosquito population depends on many factors. It's the number of births minus the number of deaths. You have to look at all the causes of birth rate and death rate.

So yes, birds kill some mosquitos. But maybe the birds and fruit also attracted animals that mosquitos feed on.

The right answer says that the birds eat the mosquitos' predators, reducing the mosquitos' death rate.

Several of the wrong answers mentioned that not all the birds eat mosquitos. This doesn't matter, because *some* birds eat mosquitos. That would normally reduce population, not increase it.

———————————

A. It doesn't matter if most birds don't eat mosquitos. Some of the birds *do* eat mosquitos. We would expect that to reduce the population, not increase it.
B. This is practically the same as A. It doesn't matter if all the birds eat mosquitos, as long as *some* of them did. We would expect the birds to decrease the population of mosquitos as long as some birds ate mosquitos. Instead the mosquito population increased.
C. **CORRECT.** If this is true, then mosquitos got lucky. The birds ate their predators. So while a few mosquitos die from birds, many more survive due to lack of predators.
D. This makes things even weirder. We would expect the dry weather to kill mosquitos. Instead, there are more mosquitos.
E. This is just a useless fact. We don't know what part of the cycle we're in. If we are in an increasing part of the cycle, this could explain things. If we are in a decreasing part, this makes things more confusing.

Question 16

QUESTION TYPE: Complete the Argument

CONCLUSION: It would be ok for Roxanne not to finish her report, assuming Luke wouldn't expect her to finish it.

REASONING: It would be ok to miss lunch if you got sick, your friend wouldn't expect you to be there. Roxanne's deadline got extended.

ANALYSIS: First, you'll want to be clear on what the analogy says. It would be *fine* to miss lunch. But you don't *have* to miss lunch.

So this argument will claim, at most, that it would be *fine* for Roxanne to not finish her report. It wouldn't be *wrong* for her to finish though, even though the deadline changed.

Second, falling sick and an extended deadline aren't quite the same thing. Falling ill is a bad thing. Getting an extension is a good thing. There's nothing stopping Roxanne from finishing on time.

So it would be ok not to finish only if Luke didn't expect her to, just like someone wouldn't expect a sick friend to show up.

———————————

A. It would not be wrong for Roxanne to finish. She just doesn't have to.
B. Not quite. The issue isn't whether Luke expected a postponement. It's whether he would be ok with her not finishing, given that there was a postponement.
C. This doesn't match the analogy, which allows people to avoid their obligations in special circumstances.
D. **CORRECT.** Here we go. It's ok for Roxanne not to finish, if Luke is fine with that.
E. It's definitely not 'wrong' for Roxanne to finish. She just doesn't have to.

Question 17

QUESTION TYPE: Weaken

CONCLUSION: TV causes children to be violent to other children.

REASONING: Children who watched a program were violent against a doll. Children who didn't watch a program were not as violent.

ANALYSIS: Pay attention anytime the question switches terms. The conclusion was that children will be violent *to each other*. The evidence is that they'll be violent *to dolls*.

Dolls are not children. Maybe TV can cause kids to be violent to objects but not to other humans.

———————————

A. We would expect some children to protest the violence. Not everyone hates poor Bobo the clown. But it's still true that children who watched TV were more likely to punch the doll.
B. This is just one child. Maybe he's unusually violent. We care about the effects TV has on all the children, on average. And this child might have been even more violent if he had watched the program.
C. **CORRECT.** This shows that TV only causes children to be violent towards dolls. They're not violent towards other children, which is what we care about.
D. Children are copycats. It's not surprising that some of them imitated the violent children. But it's still true that children were more likely to punch the doll after seeing the program.
E. This is irrelevant. The only important point is that children who watched the program were more likely to punch the doll.

Question 18

QUESTION TYPE: Principle

PRINCIPLE: Society shouldn't restrict the actions of adults, unless those actions will cause harm to others.

ANALYSIS: To violate this principle, we'd have to restrict the actions of adults, when those actions were not harming others.

Note that the principle never says we should ban things that harm others. It just says it might be ok to do that. Harm is a necessary condition for banning, but not a sufficient condition.

———————————

A. Students, homework....hey, these are kids. The principle only talks about adults.
B. This talks about *not* restricting the ability of others to profit from the invention. That's perfectly ok: the principle tells us not to restrict.
C. The principle never tells us to ban anything. It only tells us not to ban.
D. This sounds ok. We're restricting the actions of adults, but those actions harm others. The principle says we *can* restrict actions that harm others.
E. **CORRECT.** Adults only harm themselves when they ignore warning labels. The principle says not to restrict the actions of adults unless they harm *others*.

Question 19

QUESTION TYPE: Necessary Assumption

CONCLUSION: *L. rubellus* is probably the reason the goblin fern is disappearing.

REASONING: The goblin fern needs leaf litter. Leaf litter is thin where the fern has vanished. The *L. rubellus* worm is often found where the fern has vanished, and the worm eats leaf litter.

ANALYSIS: This sounds persuasive. But really, the question has just given us a correlation between the worm and the decline in the goblin fern.

Correlations never prove anything. It could be true that worms cause thin leaf litter. However, the right answer shows that thin leaf litter attracts *L. rubellus*.

The worm only comes after the leaf litter and fern are already in decline. It is an effect, not a cause.

_____

A. It doesn't matter if goblin ferns are everywhere there is leaf litter. We just need to know that leaf litter is everywhere there are goblin ferns.
B. It doesn't matter if other worms eat leaf litter. Other worms could add to the problem, but it wouldn't change the fact that *L. rubellus* appears to be harming ferns.
C. This just tells us something about what leaf litter is like *after* the fern has vanished. We only care what happens to leaf litter when the fern is still there.
D. The argument might be stronger if this weren't true. If *L. rubellus* is killing the fern, then presumably the worm sometimes appears in the same area as the fern before the fern dies.
E. **CORRECT.** This implies that something else causes the thin leaf litter. Then once the leaf litter is thin, the fern dies and the worm appears. The worm didn't cause the fern's death, it was an *effect* of the thin leaf litter.

Question 20

QUESTION TYPE: Flawed Reasoning

CONCLUSION: Most people in industrialized countries would be healthier if they took an aspirin a day.

REASONING: Aspirin prevents heart disease. Heart disease is the most common disease in industrialized countries.

ANALYSIS: This sounds persuasive. But 'most common' is a relative term. It compares heart disease to other diseases. A disease can be the 'most common' without necessarily being 'common'.

That could mean, for example, that heart disease affected 2% of people. Cancer could be the second most common, affecting 1% of people. Both diseases are far from affecting 'most' (51%) people.

In that case, it would be pointless for most people to take aspirin to prevent heart disease.

It's important to note that the evidence was about heart attacks, and the conclusion was about health. The answer didn't make note of this difference, but other questions do test your ability to realize that health is broader than heart attacks.

_____

A. Actually, the first sentence says aspirin can prevent heart disease, too.
B. **CORRECT.** Heart disease might only affect 2% of people in industrialized countries. In that case, most people wouldn't be at risk and they wouldn't need aspirin.
C. It doesn't matter if aspirin helps with other diseases. It just has to not make them worse.
D. Who cares if aspirin is not the best solution? It just has to be helpful.
E. The conclusion is only about people in industrialized nations. So it's fine that the studies only looked at people in those countries.

Question 21

QUESTION TYPE: Must Be True

FACTS:

1. Nobel prize winners are usually professional. They've all made big contributions to science.
2. Amateur scientists sometimes make big contributions to science. (C some AS)
3. Amateur scientists are always motivated by love of discovery. (AS → LD)

ANALYSIS: If two facts mention the same term, you can usually combine them.

We know amateur scientists are always motivated by a love of discovery, and some of them have made major contributions.

So some people who have made major contributions were motivated by a love of discovery.

Here's the same thing as a diagram.

C some AS → LD

Conclusion: C some LD

───────────

A. We don't know this. Maybe all the amateurs who made contributions also won a Nobel.
B. Who knows? Maybe professional scientists are *also* motivated by love of discovery. The question didn't say that only amateur scientists have this motivation.
C. **CORRECT.** This is true. Amateurs have made many contributions, and amateurs are always motivated by the love of discovery.
D. We have no idea. We know some professionals win the Nobel and make major contributions. We also know many amateurs make contributions.

   We don't know how many are in each group. It's possible that amateur scientists make more contributions.
E. We have no idea if love of discovery and significant contributions are related for professional scientists. The stimulus says nothing about this.

Question 22

QUESTION TYPE: Weaken

CONCLUSION: We should hire engineers who have no sales experience.

REASONING: Many of our best salespeople were engineers with no sales experience.

ANALYSIS: We need to know more about the group the company hired.

If the company hired many experienced salespeople, then it's surprising that engineers with no experience make the best salespeople.

But if the company mostly hired engineers with no sales experience, then it's not surprising they are some of the best salespeople.

Take a big enough group of unqualified people and some are bound to do alright.

───────────

A. Totally irrelevant. We only care what characteristics people had when they were hired.
B. **CORRECT.** If this is true, it's not surprising that engineers with no experience were the best performers. They were the largest group.
C. This might explain why engineers do well. It *strengthens* the argument.
D. This strengthens the argument. If most applicants are not engineers, then it's surprising that engineers are the most successful.
E. Answers with 'some' are very vague. This could be 2 out of 10,000 salespeople. That doesn't tell us much. It could still be the case that most people with no experience do better.

Question 23

QUESTION TYPE: Method of Reasoning

CONCLUSION: It's not necessarily true that cultures ban people from eating some animals because those animals are useful.

REASONING: It's possible. But it's also possible that cultures find other uses for animals because they can't eat them.

ANALYSIS: The anthropologist shows that the evidence for the conclusion is also consistent with a completely opposite explanation.

The anthropologist hasn't proven the conclusion is wrong. They've just proven it isn't necessarily right.

A. **CORRECT.** This is the best description. The evidence supports multiple conclusions. So more evidence is needed.
B. The anthropologist didn't prove that the conclusion is false. They say 'might', in the second-to-last line. They proved the argument isn't necessarily true, but that's not the same as proving it wrong.
C. The author hasn't shown the alternate explanation is more plausible. They say 'might', twice; they're uncertain. The author's point was that another hypothesis was just as plausible.
D. They haven't shown any evidence incompatible with the researchers' argument. They've used the same evidence to show an alternative hypothesis is plausible.
E. Not quite right. The anthropologist is doing more than switching the sequence of events. They're saying one of the events might not have occurred.

The original events were: discover animals worth more alive, create taboo against using animals.

The alternate events were: Create taboo, find other uses.

Question 24

QUESTION TYPE: Flawed Reasoning

CONCLUSION: The pledge seems to be successful.

REASONING: People who don't drink have often taken a pledge not to drink.

ANALYSIS: The pledge is *voluntary*. Who would take a pledge to avoid alcohol? Probably those who don't like to drink in the first place.

So the pledge could be the effect of not drinking, rather than the cause of not drinking.

A. Normative judgement means judging something to be right or wrong. The author didn't say whether it's morally right to tell teens not to drink.
B. The conclusion was just that the pledge seems to work. The conclusion wasn't that the pledge is the most successful measure in the history of the universe.
C. **CORRECT.** It's possible people took the pledge because they don't like drinking. People who like to drink would not take the pledge. So the pledge is an effect, not a cause.
D. There aren't any sufficient-necessary statements in the stimulus. The argument didn't say that the pledge always stops drinking, or that it is required to stop drinking.
E. The argument only made the first claim. The second claim wasn't mentioned.

If you thought this was right, look very carefully at the stimulus. Why did you choose this answer? What made you think the argument had mixed up these claims?

Question 25

QUESTION TYPE: Sufficient Assumption

CONCLUSION: Folktales can have deeper meaning.

REASONING: Folktales have the wisdom of the culture.

ANALYSIS: On sufficient assumption questions, you must connect the evidence to the conclusion.

We know folktales carry the wisdom of culture. We want to prove they have deeper meaning:

Wisdom → Deeper meaning

That statement links the two ideas. We get:

Folktales → Wisdom → Deeper Meaning

A. This doesn't help us prove that such tales have deep meaning.
B. CORRECT. Folktales let us learn about the wisdom of cultures. This tells us that they therefore have deeper meaning.
See the diagram above.
C. We don't care about tales that lack deep meaning. We want to prove that folktales *do* have deeper meaning.
D. This tells us about tales that have deep meaning. That's not helpful, because we don't know if folk tales have deep meaning. We're trying to prove that they do!
E. This tells us that folktales *could* have deeper meaning. We must prove that they *definitely* do.

Section II - Logic Games
Game 1 - Manuscript Ages
Questions 1-5

Setup

This is a linear game. It's one that can be a little difficult if you use the traditional method of 'not' rules to show where variables can't go.

I used a new type of diagram the second time through that made it much simpler.

The first two rules are straightforward:

F—H—S

GP

It's the rules involving M and L that are difficult. First, they're a bit hard to understand. They really mean that L is fifth or later, and M is third or earlier.

Second, those rules are confusing to represent. Here's the traditional way to draw these rules:

$$\overline{\cancel{L}} \quad \overline{\cancel{L}} \quad \overline{\cancel{L}} \quad \overline{\cancel{L}} \quad \overline{\cancel{M}} \quad \overline{\cancel{M}} \quad \overline{\cancel{M}}$$
$$\cancel{M} \qquad \cancel{H}$$

I've also drawn the final rule. H can't go fifth.

That's how I drew the diagram when I first I did this game, and it felt slow. I kept forgetting the rules for M and L.

Your diagrams should be clear and easy to read. Here's how I drew it the second time I did the game, and it was a lot easier:

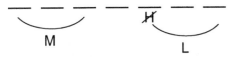

The arcs show where M and L can go. I've left the final rule as a not rule: H can't go fifth.

Now we have a simple diagram that includes three rules, and only two separate rules to remember.

Main Diagram

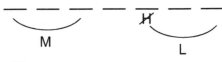

1 F—H—S

2 GP

Question 1

For list questions, go through the rules and use them to eliminate answers one by one.

Rule 1 eliminates **C.** The order is F-H-S.

Rule 2 eliminates **A.** P has to come right after G.

Rule 3 eliminates **D.** L has to come fifth or later.

Rule 4 eliminates **B.** H can't be fifth.

E is **CORRECT.** It violates no rules.

Question 2

I skipped this question at first. I wanted to develop examples that proved some letters could be third.

I eliminated **C** and **D** using that method, using the correct answer to question 1 and a scenario from question 4.

However, I got nowhere after that. It's easier to solve this question with logic.

We know M has to go in one of the first three spaces, so M probably affects who can go third.

If we place S third, then F and H have to go in spaces 1 and 2, because of the first rule.

There's no space left to put M 3rd or earlier. If S went third, we'd have to put F, H, S *and* M in the first three spaces.

A is CORRECT.

When you're stuck on a question, I recommend simply trying to draw. I figured out the logic of this question by putting S third, putting FH before, and looking at my diagram.

It took me maybe 7 seconds to draw that scenario. That's a lot more productive than staring at my page, thinking 'I don't know what to do'.

That's what I did at first, and what most students do. If you're stuck, try drawing an answer. You'll learn as you draw.

Question 3

For local rule questions, you should always draw the new rule. Here's what we get:

Then ask yourself what other rules are affected. We know M has to go third at the latest. So there are only two ways to place F-MH. Here's the diagram with M second:

Here's the diagram with M third. I also placed F, S and L:

F goes somewhere before M. S must come after H, and L comes fifth at the earliest.

This second diagram doesn't work. We still have to place GP, and there isn't a spot with two open spaces.

That leaves the first diagram, with FGH in the first three spaces. That scenario eliminates **A-D.**

E is CORRECT. This scenario proves it:

Question 4

I found it easiest to solve this question by eliminating wrong answers, using scenarios.

You can eliminate **E** because the correct answer on question one placed S fourth.

I waited to solve question 5 before I did this question. That let me eliminate **A** and **D**.

Here's the diagram from question five:

M,F, GP

__ __ __ __ L H S
         M̶

The commas indicate that the first four variables can go in any order, as long as M doesn't go fourth.

So this diagram proves that F or P could go fourth. **A** and **D** aren't right.

We're left with **B** and **C**. This diagram proves G can go fourth:

F H M G P L S
 ‿   M̶ ‿
 M   L

C is CORRECT. Let's make a diagram that shows what happens if you try to put H fourth.

The first rule gives us the order F-H-S. So F is somewhere in the first three spaces, and S is somewhere in the last three.

Rules 3 and 4 tell us that M is somewhere in the first three spaces, and L is somewhere in the last three.

So I put FM before H, and LS after H.

F M __ H L S __
 ‿   M̶ ‿
 M   L

It doesn't matter what order you put FM and LS in, or where you put them. The rules don't say anything about that. When you're to build a 'could be true' scenario, you can place variables anywhere, as long as you obey the rules.

So we could also have had M in 1, F in 3, H in 4, for example. As long as it's not illegal, go for it. There are usually multiple possible scenarios.

However, this scenario won't work. No matter where we put FM or LS, we can't place GP in this scenario. GP needs two open spaces.

Question 5

Answering this question quickly depends on your ability to see all the rules and how they interact.

First, draw the new rule:

GP
F — H — S

I don't quite know how to describe the process of getting the next deduction. Insight would be the right word, but that's not a very practical. I'll try to break it down.

M can only be in the first three places. L can only be in the final three places. This is very restrictive. When a game gives you restrictive rules, you must always keep them in mind.

The number 3 is important.

H now has three things in front of it. That means H can't be in the first three places. That means M is in front of H, since M is in the first three places.

We get this new diagram:

GP
F — H — S
M

L is the only one left out. L has to be in the final three places. H has four things in front of it. Therefore H is also in the final three places.

So, H, L and S are in the final three places.

But H can't go fifth. And H goes before S. So L goes fifth, H goes sixth, and S goes seventh.

M, F, GP
___ ___ ___ ___ L   H   S
                M

M, F and GP fill the first four spots. The only restriction is M can't go fourth.

In practice, I often get these deductions by starting to draw diagrams. If you keep all the rules in mind when you draw diagrams, you will spot these hidden points of restriction.

So don't worry that you don't have any magic insight for making deductions. I usually don't have it either. Instead, I draw, and figure things out by drawing.

D is **CORRECT.** L has to go fifth, not seventh.

Game 2 - Petri Dishes
Questions 6-11

Setup

This is a grouping game. The first question of each game usually shows a good way to draw the diagram.

Here, though, the first question puts the bottom on the top, and the top on the bottom of the diagram. That's confusing.

I reversed it, so that the bottom is on the bottom:

6̸ T __

   M __

2̸ B __

I've added the second rule to this diagram. 2 is always above 6. I drew it separately as well:

2
|
6

The first rule, I just memorized. There are at most three variables on a shelf. You could draw something like '3 MAX' if it helps you remember.

Here are the third and fourth rules:

These boxes are like reversible suitcases. The order of the variables doesn't matter. The boxes mean that 6 and 5 are always one group apart, and 1 and 4 are never in the same group.

Pay attention to the variables 1 and 4. They need two open groups. This is a three group game. Often, the questions will artificially fill one of the groups.

Then there will only be two groups left, and 1 and 4 must be split between those two groups.

The number 3 has no rules. I represent that by drawing a circle around 3:

③

There's one tiny deduction. Not even really a deduction, more of a fact. Since 6 and 5 go beside each other, one of them always has to be in the middle group.

Why? Well, they can be top and middle, or bottom and middle. Those are the only two possibilities. Here's a drawing to help you visualize it:

6̸ T 6
   M 5

2̸ B __

6̸ T __
   M 6
2̸ B 5

So one of 5 or 6 is always in the middle. You can add this to the diagram if it helps you remember:

6̸ T __

   M 6/5

2̸ B __

Of course, you won't actually draw this 6/5 when making diagrams. Usually a question will place 5 or 6 anyway. This note on the main diagram is just a reminder, assuming you figured out the deduction in the first place.

And that's it. There's no magic in this game. No amazing deductions that will let you solve everything.

There are just three main rules. Remember them, and this game is easy. Forget them and it's hard.

It's possible to memorize those three rules without much difficulty. The key is not rushing to start the questions. Spend some time on the setup.

I always read the rules once before drawing anything. I read them again while I draw. I read them once more to make sure I made no mistakes. Finally, I read them again to eliminate answers on the first question.

So I read the rules four times. This process might take me 20 seconds more than someone who reads the rules 1-2 times. You read faster each time you reread.

It is worth it. I can almost always memorize the rules effortlessly by doing this.

I mean c'mon, the rules are just a few facts. Read them four times, and you'd remember most of the rules too. So why don't you?

I guarantee you'll go *much* faster through the questions when you memorize the rules. And make less mistakes. All from 20 seconds more reading.

Main Diagram

6̸ T __

M 6/5

2̸ B __

①   2
       |
       6

②   6 | 5

③   1̸4̸

④   ③

Question 6

For list questions, go through the rules and use them to eliminate answers one by one.

Rule 1 eliminates **A.** Only three dishes max per shelf.

Rule 2 eliminates **C.** 2 has to be above 6.

Rule 3 eliminates **E.** 6 and 5 have to be beside each other, vertically.

Rule 4 eliminates **D.** 1 and 4 can't be on the same shelf.

B is **CORRECT.** It violates no rules.

Question 7

Whenever a question gives you a new rule, you should draw it. Then combine the new rule with existing rules.

We know 6 and 5 have to be one group apart. So if 6 is on the bottom, 5 is in the middle:

```
6̸ T __
   M 5
2̸ B 6|
```

The vertical line by 6 indicates that shelf is full.

Only two groups are open now. We know 1 and 4 are in different groups, so they're split across top and middle:

```
6̸ T 1/4
   M 5  4/1
2̸ B 6 |
```

There are two dishes left, 2 and 3. The middle shelf can't have four dishes (rule 1), so at least one more dish is on top.

So one of 2/3 definitely goes on top, and the other one can go top or middle:

```
6̸ T 1/4 2/3
   M 5  4/1    2/3
2̸ B 6 |
```

The hovering 2/3 indicates it can go in either open group.

The question asks who could go on the fifth shelf. We know five has to be on the middle shelf. So the answer has to be **D** or **E.**

1 or 4 also has to be in the middle.
So **E** is **CORRECT.**

Question 8

1, 2 and 3 fill up an entire shelf. That means 6 and 5 must go on other shelves.

In fact, 1, 2 and 3 must be on the top shelf, since 2 must be above 6.

Remember that 5 and 6 either go top and middle, or bottom and middle. On this question, top is full. So that means 6 and 5 take bottom and middle.

The middle and bottom shelves are reversible:

```
6̸ T 1   2   3|
   M 5⌐     4
2̸ B 6⌐
```

4 can go on either the middle or bottom shelf.

C is **CORRECT.**

Question 9

Remember that deduction about 6 and 5? It's surprisingly important this game. They go top and middle or bottom and middle.

Here are the two ways we can place 6 and 5:

6̸ T 6⌐
M 5⌐

2̸ B __

6̸ T __
M 6⌐
2̸ B 5⌐

So the middle shelf always has someone.

If one shelf has no dishes, that means that the other two shelves each have three dishes.

That's because the first rule says each shelf has max three dishes, and there are six dishes to place between two shelves.

So, the middle shelf always has dishes, and each shelf has three dishes.

Therefore the middle shelf has three dishes.

B is **CORRECT.**

Question 10

When a question gives you a new rule, draw it.

5 is alone on the bottom shelf and there are two dishes on the middle shelf:

6̸ T __
M __ __|
2̸ B 5 |

The vertical lines mean those shelves are full.

We know 6 is one above or below 5. And 2 is above 6. So 6 is in the middle and 2 is on top:

6̸ T 2
M 6 __|
2̸ B 5 |

We know 1 and 4 have to be in different groups. There are only two groups left, since 5 is alone on the bottom:

6̸ T 2 1/4
M 6 4/1|
2̸ B 5 |

Finally, only the top group has space left for 3:

6̸ T 2 1/4 3
M 6 4/1|
2̸ B 5 |

We're looking for two dishes that must be on the top shelf. That's 2 and 3.

C is **CORRECT.**

155

Question 11

Remember that one of 5 or 6 always has to be in the middle. See the setup for the explanation of this deduction.

In this question, only one dish is stored in the middle. So it has to be 5 or 6.

2 has to be above 6. Since 2 can't go in the middle on this question, 2 has to go in the top group:

6̸ T 2
   M 6/5|
2̸ B __

1 and 4 have to be split between the two other groups:

6̸ T 2 4/1
   M 6/5|
2̸ B 1/4

The question asks for two dishes that could be the only ones on the top shelf. We know that 2, and one of either 1 or 4 has to be on top.

A is **CORRECT.**

You could draw a few scenarios on this question, but it's not necessary. We already have enough information to answer the question, and it would be a lot of drawing to fill in the full placements for 6/5 and 3.

But, as a practice exercise, you might find it useful to draw the possibilities. They are:

1. 6 middle, 5 is on the bottom or top.
2. 6 bottom, 5 middle.

3 can go on the bottom or the top. Unless 5 is on top, then 3 has to go on the bottom, because shelves can have max three dishes (rule 1).

If you're not sure why these restrictions exist, draw these scenarios for practice, while referring to the rules.

Game 3 - Juice and Snacks
Questions 12-17

Setup

This game is a mix of grouping and linear. More importantly, it's one of those rare games where you can figure out almost everything before starting.

This game type used to be common, but it's rare on the modern LSAT. Now, games tend to test your memory of the rules, not your ability to combine rules up front.

However, up-front-deduction games still happen often enough that you should practice them multiple times. Once you get good at making up-front deductions, these are the easiest games on the test.

First, we'll set up the game like the first question does:

```
J __  __  __  __

S __  __  __  __
   1   2   3   4
```

I'm going to skip the first rule, and draw rules two and three. Always start with rules that are definite:

```
J __  __  __  __
               G̶

S __  __  G   __
   1   2   3   4
```

Next, the fourth rule. The first juice and the final snack are always the same. Here's a diagram to help you visualize it. The two spots by marked by an X will always be the same variable:

```
J  ✕  __  __  __
               G̶

S __  __  G   ✕
   1   2   3   4
```

Now, let's go back to the first rule. F is earlier than H, in the snacks row.

That makes snacks pretty restricted. Three rules affect the snacks row.

The final spot is particularly restricted. All three snack rules affect that spot. Who can go last?

Not G, G goes third.

Not F. F has to go before H.

So only H and I can go last in the snack row. Whenever a game offers only two possibilities, you should make two diagrams.

Let's start with I:

```
J  I  __  __  __
               G̶

S __  __  G   I
   1   2   3   4
```

F and H are the only snacks left. Rule 1 says that in snacks, F has to go before H:

```
J  I  __  __  __
               G̶

S  F   H   G   I
   1   2   3   4
```

Finally, the last juice can only be F or H. I is already first, and G can't be the last juice (rule 2):

```
J  I  __  __  F/H
               G̶

S  F   H   G   I
   1   2   3   4
```

It may seem obvious that only F/H can go last, but it's always worth drawing every deduction.

Next, let's do the diagram where H is the last snack:

J <u>H</u> __ __ <u> </u>
                Ø

S <u> </u> <u> </u> <u>G</u> <u>H</u>
  1   2   3   4

F and I are the other two snacks. They can go in either order:

J <u>H</u> __ __ <u>I/F</u>
    F, I   Ø

S <u> </u> <u> </u> <u>G</u> <u>H</u>
  1   2   3   4

The final juice is I or F. That's because G can't be last (rule 4) and H is first.

So there are only two diagrams. They cover all the rules. This makes the game very easy to solve.

With each diagram, you just have to remember which juices are left to place: G, and one of the two juices from the final space.

I want to talk about how to make these diagrams. It's easier than it looks. I just added rules one by one.

Once I added a rule, I stopped to think about what spot was the most restricted.

- Were there any spots where only two variables could go?
- If only two variables were left, did I know their order?

Once you make a deduction, stop and think again. Are there any new spots that are restricted, or where there only two variables left to place?

Each deduction you make further restricts the game. Re-examine the game whenever you make a deduction.

Main Diagram

J <u>I</u> __ __ <u>F/H</u>
                Ø

S <u>F</u> <u>H</u> <u>G</u> <u>I</u>
  1   2   3   4

J <u>H</u> __ __ <u>I/F</u>
   F, I   Ø

S <u> </u> <u> </u> <u>G</u> <u>H</u>
  1   2   3   4

Almost all questions will refer to these two scenarios. Draw them yourself, and make sure you know how we arrived at them.

If I say a question can only use scenario 1, I'll expect you to know I'm referring to one of these.

If you don't understand how I got these diagrams, try to draw them yourself. Reread the rules first, and follow along with the explanations in the setup. Don't move on until these scenarios make sense.

Question 12

For list questions, go through the rules and use them to eliminate answers one by one.

Rule 1 eliminates **C.** F has to be earlier than H in snacks.

Rule 2 eliminates **B.** G can't be the fourth juice.

Rule 3 eliminates **D.** G has to be the third snack.

Rule 4 eliminates **E.** The first juice and last snack must be the same.

A is **CORRECT.** It violates no rules.

Question 13

H is the fourth juice for this question. That has to be the first scenario from the setup. In scenario 2, only F or I can be the fourth juice.

Here's scenario one again:

J I _ _ F/H
         Ø
S F H G I
  1 2 3 4

Put H fourth, like the question says:

       G,F
J I _ _ H
         Ø
S F H G I
  1 2 3 4

G and F are the only juices left to place.

D is **CORRECT.** H is the second school for snacks in this scenario.

All the other answers don't have to be true, or can't be true.

Question 14

I is the third juice in this question. We have to use the second scenario, because in the first scenario, I is always the first juice.

Here is the second scenario diagram again:

J H __ __ I/F
   F, I   Ø
S __ __ G H
 1 2 3 4

In the first scenario, I is always the first juice.

Now let's put I third:

J H G I F
   F, I   Ø
S __ __ G H
 1 2 3 4

F and I are the only items left to place, in snacks.

C is CORRECT. F can be before I in snacks.

The other answers contradict the diagram.

Question 15

I can only be the first snack in the second scenario. Here it is again:

J H __ __ I/F
   F, I   Ø
S __ __ G H
 1 2 3 4

Now let's place I first, like the question says:

J H __ __ I/F
   F, I   Ø
S I F G H
 1 2 3 4

A is CORRECT. F could be the second juice, if I goes last.

B-D are wrong because H must be the first juice in this scenario. **E** is wrong because H has to be the last snack in this scenario.

Question 16

The best way to solve this 'could be true' question is to look at both scenarios and see whether the answer is possible in either.

Here are the two scenarios again:

Scenario 1

```
J  I  __ __  F/H
                Ø

S  F  H  G  I
   1  2  3  4
```

Scenario 2

```
J  H  __ __  I/F
     F,I         Ø

S  __ __ G  H
   1  2  3  4
```

A is wrong because F is before G in the snack row in both scenarios.

B is wrong. In the first scenario, I is before G in juices. In the second scenario, I is before G in snacks.

C is wrong. In the first scenario, I is before H in juices. In the second scenario, I is before H in snacks.

D is **CORRECT.** I could be before F in both rows in the second scenario. Here's one way it could look:

```
J  H  I  G  F
                Ø

S  I  F  G  H
   1  2  3  4
```

E is wrong. In the first scenario, H is before I in snacks. In the second scenario, H is before I in juices.

Question 17

Let's look at where G can go in the juice row, in both scenarios. Here are the two scenarios again:

Scenario 1

```
J  I  __ __  F/H
                Ø

S  F  H  G  I
   1  2  3  4
```

Scenario 2

```
J  H  __ __  I/F
     F,I         Ø

S  __ __ G  H
   1  2  3  4
```

Based on these two scenarios, G can only go 2nd or 3rd. I'll recap why this is.

The rule says G can't go fourth, so that's out. G also can't be the first juice.

Why? If G was the first juice, rule 4 says they would have to be the fourth snack. But Rule 3 says G must be the third snack, not the fourth.

The key to answering rule substitution questions is to figure out the full effects of a rule, and rephrase the rule to describe those effect another way.

B is **CORRECT.**

This question would have been hard to answer without scenarios. I take that as evidence you were supposed to figure out the scenarios.

Game 4 - Five Paralegals
Questions 18-23

Setup

This is a grouping game. Above all else, you have to remember the rules. If you remember them, there's not much to this game.

Actually, why don't you go reread the rules before you read my explanations?

I drew the last rule first - H is with S. You should always start with the most definite rules:

R __

S H

T __

Next, I drew two versions of the main diagram to show the first rule. Either F is with R and K is with T, or they both aren't:

R F   F̷ R __
S H   or   S H
T K   K̷ T __

I didn't always use these not rules when I made local diagrams. But I glanced at this diagram when drawing and reminded myself of the rule.

The second rule is a bit unique. One, but only one, of F or G is alone. I prefer just to memorize that.

It's not hard to memorize one out of three rules. That's why it's so important to draw as many rules as you can directly on the diagram.

That said, I did draw something when I did this game. It was just a placeholder to help me remember:

F | or G |

Finally, L is random. The circle indicates that L has no rules:

That's it. Not much to say about these rules. Remember that each group needs at least one person.

A few questions place variables alone in a group. Variables can only be alone in groups R or T, since H is already in group S.

So when a question tells you someone is alone, there are only two possibilities. Whenever there are only two possibilities, you should make two diagrams: One with the person alone in R, the other with the person alone in T.

Drawing both diagrams lets you find different deductions for each diagram. The LSAT makers expect you to draw two diagrams when there are only two possibilities.

Main Diagram

R F   F̷ R __
S H   or   S H
T K   K̷ T __

① __F | or __G |

② Ⓛ

Notice that, by putting two rules directly on the diagram, there's only the F/G alone rule to remember, plus the fact that L has no rules.

Putting more rules directly on the diagram makes it *much* easier to organize the game in your mind.

Question 18

For list questions, go through the rules and use them to eliminate answers one by one.

Rule 1 eliminates **A** *and* **E**. If F is with R, K needs to be with T.

Rule 2 eliminates **C**. One of F or G has to be alone.

Rule 3 eliminates **B**. H has to be with S.

D is **CORRECT.** It violates no rules.

Question 19

This is a tricky question. We're looking for a group that can't go with S. The answers list people that are with S. That part is clear.

The hard part is that you also have to consider the people *not* with S. Some of the hardest logic games questions involve unseen letters.

There's a simple trick to fixing this. Draw the unseen variables. Here's what my page looked like:

A: F, H, K   G, L
B: F, H, L   K, G
C: G, H, K   F, L
D: G, H, L   F, K
E: H, K, L   F, G

The two letters on the right are those that are with R and T, alone.

Once I drew those, I noticed that **E** had F and G in other groups. That means both F and G would be alone, which violates rule two.

E is **CORRECT.**

Question 20

As with all local rule questions, you should draw the new rule, even if it seems simple. T has exactly two people:

R __

S H

T __ __ |

Then look at the diagram, and think how it affects existing rules.

You know one of F or G is alone. In this new diagram, they could only be alone in group 1.

So we get two diagrams, one with F in R, and one with G in R.

Let's start with F's diagram. If F is with R, K must be with T (rule 1):

R F |

S H __

T K __ |

G and L fill the other two spots. One in group 2, one in group 3. There are no rules for them in this situation, they are interchangeable:

R F |

S H L/G

T K G/L |

That's the scenario with F alone. Next, put G alone. Since F is not with R, K can't be with T (rule 1):

R G |

S H K

T __ __ |

We have to place L and F. T is the only open group, so both L and F go there:

R G

S H K

T F L |

A is **CORRECT.** There's no problem with having G alone in R.

Question 21

This question says G and L are the only two people in one group.

There are only two possible diagrams. GL can't be alone in group S, because H is already there.

So GL can only be alone together in R or T.

Let's try putting them in R:

F̶ R G̲ L̲ |
   S H̲
K̶ T __

F and K are left to place. K can't go with T, since F isn't with R (rule 1).

F has to be alone, since G isn't alone (rule 2). So F goes with T, and K goes in group S:

F̶ R G̲ L̲ |
   S H̲ K̲
K̶ T F̲

Now let's try putting GL alone in group T:

F̶ R __
   S H̲
K̶ T G̲ L̲ |

So far so good. Now we have to place F and K.

We have to place F alone, since G isn't alone (rule 2).

Hmm, that won't work. F would have to go in R to be alone. But rule 1 says that if F is in R, K has to go in group T.

K can't go in T. It's full because we put GL there.

So only the first diagram works, with GL in R.

C is CORRECT.

Question 22

If you got question 21, then you could also have solved this question. In question 21, I tried to put GL alone in group T. It didn't work.

Go back and look at question 21 for the explanation.

D is CORRECT.

You can also solve this question by eliminating wrong answers. This scenario proves that either G or L could be alone in group T:

R ⁄G
S (H̲ F̲ K̲
T ↘L̲

G and L are reversible, since no rules say which group G and L should go in. So **A** and **B** are wrong.

Note that I've used a different diagram for reversibility. Sometime I draw arrows or arcs, as they're easier than writing: G/L, L/G. Go with what works.

This diagram proves **C** and **E** wrong. Once again, G and L are reversible.

R F̲
S H̲ L̲
T K̲ G̲

165

Question 23

K has to be alone for this question.

R and T are the only groups where K can be alone. H is already in group S.

Remember that, along with K, one of F or G must be alone.

So, two groups, R and T. K goes in one, and one of F/G in the other.

Let's try putting K in group T. We have to place one of F/G in the other group. It's got to be F, because of rule 1. If K is in T, F must go in R:

R F̲

S H̲

T K̲

L and G are left, we can put them in group S. This diagram works:

R F̲

S H̲ L̲ G̲

T K̲

Now let's try putting K in group R:

F̸ R K̲

   S H̲

K̸ T ___

F or G must go in T. It doesn't matter which one. L and the other F/G go in S:

F̸ R K̲

   S H̲ F/G̲ L̲

K̸ T F/G̲

That diagram works too. So either K or F can be in group R, when K is alone.

B is CORRECT.

Section III - Reading Comprehension
Passage 1 - A Plan For Small Farms
Questions 1-7

Paragraph Summaries

1. Whatley has new guidelines to help small farms thrive despite mechanized production.
2. Farms should grow at least ten crops, and grow them directly for consumers (CMCs). Farms shouldn't use chemicals if clients object.
3. Pick your own farming will let farms save on distribution costs while selling for fairly high prices.
4. Farms should be near cities, so customers can travel to the farm.

Analysis

This is a reasonable plan. Though it's odd that the LSAC specified that Whatley is African-American.

It's of course very common for the LSAC to specify that someone mentioned in a passage is a minority. But usually, that's because their ethnicity is relevant to the topic of the passage. Here, the fact that Whatley is African-American has nothing to do with farming or his recommendations. It feels like tokenism to point out his race.

This passage has a lot of details and the questions ask about them. You don't need to memorize all the details upfront, but you should have a rough idea where they are.

In other words, you should know the details well enough that a question can jog your memory when it refers to one.

Whatley's advice is to skip the middleman, offering lower costs for the farmer and lower prices for the consumer.

Normally, a farmer would have to pay workers to pick crops, and have employees drive them to stores. With this plan, the consumer will pick the crops and then drive them back to their house.

What the consumer gets:

- The fun of picking crops
- Lower prices
- Exactly the food they ask for
- The ability to ask for no chemicals

What the farmer gets:

- Year round money
- Savings on transport, labour
- Crop diversity

You should be familiar with these points before starting the passage.

There are a few other relevant details, but these are the main ones. To get familiar with details, you should do two things:

1. Try to organize paragraphs by theme, like I did in the summaries.
2. Skim the passage before starting, after you read it. This will let you see the details twice, and they'll stick in your memory much better.

Question 1

DISCUSSION: The point is that farmers might be able to avoid ruin by following Whatley's plan for selling directly to consumers.

You can first eliminate any answers that aren't true.

_____

A. **CORRECT.** The first paragraph and the final part of the last paragraph both confirm this point. Whatley has a plan for small farms, and this passage describes it.
B. We have no idea if large farming is sensitive to consumers' requests. Maybe some of it is. In any case, this is only a tiny part of the passage.
C. Whatley doesn't assess the ability of small farms to compete. He's just giving them advice.
D. This answer isn't even true. Whatley didn't say all small farms risk failure.
E. This goes too far. Whatley's plan might help small farms survive. But we don't know if it will be enough to make them dominant.

Question 2

DISCUSSION: For this type of question, you should justify your answer using a line from the passage, otherwise you risk making a mistake.

For instance, E is tempting. You might have had a vague recollection the passage said not to use chemicals.

But the passage said to avoid chemicals to please consumers, not for environmental reasons.

So that answer is both wrong. It is also misleading, because it *seems* right, if you're not 100% clear on what the passage said.

_____

A. Whatley doesn't talk about testing the market. Instead, he says farmers should only grow crops that consumers ask for.
B. **CORRECT.** Lines 26-28 say that it's important for consumers to pick their own crops. Leaving large lanes will make it easier for consumers to pick crops.
C. The final paragraph says farmers should let consumers come to them. They shouldn't go into town. (see lines 43-46)
D. Lines 26-28 say consumers should pick their own crops. If a farmer sells crops by the roadside, then the *farmer* picked the crops.
E. Close, but not quite. Whatley didn't mention the environment. He said farmers should use chemicals if consumers ask them not to. Otherwise, presumably it's ok to use chemicals.

Question 3

DISCUSSION: Start reading at line 26, where the passage talks about 'pick your own farming'. Just keep reading the sentence (it ends at line 31), and you'll see the answer.

Pick your own farming lets farmers offer cheaper prices than supermarkets, while lowering their costs.

_____

A. This sounds nice, but the author doesn't mention it as an advantage of pick your own farming.
B. This is an advantage of CMCs, but it's not necessarily an advantage of pick your own farming.
C. **CORRECT.** Exactly. Farmers save harvesting costs. So they can charge less, but make a profit. See lines 26-31.
D. This is an advantage of CMCs, listed in the second paragraph. It's not an advantage of pick your own farming.
E. Actually, the passage doesn't say how many people would be willing to drive to farms. It's a major weakness in the argument.

Question 4

DISCUSSION: Primary purpose questions are similar to main point questions. You have to figure out why the author is giving us this information.

Here, the purpose of the passage is to describe Whatley's plan for small farms.

_____

A. **CORRECT.** This sounds pretty good. Mechanization and debt are serious problems for small farms, according to the first paragraph.

The final paragraph shows that Whatley's proposals are innovative. He proposes having consumers come to farms. The traditional view is that farmers use roads to sell in town. (lines 43-46).
B. The passage only mentions one contemporary trend: the trend towards mechanization and debt. The author mentions some downsides, but doesn't discuss upsides.
C. Not quite. The passage does criticize mechanization and debt. But mainly the passage focusses on offering a solution, not a critique.
D. We only know of the advantages of Whatley's plan. The author doesn't tell us about disadvantages.
E. We don't know what impact Whatley's plan has had so far.

Question 5

DISCUSSION: For this type of question, you should try to justify your answer using specific lines from the passage.

If you do this consistently, you can go from 'sort of sure' to 100% sure, every time.

You'll get faster at it, too.

———————

A. The passage never said much about corporate farms, or whether they need loans.

B. The passage never mentions charging higher prices. The passage also doesn't talk about long run profits. Mainly, Whatley's recommendations serve to avoid debt.

   This answer uses plausible terms in ways never used by the passage. It's a misleading trap.

C. The passage doesn't say what kind of consumer would join a CMC,

D. **CORRECT.** Lines 13-17 recommend growing at least 10 different crops, to minimize the risk of crop failure. And lines 23-25 say to grow only crops that clients ask for.

   So if customers ask for less than 10 crops, then either the farm will grow crops that clients didn't ask for, or the farmer will risk crop failure by growing less than 10 crops.

E. The third paragraph implies there are no distribution costs. Customers harvest the crops themselves, at the farm.

Question 6

DISCUSSION: Lines 21-25 talk about this. To guarantee a market for all their crops, farmers should only grow crops clients ask for, and avoid using chemicals if clients don't want any.

You can use common sense to sift through the answers. If you're a farmer, you have a certain stock of produce. This question talks about selling *100%* of that stock. That's very hard, almost no business sells 100% of its inventory.

Growing different kinds of produce won't sell 100% (answer A). Watering your plants won't help you sell 100% of them (answer E).

The only real way to sell 100% of your stock is to have customers guarantee in advance that they will buy everything you produce. (lines 21-25)

———————

A. Growing 10 different crops protects against crop failure (lines 14-17). It doesn't guarantee a market for crops.

B. This low pricing is what will encourage consumers to come to the farm. But low prices don't guarantee a farmer will sell everything.

C. Clients who like fresh produce won't necessarily buy *all* of your produce.

D. **CORRECT.** See lines 21-25. If customers order all crops in advance, then presumably farmers will sell everything.

E. This helps prevent crops from dying. That won't guarantee that crops sell.

Question 7

DISCUSSION: Use your memory of the passage and your intuition to sort through answers.

But once you think you've found the right one, confirm it with the passage. There's always specific lines that will let you prove these questions with 100% certainty.

———————

A. It's hard to guarantee crops. Lines 20-21 say that the advance payment guarantees the right to *harvest*. However, there could always be drought, disease and crop failures.

No one wants diseased, failed crops. But when crops fail, that's all you get to harvest.

B. CORRECT. See lines 43-46. The traditional view is that roads let farmers take produce to consumers.

C. We have no idea how many farms a city of 50,000 can support. This simply isn't mentioned.

D. Ridiculous. The passage never mentions vehicle wear and tear, or what kind of roads people like. Roads were only mentioned to emphasize the change in direction: Rather than take food to people, take people to food.

E. We have no idea why roads were given hard surfaces. Perhaps the hard surfaces helped farmers. But that doesn't mean it was the main reason the roads were paved. There are thousands of uses for paved roads.

Passage 2 - Old Photography
Questions 8-14

Paragraph Summaries

1. Bidaut liked the detail in tintypes.
2. Estabrook wants to plant fake antique photographs in markets.
3. Old film techniques are making a comeback.
4. The old techniques are uncertain. They produce different photos each time due to errors. Artists value these errors.
5. Artists like the old photos because they're unique and intimate.

Analysis

This is a description of the renaissance in old photographic techniques. The motivations of the artists are important.

The artists like the individual variation that comes from using old photographic techniques.

Photographers used to minimize errors (lines 41-45) but these new photographers seek errors in order to add character to their pictures.

Estabrook is important, he's mentioned twice. He likes the idea of fooling people into thinking that his new photographs are old.

Lines 35-40 show that Estabrook likes the unpredictability of old techniques. He also thinks that the old techniques can change the meaning of pictures. When we think a picture is old, we project our feelings on to it.

We don't know much about the techniques themselves, apart from the fact that they produce errors. (lines 41-45)

Question 8

DISCUSSION: Go back and read the whole line. It says photography is moving forward into the past.

That's funny. As we get more and more advanced technology, some artists are rejecting it to use outdated techniques.

By adding context, the author is letting us know this situation is unexpected, and ironic.

––––––––––––––

A. **CORRECT.** One definition of irony is when something happens that is the opposite of what you would have expected to happen. As technology gets more advanced, you wouldn't expect artists to use 19th century techniques.
B. We have no idea if photographers are 'wary'. They may just think that new techniques produce less artistic results.
C. Actually, the author seems to approve of the trend towards using old techniques. The final paragraph is very positive, for example. Old-style photographs are intimate.
D. Sort of like B. You could see merit in a technique, while thinking it wouldn't produce the specific results you're looking for.

Photographers might agree, for example, that new techniques are great for people who just want nice family photos.
E. The author never implies that the use of old techniques is a fad. The line in question is just there to add context and contrast. The photographers are looking to the past, while photography in general is moving forward.

Question 9

DISCUSSION: Whenever you read a passage, you should try to figure out what the author thinks. Tone questions are very hard if you didn't catch the tone on your first read.

One thing to look for is praise or criticism. Or implied praise or criticism. Words that are usually compliments can be taken to be praise.

So when the author says that old photographs are 'intimate' (line 54), that's praise. Same with 'one of a kind' (line 50), and 'rich creamy tones' (line 2).

Meanwhile, the passage has absolutely no criticism of the techniques or the artists who use them.

The author goes to great lengths to understand the artists. So it's fair to say that they appreciate and understand the artists' work.

———————————

A. See the explanation above. The author likes the techniques. There's no hesitation.
B. CORRECT. See the explanation.
C. The author never mocks the artists.
D. The author doesn't say that new photographic techniques are bad. The author does think that what photographers are doing is interesting and valuable. But the author might also think that new techniques are useful for many purposes as well.

   It's not even clear if the photographers think new techniques are bad. The new techniques just have a different purpose than old techniques.
E. Whimsical is playful and fanciful. The author is hardly playful. They seem to take these old techniques very seriously.

Question 10

DISCUSSION: For this type of question, it's a guarantee that there's a specific line in the passage that will make you 100% certain of the right answer.

You should practice justifying your answer by finding that line. It doesn't take long once you get used to doing it.

———————————

A. We're never told about old techniques that aren't being used. Paragraph 3 only lists techniques that *are* being used.
B. Only paragraph 1 describes how tintypes work. It never mentions what chemicals are used.
C. Pinhole cameras are mentioned in paragraph 3. We have no idea who uses them.
D. Only line 21 mentions egg whites. We have no idea what effect they produce.
E. CORRECT. Lines 29-33 answer this. The new techniques were less expensive and produced photographs with fewer errors.

Question 11

DISCUSSION: The main purpose of the passage is to describe the revival of old photographic techniques, and the reasons for the revival.

A. Not quite. It's the artists who make this case. The author just describes why the artists feel the old techniques are valuable.

B. Actually, we don't really know *how* these old methods are used. All we know is that they take more effort, and they produce less consistent results.

   But how, specifically, do artists use them? We have no idea.

C. **CORRECT.** Lines 17-18 show that this development is surprising. As photographic technology advances, more photographers are using old techniques.

   This passage describes the different techniques they use, and some of the reasons why.

D. We actually don't know if these photographers have received critical acclaim. This is never mentioned.

E. Nonsense. The author only mentions Bidaut in the first paragraph, to set the scene. And they don't give much detail on Estabrook either.

   This passage is really about the general movement towards using older techniques again.

Question 12

DISCUSSION: 20th century artists use the older techniques in order to add uniqueness and character to their photos.

Newer techniques work better, but aren't as useful for achieving certain artistic goals.

The old methods are very labor intensive. They're also error prone, but the artists want the errors.

A. The herbal medicines aren't obviously worse at improving health. And there's no clear aesthetic goal to using herbs.

B. The high rise office building is still modern. To be analogous, the architect would have had to use the architectural drafting tools used by the ancients.

C. This is close. But we don't know why the engineer uses the older design. We do know the artists wanted the flaws that came with old methods.

   An engineer, on the other hand, isn't likely to want a supercharger with flaws. Presumably he's using the older design because he's judged it to be more effective.

D. **CORRECT.** This has both qualities. Older methods, and older methods used in order to produce flaws.

E. This is entirely modern. The artist isn't using old methods, and he isn't looking to include errors.

Question 13

DISCUSSION: The author mentions Estabrook in two places: the second paragraph, and lines 34-45.

I personally reread both sections before answering this question. It didn't take long to read them, and it let me answer the question with all the information about Estabrook fresh in my mind. So I answered the question much faster.

Estabrook likes the unpredictability of old processes. He also thinks that if he can fool people into believing art is from the past, then they will give it a different meaning.

A. Estabrook never mentions 19th century photographers. In fact, nowhere in the passage does the author tell us how people selected photo subjects in the 19th century.
B. **CORRECT.** This is a little vague, but it's the best answer. Lines 35-36 say that unpredictability attracted Estabrook to old techniques.

 If something is unpredictable, it's out of your control. Yet these old techniques produce exactly the results Estabrook wants.
C. This is true of *modern* photographs. We have no reason to believe that earlier photographers liked unpredictability. Lines 41-45 say that old photographs removed errors.
D. The second paragraph says Estabrook wants to fool people into thinking his photos are older than they seem. It's unlikely he thinks this is ethically questionable.
E. This is a stretch. We have no idea if the errors that occur using old techniques can be controlled after the photo is taken, or if they're instead produced at the moment the photographer takes the picture.

 Secondly, even if you *can* affect errors after the fact, Estabrook might believe that it's the subject of the photo that has the most aesthetic significance.

Question 14

DISCUSSION: Lines 38-40 best explain Estabrook's view.

He thinks that, if we believe a photograph is old, then we will add meaning to it.

So by creating pictures that seem old, Estabrook gives them new meaning. He also thinks that only old techniques can effectively fool people.

A. **CORRECT.** This shows that only old techniques can produce the effects that Estabrook wants. People see through fakes produced with modern techniques.
B. This contradicts Estabrook. Lines 38-40 show he thinks feelings are very important to a work's artistic merit.
C. If people only value accurate pictures, then that weakens Estabrook's reasoning. His old style photographs are less accurate than photos made with new techniques.
D. Estabrook's photos appear old but aren't actually old. This answer shows people *wouldn't* value his work.
E. This is just a fact about new photographic techniques. The fact that they're getting better says nothing about Estabrook's artistic goals. He purposefully avoided perfection.

Passage 3 - Patent Problems (comparative)
Questions 15-21

Paragraph Summaries

Passage A

1. The patent office is allowing obvious patents.
2. It's impossible to invent around some patents.
3. Large companies amass patents in order to sue anyone that sues them. Some companies make the mistake of not doing this.
4. It's almost impossible to make software without infringing patents, and it's incredibly expensive to find all relevant patents.

Passage B

1. Our company supports open source and abolishing patents.
2. Unfortunately, patents exist and are dangerous.
3. Many companies own defensive patents, we will do the same.

Analysis

Software patents are a big problem in the tech world. Passage A gives an overview of the problem, and passage B gives one company's perspective on how a business should deal with this problem.

Some technical solutions are obvious, says the first paragraph of passage A. And companies are now allowed to patent these obvious solutions.

One famous example is Amazon's patent on one click shopping. Their idea: Pressing a button on a sales page that lets you order and pay for an item with one click.

That seems incredibly obvious. But, in 1999, the patent office ruled it was a valuable invention. Now amazon is the only company allowed to offer one click shopping, until the patent expires.

Companies can license patents. But it gets complicated. Suppose, for example, that you want to make some new software. You'd have no idea which obvious ideas were patented.

It would cost you a lot of money to find out. And it would be very expensive to license all the relevant patents.

So some companies amass an arsenal of patents. If someone sues them, they'll sue that company. People will be hesitant to sue any company with a patent arsenal.

It's risky for a company not to have such an arsenal. That's why the company in passage B is using patents.

The company doesn't think patents should exist. But patents do exist, so the company is using them, for now, to protect itself.

Question 15

DISCUSSION: Both passages are extremely skeptical of patents. Neither passage has anything good to say about them.

Passage A criticizes the fact that obvious patents are now common.

The author of Passage B describes a defensive policy for his company, and justifies the company's use of patents.

———————

A. Passage A doesn't have anything nice to say about patents. And Passage B describes a company's policies on its own use of patents. It's not a general argument about why we should eliminate patents.
B. Passage B definitely didn't defend patents. The first paragraph calls for eliminating them.
C. CORRECT. Patenting the obvious is a good title for passage A. The passage was a complaint that patents are too easy to get, and that patents harm software. The author of passage B presents a defensive policy for his company.
D. Passage A doesn't describe a misunderstanding about patents. A passage that had this title would clear up common misconceptions about patents.
E. The author of passage B isn't apologizing to his customers.

Question 16

DISCUSSION: You should consider the fastest way to eliminate answers. You want something mentioned in passage A, and not mentioned in passage B.

So you can prove an answer wrong if it has:

• Something not mentioned in passage A, or
• Something mentioned in passage B.

It's easier to prove that something is mentioned, than it is to prove something is not mentioned. So the fastest way to eliminate answers is to prove they're mentioned in passage B.

———————

A. Passage B mentions this in lines 54-56.
B. CORRECT. Lines 31-34 mention this in passage A. Passage B never mentions this.
C. Lines 38-41 mention this in passage B.
D. Line 53 in passage B mentions the high cost of patent litigation.
E. Lines 51-52 in passage B mention that many patents should not have been granted. ('questionable nature of many software patents')

Question 17

DISCUSSION: Lines 14-15 say it's impossible to invent around a patent if it is too broad.

You can assume that 'inventing around a patent' has a straightforward meaning: finding a way around the patent.

In other words, finding a different way of achieving the same goal, which does not infringe the patent.

If a patent is too broad, there's no way to invent around it.

———————————

A. Inventing around a patent lets you bypass a patent held by a competitor. This answer instead describes bypassing the process of getting a patent in the first place. Not the same thing.

This also has a subtle error. It's not the 'use' of a product that's supposed to be non-obvious. It can be quite difficult to invent an object that seems obvious to use. (e.g. the original iPhone)

B. This describes lying, or fraud. The passage didn't recommend infringing patents. Inventing around a patent means finding a different way of achieving the same goal.

C. This sounds close, but the meaning is completely different. An example would be: "A company patents the internet, to allow people to exchange emails. You use the internet patent to allow people to shop, a use that was not intended." Inventing around the patent would be finding a different way to send emails over something similar to the internet, in a way that didn't infringe my patent.

D. The principles don't have to be entirely different. They just have to be different enough that they don't infringe on the patent. Also, the principle should be different from the competitors' patents, not different from products you own that are affected by those patents.

E. CORRECT. This lets you make use of the same ideas, while avoiding getting sued for infringing a patent.

You can read 'inventing around a patent to mean 'getting around the obstacle'.

Question 18

DISCUSSION: Passage A is a general description of the problems with patents. Passage B is a specific company's plan to deal with the threat of patent lawsuits.

———————————

A. Passage B doesn't criticize any of the ideas in Passage A. Both passages agree with each other on all points.

B. CORRECT. Patents are the problem described in passage A. Passage B describe's a company's strategy for dealing with patents.

C. Passage A says the defensive strategy is a good idea. Lines 23-25 say it's a mistake not to have defensive patents.

D. Passage B doesn't say how we can get out of the patent situation we're in.

E. Passage A only presents one side. Passage A criticizes patents, and has nothing good to say about them.

Question 19

DISCUSSION: Both authors say companies should amass defensive patents to protect against lawsuits. See lines 16-25 and lines 54-60.

A. CORRECT. See the lines references above.

B. The final paragraph of passage A says licensing is nearly impossible.

C. How would you use (exploit) a patent you don't own? This answer makes no sense, and it certainly isn't mentioned in either passage.

D. Neither author specifically warns about avoiding infringement. In fact, the final paragraph of passage A implies that it is impossible to avoid infringement.

E. The final paragraph of paragraph A says it's nearly impossible to research which patents affect your product.

Question 20

DISCUSSION: If you read around line 60, 'this same stance' refers to amassing a defensive portfolio of patents.

Lines 16-25 in passage A talk about stockpiling defensive patents. Line 20, 'a credible deterrent' is the best answer. A deterrent is something you use to warn others not to attack you.

A. This refers to the standards for issuing a patent: a patent shouldn't be for an obvious idea.

B. 'Invent around' describes the old strategy to avoid infringing a patent.

C. This phrase describes how it's now easier to patent an obvious idea.

D. CORRECT. See the explanation above.

E. You don't need to know exactly what modular components are to eliminate this answer. Modular components are mentioned in lines 26-30, those lines say software is assembled from modular components.

So modular components are part of software, not a defensive portfolio of patents.

(For the records, modular means assembling something from finished components. So a modular house would use a preset kitchen, bathroom, etc. and arrange them in a useful order)

179

Question 21

DISCUSSION: In line 39, the author of passage B says that patents impede innovation. That means they slow innovation.

To weaken this idea, we need to show that patents help innovation or at least don't hurt it.

A. 20 years is a long time in software. The world wide web is only around 20 years old. So two decades is enough time to harm innovation.

B. This doesn't show that patents hurt the reliability of software. It could be that companies that produce better products also voluntarily avoid seeking patents, for ethical reasons.

But the quality of those companies' products wouldn't suffer if the companies did seek patents. High quality causes no patents, and not the reverse.

C. Who cares *why* vendors oppose software patents? This doesn't help prove that software helps innovation.

D. **CORRECT.** If innovation were less profitable, there might be less innovation. This shows that patents may in fact increase innovation by increasing profits.

E. This doesn't tell us much. We don't know if large corporations or individual innovators produce more innovation.

Passage 4 - Dodos and Trees
Questions 22-27

Paragraph Summaries

1. Temple thought the decline in *Calvaria major* trees was caused by the dodo. He only found 13 trees, and no young trees. He assumed their seeds couldn't germinate (grow).
2. Temple thought that the seeds had a thick pit, to withstand digestion in the dodo's gizzard. Temple thought that dodos ate *Calvaria major* fruit, and that without dodos, no bird would digest the pit so the seeds could germinate.
3. Temple found that *Calvaria major* seeds could withstand passing through the stomachs of turkeys, and some seeds germinated.
4. Later ecologists found many more *Calvaria major* trees. They also found that *Calvaria major* seeds could germinate without passing through a bird's stomach.

Analysis

This passage has a different structure from most RC passages. First, it presents Temple's hypothesis, which appears to be convincing. However, the passage them demolishes this hypothesis. In the final paragraph, the author makes clear they think Temple is probably wrong.

You don't have to completely understand Temple's idea in order to answer the questions. But it helps to reread any section that confused you the first time through.

I always do this if I'm unsure about a passage. It takes less time to reread than to read. You'll answer questions faster when you understand better.

Here are the facts that support Temple's theory:

- Temple didn't find many *Calvaria major* trees. (lines 10-11)
- The youngest trees he found grew around the time the dodo disappeared. (line 12, lines 16-17)
- The *Calvaria major* seeds have thick pits. (line 21)

- This thick pit would have let seeds withstand acid in the dodo's gizzard. (lines 23-25)
- Temple suspected that Dodos often ate the fruits which contained these seeds.(lines 22-23)
- Temple thought that the seeds couldn't germinate if the pit walls were unabraded. (lines 25-28)
- Temple calculated that the pits could have withstood the dodos' stomachs (lines 34-39)
- Turkey gizzards could abrade the pit walls. Some of those seeds germinated. (lines 39-41)

That's a lot of facts to keep track of! The most important assumptions are the following:

- The youngest *Calvaria major* trees that Temple found are 300 years old.
- Temple thought *Calvaria major* seeds can no longer germinate, since they don't pass through dodo digestion.

The author only uses a couple of facts to demolish this argument:

- There are in fact many young *Calvaria major* trees. (lines 48-52)
- *Calvaria major* seeds can germinate on their own. (lines 54-57)

If you read carefully, you'll notice the author is skeptical of Temple throughout the passage.

- In line 14, they say Temple *assumed* the seeds couldn't germinate.
- In line 17, they say "what Temple *considered* the last evidence of natural germination".
- Lines 33-34 say his argument had a *semblance* of rigor.

The biggest tell of all is easy to miss. In lines 19-25, the author says that Temple *hypothesized* that dodos ate *Calvaria major* fruit.

So Temple didn't prove dodos ate the seeds! It's just a theory. It's possible that dodos never digested *Calvaria major* fruit.

A word like 'abraded' is hard, but you can get it from context on line 41. It's the verb for abrasion.

181

Question 22

DISCUSSION: The author describes Temple's theory, then shows that it is wrong.

A. This is just a fact that helps prove Temple wrong. It's far from the main point of the passage, which was to describe and discredit Temple's theory.
B. **CORRECT.** This covers everything. First the author describes Temple's theory, with skepticism. Then in the final paragraph the author's shows the theory is probably wrong. In fact, *Calvaria major* trees probably aren't even going extinct.
C. This contradicts the fourth paragraph, which shows that Temple was probably mistaken.
D. Same as C.
E. Lines 48-51 indicate that *Calvaria major* trees may in fact not be scarce.

Question 23

DISCUSSION: Lines 4-7 say that Temple was researching endangered birds.

A. **CORRECT.** See lines 4-7. Endangered birds are birds that face extinction.
B. Lines 36-37 mention that certain test results let Temple figure out the crush resistant strength of the seeds. The lines don't tell us exactly what test results Temple used.

The bird studies mentioned nearby (lines 34-35) didn't measure pit strength. They just let Temple estimate the abrasive force in Dodo gizzards.
C. The studies in lines 34-35 let Temple estimate the abrasive force in Dodo gizzards. But that doesn't mean any modern birds have the same abrasive force in their gizzards.

In fact, if some modern bird gizzards have the same force as Dodo gizzards had, then Temple probably would have concluded that those birds could let *Calvaria major* pits germinate.
D. The author never describes the quality of Temple's studies. The author only says that the studies lent Temple's theory a 'semblance' of rigor (lines 33-34). That indicates that the general theory wasn't rigorous. It's possible the studies were rigorous.
E. Actually, Temple's major research topic was the endangered birds of Mauritius (lines 4-7). His research into *Calvaria major* pits was an offshoot of his original research (line 6).

Question 24

DISCUSSION: Semblance means impression. Something not real. If someone has a semblance of intelligence, they seem intelligent, but are not.

So this indicates that Temple's overall study was not rigorous, even though his tests made it seem rigorous.

———————————

A. This is tempting, but not quite right. The phrase refers to Temple's overall study. So his experimental findings about the pits may have been accurate.

However, those experimental findings were not enough to make his overall study scientific.

B. Actually, line 31 is the line that shows direct proof was unobtainable. The 'semblance of rigor' line has a different purpose: it shows Temple's study was not actually rigorous.

C. Lines 33-34 don't actually say whether the studies Temple used were firsthand studies he did himself.

In any case, the passage definitely didn't contrast the bird studies with the information about the age of the trees. As far as we know, the foresters were credible when they said the trees Temple found were over 300 years old.

D. CORRECT. Temple's studies of the *Calvaria major* pits were the only direct, quantitative evidence he produced. The studies made his theory *appear* scientific, even though it actually was not a very scientific theory.

E. Temple fed some seeds to turkeys, and checked what they pooped out. While that was interesting work, it's hardly an exceptionally precise or creative experiment.

In any case, scientists didn't praise Temple, and if you were going to praise an experiment's rigor, 'semblance' is not the word you would use.

Question 25

DISCUSSION: You'll want to justify your answer using the passage. These questions almost always have a line reference that lets you prove an answer is correct, with 100% certainty.

———————————

A. CORRECT. See lines 54-57. Speke showed that *Calvaria major* seeds can germinate even if they haven't been abraded by bird gizzards.

B. Lines 39-41 contradict this. Turkey gizzards destroyed many of the seeds.

C. Lines 39-41 indicate that turkey gizzards could abrade *Calvaria major* seeds. This suggest dodos could also have abraded *Calvaria major* seeds.

D. Very tricky. Lines 19-25 show that Temple *hypothesized* that Dodos commonly ate the *Calvaria major* fruit.

He had no proof for this idea. How could he? The dodo is extinct. And he didn't find any *Calvaria major* pits inside dead dodos.

Temple's theory was just that: a theory. He didn't prove that dodos had anything to do with *Calvaria major* trees!

E. The passage never mentioned natural forces that could abrade the pits of *Calvaria major* seeds. This answer is a wild goose chase.

Question 26

DISCUSSION: The fourth paragraph shows that the author is extremely skeptical of Temple's theory.

There are more *Calvaria major* trees than Temple realized (lines 48-52). The seeds can germinate without abrasion by bird gizzards (lines 54-57).

Lines 58-62 do indicate that the author is not 100% certain Temple is wrong. The author says the decline in the tree 'could easily be due' to other factors.

The author doesn't say that other factors are *definitely* the cause.

————————

A. The fourth paragraph almost completely contradicts Temple's theory.
B. Same as A.
C. Debatable. Temple's theory is almost certainly wrong, so it's hard to say it is a valuable theory.
D. It's not useful to have a precisely formulated theory if the theory is wrong. In the fourth paragraph, the author shows that they think Temple was wrong.
E. **CORRECT.** See lines 48-52 and 54-57. Contrary to Temple's ideas, there are many *Calvaria major* trees, and their seeds can germinate.

Question 27

DISCUSSION: You can disprove wrong answers with lines in the passage. This doesn't take that long once you practice.

Look for line references when you review, and you can answer this type of question more quickly.

————————

A. Paragraph four contains information about Temple's critics. The paragraph doesn't say why *Calvaria major* fruit developed thick walls.
B. See lines 58-62. They said the decline 'could easily be due to other factors'. So the author isn't 100% certain Temple was wrong.
C. **CORRECT.** Lines 54-57 suggest that *Calvaria major* seeds have a low germination rate. So it's actually to be expected that there aren't many *Calvaria major* trees.
D. See lines 57-58.
E. See lines 54-57.

Section IV - Logical Reasoning

Question 1

QUESTION TYPE: Identify The Conclusion

CONCLUSION: Scientists should reassess the view that no deep sea creatures can detect red light.

REASONING: There is a deep sea creature that has red lights that probably act as lures.

ANALYSIS: Identifying conclusions is a very important part of arguments.

Anytime the author gives a recommendation (should, need to, ought to), that's almost certainly the conclusion. Especially here, where 'need to' comes after 'but', a word that indicates the author's own opinion.

A. This is evidence that scientists ought to change their opinion.
B. This is evidence that those red lights are lures.
C. This is just a fact. For this to be the conclusion, the whole argument would have had to be devoted to proving that this creature had been discovered.
D. This is a belief that the author argues is mistaken.
E. **CORRECT.** The red light lures are evidence that some deep sea creatures can see red light.

Question 2

QUESTION TYPE: Most Strongly Supported

FACTS: Acrylics provide everything a house paint should have. But acrylics can't correct surface defects. Those need repair.

ANALYSIS: The only real conclusion we can draw is that house paints don't need to be able to correct surface defects.

Acrylics are a good house paint, and they can't correct surface defects.

A. The passage never said what causes cracked paint. Harsh weather is never mentioned, so we can't rule it out.
B. Nonsense. It's true acrylics provide everything a house paint should have. But the author never said they're the only paints that do this.
C. The author never mentions painting over other types of paint. We have no idea if this is a good idea or not.
D. **CORRECT.** Acrylics are good house paints, and they can't repair surface defects. So it seems as though correcting surface defects is not a requirement for house paints. Otherwise acrylics wouldn't make good house paints.
E. The author never mentions paint color. We know absolutely nothing about this.

Question 3

QUESTION TYPE: Flawed Reasoning

CONCLUSION: Private business is inefficient.

REASONING: One private business is inefficient.

ANALYSIS: You have to read between the lines to see the author's real conclusion.

The author is claiming that philanthropists are already more efficient then private business. They thinks private business is inefficient.

Their evidence? Bywords Corporation is inefficient.

That's a pretty lousy argument. There are millions of private businesses. Perhaps most of them are very efficient, even if Bywords Corporation isn't.

A. This is a different error. It's like saying "we ought to eat junk food, because we do eat junk food"
B. **CORRECT.** The author assumes that all business are inefficient since Byworks corporation posts losses.

   That's a very bad argument. The author would have to examine a representative sample of businesses to properly draw that conclusion.
C. The editor is the proponent of the claim. The author is responding to the editor.

   The author makes no personal attacks against the editor. In fact, they tell us nothing at all about the editor. Definitely not ad hominem.
D. This is a different error. It's like saying "There's no evidence John is a good candidate, so he must be a bad candidate".
E. This is a different error. It's like saying "Coffee made me jittery, so I must be a warm, brownish liquid".

   I could have thought of a more sensible example, but this made me laugh.

Question 4

QUESTION TYPE: Method of Reasoning

CONCLUSION: Crime statistics aren't accurate. They mostly tell us about the motives of those who produce crime statistics.

REASONING: A variety of people that produce crime statistics have incentives to raise or lower reported crime rates.

ANALYSIS: This argument lists several examples to prove its point.

Not much else to it.

A. The argument doesn't give any evidence against its conclusion.
B. **CORRECT.** The argument lists various organizations that have incentives to misreport crime rates.
C. This is completely different. You make a general statement, then think of what would be true if that statement were true. Here's an example. "I'm sure all Canadians must wear clown wigs. That must mean they look funny when they travel. And you can spot one at a distance. And clowns can blend in with crowds. And...."

   Note: I'm Canadian. I haven't worn a clown wig since I was a kid.
D. This is different. It's like saying: "There are unemployed people. And there aren't enough daycares. We should hire unemployed people to run a daycare."

   Two problems, solved by a single solution.
E. This is completely different. An example would be saying "Don't worry that the new CEO has no experience. That just means he doesn't know what can't be done!"

Question 5

QUESTION TYPE: Paradox

PARADOX: Dairy has lots of calcium. Calcium prevents osteoporosis. But countries that get calcium only from fruits and vegetables have less osteoporosis.

ANALYSIS: There are a few possibilities. One would be that the form of calcium in fruits and vegetables is easier to absorb.

The other would be that there's something present in dairy that prevents calcium absorption.

A. This shows that eating too much calcium isn't bad. Who cares? We need to explain why dairy seems harmful.
B. That's nice that some people eat dairy. So what? The stimulus considered countries where people *don't* eat dairy. We want to explain why they get less osteoporosis.
C. This shows that calcium deficiency doesn't *always* lead to osteoporosis. That's fine. Calcium deficiency just has to increase the risk of getting osteoporosis.
D. This shows that some deficiencies go together. But it doesn't explain why people have less osteoporosis when they don't eat dairy.
E. CORRECT. This shows that people who eat dairy don't absorb all the calcium that's in dairy.

So effectively, you get more calcium from eating fruits and vegetables.

Question 6

QUESTION TYPE: Principle

PRINCIPLE:

First term board member → accountant OR has support of full committee

Contrapositive:

~~Accountant~~ AND Lacks Supports of at least one member → Should not be first term member

ANALYSIS: This principle gives necessary conditions for being on the board as a first term member.

If someone is on the board, we can conclude they should meet at least one of the necessary conditions. If someone fails to meet both, we can conclude they should not be on the board.

(They might still be on the board, of course. People do lots of things they *shouldn't* do)

The principle says nothing about people who aren't first term members. You can eliminate three wrong answers because they don't specify 'first term'.

A. Simkins might still be ok, if he has the support of all committee members.
B. The principle was about first term members. We have no idea what rules apply to third term members like Timmins.
C. Ruiz could be a second or third term member. In that case, the principle wouldn't apply to him.
D. CORRECT. Klein is a first term member, so the condition applies. Look at the contrapositive in the 'principle' section. If someone is not an accountant and lacks support from some members, they should not be on the committee.
E. We have no idea if this is true, because we don't know if Maber is a first term member. The principle only applies to first term members.

Question 7

QUESTION TYPE: Weaken

CONCLUSION: The survey shows that it's more fun to listen to a novel than to read it.

REASONING: People who listened to a particular novel enjoyed it. People who read it didn't enjoy it.

ANALYSIS: This survey doesn't have a great sample. It only looks at people who read or listened to *one* book.

There are millions of books. Maybe there's something special about this book that makes the audio book better. For example, perhaps the author gave a very passionate, personal reading.

It could be that in most cases, people prefer to read rather than listen. So to weaken the argument, we can show that this book is not representative of all books.

Maybe this audiobook was particularly good, or the written book was not so good.

A. If you *listen* to a book, you must know whether you enjoyed *listening* to it. It doesn't matter if you also read the book. And vice-versa.
B. We don't know what this means. Do people enjoy reading books because they can rush through them? Or do they like listening to audiobooks because the enjoyable experience of listening to them lasts longer?
C. This is useless. It lumps everyone together. We need an answer that lets us distinguish between those who listen on tape and those who read.
D. Worthless. If there's no audio version of a book, then there's no point in making a comparison. You can't prefer an audiobook version that doesn't exist.
E. **CORRECT.** This shows that the novel was an exception. The book is hard to understand if you read it, but easier to understand if you listen to it.

So the survey results can't tell us about books in general. Most books aren't hard to read.

Question 8

QUESTION TYPE: Necessary Assumption

CONCLUSION: If you're a recognized medical specialist, then you're competent in your specialty.

REASONING: You must study for quite a while and pass an evaluation to be a medical specialist.

ANALYSIS: Doing something for a long time doesn't automatically make you competent. It's possible these medical graduates don't know what they're doing, even after all their training.

The argument has to assume that anyone who has trained that long is competent. Or anyone who is a recognized medical specialist is competent.

A. The conclusion is about competence. This answer is about motivation. Unfortunately, being motivated doesn't automatically make you good.
B. This isn't quite good enough. Being a doctor is hard. Maybe being among the most talented people doesn't guarantee you are competent.

For instance, only the most talented students apply to Yale, but that doesn't guarantee they all get in.
C. **CORRECT.** This works. It's a conditional statement: complete evaluation → competent

We know that the doctors completed an evaluation. Using that condition is a required link in the argument.

This is actually a sufficient assumption as well as a necessary assumption. If we know this is true, the argument is 100% correct.
D. 'Usually' isn't enough. The conclusion says 100% of specialists are competent. No exceptions.
E. This is like D, except worse, because it's saying studying is a necessary condition for competence, rather than sufficient. So this answer can't even guarantee competence in any cases.

Question 9

QUESTION TYPE: Most Strongly Supported

FACTS:

1. Archaeologists found 10,000 years old plant remains at a site.
2. If the plants were cultivated, then the people discovered agriculture thousands of years before others did.
3. If the plants were wild, then the people ate a wider variety of plants than others did at the time.

ANALYSIS: There's not much to say here. There are two possibilities, and you can't combine them.

It's safe to say that wild plants are the opposite of cultivated. So there are only two possibilities: early agriculture discovery, or wider use of plants.

This is a most strongly supported question. It means there's some wiggle room in the right answer. On this question, it's so subtle that you probably didn't even notice it. I'm going to write a note explaining the wiggle room on the other side of the page. Only read that if you really want to dig deep into how this test works.

A. We have no idea. Maybe the archaeologists won't be able to figure out how the plants were used.
B. **CORRECT.** This is probably true. Either the plants were cultivated, or the group ate plants no one else ate. See the opposite page for a more precise explanation.
C. This doesn't follow. It's possible the group had reached a more advanced stage with wild plants, *and* had also discovered how to farm some plants.
D. It's possible the group discovered agriculture, but didn't cultivate plants at that site. Or maybe all the cultivated plants disintegrated and we won't find evidence.
E. We have no idea which of these two possibilities is more likely. We know one of them is true, but we can't say which one.

Question 9 Note

Let's call the people at the site the uggs. We know for sure that they ate a wider variety of plants than anyone else.

But how do we know they used plants in a way that no one else did? We actually don't. It's just fairly strongly supported.

Suppose there were 1000 types of plants. The uggs ate all 1000 of them at the site.

Other tribes only used 1-2 of these plants each. Perhaps all the other tribes in the world used a total of 200 plants between them.

That means there were 800 plants the uggs used, that no one else used in that way.

Now, suppose the other tribes only used 1-2 types of plants each. But between all the other tribes, there was at least one tribe that ate each one of the 1000 types of plants.

In that case, there would be *no* plants that the uggs used in a way that no one else did. No tribe used as many plants as the uggs, but at least one tribe used each of the plants the uggs used.

Make sense? So we can't say for sure that answer B is true. But it's pretty strongly supported.

Question 10

QUESTION TYPE: Parallel Reasoning

CONCLUSION: Car X is more efficient than car Y.

REASONING: The two cars had the same mileage, even though car X was driven less efficiently.

ANALYSIS: This is a good argument. Car X performed just as well as Y, even though X wasn't used as efficiently.

So car X had spare capacity that could be used to make it even more efficient than Y, if car X was driven properly.

_____

A. This isn't a good argument. It's possible X and Y experience pain the same way, but describe it differently.
B. **CORRECT.** This is a good argument. Weight gain is like fuel efficiency. Eating more is like driving less efficiently. If our hamster ate fewer calories, presumably it would have gained less weight than the other hamster. Our hamster had spare calorie burning capacity.
C. This argument would be more parallel if Ronald went the same speed coasting down the hill and pedaling on level ground. Then we might say he has more potential speed on the hill.

  As it is, he might already be coasting at his max speed down the hill.
D. The estimates are only lower on *average*. It's possible that the estimates matched in a few cases because both people knew a lot about those particular pieces. So they could have had accurate estimates for those two, and be all over the map for everything else.
E. This makes an error between absolute level, and relative level.

  Let's say you have 20/20 vision. You see well. You put on some mild prescription glasses. You see *less well,* but still pretty well, since you have good vision.

  Just because you do well with glasses on, doesn't mean you do *better* with them on.

Question 11

QUESTION TYPE: Flawed Reasoning

CONCLUSION: The certification isn't difficult.

REASONING: The written part of the certification is easy.

ANALYSIS: This is a part to whole flaw. It's like saying: It's easy to get in to Yale law school, because it's easy to fill out their application form.

Filling out the form is the easy part of getting into Yale. Overall, it's very hard to get in to Yale.

Likewise, it could be that the written part of the certification is easy, but the practical part of the certification is very, very hard.

_____

A. There's no conditional statement in the stimulus. Sufficient and necessary conditions aren't relevant here.
B. The conclusion was about whether the certification was hard. The argument didn't say whether plumbers need to be certified.
C. I found this tempting. But if you read the start of the second sentence, the author admits that Plumb-Ace plumbers may be more qualified.

  The conclusion is only about whether or not the certification process is *difficult*. That has nothing to do with whether it is *harder or easier* than other certification processes. Difficult is an absolute term, harder is a relative term.
D. This is a different error. It's like saying: "There's no proof we'll get out of recession, so we won't." The only correct conclusion would be "so we might stay in recession".
E. **CORRECT.** The written part was easy. That doesn't mean the whole thing was easy.

Question 12

QUESTION TYPE: Role in Argument

CONCLUSION: Building ceremonial architecture wasn't frivolous.

REASONING: Impressive architecture let ancient Egyptian Pharaohs spend less on the military.

ANALYSIS: This is a reasonable argument. The claim that the ceremonial architecture was not frivolous is the conclusion.

Notice the word 'however'. That indicates the author's opinion, which is usually the conclusion.

The word 'for' usually indicates that the previous words were the conclusion, and the words that follow are evidence.

A. **CORRECT.** The appeal to the psychological effects comes after the word 'for'.
B. There's no support for this claim. It's just a fact we're supposed to accept as true.
C. It's the other way around. Saying that the pyramids were not frivolous is a judgment, which needs to be justified. The justification is that military force was not required.
D. The argument never made this claim. Pharoah's authority ultimately depended on force. People realized that he had the force to control the natural world, so they didn't even try to rebel.
E. The architecture had more than military utility. It also had ceremonial utility.

Religious ceremony was an important part of ancient egyptian life. I'm mentioning that only to emphasize that you can't just discard something like ceremonial utility.

Question 13

QUESTION TYPE: Sufficient Assumption

CONCLUSION: The patent law change will harm scientific research.

REASONING: The proposed change will slow down communication of discoveries.

ANALYSIS: The conclusion is that the legal change will have a chilling effect on science. But we have no idea what a chilling effect is.

I like to read these as if it said "therefore the proposal will force scientists to wear funny hats".

You no longer have to think about what argument means. You just need to connect the premises to that nonsense statement. The answer would be:

Slower sharing of papers → Scientists forced to wear funny hats

That type of connection is the basis of almost all sufficient assumption questions. Just connect whatever they give as evidence to whatever they claim in the conclusion. You don't have to think about meaning, just match terms.

A. This doesn't mention chilling effects. This answer would have to tell us how more patent applications could chill science.
B. This doesn't mention chilling effects. It's possible the proposed change would encourage even more advances than the current system allowed.
C. **CORRECT.** The proposal will cause delays in the communication of discoveries. This says that therefore the proposal will have chilling effects on science.
D. It doesn't matter what researchers think. We don't know why they oppose the changes. Even if they think the proposal will have chilling effects, they could be wrong.It's important to distinguish between people's beliefs and actual facts.
E. That's nice. It's possible that the new rules will facilitate progress even more effectively, by some other means. This doesn't tell us the proposal will have chilling effects.

Question 14

QUESTION TYPE: Flawed Parallel Reasoning

CONCLUSION: People only want pleasure

REASONING: You feel pleasure when you get what you want.

ANALYSIS: *One* effect of getting what you want is pleasure. There may be others.

Just because something has an effect doesn't mean that's the only reason you do something. Any action has multiple effects.

Maybe you go after what you want because you like the feeling of power that comes from getting it. Pleasure is a pleasant side effect, but not the main reason you do things.

I got this question wrong when I took the test. I completely failed to understand the argument, and didn't review this question properly. You should always review questions you have doubts about, if you have time.

––––––––––––

A. This is a bad argument, but it's a different error. The author is probably *glad* he came, but that doesn't change the fact that he didn't want to come originally.
B. This is a different error. You might want to do something even if you're afraid of it.
C. **CORRECT.** A stomach ache is one of the many effects of eating pizza. That doesn't mean you eat pizza only because you want that particular effect. Eww.
D. This is a reasonable argument. Expecting something is not the same thing as being 100% certain of it. I expect, reasonably, that there won't be nuclear war in 2013. But there could be.
E. This is a bad argument, but it's a different error. If the author really likes basketball, he might enjoy a basketball game even if he doesn't eat hot dogs.

Question 15

QUESTION TYPE: Flawed Reasoning

CONCLUSION: The two sentences don't have the same meaning.

REASONING: The two sentences aren't identical, the word order is different.

ANALYSIS: The philosopher is being a pedantic nerd. Meaning doesn't have to do with word order. Here's an example using math: $3 + 2 = 2 + 3$

Both expressions equal 5. It doesn't matter what order you add the numbers in.

The math equations are different (different order), but they have the same meaning.

- Word order doesn't always affect the meaning of sentences.
- The meaning of sentences isn't always affected by word order.

See what I just did there?

––––––––––––

A. The question isn't whether the sentences are identical. It's whether they have the same meaning.
B. This helps you prove that two sentences *don't* have the same meaning. We want to prove that these two sentences *do* have the same meaning.
C. Tempting. This is certainly a true fact about what the sentences mean.

But this true fact doesn't prove the two sentences are the same, or that they have the same meaning.
D. **CORRECT.** Exactly. The two sentences can mean the same thing even if the word order is different.
E. This is an appeal to authority, which is almost always a bad argument.

A linguist has expertise on the meaning of words, but so does a philosopher.

Question 16

QUESTION TYPE: Flawed Reasoning

CONCLUSION: The salespeople lie about their products' quality.

REASONING: The salespeople are paid on commission. They recommend the products which get them the highest commissions.

ANALYSIS: The salesmen certainly have a motive to lie. And it's suspicious that they only recommend items which earn them the highest commissions.

But, it's possible the salespeople only make true claims, while still recommending only those products that earn them the highest commissions. There are two ways that this could happen:

1. Salespeople use true but misleading claims.
2. The products with the highest commissions are the best products.

So, this argument makes an ad hominem error. We can't say that salespeople lie just because they have an incentive to lie.

A. This answer means 'circular reasoning', i.e. an argument with no evidence. But the argument did have some (faulty) evidence. It claimed the salespeople couldn't be trusted because of who they were.
B. **CORRECT.** The source of the claims is 'a salesperson with an incentive to lie to you'. You can't conclude a claim is wrong just because of who said it.
C. This is a different error. It's like saying "Dutch people are, on average, taller than the average American adult. Therefore this Dutch baby is taller than the average American adult".
D. There was no statement sufficient to prove the conclusion. And the argument never mixed up sufficient and necessary.
E. Which authority? The stimulus never mentions anyone who is an expert on salespeople, or lying, or any other subject.

Question 17

QUESTION TYPE: Principle - Strengthen

CONCLUSION: Predicting the advance of the perihelion isn't evidence for Einstein's theory.

REASONING: The advance of the perihelion was well known. Einstein could have adjusted his theory to account for it.

ANALYSIS: This is a reasonable argument. No scientist would publish a theory that made obviously wrong predictions. So it's likely Einstein made sure his theory predicted things like the perihelion.

If the perihelion had been discovered after the theory was published, that would have provided better evidence that Einstein's theory was right. It's impressive to correctly predict something unknown.

Many wrong answers assume that you were confused about the conclusion. The conclusion is: the advance of the perihelion should not be considered evidence that the theory is correct.

A. No one claimed the theory discovered the perihelion. The perihelion was well known before Einstein made his theory.
B. This is a good answer until the end. It says "unless the theory was developed with that phenomenon in mind."

It should be "unless the theory was developed *without* the phenomenon in mind". Predicting something is not impressive if you know about it.
C. We're not arguing about whether Einstein's theory is well supported. We're arguing about whether the fact that Einstein accounted for the perihelion should be evidence for his theory.
D. **CORRECT.** Einstein probably did adjust his theory to account for the perihelion. So this shows that we shouldn't count the perihelion as evidence for his theory.
E. The first part of this is right. The second part isn't. We're not arguing whether or not the theory predicted the perihelion. We want to know if *accounting* for the perihelion should be evidence for the theory.

Question 18

QUESTION TYPE: Flawed Reasoning

CONCLUSION: We should sell only low end models.

REASONING: We make a higher profit *margin* on low end models. So we'll make more *profits* by selling low end models.

ANALYSIS: Note that any sentence with 'should' is usually the conclusion.

This argument confuses profits and profit margins. Profit margins are percentages: you make, for example, 8% of the sale price.

Profits are dollar amounts: you make, for example, $500 whenever you sell a certain computer.

High end computers might be more profitable, even if they have a lower margin. I'd rather make 5% of a $2000 sale than 10% of a $400 sale. That's $100 instead of $40.

A. **CORRECT.** See the explanation above. I'd rather get more *money* from a high end sale, even if the profit *percentage* is lower.
B. This doesn't quite work. If you sell the same amount of computers of each type, you're still making a higher margin on the low end models.
C. So? The point is that lower end models have a higher profit margin. You might *prefer* that the customer buys the low end model.
D. The manager doesn't say profits are the only objective. But his proposal seems like it will increase profits without harming other objectives. That's a win.
E. Well duh. Sales are always going to fluctuate. But there's no reason to believe low end sales will be consistently worse than high end sales in the future.

Question 19

QUESTION TYPE: Weaken

CONCLUSION: Economists are wrong to say that lottery tickets are a waste.

REASONING: You get less on average than you pay, when you buy lottery tickets. But you get less on average than you pay from insurance as well. Insurance is a good purchase.

ANALYSIS: The professor is implying that the chance of getting rich makes it worthwhile to buy some lottery tickets, just like the chance of avoiding disaster makes it worthwhile to buy insurance.

Both lottery tickets and insurance on unprofitable, on average. Some winners, mostly losers.

There's a difference though. Most people fear loss more than they value gains. So maybe it's worth losing money on insurance, but not worth losing money on lottery tickets.

A. This doesn't tell us that people shouldn't spend money on lottery tickets.
B. This helps the argument. Lotteries keep a smaller portion of your money than insurance does.
C. This doesn't tell us that it's *not* worth taking risks on the lottery. We want to show the risks of the lottery aren't worth it.
D. The odds of winning don't matter that much. I'd like to have a small chance of a $10,000,000 lottery payout. That would change my life.

Getting $500 from insurance is nice, but not life changing.

You can't just look at the odds of winning. You must look at the odds multiplied by what you get if you win.

E. **CORRECT.** If this is true, then insurance is more valuable than the lottery. It might be worth losing money on insurance, but not worth losing money on the lottery.

Question 20

QUESTION TYPE: Must Be True

FACTS:

1. There were many big tropical forest fires in 1997.
2. An unusually strong el Nino caused more drought that year.
3. Many scientists think air pollution caused global warming, which made el Nino stronger.

ANALYSIS: Pollution might have made the fires stronger, or it might not have. To clarify the scenario where it didn't, let's give the drought a strength from 1-100. A level 1 drought is a weak drought. Level 100 is a terrible drought that wrecks the forest.

Let's say you need a drought level of 65 to make the forest susceptible to large fires.

Without pollution, El Nino causes a level 70 drought. With pollution, El Nino causes a level 75 drought. *Either way,* the drought is strong enough.

We can say, if the scientists are right, that pollution contributed to the strength of the drought.

We can't really say it contributed much to the size and intensity of the fires. It could be that past a drought level of 65, drought isn't really a big factor on the size and strength of forest fires, and other factors become more important.

———————————

A. Not true. Air pollution *might* have made El Nino stronger. But the drought could still have been strong enough even without the air pollution.
B. It's possible that even a normal El Nino would have caused enough drought to create large forest fires. See the examples above.
C. We don't know much about El Nino. That year it caused drought. Maybe it has other effects in other years. Or maybe other factors could prevent fires in those years.
D. The scientists would think that pollution enhanced drought. But the drought might still have been strong without air pollution.
E. **CORRECT.** El Nino caused drought. So if El Nino were stronger, then it probably made the drought stronger.

Question 21

QUESTION TYPE: Sufficient Assumption

CONCLUSION: Skiff will be promoted if his book is as important and as well written as he claims.

REASONING: If Skiff releases his book this year, Nguyen will recommend promoting him, and the dean will listen.

ANALYSIS: Who cares if Skiff's book is important and well written?

He has to release it *this year* to get Nguyen's recommendation.

On sufficient assumption questions, you must connect the evidence to the conclusion. We get:

Important OR well written → published this year

That will let Skiff get Nyugen's recommendation. Here's the full diagram:

Important OR well written → published this year → Recommendation → Promotion

Three of the wrong answers add necessary conditions for Skiff to get promoted. Necessary conditions can never help you prove something will happen. They can only prove that something *won't* happen, when the necessary condition is missing.

———————————

A. **CORRECT.** See the explanation above.
B. This doesn't tell us Skiff will publish in time to get Nguyen's recommendation. It just adds another useless necessary condition Skiff needs to fulfill before getting promoted.
C. It doesn't matter whether Nguyen thinks the book is well written. We only know Nguyen will recommend Skiff once he publishes. We need to know that Skiff will publish this year.
D. Same as B. This adds an additional necessary condition. That doesn't help us prove that the book will be published this year.
E. Same as B and D. This adds a necessary condition. That makes it *harder* for Skiff to get promoted.

Question 22

QUESTION TYPE: Flawed Reasoning

CONCLUSION: The magazine won't be the largest selling martial arts magazine in ten years.

REASONING: If circulation keeps rising, the magazine will be the best selling martial arts magazine. But circulation won't keep rising.

ANALYSIS: This sounds like a good argument, but really it just incorrectly negates a conditional statement. We have:

Rising fast → Best seller

The argument incorrectly assumes:

~~Rising fast~~ → ~~Best seller~~

It's possible the magazine will be the best selling magazine in ten years even if sales stop rising. Maybe the magazine is *already* the best seller. Maybe other magazines will see circulation drop.

———————————

A. This is a different error. The author doesn't have to prove that the changes are the *only* necessary condition. They just have to prove that the changes *are* a necessary condition. Failing to meet *any* necessary condition will negate a sufficient condition.
B. The argument doesn't say that slower growth will cause circulation to shrink. The author only says that the magazine will not be a best seller if growth slows.
C. The argument didn't use circular reasoning. They have some evidence for the conclusion: circulation won't increase at the same rate.
D. Actually, a single fact incompatible with a general claim is always enough to prove a general claim false. If I say 'all swans are white', then you just need to find *one* black swan to prove the statement wrong.
E. **CORRECT.** A continued rise in circulation will ensure that the magazine is the best seller. But the rise in circulation may not be necessary. Maybe the magazine is already the best seller. Maybe other magazines' circulation will shrink.

Question 23

QUESTION TYPE: Strengthen

CONCLUSION: Pesticide resistance would spread from crops to their relatives that are weeds.

REASONING: Flower color spread from domestic radishes to wild radishes. Pesticide resistance is genetically engineered.

ANALYSIS: We don't know much about the spread of genetic traits.

• Maybe flower color is easier to spread than other traits.
• Maybe traits can spread easily in radishes, but not in other plants.
• Maybe genetically engineered traits are hard to spread.

To strengthen this argument, we could prove the opposite of one of those statements.

For example, suppose traits are harder to spread in radishes than in other plants. Then the fact that the trait did spread in radishes is evidence that traits could spread in other plants too.

———————————

A. It doesn't matter how easy it is to spread a trait from a wild to a domestic. The stimulus only talks about spreading from domestic to wild.
B. This is vague. Maybe it took a 50% increase in the ratio to increase spread speed by 1%. What does that tell us? It's not clear what effect this has on the spread of other traits.
C. If radishes are not representative, then the argument is *weaker*. Radishes may not prove anything about other plants.
D. Pesticide resistance is a genetically engineered trait. The argument would be *stronger* if flower color were genetically engineered too. That would prove that genetically engineered traits could spread. This is a weaken answer.
E. **CORRECT.** This shows that almost any other genetic trait could spread more easily than radish color. So this experiment is fairly strong evidence that other traits such as pesticide resistance could spread.

Question 24

QUESTION TYPE: Identify The Conclusion

CONCLUSION: Parents hurt their children's self esteem if they praise children for everything they do.

REASONING: Children will distrust praise if they are praised for everything.

ANALYSIS: The word 'actually' indicates the conclusion here. Any contrast words, such as 'but', 'although', 'actually', etc. indicate the author's opinion, which tends to be the conclusion.

A. The author says children need praise for their achievements, but this isn't the conclusion.
B. This is evidence that supports the conclusion that constant praise is harmful.
C. Where the hell did this come from? The stimulus never mentioned expectations or capability. The conclusion normally is something that was explicitly mentioned.
D. **CORRECT.** The first sentence mentions this. The word 'actually' is a sign that this is the conclusion.
E. The author doesn't even say this. He says children require praise for their achievements, but he doesn't say what will happen if they don't get praise.

Question 25

QUESTION TYPE: Agreement

ARGUMENTS: Pauline says that if the dams are breached, electricity costs will increase. Population and industry are growing.

Roger says the dams are already producing as much electricity as they can. We need new electricity sources.

ANALYSIS: You have to read in between the lines here.

When Pauline says that population and industry are growing, she means that the region will soon use more electricity. Otherwise we wouldn't need new sources of electricity.

When Roger says we'll have to expand the dams, that can only be because electricity use is growing. Otherwise, the existing dams would be enough.

So they agree electricity use is likely to increase, or at least not decrease.

Note that this is an agreement question, not a disagreement question. There are two agreement questions on this test, whereas they are extremely rare on earlier tests. Read questions stems more carefully from now on when there are two speakers.

A. Roger never says whether we can compensate for closing the dams.
B. **CORRECT.** See the explanation above.
C. Roger never mentions whether costs will rise, or whether we'll get new capacity to keep costs down.
D. Roger says nothing about environmentalists.
E. Neither of them say whether or not we can decrease prices by finding new sources of electricity.

Preptest 70
Section I - Logical Reasoning

Question 1

QUESTION TYPE: Sufficient Assumption

CONCLUSION: The *Messenger* won't interview Hermann.

REASONING: The *Messenger* won't do anything that its editors think would compromise its integrity. Hermann wants to approve the interview before publication.

ANALYSIS: This is a sufficient assumption questions, not a 'complete the argument' question. The questions asks you to *prove* the conclusion. The way to answer sufficient assumption questions is to arrange the evidence, find the gap, and add a new premise that lets you draw the conclusion.

H wants approval　　[gap]　　Editor believe compromise integrity → Won't do it

Just put an arrow where the gap is, and you'll see that the missing statement is:

H approval → Editor believe compromise integrity

_____

A. CORRECT. Hermann wants the right of approval. This answer shows that the editors think that would compromise the *Messenger's* integrity. And the editors don't do anything if they think it will compromise integrity.
B. The past doesn't guarantee the future. Sure, the editors have never given approval before....but they might change their minds for Hermann.
C. This tells us that most TV stars are different from Hermann. So what? This answer doesn't tell us that the editors will deny Hermann's request.
D. We know exactly *one* reason that the editors will refuse to do something: if they believe that an action compromises their integrity, they won't do it. It's not clear that the editors believe substantial changes will compromise integrity.
E. This explains why Hermann wants the right of approval. But it doesn't prove that the editors will reject his request.

Question 2

QUESTION TYPE: Flawed Reasoning

CONCLUSION: It's silly to say that GIAPS makes people create bad presentations.

REASONING: GIAPS is just a tool, and therefore isn't responsible for bad presentations. The blame lies with people that use tools poorly.

ANALYSIS: This question is unusual in that the right answer asks you to contradict a premise. The premise is "the tool therefore isn't responsible for bad presentations". Technically, the premise in question is an intermediate conclusion. It starts with "therefore". All conclusions are fair ground for contradiction, though its rare that the LSAT will require you to contradict intermediate conclusions.

You've probably heard that you're "not allowed" to contradict premises. This isn't true. It's just rare that an answer *actually* contradicts a premise. If you think that an answer contradicts a premise, it's more likely you've misunderstood something.

_____

A. Which claims? There's no inconsistency. To choose this answer, you'd need to find two contradictory claims, i.e. "The software is expensive" and "the software is cheap"
B. The argument didn't say this! Search this question all you want, the author did *not* say anything about good presentations.
C. The argument didn't mention popularity. An answer can't be the flaw if it didn't happen.
D. CORRECT. This is a good objection. Maybe the software is really, really bad.
"So it cannot be responsible...." is an intermediate conclusion and it's not supported by good evidence. That's why it's contradictable.
E. This answer describes an ad hominem flaw. An example is "We shouldn't wear clothes because Hitler wore clothes!". You have to evaluate *what* an argument says, not *who* said it. But this argument doesn't attack anyone's character.

Question 3

QUESTION TYPE: Strengthen

CONCLUSION: Alphin Bay shows that there will be damage to the environment.

REASONING: Opponents claim that modern drilling techniques are clean. But drilling began five years ago at Alphin Bay, and it's messy.

ANALYSIS: This is a classic example of a term shift. We don't know what 'modern' is. Drilling at Alphin Bay began five years ago. Were 'modern' techniques used at that time?

Maybe drilling is changing rapidly. If so, pollution at Alphin Bay doesn't prove anything, and the critics might be right.

We can strengthen the argument by showing that Alphin Bay used 'modern' drilling techniques.

———————————

A. The argument is about whether oil drilling will *cause* pollution. This answer is about whether we should *allow* pollution. Not the same thing.
B. We care whether the techniques will *actually* cause pollution. Who cares what the company *says*? They could by lying or mistaken.
C. The argument is about whether drilling will cause pollution, not whether we *should* drill.
D. **CORRECT.** If drilling techniques haven't changed in five years, then the techniques used at Alphin Bay were likely modern techniques, too. Therefore, this answer tells us that modern drilling techniques would probably pollute the nature reserve as well.
E. So what? The argument is about whether oil drilling will cause pollution. Other industrial activity shouldn't affect whether oil drilling causes pollution.

Question 4

QUESTION TYPE: Point At Issue

ARGUMENTS: James says that community colleges meet the educational needs of their communities, and universities don't.

Margaret says that universities work to serve the communities they're located in. People attend college and university to get a job.

ANALYSIS: This question shifts terms frequently. James says community colleges 'work towards' serving their communities. You can assume that this is the same thing as 'having a goal', which is the language that Margaret uses.

Many topics are only mentioned by one author. For instance, Margaret tells us nothing about the goals of community colleges. And James doesn't tell us why people go to school, so the last half of Margaret's argument is irrelevant.

James says 'educational needs' and Margaret simply says 'needs'. These aren't the same thing; this seems like a minor flaw since the credited answer talks about *educational* needs. However, the question stem just says 'most support', so we don't need 100% proof of disagreement.

———————————

A. **CORRECT.** James says community colleges work towards this, but universities don't. Margaret says universities want to serve the needs of their communities. Presumably this includes educational needs.
B. Neither James nor Margaret says whether universities serve educational needs in practice. They both talk about *goals,* while this answer is about what *actually happens.*
C. James doesn't say why people go to university.
D. James doesn't mention the primary educational need in a community, so how could he disagree? For that matter, Margaret also doesn't say what a community's main need is.
E. Margaret agrees, but James has no opinion on this point. So they can't disagree.

Question 5

QUESTION TYPE: Paradox

PARADOX: People who take an organizational seminar tend to become more organized, but they usually don't become more efficient.

ANALYSIS: We associate organization with efficiency, but they're not the same thing. I knew someone who carefully planned every day, and got nothing done.

The best answer will show that the seminar somehow causes people not to gain efficiency.

_____

A. 'Some' is a very vague word, it can refer to one person out of 150,000. Not a useful word in most cases. One person's case can't explain what happens to an entire group.
B. The question talked about people who *do* take organizational seminars. This answer talks about people who do *not* take seminars.
C. This just tells us a random fact about people who take organizational seminars. It's not clear how management training relates to efficiency.
D. This might explain why those people took organizational seminars – those workers knew that they were poorly organized. But this answer adds no information about efficiency.
E. **CORRECT.** Efficiency refers to how much you can get done in a certain amount of time. This answer helps explain why better organizational skills don't make you more efficient: you now have to spend a *lot* of time organizing yourself. So you have less time to actually get things done.

Question 6

QUESTION TYPE: Principle

SITUATION: Some customers incorrectly believed their coupons had expired. This was because the company screwed up. The situation was unfair.

PRINCIPLE: If you cause an unfair situation, you must fix the results of that situation.

ANALYSIS: This question tests your precision. The principle tells you *one* thing. "If you make a bad situation, fix it".

All the wrong answers talk about totally different things. Don't pick an answer because it sounds "reasonable". The answer has to relate to the *one* thing that the principle tells you.

We know that Thimble created an unfair situation. So according to the principle, Thimble must pay. This is a quick way to eliminate answers – anything that says Thimble doesn't need to pay is wrong.

_____

A. Nonsense. We're looking for an answer that forces Thimble to rectify the situation. This answer tells Thimble *not* to give rebates.
B. This answer is about how to assign blame. The principle doesn't tell us how to assign blame. It tells us what Thimble should do if they are guilty.
C. **CORRECT.** This fits with the principle. There's a chance that these consumers failed to get the rebate because of Thimble's mistake. So according to the principle, Thimble must try to rectify the unfair result by giving rebates to anyone who might have missed out.
D. This is insane. Thimble made a promise to give a discount. Rather than tell Thimble to fix the situation, this answer tells Thimble to break their promise, to all consumers. That's *very* unfair.
E. There might be other situations that obligate Thimble to offer a rebate. If someone was unfairly denied a rebate due to ethnic or religious background, then perhaps Thimble is obligated to offer a rebate in that situation too.

Question 7

QUESTION TYPE: Sufficient Assumption

CONCLUSION: The biography doesn't explain what's interesting about Shakespeare.

REASONING: The biography doesn't explain what made Shakespeare different from his peers.

ANALYSIS: The first sentence is the conclusion. If you had trouble identifying this, notice that the conclusion is an opinion. Any idea about whether something is 'good' or 'bad' will usually be the author's opinion. The word "but" in the final sentence indicates evidence for the conclusion.

As with all sufficient assumption questions, there is a gap. In this case, a diagram doesn't help. Just focus: we know exactly *one* negative fact about the book. The book didn't explain what made Shakespeare different.

We want to link that to the idea that the book didn't explain why Shakespeare was interesting. If Shakespeare was interesting *because* he was different, then the single fact proves the conclusion. The thing that made Shakespeare different is also what made him interesting.

———————————

A. This might excuse the author's failure to tell us what made Shakespeare different. But it doesn't tell us whether the biography told us what made Shakespeare interesting.
B. Shakespeare wasn't the average man. I have no idea what this answer is supposed to tell us.
C. This might show that the biography *should* have explained why Shakespeare was different. But it doesn't link being different to being interesting.
D. At best this shows that the biography wasn't a good biography. A bad biography might still manage to explain why Shakespeare was interesting.
E. **CORRECT.** This shows that what made Shakespeare different is what made him interesting. So if the biography fails to explain different, then it also fails to explain interesting.

Question 8

QUESTION TYPE: Must be True

FACTS:
1. Whipping cream in a blender produces a crappy, velvety substance.
2. The blender fails because it doesn't let in enough air to whip cream effectively.
3. A special attachment in the blender can help.
4. But the special attachment can't fully compensate for the air intake problem.

ANALYSIS: Must be true questions ask you to combine facts from the stimulus. To do this, you need to have a clear understanding of each fact.

Usually you can't prephrase must be true questions. Instead, you need to load the facts in your short term memory so that you can spot which answer correctly combines two or more facts.

———————————

A. There could be *thousands* of methods of whipping cream poorly, and maybe some don't produce the velvety substance that comes from blenders.
B. **CORRECT.** This combines the end of the final sentence with the second sentence. An attachment helps, but it can't change the fact that there isn't enough air in a blender.
C. Be careful of "always". It's a very extreme word. This answer says that an attachment will *never* produce a worse result. That's ridiculous – surely an attachment could malfunction at some point.
D. A very tricky trap answer. The attachment makes things *better,* but maybe to make the result *good* you still need the same quantity of air.

Suppose you need $1500 a month to meet your living expenses, or you'll be all sad and velvety. The moral support of your friends will *reduce* your sadness. But to *solve* the problem you still need the same amount of money, $1500 worth. Moral support can't reduce the money you need.
E. We have no idea which method is the most common. Maybe most people are fools, and use blenders even though they don't work well.

Question 9

QUESTION TYPE: Flawed Reasoning

CONCLUSION: There is good reason to think that the hypothesis is false.

REASONING: There's no evidence for the hypothesis.

ANALYSIS: I intentionally simplified the conclusion and reasoning to make the error clearer. You can't conclude that something is wrong just because there's no evidence to support it. To prove that something is wrong you need actual evidence *against* it.

The astronomer only has *lack* of evidence. He should have concluded "I don't know if the hypothesis is right or wrong. I have no evidence for or against it."

Instead, he assumes that the hypothesis is wrong. When you have no evidence, you can't do that. You have to say "I don't know". Something can be right even if you currently lack evidence that it is.

Don't let the science talk frighten you. Almost all of it is fluff. The entire argument is in the final sentence.

––––––––––––––

A. **CORRECT.** The astronomer says there is 'good reason' to think that the hypothesis is false. Good reason = evidence. Why does the astronomer think that there is evidence against the hypothesis? In the final sentence, his only proof is that there is no evidence *for* the hypothesis.

B. The astronomer *didn't* say that the hypothesis is inherently implausible. He just said that there's currently no evidence for it.

C. The astronomer didn't mention any hypothesis that is equally likely to be true.

D. Which premises contradict the conclusion? If the flaw didn't happen, then an answer can't be correct.

E. This isn't a flaw. If your opponent makes a true claim, then you *must* grant that it's true, even if it weakens your argument.

Question 10

QUESTION TYPE: Flawed Parallel Reasoning

CONCLUSION: VIVVY is a good program.

REASONING: Three people have had success with VIVVY.

ANALYSIS: This is an unusually stupid argument, though it's very common in advertising.

Suppose that 3,000,000 used VIVVY. Amy, Matt and Evelyn went on to become successful, and the other 2,999,997 students became hobos. Yikes. Would you have your child use VIVVY?

For parallel reasoning, you need to find an abstract way to describe the argument, then find the answer that matches that description. Here, the argument extrapolates from a small sample without indicating how many people the sample was taken from.

––––––––––––––

A. **CORRECT.** This works. We have no idea how many people play the lottery. It's quite possible that Annie, Francisco and Sean won due to chance and not due to their good luck charms.

B. This is very different. Here, Jesse is in the group of three people, and the conclusion is about Jesse. In the stimulus the conclusion was about everyone.

C. This makes a different error. It confuses necessary and sufficient. Yes, we can expect that those three will be laid off, since everyone hired in the past year will be laid off. But maybe many others will be laid off as well – we can't conclude that these three will be the only victims of layoffs.

D. This is like B. The evidence and the conclusion concerns only the group of three people. In the argument, evidence from three people was used to make a claim about *everyone* who uses VIVVY.

E. This is a flawed argument, but it's a different flaw. Just because *most* people get jobs, you can't say that those three *definitely will* get jobs. Here, evidence from the whole university is used to make a claim about the group of three. In the stimulus, evidence from the group of three was used to make a claim about all users of VIVVY.

Question 11

QUESTION TYPE: Argument Evaluation

CONCLUSION: This new sewage sludge fuel technology will help us meet our energy needs with less environmental harm and without nuclear power.

REASONING: The new technology can produce oil from sewage sludge.

ANALYSIS: The stimulus lists an advantage to sewage sludge: it's not nuclear power. But that's all we know.

There are many other questions:

- Does sewage sludge pollute? Several answers address this.
- Is sewage sludge expensive?
- Is there enough sewage sludge to make an impact?

The wrong answer mentions that sewage sludge production has *improved*. I care about whether something is good *now,* not whether it recently got better.

A. If using sewage as fuel lets us *avoid* dumping sewage sludge, then this technology will be even more useful for protecting the environment.
B. **CORRECT.** It doesn't matter whether the processes have *improved*. That's a relative term. We care whether the processes are currently *good* or *bad*. Those are absolute terms.

    If you get into a car, you care whether it is *safe,* not whether it is *safer* than it used to be. A car could be *safer* and still be a deathtrap.
C. If sewage fuel is too expensive, then it can't replace nuclear.
D. If sewage fuel produces harmful gases, then switching to sewage from nuclear could increase pollution.
E. If sewage fuel produces harmful waste, then it's hard to see how it would be better than nuclear.

Question 12

QUESTION TYPE: Paradox

PARADOX:
1. The most common species reproduce the most, and the rare trees live longer.
2. This is true no matter which species is common and which is rare.

ANALYSIS: Your first task on paradox questions is to understand the paradox. Let's imagine that there are only two trees in forests: spruces, and elms.

- In one forest, spruces are most common, and elms live longest.
- In another forest, elms are most common, and spruces live longest.

So it's not some feature of each tree species that causes them to live longer. It's the fact that trees are rare that seems to cause them to live longer. The species that reproduces best within a forest is also the shortest lived. That seems odd, and it's what you have to explain.

A. This explains why one species is more common, but it doesn't explain why the rare species lives longer.
B. This explains nothing. It doesn't tell us why trees live to be old in the first place.
C. Good, this shows the scientists were smart enough not to introduce an uncontrolled variable into their experiments. But this doesn't *explain* anything, it just means that the experiments were well done.
D. This shows that it is *useful* for the rare species to survive. But that doesn't explain *why* they survive. Plenty of useful things never happen.
E. **CORRECT.** If there's more competition, then we can expect some trees of the more common species not to have enough resources, and to die. The rare species are living a life of luxury, as there's little competition for resources. Thus they live longer.

Question 13

QUESTION TYPE: Necessary Assumption

CONCLUSION: The TV station's ad is worse than the producers' ad.

REASONING: The TV station's ad is grossly misleading.

ANALYSIS: This is a classic LSAT error. It makes a comparison, but only tells you about one of the two ads.

The argument tells us that the station's ad was grossly misleading. But the argument doesn't tell us anything about the producers' ad. The argument merely *implies* that the producer's ad wasn't also grossly misleading. So the argument merely *assumes* that the producers' ad is better.

———————————

A. The stimulus wasn't about how viewers discover the program. The stimulus was only about how effective each ad would be.

B. **CORRECT.** The negation of this answer wrecks the argument. There's no difference between the ads if this answer isn't true.

   Negation: The producer's ad would have been grossly misleading as well.

C. Same as A. The stimulus is not about how most viewers found the program. The argument is about whether or not the TV station's ad was effective, compared to the producers' ad.

D. This goes too far. The stimulus didn't say that the producers' ad was the greatest ad in the history of the known universe. The argument only said that the producers' ad would have been *better* than the TV station's ad.

E. Same as A and C. The stimulus was about whether the TV station's ad was worse than the producers' ad. This answer doesn't even talk about the ads, it just gives us a useless fact about the audience.

Question 14

QUESTION TYPE: Principle

SITUATION: Sharon's favorite novelist criticized a political candidate that Sharon supports. Sharon decided that the novelist was not so smart, and kept her opinion of the political candidate.

ANALYSIS: This principle question gives you an individual situation. You need to find a principle that matches the information in this stimulus.

Sharon seems to trust her political candidate more than she trusts the novelist. That's about all we know. She liked both the writer and the candidate for a long time, but supported the politician when the two of them disagreed.

There are a few possible interpretations:

- Given a choice between a long favored novelist and a long favored politician, some people will choose the politician.
- If someone contradicts your opinion, you'll probably disagree with them and stick to your opinion.

———————————

A. This isn't supported. Sharon was one of the novelist's most dedicated fans, yet she wasn't influenced by the novelist.

B. This is far too broad. It matches none of the elements of the stimulus, and it tells us that we should almost always reject the political opinions of artists. But Sharon might have listened to the novelist if she hadn't been a long term supporter of the politician.

C. This is too broad. We don't actually know that the artist was wrong to speak out. The novelist lost Sharon's support, but maybe many others agreed with the novelist.

D. **CORRECT.** This works. Sharon had supported the politician for a long time. The novelist contradicted her. Rather than reassess her opinion, Sharon rejected the novelist.

E. This doesn't work. Sharon's allegiance to both the novelist and the politician was longstanding.

Question 15

QUESTION TYPE: Flawed Reasoning

CONCLUSION: Sparkle Cola was the best cola.

REASONING: The participants were evenly divided into five groups. Most people preferred Sparkle cola.

ANALYSIS: This tests your understanding of the word 'most', and your ability to visualize five different groups. I'll use an analogy. Let's say that we're determining the highest rated food. There are five groups, and each group is given the choice between spinach and one other food. Here are the alternate choices for each group, numbered 1-5:

1. Liver
2. Garbage
3. Rotten meat
4. Jellyfish
5. Ice Cream

Bleuck! Ugh! Ewww! Ick! ....Yum!

Groups 1-4 choose to eat spinach. They hate it, but the alternative is worse. Group 5 chooses to each ice cream, and loves it. So 'most' people chose spinach, but ice cream was the most highly rated food.

A. **CORRECT.** It's possible that one group had the cola of the gods, Ambrosia-Coke. They *loved* it, and preferred it to Sparkle Cola. The other groups preferred Sparkle cola, but gave it a low rating. Ambrosia-Coke got the highest rating of any of the colas.
B. The argument didn't say anything about what the volunteers would *buy*. An answer can't be a flaw if it doesn't happen.
C. This isn't a flaw! The study compared sparkle cola to other colas. The study didn't claim that sparkle was the best cola in the world. The ad just said that Sparkle was the best in the study.
D. This answer tests whether you read the question. The volunteers were *blindfolded!* Obviously, they didn't choose colas based on packaging.
E. So? The study was just a comparison of *colas*. You don't need to ask people about wine or milk when you're studying their cola preferences.

Question 16

QUESTION TYPE: Weaken

CONCLUSION: TV makes people overestimate risk.

REASONING: There is a correlation between how much TV someone watches and how likely they think they are to suffer from a natural disaster.

ANALYSIS: Repeat after me: correlation does not equal causation. Correlation does not equal causation. Correlation does not equal causation.

Anytime two things happen together, that's just a *correlation*. In this stimulus, we have two things happening together: TV watching, and fear of natural disaster. Here are the four possibilities:

1. TV causes fear
2. Fear causes more TV watching
3. A third factor (e.g. living in a certain area) causes both fear of disaster and TV watching.
4. It's just a coincidence

You can weaken an attempt to draw causation from correlation by showing that one of the alternate possibilities is true. In this situation, it's also possible that TV watchers are the ones with a correct view of the risk of natural disaster, and therefore TV isn't misleading.

A. So? This doesn't show that TV doesn't cause fear.
B. This heightens the tension. The people who watch the most TV have the greatest fear of natural disasters AND live in the regions with the fewest disasters.
C. Tempting, but this is talking about the wrong group. If this answer had said that people who watch more TV have an accurate view, then *that* would weaken the idea that TV misleads.
D. This shows that Television isn't responsible for educating people about natural disasters. So this answer doesn't weaken the idea that TV is a bad influence.
E. **CORRECT.** This is number three from my list above. A third factor (risky location) leads people to watch lots of television, and to have an above average estimation of natural disaster risk.

Question 17

QUESTION TYPE: Role in Argument

CONCLUSION: Heavy rains will happen more often if the earth's atmosphere becomes much warmer.

REASONING: A warm atmosphere leads to:

1. Warmer oceans, which cause fast evaporation, which means rain clouds form more quickly.
2. More moisture and larger clouds.
3. Large clouds lead to heavier downpours.

ANALYSIS: You don't need to get too technical for role in argument questions. Just identify the conclusion and premises. The conclusion is the first sentence. The fact that it says "likely" indicates that it's probably an opinion and thus the conclusion.

The stimulus lists three facts to support the conclusion. You can combine the facts into one statement: "Warming will cause faster accumulation of large clouds that cause heavier downpours". This statement supports the slightly more direct idea that a warm atmosphere leads to more heavy rains.

The sentence in question is just a fact. The term "in general" is a clue: it's not a conclusion indicator.

A. The first sentence is the conclusion.
B. The first sentence is the *only* explicitly stated conclusion. Explicitly stated = written down.
C. This answer tempted me. But to choose this, you'd have to say which of the first two facts supports the third. Neither of them do: the third fact stands on its own and doesn't need support.
D. **CORRECT.** See the explanation above. The three facts stand independently of each other, and combine to support the first sentence, which is the conclusion.
E. Nonsense. There was no phenomenon in the conclusion, only a prediction of a phenomenon. So the premises don't explain the phenomenon. Instead, they support the likelihood of the prediction. That's the second way to eliminate this answer: the third sentence definitely supports the conclusion.

Question 18

QUESTION TYPE: Identify The Conclusion

CONCLUSION: Anthropologists overrate the usefulness of field studies.

REASONING: Living in a community affects that community, and anthropologists underestimate how much communities are affected.

ANALYSIS: The word 'however' is *very* important in arguments. It indicates two things:

1. Contrast with what was said before.
2. The author's opinion.

Author's opinion = the main conclusion. Usually, anyway. So typically, the phrase that follows "however" is the conclusion. That's all you need to know for this type of question.

The first sentence provides context. The final sentence shows *why* anthropologists overrate field studies.

Note that the argument is *not* claiming that field studies aren't helpful. The claim is that they are overrated: i.e. They're not *as* helpful as they seem.

Note: Sometimes, the phrase after "however" is evidence for the conclusion. In those cases, the conclusion will directly follow, after a word like "so".

E.g. "However, I don't like the opera. *So,* I won't be using the free tickets."

A. **CORRECT.** See the explanation above. "However" indicates the conclusion in this case.
B. This is just context that tells us about field studies.
C. Same as B. This is just context.
D. This is just a fact that shows anthropologists aren't completely clueless.
E. This is the main premise that supports the conclusion. *Because* anthropologists underestimate their own impact, they *therefore* overestimate the usefulness of field studies.

Question 19

QUESTION TYPE: Parallel Reasoning

CONCLUSION: The proposal will probably be rejected.

REASONING: Juarez says:

Not rewritten → Rejected

Two facts:

1. Juarez is very reliable.
2. The proposal won't be rewritten.

ANALYSIS: This is a good argument, with a unique structure. Juarez makes a conditional statement.

The argument says that we can trust Juarez, and it says that the sufficient condition of the conditional statement is true. The conclusion is probabilistic, not certain.

So look for an answer that matches this structure. This is the key to answering long parallel reasoning questions quickly. You can skip over answers that don't seem to match. I'll point out the structural differences that let you quickly eliminate answers.

A. Here, the science journal (i.e. Juarez) provides a fact, not a conditional statement. Wrong! Next answer, please.
B. Same as A. The science journal provides a fact, not a conditional. Also, we don't have the same probabilistic conclusion. This argument concludes that the medication is *definitely* safe.
C. **CORRECT.** This mirrors the structure exactly. Science Journal says:

Data accurate → Drug Safe

Two facts:

1. Journal usually right.
2. Data accurate.

D. Here the journal made *two* claims. Juarez made one. Wrong! Next answer, please.
E. Here the journal states a fact. Juarez stated a conditional. Wrong!

Question 20

QUESTION TYPE: Flawed Reasoning

CONCLUSION: Most people could save hundreds of dollars by switching to Popelka.

REASONING: People who have switched to Popelka saved hundreds of dollars on average.

ANALYSIS: The LSAT expects you to understand the scientific method. One key to science is that samples should be *random*.

The sample here is not random. The people who saved hundreds of dollars *chose* to switch to Popelka. Maybe they switched *because* they knew they would saved hundreds. Maybe the people who haven't switched to Popelka would *not* save hundreds, and that's why they don't switch.

To put it another way, imagine I run a program called "Auto insurance for Bob". Anyone named Bob can save $1,000 with my program. So the average savings is $1,000, because only Bobs enroll in my program. But this Bob-related evidence doesn't prove that Jim will save money if he switches.

A. 'Some' is a useless word. Drill this into your head. 'Some' can refer to 1-2 people. Who cares if 1-2 people didn't save money. Thousands of others might have saved money!
B. The first test of whether an answer is the flaw is: did this even happen? This answers says "if you're new, you pay as much as older customers". The argument didn't say or assume that! So this can't be the flaw.
C. Who cares? This isn't a flaw. The conclusion is "Popeka will save you money". The argument didn't claim that "Popeka will save you more money than any other company will".
D. If policyholders underreported their savings, then the argument is *stronger*. The actual savings would be higher, which supports the conclusion. This is not a flaw!
E. **CORRECT.** This means "People switched to Popeka *because* they could save money". Maybe others don't switch because they know they can't save money. See the explanation above.

207

Question 21

QUESTION TYPE: Necessary Assumption

CONCLUSION: Front-loading machines require a special detergent in order to properly clean clothes.

REASONING: Ordinary powder detergent doesn't fully dissolve in front loading machines.

ANALYSIS: Pay close attention anytime terms switch, especially when it seems "reasonable" to assume that they mean the same thing.

The evidence is that "powder won't dissolve fully". The conclusion is that "clothes won't get fully clean". That sounds reasonable, but who says powder needs to dissolve fully in order to clean clothes? That's just an assumption the argument is making.

————————————

A. Negate this: "One top loading machine in Mongolia uses half an ounce more water than other top loading machines". That certainly doesn't wreck the argument.
B. Negate this: "A detergent designed for front loading washers also dissolves well in top loading washers". That just shows that the detergent can work in both types. Great!
C. This answer refers to all washing machines. So you could negate it by saying "Front loading machines require special detergent, but top loading machines can use any kind". The argument is only about front loading machines.
D. **CORRECT.** I don't think this answer is properly formulated. I think it should have said "An ordinary powder detergent does not get clothes really clean unless it dissolves readily". You could negate the answer as written by saying that liquid detergent doesn't need to dissolve readily, but powder detergents do. That wouldn't wreck the argument. That said, this is the best answer. **Negation:** A detergent can get clothes really clean even if it doesn't dissolve readily.
E. We know that top loading washers use more water, and they may get clothes cleaner with ordinary detergent. But that doesn't mean that more water is *always* good. Maybe there's a washer that uses *even more* water but doesn't work well.

Question 22

QUESTION TYPE: Must Be True

FACTS:
1. Most physicians don't think that they're influenced by gifts.
2. Most physicians think that other physicians are influenced by gifts.

ANALYSIS: This question tests a rare deduction. If you combine two most statements, they have to overlap, and you can conclude a 'some' statement. I'll prove it with a small example. Let's imagine three doctors: Smith, Lopez and Dietrich.

There are just three doctors, so two out of three of them equals 'most' doctors. So let's say that Smith and Lopez both believe that the other two doctors are guilty AND let's say that both Smith and Lopez believe that they themselves are innocent.

- People who think they are innocent: Smith, Lopez
- People blamed by other doctors as being influenced: Smith, Lopez, Dietrich

Obviously, someone is wrong. Every doctor has been accused of being influenced, yet two of them believe they aren't influenced.

And that's exactly what we can conclude. At least some doctors are wrong.

————————————

A. We have no idea what effect gifts actually have. The stimulus only gives us evidence about physicians' *beliefs*.
B. The stimulus doesn't mention guidelines. A 'must be true' answer must be based on something from the stimulus.
C. **CORRECT.** See the example above. There are at least some doctors who believe that they are innocent and yet are accused by some other doctors.
D. The stimulus never mentioned *any* physicians who admit that they were influenced. We only know that 'most' physicians think that they are innocent: most can mean 'all'.
E. Same as D. We have no proof that any physicians admit guilt.

Question 23

QUESTION TYPE: Principle – Strengthen

CONCLUSION: The country is not a well-functioning democracy.

REASONING: Most people want the bill, but influential people oppose it. The bill won't violate human rights.

ANALYSIS: Principle questions are sometimes like sufficient assumption questions. The stimulus will give you a bunch of facts, then give a moral judgment. You need to show that those facts justify the moral judgment. So we need an answer that says one of the following:

Well functioning → pass into law if benefits and no violations within a few years

NOT pass into law if benefits and no violations within a few years → NOT well functioning

Be very precise. Two wrong answers sound good, but have the wrong timeline.

A. This is almost right. But the stimulus said most people *favored* the bill. This answer talks about bills that *benefit* most people. Those are different things.
B. This sounds good, but look at the timeline. The stimulus complained that the bill wouldn't be passed into law for a few years, but it might be passed eventually. So the situation might not violate the criterion in this answer choice.
C. This answer supports the idea that we *are* in a well functioning democracy. It says that it's normal for such a democracy not to pass useful bills if influential people oppose them.
D. This describes bills that *are* passed. The question was about a bill that is *not* going to be passed.
E. **CORRECT.** This answer fits the facts. It says that in a well functioning democracy, beneficial bills will be promptly passed into law. In the stimulus, the beneficial bill wouldn't be passed for a few years, if at all.

Question 24

QUESTION TYPE: Must Be True

FACTS:
1. Most commercial fertilizers just have macronutrients.
2. Plants also need micronutrients.
3. Raking grass removes micronutrients.

ANALYSIS: You can combine all three statements to say:

"If grass is raked away, then commercial fertilizers alone won't be enough to keep plants healthy"

That's all we know. All the wrong answers mix up sufficient and necessary.

A. The stimulus said that the most *widely available* fertilizers only have macronutrients. But there could be some less common fertilizers that include micronutrients as well.
B. This answer reverses sufficient and necessary. The stimulus says that commercial fertilizers are a *sufficient* condition for having macronutrients. But other things could also have macronutrients. Heck, you can buy potassium pills.
C. **CORRECT.** This combines all three facts. If you rake away grass, then the soil will be missing micronutrients. Yet most commercial fertilizers don't contain micronutrients.
D. This is very tempting. Its true that commercial fertilizer + grass clippings seem like a *sufficient* condition for soil health. But this answer says that they are a *necessary* condition. We don't know that. Maybe soil doesn't need commercial fertilizers – forests don't need fertilizer.
E. If you rake up grass clippings, your soil will lack micronutrients, true. But there might be ways to restore micronutrients.

Question 25

QUESTION TYPE: Strengthen

CONCLUSION: Manufacturers can't dilute their waste to bring it below the acceptable level.

REASONING: No reasoning was given.

ANALYSIS: The question is quite specific. It asks us to justify the anti-dilution provision mentioned at the very end. Most of this stimulus is just fluff. The stimulus didn't give any justification for the rule that stops manufacturers from diluting their waste.

So practically any reason will do. You just have to identify which answer gives us a reason not to dilute waste. Only two answers even mention diluted waste, and only answer B mentions that diluted waste can be harmful, so it's correct.

A. This explains why we should be careful with waste. But the question asks about the anti-dilution provision, and this answer doesn't address that.

B. CORRECT. "Undiluted" in this case refers to waste that has more than 500 parts per million. You wouldn't bother describing waste as undiluted if it didn't have a high concentration. This answer shows that diluted waste is still harmful. If you group a bunch of it together (say, by putting it in a dump) then it's dangerous.

C. This reduces the risk of XTX. It doesn't help explain why we shouldn't allow the dumping of diluted XTX waste. We need an answer that shows a *danger*.

D. This explains why dump owners won't accept undiluted waste. But the question asks about a law that prevents us from dumping *diluted* waste.

E. This explains why manufacturers might want to dilute waste. It doesn't explain why the law prevents them from diluting waste.

Section II - Reading Comprehension
Passage 1 - Prion Pathogens
Questions 1-7

Paragraph Summaries

1. Scientists used to assume that pathogens had DNA in their cell structure.
2. CJD is caused by prions. Prions are a pathogen composed mostly of protein. They have no nucleic acid or genetic material in their cell structure.
3. **First half of 3rd paragraph:** Prions are normal cells. But they can go weird, become dangerous, and replicate themselves. This replication creates a plaque that kills nerve cells. **Second half of 3rd paragraph:** The immune system can't fight prions, as they are normal cells. So there's no way to stop prions, and CJD is fatal.
4. Scientists were skeptical of prions, but now they accept that prions cause CJD and maybe other diseases. But we don't really understand the mechanisms by which prions replicate and destroy cells.

Analysis

This is a very dense passage. If you dislike science then you probably weren't happy to see this first. If you find scientific language off-putting, I recommend checking out ~20 back issues of the Economist from the library. Each issue has about three pages of well written science articles. Reading them is an excellent way to become familiar with scientific language and concepts.

Another good idea is to reread any sections of the passage that you don't understand. I've timed students, and they greatly overestimate how much time it takes to reread a paragraph. When you read something twice you understand it much better and you can go faster on the questions.

The gist of this passage is that prions are a new type of pathogen. Pathogen just means something that causes disease.

We used to think that all pathogens had DNA (also known as nucleic acid). But prions don't have DNA (line 22). This is the most important fact in the passage, so **I'll repeat it: Prions lack DNA.**

Prions sound pretty nasty. They're ordinary proteins in your body, so your immune system won't attack them (lines 40-42). Unfortunately, sometimes prions go wonky and get a strange shape (lines 29-30).

When prions take this new shape, they start reproducing. Scientists aren't really sure how prions reproduce (lines 58-60), but the result is quite deadly.

The immune system can't stop the prions, and we haven't found therapies to stop them, either. So prions just keep reproducing, and eventually kill you (line 45).

CJD is the main disease mentioned in the passage, and it's caused by prions. When prions in the brain reproduce, they create a plaque that kills nerve cells (line 39).

A few answer choices talk about prions being contagious. This is a red herring. The passage never says if prions can spread from person to person. Line 31 mentions that prions are "infectious", but this just means that prions spread quickly *within* your body. If prions spread to someone else, that person's immune system would likely attack the prions, because immune systems attack things that come from outside the body.

It's important to note that we're not *sure* about much. The theory of prions as disease agents is fairly well supported (lines 50-56), but we don't fully understand prions (lines 56-60). We're not even 100% certain that prions cause CJD. The passage is not clear on this point, but lines 12-15 say that the prion theory has merely *challenged* conventional wisdom. Researchers haven't yet definitively proven that conventional wisdom is wrong.

Question 1

DISCUSSION: The main point of the passage is that prions are a newly discovered pathogen that cause CJD and other diseases. Prions are special because they replicate but don't have DNA.

A. This isn't even true. The passage never mentioned whether most organisms can produce several kinds of protein. Also this answer completely ignores disease, which was a major focus of the passage.

B. **CORRECT.** This covers all the main points: disease and a new way for pathogens to replicate.

C. This just covers part of the final paragraph. A main point answer should cover the whole passage.

D. This answer covers only a few words: the first half of the first sentence of the final paragraph. The rest of the passage doesn't talk about scientific skepticism. Indeed, it seems that now scientists accept prion theory. See line 52.

E. This is just a small part of the passage. This answer completely ignores disease and pathogens.

Question 2

DISCUSSION: On this type of question, narrow it down to 1-2 answers, then check the passage for confirmation. You can almost always prove a 'most strongly supported' question by reference to the passage.

A. **CORRECT.** Lines 9-11 say that scientists traditionally believed that pathogens had DNA. The rest of the passage says that prions are a pathogen that has no DNA yet causes CJD.

B. The passage never mentions how CJD spreads or if prions are contagious. The passage implies that prions aren't contagious, because they are produced within *our* body (line 40). That's why our immune systems don't attack them.

If your prions entered someone else's body, their immune system would likely react. You *can* use outside knowledge to make warranted assumptions: we know immune systems often reject foreign tissues.

C. Unfortunately, we don't really understand why prions reproduce and cause disease (lines 57-60), so we don't know how to stop CJD.

D. Lines 45-47 directly contradict this answer. There are wide variations in how the disease progresses.

E. Lines 50-51 make clear that the prion theory of CJD now has considerable support. There was only *initial* skepticism.

Question 3

DISCUSSION: This question says that the passage helps to answer the question asked by the right answer.

So you should narrow things down to 1-2 answers, then check that the passage actually *does* answer the question in the answer choice you choose.

_____

A. We don't know what causes prions to replicate (lines 56-60), so it's not clear whether blows to the head are relevant.
B. *Chronic* insomnia is a symptom of CJD (line 19), but *occasional* insomnia isn't mentioned as a symptom. Lots of people have occasional difficulty sleeping.
C. Radiation or gene damage isn't mentioned in the passage. Heck, prions don't *have* genetic material. See line 22, prions lack nucleic acid.
D. The passage never says whether heredity is risk factor for CJD.
E. **CORRECT.** Lines 36-39 show that prions damage the brain by creating thread like structures.

Question 4

DISCUSSION: Another specific detail question. As with questions 2 and 3, you can answer this by referencing a specific line in the passage.

If you don't do this, you *will* make mistakes. With practice, it only take 5-10 seconds to confirm your answer and achieve 100% certainty.

_____

A. The passage never talks about transmitting CJD. And the passage implies that prions aren't contagious. The immune system doesn't attack them because they are part of the body (line 40). But the immune system normally attacks things that come from other people's bodies, such as transplanted organs.
B. This goes too far. The point of the passage is that prions are pathogens, and therefore not *all* pathogens replicate via DNA. But it still could be true that most pathogens have DNA.
C. **CORRECT.** Lines 30-40 support this. Prions are dangerous because they reproduce within the body and create plaque. The plaque kills nerve cells. Without replication, prions couldn't create plaque.
D. Lines 54-56 only say that prions *may* be involved in Alzheimer's and Parkinson's disease. We can't say for certain what causes those diseases, so this answer isn't supported.
E. The passage never compares the aggressiveness of prions to other pathogens. It's true that CJD is fatal, but that's not because CJD is particularly aggressive. It's because we have no defense against prions. So they have all the time in the world to kill us.

Question 5

DISCUSSION: I was stuck on this question, because I forgot that it was a LEAST likely question. Make sure to double check question stems if you're stuck.

For this type of question, if you're stuck between two answers: remember that all the wrong answers can be eliminated by reference to the passage.

_____

A. This is very well supported. Abnormal prions are the ones that replicate and cause CJD (lines 30-40).
B. **CORRECT.** Unfortunately, line 45 says that CJD is *always* fatal.
C. Line 22 supports this. Prions lack nucleic acid, yet they still reproduce.
D. Lines 40-42 support this. Our immune system doesn't attack prions, and the passage doesn't mention any other natural defenses.
E. Lines 56-60 support this.

Question 6

DISCUSSION: A pathogen is something that causes diseases and replicates itself (lines 2-5). Prions appear to be pathogens (see lines 19-24).

We used to think that pathogens had DNA, but prions lack DNA (see line 22).

This question asks us to assume that all the facts we learned about prions are true. Remember, we're looking for things that must be false. It's possible that certain answers *could* be false, but that's not enough. B and C aren't necessarily true, for instance, but they could be true, and that's all you need.

_____

A. **CORRECT.** The contrapositive of this answer is: pathogens have nucleic acid. But the theory says that prions are pathogens and that they lack nucleic acid (line 22). So this answer contradicts the passage.
B. This seems true. The passage implies that the discovery of prions was recent.
C. Lines 1-3 support this. Pathogens are things that cause disease.
D. If the prion theory is correct, then prions are pathogens, and prions cause CJD. So this answer would be true.
E. This seems true. If the prion theory is correct, then prions are also pathogens. Prions are not bacteria, viruses, fungi or parasites.

Question 7

DISCUSSION: Scientists haven't proven that prions cause CJD. They've just noticed a correlation. Prions replicate, and CJD progresses. This isn't *extremely* clear in the passage, since the third paragraph indicates that prions are definitely the cause. But paragraphs 2 and 4 make clear that there's still some doubt about whether prions actually cause CJD. See lines 48-52 (They say the experiments "*supported* the conclusion"....not *proved*), and lines 12-14 (They say that the "assumption has been *challenged*"....not *disproven*).

So there may only be a correlation between prions and CJD. We can weaken the idea that prions cause CJD by showing that prions aren't harmful, or that something else causes CJD.

A. Tempting, but many diseases share the same symptoms. CJD's symptoms cause loss of mental acuity and insomnia. That describes two of the symptoms of the common cold!

Either a disease is CJD or it isn't. To be right, this answer would have had to link the viral infection to patients actually diagnosed with CJD, or with those experiencing a disease so similar that it could also be classed as a neurodegenerative disease.

B. If the therapies cured CJD, then this would be the right answer. But the therapies could be totally ineffective, so the fact that the therapies don't block prion reactions doesn't mean prion reactions aren't the cause of CJD. The mere fact that we use remedies doesn't prove that the remedies work, unfortunately. The therapies might just treat secondary effects or relieve pain.

C. This doesn't show that prions don't cause CJD. This answer just shows that prions cause even more problems. 2

D. The stimulus never mentioned whether malfunctioning prions were hereditary. So this answer tells us nothing about prions.

E. **CORRECT.** Prions aren't bacteria. So if an anti-bacterial drug reverses CJD, then it sounds like bacteria are the cause, not prions. This answer is especially significant since up until now CJD was fatal – we had no way to reverse it (line 45).

Passage 2 - Dunham's Anthropological Dance
Questions 8-14

Paragraph Summaries

1. Dunham's training as a dancer and researcher let her bring dance-isolation to mainstream North American dance.
2. Before Dunham, social scientists neglected dance because they didn't consider it scientific, and because they lacked training in dance.
3. Dunham researched the African origins of Caribbean dance. Against the advice of colleagues, Dunham took part in the dances herself. This let her understand them, and learn the techniques.
4. Dunham created performances using the styles she learned. She managed to include African-American themes in modern dance.

Analysis

In a passage with multiple viewpoints, you should know what each side says, and who the author agrees with.

On one side we have the stodgy, traditional social scientists. Probably, they were white males, though this isn't indicated. The social scientists neglected to study dance (lines 19-23), they advised Katherine Dunham not to dance (lines 33-35), and they couldn't dance (lines 23-25). Losers.

The social scientists had a very formal approach. They thought dance wasn't "scientific", whatever that means. They also thought that an anthropological researcher should stay strictly separated from the people she was studying.

Lines 37-40 shows that the author believes the social scientists were unrealistic in thinking that detachment is good or even possible. The passage also implies that the author agrees with Katherine Dunham's methods, and thinks that Dunham learned valuable things by dancing with those that she studied.

Dunham was a researcher and a dancer. This combination was unique (lines 23-27). As you surely know, dance is a practical skill – it requires training and practice. The author implies that to understand dance, you must be able to do it. Dunham's background in both research and dance thus gave her the ability to study Caribbean dances and their African origins.

I mentioned lines 23-27. They are particularly notable since they suggest that Dunham was the only person trained in both dance and social science – no one else was qualified to study the dances the way that she did.

Paragraphs 1-4 talk about the results of Dunham's work. Her achievements were *very* impressive for a researcher. Normally researchers study things, but they do not *do* things. Dunham did many things. The first paragraph shows that she introduced a completely new technique to North America and Europe. The next time you watch a music video, see if you notice one of the dancers moving one part of their body in isolation. It would seem that's thanks to Dunham!

The final paragraphs show that Dunham was able to create theatre performances that set the stage for the wider inclusion of African-American themes in North American dance.

This isn't in the passage, but Katherine Dunham was African-American herself. She's worth googling, she was as influential as this passage suggests. She even starred in a major Hollywood movie, at a time when it was very rare to feature African-Americans as leads.

You could sum up the main point of the passage as: "Intrepid researcher-dancer defies backwards, traditional ideas about anthropology. She dances with her research subjects, and uses what she learned to make a lasting impression on North American dance."

Question 8

DISCUSSION: The main point is that Dunham had special expertise in dance and anthropology that let her study Caribbean dances. She used what she learned to impact North American dance.

A. Not necessarily true. Katherine Dunham *defied* anthropology (lines 31-33). It's not clear that she transformed it. Anthropologists eventually recognized that they couldn't stay isolated from their research subjects (line 38), but this might not have been due to Dunham.
B. Not even true. Katherine Dunham was the first to incorporate dance-isolation and African-American themes in North American dance. But there are thousands of traditional cultures in the world – some of these other traditions might have already been used in North American dance.
C. Where did this come from? The passage never mentioned African-American dancers, choreographers, or their aesthetic and political concerns. I don't know how to explain that this is wrong. If you picked this, try to figure out what your thought process was, as the answer is completely unsupported.
D. The passage never says that Dunham discovered the link between Caribbean dances and African dances. It just mentions that there *was* a link (lines 28-31), and that Dunham was interested in studying it.
E. **CORRECT.** This covers the main themes of the passage. Dunham was uniquely suited to study dance (lines 23-27). Paragraphs 1 and 4 show that her studies let her impact modern dance.

Question 9

DISCUSSION: See lines 31-40. Dunham actually danced with the people she was studying. Other anthropologists avoided this, as they thought that they should be neutral observers, and that dance was physically challenging.

The wrong answers simply aren't mentioned in the passage. It's difficult to explain why they're wrong. They're completely unsupported.

If you picked a wrong answer, try to see how you were fooled by the answer choice, and how you could have avoided the error.

A. The passage never mentions how long various anthropologists studied in the field.
B. The passage actually doesn't mention Dunham's own culture. And it doesn't say whether or not other anthropologists related their research to their own cultures.
C. **CORRECT.** Participative approach = Dunham participated in dances with her research subjects. Lines 31-40 show that Dunham did this and that other anthropologists didn't.
D. The passage never mentioned politics. African-American politics are a common LSAT theme, but that doesn't mean that *every* African-American passage will be political.
E. The passage says that Dunham was familiar with dance, but it doesn't say if Dunham was familiar with Caribbean cultures.

Question 10

DISCUSSION: When a question quotes a specific line, you should read around that line for context. You can answer this question simply be reading the full sentence, which is lines 19-23.

Social scientists valued things that were 'scientifically rigorous'. They avoided studying dance, so presumably they thought that they couldn't study dance with scientific rigor.

The 'peers' are those judging the social scientists' work. If you're a social scientist, your peers will decide if your work is scientifically rigorous and therefore valuable.

———————————

A. Lines 19-23 indicate that social scientists largely ignored dance. So the 'peers' wouldn't have had an opinion on whether dance was interpreted correctly or incorrectly.

B. Lines 19-23 say that social scientists didn't think that research on dance could be scientifically rigorous. Therefore they would probably think that it's *difficult* for social scientists to obtain reliable data, even if those social scientists were well versed in dance traditions.

C. CORRECT. This is why social scientists avoided studying dance. They feared that their peers would not think dance could be studied with scientific rigor. See lines 19-23.

D. Lines 26-27 explain why dance experts didn't study dance ethnology. It was because they weren't trained in social science. It had nothing to do with being preoccupied.

E. It's true that social scientists don't think that dance can be studied with rigor. But lines 19-23 don't say *why* rigor was impossible. The passage doesn't say anything about dance forms being too variable.

Question 11

DISCUSSION: Read the whole sentence, lines 23-27. These lines show that Dunham was unique. She had training in both dance and anthropology.

All other experts only had training in social science or dance, but not both. That explains why no one had previously conducted Dunham's studies.

———————————

A. Lines *19-23* explain why social scientists didn't study dance. This question is asking about lines 23-27.

B. This is tempting. But lines 23-27 only talk about why groups are *not* qualified to study dance. This answer has the wrong emphasis: the passage wasn't trying to prove that any group *was* qualified to study dance (apart from Dunham).

C. We're not told why Dunham chose to study dance. Dunham may not have been aware that she was the only dancer qualified to study dance.

D. CORRECT. Lines 23-27 show that no dancer had studied dance because they weren't trained in social science research.

E. What? The dancers mentioned in lines 23-27 did not *have* a field of research. That was the point of mentioning them – they were qualified to understand dance, but they weren't researchers.

Question 12

DISCUSSION: In 1935, Dunham began studying the dance forms of the Caribbean. These dances had origins in African dance (lines 28-31).

The passage contradicts all the wrong answers.

_____

A. Lines 10-11 show that both Caribbean and Pacific-island cultures used body isolation. But that's just one technique – we have no idea how similar the two dance cultures were in other respects. Meanwhile, the passage implies that Caribbean dance culture was most similar to *African* dance culture, since Caribbean dance had its origins in African dance.

B. Lines 10-11 mention that Pacific-island dance cultures also used body-isolation. So they might have used these techniques before Caribbean dancers started using them.

C. Lines 45-47 show that Dunham used her Caribbean experience to create *new* forms of ballet.

D. Lines 1-5 show that Dunham was the first to incorporate Caribbean body-isolation techniques into modern American dance.

E. CORRECT. Lines 10-11 support this. Caribbean dance culture was influenced by its origins in African dance culture.

This is a fairly straightforward answer, if you get to it. You should always glance over all five answers before spending too much time on any one of them.

Question 13

DISCUSSION: The key points of Dunham's work are the following:

- Expertise in research and in dance
- Immersion in the culture she was studying
- Teaching what she learned to dancers in her own culture.

So you want an answer where someone uses their expertise to immerse themselves in a foreign culture and teach what their learned to their own culture.

The key is participation. None of the wrong answers mentions a researcher participating in what they study.

_____

A. Dunham actually danced the dances she was studying. This answer should have told us the French archaeologist learned to play the instruments she was researching.

B. Same as A. This answer should have said the Australian researcher tried the plants she was researching.

C. This answer says the techniques were used in both countries. Dunham studied techniques that weren't present in her own country.

D. CORRECT. Dunham participated in the dances she was studying, and introduced the techniques to America. Here, the teacher actually taught in order to learn the techniques, and he introduced them to Brazil. Everything fits.

E. This answer has no participation. The clothing designer should have actually learned to design foreign clothes himself.

Question 14

DISCUSSION: Read the whole section, lines 31-40. Line 38 is key, the author says that the traditional social scientists' ideas are now "fortunately recognized as unrealistic".

So the author disagrees that anthropologists should remain separate from the people they study, and the author thinks that Dunham was correct to participate in Caribbean dances.

————————

A. The author thinks Dunham made the right decision by participating in dances. So if the social scientists thought that there was a risk of injury, the author wouldn't agree with them.

But it's not even clear that the social scientists did think that there was a risk of injury. Lines 35-36 mention that the dances were physically demanding, but the social scientists actually didn't mention risk of injury per se. The social scientists might simply have considered dancing to be hard work and too much exercise.

B. The social scientists didn't recommend "initial caution". They recommended Dunham avoid dancing altogether!

C. It's true that the author thinks that the researchers were incorrect. But lines 31-40 don't mention scientific rigor. The author never expresses an opinion about the scientific rigor of anthropological research.

D. **CORRECT.** Line 38 supports this. It's now recognized that anthropological researchers can't remain entirely separate from the people they study.

E. Only lines 19-23 mention scientific rigor. The author never says to what extent they think scientific rigor is possible in the study of dance.

Passage 3 - Happiness Paradox (comparative)
Questions 15-20

Paragraph Summaries

Passage A

1. Happiness paradox. Richer people are happy, richer societies are not happy.
2. Our happiness depends more on the increase in our income than the level of our income. We are not good at understanding this and we over-invest in material goods.
3. Rivalry: A study showed that most people would choose to be poor, but richer than others. East Germans are richer than they used to be. But now they compare themselves to West Germans, so now they feel poorer.

Passage B

1. Does the Solnick-Hemenway study show that we still seek advantages over our rivals via bigger houses?
2. Actually, the data show that richer people feel happier because they're more successful and feel that they have created more value.
3. Two equally successful people will be equally happy, even with different incomes.
4. Wanting to be successful is a noble desire, it means that we want to create value. Fortunately, it also makes us happy.

Note: Paragraph summaries get a bit imprecise on some comparative passages. These two passages have 11 paragraphs between the two of them.

Obviously, I don't keep mental notes on what every single paragraph says. That's only useful for passages with fewer, longer paragraphs (including some comparative passages).

Instead, these notes represent the main points from each passage. They're what I retained from each passage before I moved on to the questions.

Analysis

One of your most important tasks on a comparative passage is to figure out the main point of each passage, and how the two passages relate to each other. In particular, you should know where the authors agree and where they disagree.

Both authors mentions a study, the Solnick-Hemenway study. Both authors give their *interpretations* of the study.

A study has no objective truth. The Solnick-Hemenway merely reported some observations. Lines 24-33 report the results of the study. The study found that people would prefer to have a smaller amount of money if they were richer than other people.

The author of Passage A thinks that this means we experience rivalry with our peers. We compare ourselves to others, and want to have more money than them.

The author of Passage B has a different interpretation. They say that data shows that we actually care about being successful (lines 50-53). It's true that people with money often feel more successful (lines 55-56), but this is just a correlation. It's the success itself that makes us feel happy (lines 56-57).

Further, we have a noble reason for wanting to feel successful. When we're successful, it's usually because we created value for others. So really we want to feel like we've made contributions to society. (lines 60-66).

So, Passages A and B agree that the study is worthwhile. They disagree on how to interpret the study, and whether rivalry is noble or ignoble.

Passage A also talks about habituation – a topic ignored in passage B. Habituation means that we get used to additional income. If you move from $40,000 to $50,000, you will be happy, for a time. But then you'll get used to $50,000. It will feel 'normal'. You'd have been just as happy at $40,000, and you'd probably have had more leisure time.

We're not very good at understanding this. So we keep chasing after money, even though it doesn't make us happier (lines 20-23).

The questions completely ignore the phenomenon of habituation, possibly because only one passage deals with it. This doesn't mean you should ignore something that is only talked about in one passage – that information can give you clues about the author's attitude. Still, a topic is more likely to be useful on comparative passages if it's mentioned in both passages.

Question 15

DISCUSSION: The questions asks about the purpose of both passages. You can answer these questions with 100% certainty. You're looking for something that's mentioned in *both* passages.

Don't just go off of a vague feeling. Check! LSAT students consistently overestimate how much time it takes to refer to the passage. With practice you can learn to find the right lines within 5-10 seconds. This technique lets you be 100% certain that your answer is correct.

You can also eliminate wrong answers by checking the passage. Suppose you know that a concept is mentioned in passage A, but you're not sure if it's in passage B.

You can eliminate the answer by skimming passage B to see if it mentions the concept. Again, this is something you can practice. Have a friend quiz you on whether a passage contains an idea. See how fast you can go.

A. Only passage B mentions value.
B. CORRECT. See lines 1-2 and lines 57-58.
C. Only passage B mentions biology (lines 42-45).
D. Only passage A mentions habituation.
E. Only passage A mentions required income (lines 13-15). Required income relates to habituation, and passage B doesn't mention habituation.

Question 16

DISCUSSION: Several of the wrong answers bring in concepts from passage A in an attempt to confuse you. This should tell you two things:

1. It's very useful to spend extra time reading the passages. If you're 100% clear about what A and B say, then you can easily eliminate wrong answers and save time.
2. If in doubt, check the passage. It doesn't take long, and you can realize that passage B doesn't even talk about most of the things mentioned in the wrong answers.

A. Lines 48-50 show that the author of passage B only mentions genetics in order to disagree with the theory of rivalry. The author never says why we desire to create value – maybe it's a cultural phenomenon.
B. The author never mentions standards of living. This answer is just trying to confuse you with a concept that the author of passage A talked about.
C. **CORRECT.** If you read lines 50-65, it's clear that the author of passage B thinks that success and the feeling of providing value are what make us happy.

   If you win the lottery, that isn't what most people would call success or creating value. So the author of passage B would think that winning the lottery or getting money from luck won't make people happy.
D. This refers to habituation, which was discussed in the first half of passage A. The author of passage B never discusses habituation or small salary increases.
E. The author of passage B never talks about the happiness of society as a whole. But presumably the author would think that society would become happier if the added wealth were due to success. So they wouldn't agree with this answer.

Question 17

DISCUSSION: Line 24 is in passage A. The author thinks that the Solnick-Hemenway study shows we view others as rivals and want to earn more than them.

In lines 41-50, the author of passage B introduces the theory of rivalry, and then completely disagrees with it. The rest of passage B shows that the author thinks that we value success, and that money often accompanies success.

Lines 62-64 show that the author of passage B thinks his opponents are mistaken about human nature. We are not motivated by greed. Instead we crave success because it demonstrates that we have provided value.

Overall, we can say that the author of passage B thinks that passage A's interpretation of the study is wrong in its conclusions, and also unflattering in that it portrays us as greedy and competitive.

A. **CORRECT.** Lines 48-50 show that the author thinks the interpretation is mistaken. Lines 62-64 show that the author thinks that scholars are mistaken about human nature as well. We're motivated not by greed, but to create value.
B. Rivalry is *not* flattering. If the theory of rivalry is true, then it means that we're greedy and we compete with everyone.
C. Lines 62-64 show that the author of passage B thinks that his opponents are mistaken about human nature.
D. Lines 48-50 show that the author of passage B thinks that the conclusions are not valid.
E. This is the complete opposite of what the author of passage B thinks. See lines 41-50 and 62-64.

Question 18

DISCUSSION: Passage A mentions the study in order to introduce the phenomenon of rivalry.

Passage B mentions the study in order to disagree with certain interpretations of it. The author of passage B then introduces their alternate theory: we want to feel successful.

I found the passage B section of these answers harder. I would have said "to present a view that will be argued against".

This shows why you can't get stuck on prephrases. There are multiple ways to say anything. Instead of my version, you can also say: passage B mentions the study in order to introduce the main topic.

Also, the author of passage B technically doesn't disagree with the study. They disagree with certain interpretations of the study. So the study itself isn't introduced as a "view to be argued against".

Meanwhile, passage A doesn't introduce the study as the main topic. Most of passage A is about habituation, which has nothing to do with the study.

A. The author of passage A uses the study as evidence. It isn't a view to be argued against.
B. Same as A.
C. The first part of this is fine. The second part is wrong. The author of passage B introduced the study along with a view that they *disagreed* with. There was no additional evidence for this view.
D. **CORRECT.** Passage A uses the study as support for their idea: the phenomenon of rivalry. Passage B uses the study as a way of launching into their main topic: the relationships between wealth, success, value and happiness.
E. The first part makes this answer wrong. The main topic of passage A was arguably habituation. The study only introduced the phenomenon of rivalry, which was the smaller part of passage A.
The second half sounds right. Though technically the author of passage A didn't argue against the study itself. But I would have picked this answer if it had had the first half from answer D.

Question 19

DISCUSSION: The question asks what each author would think of a person who wants to be richer than their neighbors.

The author of passage A thinks that such a person is motivated by rivalry.

The author of passage B thinks that such a person is motivated by the desire to feel successful and to feel that they have provided value to others.

A. Nonsense. Insular means "isolated, withdrawn, like an island". Cosmopolitan means "worldly". Neither word makes sense in context.
B. Arguably, these are reversed. The author of passage A would say that such a person is focussed on themselves, and thus egocentric. The author of passage B would say that such a person wants to provide value to others, and thus is altruistic.
C. Neither author would say how happy such a person is. The question talks about a person who wants to make more money than their neighbors. So we don't know if that person *is* richer than their neighbors or just *wants to* be.
D. **CORRECT.** The word misguided is supported by an overall view of passage A. Lines 20-23 show that we are not good at predicting how extra money will affect our happiness. So someone seeking extra wealth is being silly. The author of passage B thinks that someone who wants to be rich really just wants to help others and provide value (lines 62-66). So wanting to be rich is a good thing.
E. This is completely unsupported. Neither passage mentions luck. Luck is only mentioned in answer C of question 16.
And lines 48-50 show that the author of passage B disagrees with the theory that we are motivated by primeval urges of rivalry.

Question 20

DISCUSSION: As with all questions of this type, you can prove the answer 100% correct by finding references in both passages.

If you're reading this explanation, there's good odds that you chose answer D. But only passage A mentions a paradox. Watch out for this on comparative passages. Passage A does *not* determine what's true in passage B.

You might have hesitated about E because passage A doesn't directly mention data. But passage A cites a study. Everyone would agree that a scientific study is data. That's an example of a warranted term shift.

A. Lines 48-50 show that the author of passage B disagrees with biological origins. Passage A never mentions biology.

B. Neither author does this. I have no idea what this answer refers to – neither passage mentions what popular opinion thinks of the theories discussed. If you picked this, you have some self-examination to do. Ask yourself what gave you the impression this was correct – you'll avoid many errors if you figure out why you chose this.

Note: lines 48-50 show that the theory is commonly heard, but that could just mean several researchers mention it, but not the general public.

C. Same as B. This is completely unsupported. Examine your thought process to see why you found this tempting.

D. Very tempting. Lines 1-2 show that the author of passage A believes that the data represent a paradox. But the author of passage B never mentions a paradox. They seem to think that the situation is perfectly clear: we're motivated by success and value, end of story.
This answer is hard because the early mention of 'paradox' sets the tone for both passages. Remember not to carry ideas from passage A into passage B.

E. **CORRECT.** The author of passage A cites a study (lines 24-33). That's data.
The author of passage B mentions data directly: see lines 50-53.

Passage 4 - Risk and Voluntariness
Questions 21-27

Paragraph Summaries

1. Policy experts care about how many lives can be saved. Laypeople care about whether a risk is voluntary. But 'voluntary' is ambiguous.
2. Most things are part voluntary and part involuntary. Laypeople mistakenly focus only on the moment an accident occurs, and not what lead up to the accident.
3. "Voluntary" often means "I don't like what that person is doing and I don't want to pay money to help them".
4. The government should simply try to save as many lives as it can. Voluntariness per se should not be a criterion.

Analysis

This is a somewhat complex passage. It's not a good idea to read a passage like this once and move on to the questions. If there are parts you didn't understand, you should go back to reread them. You'll go a lot faster on the questions if you understand the passage. Rereading can save you time.

The passage talks about how the government should improve safety. Most people agree that the government should act to reduce risks.

But normal people and experts disagree. Regular people focus on whether a risk is voluntary. Experts focus on how many lives can be saved for a certain amount of money.

The author agrees with the experts. The central point of the passage is that "voluntary" is not a good way to decide how to reduce risks.

When deciding whether something is voluntary, normal people just focus on the moment in which danger occurs. An airplane passenger is an example. If you're on a plane, you can't move, so the situation feels "involuntary".

But the author points out that people *choose* to go on airplanes. Almost everything is at least partly voluntary (lines 21-25).

The third paragraph says that if we don't like an activity, we'll label it "voluntary" in order to avoid paying for safety improvements. Yet we'll pay to improve the safety of voluntary activities if we like those activities. So we're supportive of protecting firefighters but not skydivers, even though both activities are voluntary.

The final paragraph is a bit cryptic. It says that we should listen to experts and save as many lives as we can – that part is clear.

But what does the second half mean? Departures from the principle should be based on "specific considerations for which voluntariness serves as a proxy". What?

I'll illustrate with an example. Why do people *actually* think fireman deserve to be safe? It's because firemen risk their lives to *protect us*. Skydivers don't protect anyone. Further, people who don't like skydivers think that they risk their lives foolishly.

This distinction causes regular people to say that firefighters deserve support, but sky diving is voluntary.

So the final paragraph suggests that we can make an exception to save firefighters, even if it would be more cost effective to save sky divers. But the exception should be made because fire fighters protect us, not because of voluntariness. "They protect us" is the thing that voluntariness is serving as a "proxy" for, so that's what we should use to justify exceptions.

So the author doesn't think that laypeople are completely wrong. Sometimes their intuitions are valuable. But we should focus on the reasons that make people label something "voluntary". Voluntariness itself is not a useful concept. (lines 50-54)

Most of the wrong answers for these questions are nonsense. When a passage is difficult, the LSAC intentionally writes nonsensical, confusing answers. They assume that you were hallucinating when reading the passage, because most of the wrong answers have nothing to do with anything. There are a few ways to fix this:

1. Reread the passage until you're clear on what it says.
2. Treat the answers as your enemy; assume they're lying.
3. Read all the answers before spending too much time thinking about them. This helps on questions where the right answer is D or E, and is obvious once you reach it.
4. Try to figure out what an answer actually refers to.
5. Justify the answers using actual lines and ideas from the passage. Don't just use your gut.

The most important thing you should know about this passage is that voluntariness is *not* useful. It's a sideshow. See lines 14-19 and 50-54. We should not be using voluntariness for anything.

Question 21

DISCUSSION: This passage is an argument. The main point is that we shouldn't listen to laypeople and their ideas about voluntariness. When we're acting to reduce risks, we should listen to policy experts. Experts say to choose things that save the most lives for the least money.

There are multiple indications that this passage is an argument. Lines 14-19 say that voluntariness is not useful. Paragraphs 2-3 say that voluntariness is vague and arbitrary. Paragraph 4 concludes that we should judge interventions by how many lives they save.

A. This is true, but it's just a fact that supports the main point of the passage. The main point is that we shouldn't consider voluntariness important.
B. **CORRECT.** The final paragraph supports this. The passage is making an argument and the fourth paragraph is the conclusion.
   If you didn't realize that the passage is an argument, look at lines 14-19. The author says that voluntariness is not useful. Paragraphs 2-3 support this assertion, and this in turn leads to the conclusion in paragraph 4.
C. The whole point of the passage is that voluntariness is not a useful concept.
   See lines 14-19, and 50-54. We shouldn't use voluntariness, whether or not experts decide what is voluntary.
D. This isn't even true. The whole point of the passage is that voluntariness is not a useful concept. See lines 14-19 and 50-54.
E. This is true, according to the passage. But it's just a fact that supports the main point. The main point is that therefore voluntariness is not useful for making decisions.

Question 22

DISCUSSION: You're not going to like hearing this, but if you got this question wrong it's because you completely misunderstood the passage.

Lines 12-13 say the right answer. If you found those lines, then this was a very easy question.

All of the wrong answers assume you had no idea what experts believe and what laypeople believe.

This question illustrates why it's extremely important to review a passage if you're not clear on what it says. The wrong answers are designed to trick people who have only a partial understanding of what they read.

———————————

A. Lines 34-49 directly contradict this. Laypeople wouldn't support saving skydivers even if there were a good ratio of dollars to lives saved.
B. Experts care about lives saved, not voluntariness. If laypeople deferred to experts, then laypeople wouldn't care about voluntariness.
C. **CORRECT.** Lines 12-13 say this directly.
D. Lines 11-12 say that this is what *experts* focus on.
E. Lines 46-49 say that this is what the author recommends *the government* consider. Total resources available wasn't mentioned as a factor that laypeople consider.

Question 23

DISCUSSION: Lines 33-35 are key. They say that if people don't like something, they will call it "voluntary" and oppose public spending to improve public safety for that activity.

Thus people call skydiving voluntary, and call firefighting involuntary, even though both involve a choice (lines 35-42).

———————————

A. Space travel isn't mentioned in the passage.
B. Lines 33-42 indicate that people would call skydiving voluntary in order to avoid spending money to make it safer.
C. I was tempted by this, because people support spending money on firefighters. But line 42 clearly says that firefighting is voluntary. The point of mentioning firefighters was to illustrate that people don't care about voluntariness in a consistent way.
D. **CORRECT.** Lines 25-27 say this directly.
E. Mountain climbing isn't mentioned in the passage.

Question 24

DISCUSSION: For questions like this, there will be a few lines that *directly* support the right answer. If you don't find those lines, you're just guessing. With a small bit of practice you can learn to find lines within 3-5 seconds.

———————

A. Lines 48-50 and 38-39 directly contradict this. The author cares mainly about how many lives we can save.

B. CORRECT. Lines 9-13 support this. Voluntariness is a difference between expert judgments and regular judgments. Experts care about lives saved, regular people care whether an activity was voluntary.

C. The passage never says what other risks airline passengers face, apart from crashes.

D. The whole point of the passage is that voluntariness is not a useful concept. The author doesn't care whether or how we decide that something is voluntary.

E. Lines 21-25 touch on this. The author doesn't give an exhaustive opinion on what risks are completely involuntary. They only mention asteroid risks – there could be other involuntary risks as well.

Question 25

DISCUSSION: Read the whole third paragraph and you'll see that the point is that voluntariness is not a useful concept when we're deciding how much money to spend on safety.

So when the author says that voluntariness has "no special magic" he means that it's not a concept we ought to attach any importance to.

I'm unusually insulting about the wrong answer choices below. They make me mad. They're total nonsense designed to trick you. None of them make any sense or refer to anything mentioned in the passage.

———————

A. What? No. By definition, a risk is either voluntary, involuntary, or a bit of both. The two words *do* exhaustively categorize the risks we face. With this answer, the LSAC expected you to be confused about what the word "exhaustively" meant.

B. I think this answer is meant to play on the anti-government paranoia that has long been popular in the United States. The passage doesn't talk about the government "concealing" anything. This is total nonsense.

C. What junk. The author never talked about the meaning of voluntary and involuntary. The point wasn't whether voluntary has a "special meaning". The question is: Is voluntariness a useful concept with which to make decisions?

D. Total rubbish. "Inform people's understanding of the consequences of risk"....what the hell does this refer to? It wasn't in the passage! The phrase I quoted means "how people decide how dangerous an activity is". That simply isn't discussed anywhere.

E. CORRECT. Lines 14-19 and 50-54 support this. The point of the passage is that voluntariness is not a useful concept. So when the passage says that there is no special magic to voluntariness, the author means that we shouldn't consider voluntariness as being particularly important.

Question 26

DISCUSSION: As with the other specific detail questions on this passage, you can and should support the right answer using a few lines from the passage.

The wrong answers all refer to concepts out of context. They're intended to trick you, if your understanding of the passage was incomplete.

A. This is very extreme. *Any* activity could involve a loss of human life....even getting out of bed! The author doesn't necessarily think that every activity must be made safer. Especially since we have a limited budget (lines 48-49).

B. **CORRECT.** Lines 21-25 support this. Most risks are voluntary to a certain degree, including environmental risks. Presumably some environmental risks are therefore risky to a greater degree than others.

C. It's true that the author supports policy experts. The author thinks experts are right that we should focus on saving lives.
But the author doesn't think that experts are necessarily any good at judging what is voluntary. The point of the passage is that voluntariness is not important.

D. Lines 48-49 say that we have limited resources. The author did *not* say whether those resources should be increased.

E. Actually, the author spends two paragraphs trashing the beliefs of ordinary people. We ordinary folk focus on voluntariness, but voluntariness is not a useful concept. Nowhere does the author say that it's important to listen to us regular people.

Question 27

DISCUSSION: For author's attitude questions, look for judgments. Authors tend to be quite subtle. Assume that any small positive/negative judgment implies that the author completely agrees/disagrees with a given group.

A. The author didn't say that people misunderstand risk. For instance, lines 35-39 imply that people *do* understand the risks faced by skydivers.

B. It's true that the author doesn't recommend listening to ordinary people. But the author's concern seems to be that regular people don't support *enough* regulation. For instance, the author supports regulating the safety of skydivers (see lines 35-39), whereas ordinary people wouldn't want to spend money improving skydivers' safety.

C. **CORRECT.** Lines 30-35 show two reasons that the author is skeptical of ordinary people's views on voluntariness. Ordinary people only look at part of the situation, and ordinary people decide whether something is voluntary based on whether or not they like the activity.

D. Actually, lines 47-49 show that the author *is* mainly concerned with saving lives.

E. The author *never* criticizes experts. Instead, the author spends paragraphs 2-3 criticizing common people.

Section III - Logic Games
Game 1 - Benefit Concert Bands
Questions 1-7

Setup

This is a linear game, with a few twists. It's not a particularly difficult game. Nonetheless, it's worth noting that all of the game types are becoming less standard.

The LSAC is aware that people are prepping more intensely, so they're reducing the number of games that can be learned from a strategy guide.

To get better at non-standard games, you should repeat them. This way you'll develop an intuition for the underlying patterns on logic games, and you'll be able to handle new, non-standard rules. It's a good idea to repeat the game on your own before reading these explanations.

Now, for the setup. First, you hopefully know that linear diagrams should have a series of horizontal slots:

$$\underline{\quad}\ \underline{\quad}\ \underline{\quad}\ \underline{\quad}\ \underline{\quad}\ \underline{\quad}$$
$$1 \qquad 2 \qquad 3 \qquad 4 \qquad 5 \qquad 6$$

Next, this game has some pure sequencing rules. These often appear in linear games. Here's the first rule:

V — Z

Here's the second rule:

Z
⟩X
W

The first two rules can and should be combined. Notice that Z is in both rules. You can join both diagrams together using Z:

V — Z
⟩X
W

Always watch for multiple rules that mention the same variable.

The third and fourth rules are fairly rare. They say that U must be in the final three spots, and Y must be in the first three.

You *could* just write these in your list of rules, marking something like "U = last 3". Or you could draw a "Not U" symbol under slots 1-3.

I think both of those methods add visual clutter without clarity. I *do* use "not" rules, but not when six of them are required to represent two rules. Instead, here's how I drew these rules:

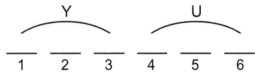

Notice that this diagram is both clear and minimal. Y goes somewhere in the first three and U goes somewhere in the final three.

One glance at the main diagram is enough to remind you of *exactly* what the rules say. I also find this helps me visualize where Y and U can go.

You should always check for deductions before starting. Look for restricted points. The main deduction is that only U or X can go last.

Y must go in the first three spaces, and V, Z and W must go before X. So only U or X are left to go sixth. You *could* draw this on the diagram:

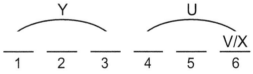

However, I would only do this if you're prone to forgetting this type of deduction. If you're an advanced student of logic games, this type of deduction is likely second nature to you.

It might be worth adding Y – X on your ordering diagram. X has three variables before it, so X can't go in the first three spaces. However, I haven't drawn this on mine, as it's easy for me to see this.

Main Diagram

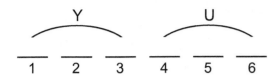

```
 ___  ___  ___   ___  ___  ___
  1    2    3     4    5    6
```

V — Z
      ⟍
       ⟩ X
      ⟋
  W

Notice that all six variables are represented, along with their rules. This setup makes it pointless to draw a separate list of the variables (UVWXYZ). Such a list adds no value, and wastes space and time.

This setup also makes it easy to visualize possibilities. You don't have to hold any rules in your head.

It's difficult to explain what you see inside your own head. But when I look at these, I can see V – Z – X floating over the diagram and interacting with Y and U.

Obviously, whether or not you can do this depends on your visualization skills. But I expect it's a learnable skill to some extent. Practice seeing the variables move around over the diagram: it really comes in handy for sequencing games.

Question 1

Unusually, this question is not an 'acceptable order' question. Usually first questions are. If the first question is *not* an acceptable order question, it's a sure sign that you were expected to make a deduction in the setup.

Here, the only deduction is that you can combine rules 1 and 2 to get this diagram:

V — Z
      ⟍
       ⟩ X
      ⟋
  W

Since it's the only deduction, this diagram is almost certainly what will let us get the right answer. We're looking for something that can't go fifth. That means something that has more than two other variables after it.

That's V. Both Z and X have to go after V, so V can go fourth at latest.

B is CORRECT.

Question 2

When a question gives you a new rule, you can combine it with the existing rules to make a deduction.

We know Z is after V and before X:

V — Z
    ╲
     ╲ X
  W ╱

This question also places Z before Y. And we know Y can go third at latest.

So Z is after V, and before Y. That's three variables. Since Y can't go later than third, we must place these three variables in slots 1-3:

```
              ___U___
              /       \
 V    Z    Y   ___  ___  ___
 1    2    3    4    5    6
```

The question asks about the earliest we can place W. Let's first look at the remaining variables. W comes before X. U is the only variable left, and the only rule for U is that it goes somewhere 4-6. Here's how I draw this:

```
                  W — X , U
 V    Z    Y   ___  ___  ___
 1    2    3    4    5    6
```

The line between W – X shows that W comes somewhere before X. The comma between W – X and U means that there are no rules governing where you can place U. It could go before W – X, in between them, or after them.

This way of drawing "W – X, U" is a flexible method of visualizing everything that can be true, without clutter.

There is no reason we can't place W fourth, so **C** is **CORRECT.**

Question 3

This question tests your ability to apply the ordering rules. Let's look at them again:

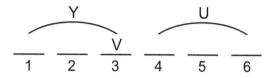

The question places V third:

```
        ___Y___           ___U___
       /       \         /       \
  ___  ___  ___  ___  ___  ___
              V
   1    2    3    4    5    6
```

We know that Y has to go in slots 1-2. Who else can go there?

Not U. They must go 4-6.
Not Z. They must go after V
Not X. They must go after Z.

So only W can also go in slots 1-2. We get this diagram:

```
  Y , W              Z — X , U
 ___  ___  ___  ___  ___  ___
             V
  1    2    3    4    5    6
```

The commas indicate that variables are interchangeable, while the line between Z – X indicates that there's an ordering rule for them to obey.

You might have seen Powerscore draw Y and W like this: Y/W W/Y

That works too. However, that method doesn't work well for slots 4-6, which is why I prefer my more flexible method. You get a very clear view of where every variable can go.

B is **CORRECT.** W has to be 1st or 2nd, so they are always before Z in this scenario.

A, C and **E** are wrong because U could be before Z – X, in between them, or after them.

D is wrong because Y and W are interchangeable in this scenario.

Question 4

For this question, ZW are a block. Let's look at what other rules apply. We know that X is after ZW, and V is before ZW:

$$V - \boxed{ZW} - X$$

This is not an easy group of variables to place. In fact, ZW can *only* go third and fourth.

You may be thinking "how can you *know* that"? If so, I encourage you *not* to think. Instead, draw.

Make a diagram with ZW second and third. Doesn't work: V has to go first, and there's no space to put Y in 1-3.

Make a diagram with ZW fourth and fifth. Doesn't work, X has to go last, and there's no space to put U in 4-6.

I'm sure you can see why we can't put ZQ in 1-2 or 5-6. It's because V has to go before them, and X has to go after.

So with two diagrams, you can prove that this is the only possible setup:

With practice, you can draw 2-3 test diagrams in about 15 seconds. If you find it slow going, it's because you haven't practiced, and because you don't have the rules memorized. But you can learn to be faster.

I don't "think" about most logic games. I just try stuff, and then I "see" what works and what doesn't. Logic games are a very mechanical process. Usually the new rules for individual questions are quite restrictive.

Anyway, **E** is **CORRECT.** Z has to go in slot 3.

A and **C** are wrong because U and X are interchangeable in this scenario.

B and **D** are wrong because V and Y are interchangeable in this scenario. Either one could be first or second.

Question 5

It can be helpful to identify the groups that *can't* perform first.

U can't perform first, because they must go 4-6.

Z can't perform first, because they come after V.

X can't perform first, because Z, V and W come before X.

That leaves V, Y and W. They have no variables in front of them, so they all could go first.

D is CORRECT.

Question 6

This question places W immediately before X. That rearranges the ordering rules:

$$V - Z - \boxed{WX}$$

Nobody but U can go after X. So in this question, WX and U fill the final three spots:

$$V - Z, Y \quad \Big| \quad \boxed{WX}, U$$

$$\underline{\quad}_1 \quad \underline{\quad}_2 \quad \underline{\quad}_3 \quad \underline{\quad}_4 \quad \underline{\quad}_5 \quad \underline{\quad}_6$$

I put a dividing line in the middle to make clear which side the floating variables go on. Though on my own sheet I just drew the blocks a bit further apart. I find these floating variables the easiest way to visualize who can go where. No need to draw five separate scenarios – this one diagrams lets you see them all in your head.

A doesn't work because U can only go before WX or after, so U can only be fourth or sixth.

B doesn't work because V is before Z. Since Z is third at the latest in this scenario, V can only go first or second.

C doesn't work because W has to go in the final three slots in this scenario.

D is CORRECT. This diagram proves it:

$$\boxed{WX}, U$$

$$\underset{1}{V} \quad \underset{2}{Z} \quad \underset{3}{Y} \quad \underline{\quad}_4 \quad \underline{\quad}_5 \quad \underline{\quad}_6$$

I filled in only the first half in order to emphasize how you should view these diagrams. This is a "could be true" question, so you just have to show that an ordering is possible.

You don't have to prove everything, or even finish the scenario, since you know that any order for 4-6 is legal as long as it fits the constraints we set up for this question. WXU or UWX are both fine.

E is wrong because Z has to go in slots 1-3 for this question.

Question 7

If you're like most LSAT students, I'll bet you *hate* rule substitution questions. If I told you they don't have to be hard, would you believe me?

The trick is to look at the full effect of a rule, and describe it another way. Let's look at what we know about X:

V — Z
        ⟍
          ⟩ X
        ⟋
   W

X comes after Z, V and W. X also comes after Y, because Y has to be in one of the first three places, and X already has three people in front.

So Z, V, W and Y comes before X. Only U *could* come after X. That's the full extent of the rule.

And now that's we've looked at the full extent of the rule, it's obvious that **A** is **CORRECT.**

You can also answer these questions by elimination. An answer is wrong if it allows something that shouldn't be allowed, or if it prevents something that normally would be allowed.

B is wrong because it puts V before W. Normally, it's possible for W to go before V.

C is wrong because it leaves out Z. With the rule in this answer, it would be possible for Z to go after X.

D is wrong because it allows Z to go after X. For example, this order is normally illegal, but it would be allowed with this rule:

V	W	Y	U	X	Z
1	2	3	4	5	6

That diagram also proves that **E** wrong. **E** allows Z to be after X as long as X is in five. That is different from the normal rules.

Game 2 - Research Team
Questions 8-12

Setup

This is an in-out grouping game. If you found this game hard, you're not alone. Most students find that in-out grouping games are one of the hardest game types on the LSAT.

But I've got good news for you: this is also one of the most common and standard types of games on the LSAT. That might not seem like good news, but it means you can practice many games of this type.

You'll find that once they practice this type of game, it becomes one of the *easiest* game types. So if you work at it, you can turn in-out games from a disadvantage to an advantage.

I'll note that if you look at games classifications online, they lump a bunch of different games together as "in-out grouping games". The type I'm referring to here has the following characteristics:

1. All of the rules are conditional statements.
2. All of the rules can be connected together to form one big diagram and its contrapositive.

Now, since all the rules can be combined, it is *not* sensible to draw them separately. It's better to just start combining them right off the bat.

Some students don't agree, at first. They worry and fret and feel they can't do it. Instead, they draw all the rules separately, and the contrapositives, and end up with a jumble of rules. They then spend 3-4 minutes looking for deductions, but their drawing is so confusing that they never make a single one. I've never seen a student make proper deductions when they start by drawing the rules separately.

Don't be like that. You *can* do this. Just follow along, and draw the diagram for yourself on paper. Do it a few times and it will feel like second nature.

The key to combining rules is to look for multiple rules that mention the same variable. You can always connect two rules if they have a variable in common. You might have to take the contrapositive of one of them, if the common variable is in the form "M" and "Not M" (i.e. negated) form.

Enough preamble, let's look at the first rule:

$$M \nearrow^{\varnothing}_{+} \searrow_{\cancel{P}}$$

This means that if M is in, both O and P are out. Don't ever forget the + and 'or' signs in between arrows. They're very important.

The next rule looks like this:

$$S \nearrow^{P}_{+} \searrow_{T}$$

It may not be obvious how this connects, but both rules mention P. So let's take the contrapositive of rule 2:

$$\begin{array}{c} \cancel{P} \\ \text{or} \searrow \cancel{S} \\ \cancel{T} \nearrow \end{array}$$

To take the contrapositive, you reverse the terms, and negate them. You also change "and" to "or" and vice-versa.

Now both the first and second rule have a "not P". We can connect the two rules like this:

It's a mistake to move on to the third rule if you don't first combine the first rules like we just did.

The third rule mentions M, and M is already on the diagram, so you can connect the third rule like this:

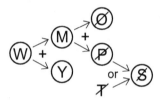

That's it! That one big diagram covers all the rules.

Learning how to draw it is one thing. You also need to know how to read it. You must read these diagrams left to right.

As an example: if W is in, then both Y and M must be in as well. Since M is in, O and P and S are out. We don't know anything about T, it could be in or out. I've circled what we know, *if* W is in:

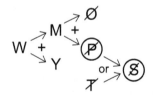

Let's look at another example. What happens if P is out? We only know one thing: S is also out:

We don't know anything about the other variables. Maybe M is in, or maybe it is out. P being out is just a *necessary* condition for M being out, so it doesn't tell us anything about M.

The more you do these games, the more this type of diagram will make sense. It's like learning a language, you can't read them fluently at first. But once you *can* read this diagram, it's by far the most powerful way to solve these games.

Now, we also need to take the contrapositive of the main diagram. You do this just like you'd take any other contrapositive:

1. Reverse the order
2. Negate everything
3. Change 'and' to 'or', and vice versa.

Here it is:

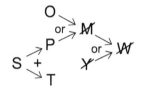

I *highly* recommend you draw this yourself on paper and practice the three steps. Taking contrapositives is a very mechanical process, which means it gets easy with practice.

There is one other rule that doesn't fit on this diagram. At least four variables are selected. There could be more than four selected as well of course – four is just the minimum.

This rule was in the opening paragraph – you should always scan the opening paragraph to see if there's any rules hidden in there.

Lastly, there are no rules for Z. A good way to represent this is to draw Z with a circle around it. I drew this near my other two diagrams.

(Z)

Main Diagram

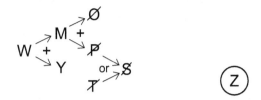

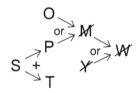

At least four employees are selected.

Question 8

For acceptable order questions, go through the rules and use them to eliminate answers one by one.

I do not recommend using your diagram to solve acceptable order questions, even on in-out grouping games. It's faster to use the rules, and reading them again helps you to memorize them.

Rule 1 eliminates **A.** M and P can't go together.

Rule 2 eliminates **C** and **D.** If S is on a team, then both T and P must be there.

Rule 3 eliminates **E.** If W is on a team, then M must also be on that team.

B is **CORRECT.** It violates no rules.

Question 9

This is a common question type on in-out games. It asks which two people can't go together.

You're looking for the following relationship:

1. The variable on the left is in positive form. i.e. "S"
2. The variable on the right is in negative form i.e. "M̶"
3. **Example:** S → M̶, M → S̶

In other words, one variable being *in* forces the second variable *out*. This method works whether you look at the main diagram or the contrapositive. Pick a pair of variables from an answer and look for the left most variable on either of the diagrams. Then see if it matches the form I described above.

A is wrong. There are no arrows connecting M and T.

B is wrong. There are no arrows connecting O and Y.

C is wrong. Z has no rules, it can never force another variable out.

D is **CORRECT.** If S is in, W is out:

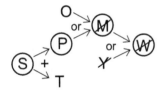

(T is in too of course. I've only circled the variables leading from S to W in order to clarify the relationship you're looking for on this question.)

E is wrong. If W is in, Y is in. Clearly, those two can be together.

Question 10

I found this question hard. I eventually figured out what I was missing: I had forgotten that at least four employees must be selected.

This question places Y out. That also forces W out. You can draw this as an in-out diagram, it may help you to keep track:

I	O
__	Y
__	W
__	
__	

We need at least four variables in. I've drawn that as a reminder in this diagram, but I won't always repeat it.

So, Y and W are out. Since we need at least four employees in, we can have, at most, two more employees in the out group.

The answers ask who *can't* be placed in. The right answer will be an employee that forces more than two other employees out if they are in.

That's M. Refer to the diagram, look at "M in", and you'll see that O, P and S must be out. That's five people out total, which is too many:

I	O
	Y
	W
	O
	P
	S

E is **CORRECT.**

This listing shows that all the others could be in together:

I	O
T	Y
Z	W
P	M
O	
S	

This scenario is actually just the contrapositive of the main diagram:

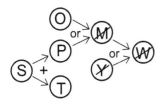

(I added Z in the in/out diagram above too, since Z can always be in)

Question 11

Another tricky question. I found trial and error to be the most effective method. If P is out, then S is out.

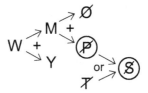

Only a max of four employees can be out. So we've only got two employees left to place out, at most.

All of the wrong answers force three people out, which makes a total of five out. That's one too many.

A places M and O out. M out means W is out, for a total of five out: P, S, M, O, W

B places M and T out. M out means W is out, for a total of five out: P, S, M, T, W

C places M and Z out. If M is out, then W is also out. That makes a total of five out: P, S, M, Z, W

D is **CORRECT.** This answer places O and T out. O being out doesn't force anyone out.

T being out only forces S out, and S was already out on this question. Here's the in-out diagram for this that shows this answer works:

I	O
Y	P
Z	S
W	O
M	T

In fact, this answer is just the main diagram, plus Z. So it obeys all the rules:

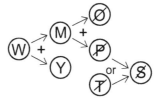

E places O and Y out. If Y is out, then W also has to go out. That makes a total of five out: P, S, O, Y, W

Question 12

This is a slightly unusual question. *Normally,* when looking for a pair where at least one has to be in, you would look for a pair with the sufficient negated, and the necessary in. E.g. Q̶ → M

But there are no pairs like that in this game. So we'll have to use a different method to find out what variables must be in.

The fast way to solve this question is to find a couple of working orders. If you find an order that works, you can use it to eliminate wrong answers. Any variables not included in your working order obviously don't *have* to be in.

To quickly make two working scenarios, I used the main diagrams. I just started from the left and fulfilled all the sufficient conditions. Like this:

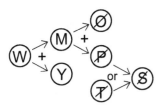

For the first diagram, that gives us WYM in, and OPST out. Add Z in to make four variables in.

Let's make another working scenario, using the second diagram. If you activate all the sufficient conditions, SPTO are in, and MYW are out.

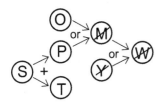

I also left Z out, because this question is asking who *has* to be in. Z doesn't have to be in if we already have four variables in.

So now we have two groups of employees that fulfill all the rules:

WYMZ and   SPTO

You can use these groups to eliminate answers.

A is wrong. The first group doesn't include O or S.

C is wrong. The first group doesn't include P and S.

E is wrong. The second group doesn't include Y or Z.

Hopefully this method makes sense. I'm attempting to describe the kind of short cut that high scorers use routinely.

Under timed conditions, it took me all of 10 seconds to create those two groups. It takes longer to explain it, because I'm walking you through the steps I went through instantaneously in my head. I recommend practicing this question a few times to get better at quickly creating scenarios to disprove answers.

So now we've narrowed things down to **B** and **D**. If you use a quick method to eliminate three answers, you can afford to spend more time testing the remaining two. Let's see if we can create a scenario without OW or without TY.

This scenario eliminates **B**. MYZT. It obeys all the rules, and doesn't include O or W. For purposes of illustration, I'll highlight all the variables I selected across both diagrams. MYTZ are in, POSW are out.

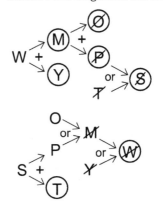

You must read the diagrams left to right. We've covered all seven variables across both diagrams, and none of the rules conflict.

D is **CORRECT.** It's impossible to construct a correct scenario without either T or Y.

Game 3 - Repertory Theatre
Questions 13-18

Setup

This game is a mixture of linear and grouping. I don't classify games beyond that. Few people who score well on logic games really care about games classifications. That's just something prep companies invent to sell books and courses, and also because they enjoy classifying things.

It's more important to repeat games and develop an intuitive sense of how to draw the rules.

Ok, let's look at the setup of this game. First, you need to think about how to draw this game. There are three groups, and three time slots. The first question is a good guide to how to represent this. They've arranged the groups vertically, and the times left to right. I've added a slight modification to make clear that 8 o'clock is after 7 o'clock.

1 __   __

2 __   __

3   __

    7   8   9

I'm just going to draw the diagram like this once, so that it's perfectly clear to you where 123 and 789 are. But for future diagrams, I'm going to leave off the 789, like this:

1 __   __

2 __   __

3   __

The 789 diagram is very cluttered. If you put too much stuff on your diagrams, your brain won't be able to make sense of them.

And actually, my own diagrams are even more minimal. My main diagram has the 123, but my diagrams for individual questions generally don't have numbers. Here's a scenario from question 17, drawn the same way I'd draw it on my page:

W̲   S̲

—   —

    R̲

It's lightning fast to draw a diagram like that, and by glancing at the main diagram I can orient myself easily. My main diagram is on the second page, beside the questions.

Even looking at this, without checking my main diagram, I find it obvious to see which groups are 123 and 789.

However, I'll be including the 123 for the rest of the explanations, for clarity. However, I encourage you to experiment with the most minimal diagrams that make sense to you.

I've just given you a little peek behind the curtain. The explanations in all of my books are very similar to what I would draw on test day, but they're not identical.

This is true of *every* set of logic games diagrams you might find online. LSAT instructors need to add some complexity in order to make diagrams clear for explanatory purposes. But you should leave off any details you don't find essential. Your diagrams only have to make sense to you.

Ok, now, for the rules. I'll start with rules 1 and 4, as they can't be drawn on the diagram. Rule 1 says that W is before H:

W—H

You could also add this rule to the diagram as "not" rules, where you draw "not H" under slot 7, and "not W" under slot 9. I'm avoiding this, because that's a tactic for beginning students. Advanced students can tell just by looking at W – H that H can't go at 7 o'clock and W can't go at 9 o'clock.

Rule 4 says that H and M don't go in the same group:

You may recognize this as a diagram that's also used in linear games. I've never run into a problem using it for both linear and grouping games.

If this were a linear rule, it would mean that HM can't go beside each other, in either order. As a grouping rule, it means that H and M can't be in the same group.

Rules 2 and 3 can be drawn directly on the diagram. I put them as 'not' rules to the right of each group. R can't go in group 2 and S can't go in group 3:

1 __ __

2 __ __ R̸

3 __ S̸

Main Diagram

1 __ __

2 __ __ R̸

3 __ S̸

(1) W—H

(2) H̸M̸

244

Question 13

For acceptable order questions, go through the rules and use them to eliminate answers one by one.

Rule 1 eliminates **B.** The western is supposed to begin earlier than the horror film.

Rule 2 eliminates **D.** The sci-fi film can't be shown on screen three.

Rule 3 eliminates **E.** The romance can't be shown on screen two.

Rule 4 eliminates **C.** The horror and mystery films must be shown on different screens.

A is **CORRECT.** It violates no rules.

Question 14

This is another type of acceptable order question. Remember that the two movies in the answers are on screen two. They are shown at 7 and 9.

It's best to go through the rules one at a time to see if a rule proves an answer correct.

The first rule proves that **C** is **CORRECT.** The western must go before the horror film. That means that W can't go at 9.

You should, of course, check that none of the answers violate rules 2-4. And all the other answers are fine.

I'm not going to bother proving that the other answers work. It's not something you'd ever want to do under timed conditions.

If you think that one of the other answers also doesn't work, then you're misreading the rules. I don't know which rule you're misreading, so I can't solve the problem except by telling you to read the rules again and find your mistake.

Question 15

I actually got this question wrong when I took the test under timed conditions. (Yes, I make mistakes)

I chose **A,** because I forgot that the romance film can't go in group 2.

But I'm getting ahead of myself, I'll show you the diagram we can draw based on the new rule this question gives us.

This question says that W and S are in the same group. That means they're in group 1 or 2, because only those groups have two spaces.

We can also figure out the order of W and S. The western has to go before the horror film, so the western can't go in group 3. Therefore the western goes at 7, and the sci-fi goes at 9.

So we get these two diagrams:

```
1   W        S
    __       __

2            R̸
    __       __

3            S̸
             __
```

```
1   __       __

2   W        S   R̸
    __       __

3            S̸
    __
```

But actually, the first diagram won't work. The romance film can't go in group two, so it would have to fill group three.

That would leave the mystery and horror films to go in group 2. And that violates rule 4.

So we're working from the second diagram. One of M/H goes in group 3, because they can't go together:

```
    R, M/H
1   __       __

2   W        S   R̸
    __       __

3   M/H          S̸
    __
```

The romance film and the other one of M/H fill group 1. Just remember that the horror film can't go at 7 o'clock, because it comes after the western.

This is a could be true question.

A can't be true. The second screen is filled by the western and the sci-fi film.

B is CORRECT. This diagram shows that it works:

```
1   R        M
    __       __

2   W        S   R̸
    __       __

3   H            S̸
    __
```

C doesn't work. If the romance film is on screen three, then the mystery film and the horror film would have to go together, which violates rule 4.

D can't be true. If the sci-fi film starts at 7, then the western would start at 9, since they're in the same group. But the western can't start at 9 – it has to go before the horror film (rule 1).

E doesn't work. This question says that the western is on the same screen as the sci-fi film. Only screens 1 and 2 have two spaces, and neither of them have a show starting at 9 o'clock.

246

Question 16

This question places the romance before the western. We also know that the western is before the horror film. So we get this order:

R – W – H

That means the romance is at 7 o'clock, the western is at 8 o'clock, and the horror film is at 9 o'clock.

The romance film can't go in group 2, so it must be in group 1. The western is in group 3, as that's the only screen with an 8 o'clock showing:

1 R   __

2 __   R̶

3   W   8̶

Next, the mystery and horror films must be in different groups (rule 4). That means one of them is in group 1, and the other in group 2:

1 R   M/H

2 __   __ S, H/M

3   W

The sci-fi film also has to go in group 2, as it's the only group left open. **E is CORRECT.**

In case you were wondering, I drew S and M/H to the right of group two, with a comma, to indicate that they both go in that group, in either order.

Question 17

This question appears similar to question 14. It looks like a rule based "acceptable order" question.

Unfortunately, I went through every rule and none of them seemed to directly eliminate any answers.

When you're stuck, you should consider the most restricted variables. In this game, the horror film and the mystery film are quite restricted, as rule 4 says they can't go together.

Notice that answers **A-D** all include one of the horror and mystery films. So they automatically fulfill our toughest rule.

E does not have either the horror or the mystery film, so let's start there.

The western and the sci-fi film fill group one, and one of H/M fill group 3:

1 W   S

2 __   __ R, H/M

3   H/M

So the romance film and the other H/M go in group 2. But this doesn't work: rule 3 says that the romance film can't go in group 2.

E is CORRECT.

This is a hard question, but it fits a pattern. If a question seems impossible, look for what's *not* included in the answer choices. The LSAC knows that people aren't very good at imagining things that aren't listed, so they're pretty predictable at using this trick to make hard questions.

Question 18

This question places sci-fi and romance on the same screen. Rule two says that the sci-fi film can't go on screen 3. Rule three says that the romance film can't go on screen 2.

So if the sci-fi and romance film are together, they have to be shown on screen 1, in either order:

```
1  S/R      R/S
       ——        ——

2  ——        —— R̸

3       ——      S̸
```

We have the western, the horror film, and the mystery left to place. We know the horror and the mystery have to fill two groups, so one of H/M fills group 3:

```
1  S/R      R/S
       ——        ——

2  ——        —— R̸

3  H/M       S̸
      ——
```

The western and the other H/M goes in group 2. The western has to go in 7 o'clock, because rule 1 says the western is before the horror film:

```
1  S/R      R/S
      ——        ——

2  W        M/H R̸
     ——         ——

3      H/M       S̸
          ——
```

A is **CORRECT.** The western must start at 7 o'clock.

B-E all could be true, but don't have to be. R/S and H/M are interchangeable for this question.

Game 4 - Lectures on Birds
Questions 19-23

Setup

This is a linear game, with each lecture assigned to one hall.

It's best to keep your diagrams as simple as possible, so I draw the lectures above the slots, and the halls underneath the slots. I'll demonstrate by drawing the main diagram with the first and second rules:

Notice that I haven't included numbers. If you make diagrams without numbers, you'll very quickly learn to see which slot is which. You'll also be able to draw diagrams much faster, with less space.

I usually include numbers in my diagrams for explanatory purposes, but with only five slots it's better to show you how I would *actually* draw this.

There's not much we can do with the third rule. It says that three of the lectures are in Gladwyn hall. It's best just to memorize rules like this, though it's not a bad idea to include a note in your list of rules, like so:

3 G

The most important thing you must realize about the first rule is that if there are three Gs, then there are only two Hs.

This comes up over and over, so I'll repeat it:
there are only two Hs.

The next two rules also can't be drawn on the diagram. The fourth rule says that S is in Howard Auditorium, and that S is before O:

$$\frac{\text{S}}{\text{H}} \ \underline{\quad} \ \frac{\text{O}}{}$$

Once again, this diagram includes as much detail as necessary, but no more.

The fifth rule is similar. T is before P, and P takes place in Gladwyn Hall:

$$\frac{\text{T}}{} \ \underline{\quad} \ \frac{\text{P}}{\text{G}}$$

That's it. As with most modern logic games, there's no way to combine these rules to draw deductions. The most important things on modern logic games are making a clear representation of the rules, and memorizing the rules.

Is it possible to make a couple of scenarios. We know that there are only two Hs, and S has to take place in H.

S is also in front of O. So either S can go fourth, or S can go in one of 2/3.

If S is fourth, we know that O is last:

$$\frac{}{\text{G}} \ \underline{\quad} \ \underline{\quad} \ \frac{\text{S}}{\text{H}} \ \frac{\text{O}}{}$$

If S is 2/3, then the placement of G and H is completely determined, because we've placed both Hs:

$$\frac{}{\text{G}} \ \frac{\text{S}}{\text{G}} \ \frac{}{\text{H}} \ \frac{}{\text{H}} \ \frac{\text{O}}{\text{G}}$$

O is floating to the right of S in the second diagram. This is a way of placing the fourth rule directly on the diagram: O is after S. That way it's harder to forget the rule.

The line above the second and third slots indicates that S could go second or third (you have to move H too).

There are no added deductions you can make by placing S 2nd or 3rd, so I represented both possibilities as one scenario. The two positions are interchangeable.

The scenarios on the previous page are very rough diagrams. They are useful because they let you see how limited the game is. S can only go second, third or fourth.

I find that when I make these diagrams in advance, I see things that I wouldn't have noticed otherwise. Many questions become very obvious, as I've realized the possibilities are quite limited.

I encourage you to sketch out a couple of scenarios before you start games. You may be surprised at the insights you gather. Try to split the scenarios based on an objective factor, such as "S is fourth, or S is 2/3". Don't just draw randomly.

I normally only draw scenarios when I can make a clear division between two exclusive possibilities. i.e. Things can only go one way, or another way.

Main Diagram

G   __   __   H   __

(1)   3 G

(2)   S / H   __   O

(3)   T   __   P / G

Two scenarios

S fourth

__   __   __   S/H   O
G   H

S second or third

         ⌒   O
         S
__   __   __   __   __
G   G   H   H   G

Question 19

For acceptable order questions, go through the rules and use them to eliminate answers one by one.

On this question, you must combine two rules to eliminate **D** and **C**. That's unusual, but the process is the same.

When I solved this, I eliminated all the answers I could get rid of with a single rule, then I examined the remaining answers in more detail to see if they violated a combination of rules.

Rule 5 eliminates **A** and **B**. Petrels must be lectured on earlier than Terns.

None of the other rules eliminate any answers on their own.

Rules 1 and 4 eliminate **D**. The first lecture is in Gladwyn Hall, and the Sandpipers lecture is in Howard Auditorium. So Sandpipers can't go first.

Rules 2 and 5 eliminates **C**. Petrels must go in Gladwyn Hall, and the fourth lecture must be in Howard Auditorium. This answer places P fourth.

E is **CORRECT.** It violates no rules.

Question 20

Open-ended "must be false" and "must be true" questions can be among the hardest logic games questions.

Sometimes you have a flash of insight and you can get the answer right away. Other times you have no choice but to try every answer, using trial and error.

I'm going to try to help you get that flash of insight. The key is to look at the answers and see what rules they relate to. Here the answers place G and H. Let's see what rules relate to G and H:

- There are three Gs. Therefore there are two Hs.
- A G is first
- An H is fourth.

The right answer will violate one of these rules. None of the answers violate the rules about putting G first or H fourth. So the right answer almost certainly violates the first rule: there are three Gs and two Hs.

Let's look at the answers that mention H, because H is the more restricted variable. One of the two Hs is already fourth, thanks to rule two. So only one of the other lectures can take place in H.

B puts H in second and third. We also know H is fourth. That's three Hs, which is too many, so **B** is **CORRECT.**

D places two Hs, but one of them is fourth. Since there was already an H fourth, this answer only requires two Hs total. So **D** is possible.

There's basically no way for **A, C** or **E** to violate a rule. Three lectures take place at G, so there's no way for an answer to place too many Gs.

I hope this helps you see that there's usually a *method* that you can apply to quickly solve "must be false" questions. The right answer was simply based on combining two rules: rule 2 and rule 3.

Question 21

When a question gives you a new rule, there is always a way to combine that rule with one of the existing rules. To do this effectively, you should have the regular rules memorized.

When you have all the rules in your head, it's *much* easier to combine them.

This question says that terns are lectured on in H. Here are the existing rules that relate to that:

- Sandpipers are lectured on in H (rule 4).
- Only two lectures are H (rule 3).
- One of the H lectures is fourth (rule 2).

Whew, there are quite a few involved in this question. Let's go through step by step.

There are two Hs. For this question, S and T are the lectures that take place in H.

Since one of the Hs is fourth, that means that one of S and T will be fourth. Whenever there are only two possibilities, you can split things up into two scenarios. Separate scenarios will let you get more deductions:

$$\frac{\quad}{G} \; \frac{\quad}{} \; \frac{\quad}{} \; \frac{S}{H} \; \frac{\quad}{}$$

$$\frac{\quad}{G} \; \frac{\quad}{} \; \frac{\quad}{} \; \frac{T}{H} \; \frac{\quad}{}$$

This may seem a lengthy process when I explain it. But it actually takes longer to explain than to draw. Success at logic games comes from experience. A skilled student of logic games can get the two scenarios above with 5-10 seconds of drawing and deductions.

Likewise, a skilled student will make all the deductions I'm about to walk you through, and they'll make them very quickly. If you move on without understanding this question intuitively, then you won't learn that skill. Keep practicing questions like this until they're second nature. Draw the diagrams on your own, too.

Ok, so we made two scenarios, with T and S fourth. Other rules mention those birds. T is before P, and S is before O. (rules 4 and 5)

$$\frac{\quad}{G} \; \frac{\quad}{} \; \frac{\quad}{} \; \frac{S}{H} \; \frac{O}{G}$$

$$\frac{\quad}{G} \; \frac{\quad}{} \; \frac{\quad}{} \; \frac{T}{H} \; \frac{P}{G}$$

In both cases, the fifth lecture takes place in Gladwyn Hall. This is because on this question, S and T are the lectures that take place in Howard Auditorium. (Also, rule 5 says that P takes place in Gladwyn Hall)

Ok, so now we have to place T in the first diagram, and S in the second. S and T both take place in H, so they can't go first. And they both have something after them, so they can't go third. Therefore they each go second:

$$\frac{\quad}{G} \; \frac{T}{H} \; \frac{P}{G} \; \frac{S}{H} \; \frac{O}{G}$$

$$\frac{\quad}{G} \; \frac{S}{H} \; \frac{O}{G} \; \frac{T}{H} \; \frac{P}{G}$$

The next step would be placing R first in both diagrams. I left that off to make the previous step easier to follow.

A is **CORRECT.** In the second diagram, O is third and is in Gladwyn Hall.

These dual scenario deductions are a very common pattern for some "could be true" and "must be true" questions. The question can be split into two scenarios. When you fill them both out, you'll then see what can be true in both diagrams, and what must be true in both.

As I said, you can get quite fast at this with practice. The alternative is trial and error. That can be a perfectly acceptable method. You can get lucky, try A, and see that it's the right answer. But the problem with trial and error is that you don't usually know where to start, and you may have to try every answer.

Question 22

The diagrams from question 21 let us solve this question. **A is CORRECT.** O can be fifth, and in Gladwyn Hall.

Here's the diagram that proves it:

$$\frac{R}{G} \quad \frac{T}{H} \quad \frac{P}{G} \quad \frac{S}{H} \quad \frac{O}{G}$$

You can also eliminate some answers using the rules.

B is wrong because rule four says that petrels are lectured on in Gladwyn Hall.

D is wrong because rule four says that sandpipers go before oystercatchers. So sandpipers can't go fifth.

E is wrong because rule five says that terns are before petrels. So terns can't go fifth.

C is slightly trickier to eliminate. If rails are fifth and in Howard Auditorium, then we know the placement of both Hs:

$$\frac{}{G} \quad \frac{}{G} \quad \frac{}{G} \quad \frac{}{H} \quad \frac{R}{H}$$

Rule four says that sandpipers have to be in Howard Auditorium. But rule four *also* says that sandpipers must be before oystercatchers.

That's not possible on this diagram. The only H where we can put sandpipers is in slot 4, and that leave no room to place sandpipers ahead of oystercatchers.

Question 23

This question places sandpipers third. Let's do that and see what happens. Remember, rule 4 says that sandpipers are in Howard Auditorium:

$$\frac{}{G} \quad \frac{}{} \quad \frac{S}{H} \quad \frac{}{H} \quad \frac{O}{}$$

I also placed O to the right of S, as a reminder that rule 4 says that O comes after S.

So far, there are two Hs and one G on the diagram. Rule 3 says that there are three Gs, so we have to make the other two slots G:

$$\frac{}{G} \quad \frac{}{G} \quad \frac{S}{H} \quad \frac{}{H} \quad \frac{O}{G}$$

This diagram easily eliminates **A-C.**

A is wrong because O has to be after S. So O can't go second.

B and **C** are wrong because in this diagram the Hs are third and fourth, not second or fifth.

This diagram proves that **D** is possible:

$$\frac{R}{G} \quad \frac{T}{G} \quad \frac{S}{H} \quad \frac{O}{H} \quad \frac{P}{G}$$

D is **CORRECT.**

That diagram should also make clear why **E** is wrong. Rule five says that P is after T. So if T is fourth, then P has to go fifth.

But we also know that O has to go fourth or fifth, because rule four says that O is after S. So If we placed T fourth, then T, P and O would have to go in fourth and fifth. There's no space for that.

253

Section IV - Logical Reasoning

Question 1

QUESTION TYPE: Strengthen

CONCLUSION: We can't be certain enough to justify punishing the auto repair shop.

REASONING: There is some evidence that the auto shop is responsible for the pollution. But the penalty is very severe.

ANALYSIS: We're trying to judge whether the auto shop is responsible: should we convict them, or not? The argument says that stronger evidence is needed, because the penalty is harsh.

We need a principle that says this is correct. So the right answer will say that we *should* require strong evidence in order to impose harsh punishments. Principle questions are about what 'should' happen.

Answers B, C and E are about how to set a penalty for a crime. That's irrelevant. The penalty for this crime is already set.

A note on logical errors: did you *feel* that the auto shop was at fault? There's very little proof. 'Some' evidence 'suggests' the auto body shop is guilty. If you instantly decided the auto body shop was guilty, then that's a mental error you need to eliminate.

––––––––––––––

A. **CORRECT.** This matches what the stimulus said. The penalty is severe, so this answer tells us that we *should* wait for stronger evidence.
B. This tells us how severely you ought to punish crimes. But the stimulus was about whether we could conclude that the auto shop was guilty.
C. Same as B. This is about how to *set* the penalty for a crime. But we are trying to decide whether the auto shop is guilty. The penalty is already set.
D. No one has confessed. This is irrelevant. Admission of guilt is just a factor that *might* let us avoiding debating whether we have enough evidence to convict the auto body shop.
E. This tells you how to set a penalty. It doesn't tell you how to know whether someone is guilty.

Question 2

QUESTION TYPE: Most Strongly Supported

FACTS: Lots of nursing home residents suffer from depression. A study found that those who bond with pets are less likely to have depression.

ANALYSIS: We know *one* thing. Pets helped reduce depression.

That doesn't mean pets are the best method. Nor does it mean that pets will completely solve the problem. Likewise, we can't conclude that pets are essential to solving the problem.

We just know that pets help. They're solving a problem. Presumably, the people in nursing homes lack personal bonds, and pets help make up for that.

––––––––––––––

A. Careful. Maybe depression is a serious problem for everyone, not just nursing home residents. The question didn't compare nursing home residents to any other groups.
B. This goes too far. The question only told us that pets *help*. The question didn't compare pets to any other methods: maybe human companionship is even more effective.
C. **CORRECT.** This is fairly well supported. If you form a personal bond with a pet, then you have a new companion. The fact that pets reduce depression show that nursing home residents may be lacking companionship.
D. This goes too far. There might be people who are happy without animal companions. For instance, maybe people with many human companions don't need pets in order to be happy.
E. This goes too far. We know that pets *helped*. That doesn't mean they can eliminate the problem entirely.

LSAT 70 - SECTION IV, LR

Question 3

QUESTION TYPE: Flawed Reasoning

CONCLUSION: Only funny ads work well.

REASONING: Funny ads hold people's attention. Ads only work if they hold your attention.

ANALYSIS: Funny ads are *sufficient* to hold your attention. But other ads could also hold your attention – the stimulus didn't show that funniness is *necessary*.

You can diagram this if you'd like. There are two conditional statements that don't link up:

Funny → holds attention
Effective → holds attention

A. **CORRECT.** Maybe emotional ads can also hold people's attention. Then funny ads wouldn't be the only kind that could be effective.
B. The argument doesn't do this. The second sentence says that funny ads attract *and* hold your attention.
C. I found this very tempting. The argument implies that funny ads are effective, when all we know is that funny ads meet a *necessary* condition for effectiveness.

   So why isn't this right? It's because the main point of the conclusion is that funny ads are the *only* effective ads i.e. that no other ads can be effective. So A is the best answer. Though there is a case to be made that this answer is also right and that the question is flawed.
D. The stimulus uses "effective" the same way each time. To pick this type of answer, you have to say what the two different definitions of effective are.
E. The stimulus didn't even talk about the purpose of an advertisement. An answer can't be the flaw if it didn't happen.

Question 4

QUESTION TYPE: Strengthen

CONCLUSION: We shouldn't be concerned by stories about people getting sick after vaccination.

REASONING: Millions of people get vaccinated every year. We can expect that some will get sick afterwards by coincidence.

ANALYSIS: The doctor has shown that the illnesses *could* be caused by coincidence. To strengthen his argument, we should show evidence that helps prove that the illnesses *are* due only to coincidence.

The right answer does this by showing that there is no increased risk of illness following vaccination. That's pretty convincing.

A. This may weaken the argument. If illness only follows new vaccines, then maybe the vaccines weren't properly tested and they *do* cause illness.
B. This tells us whether or not to vaccinate people. It doesn't show whether vaccines are safe.
C. **CORRECT.** Suppose this wasn't true. Imagine 50 people a day get sick on average, but 600 people get sick the day after being vaccinated. That would imply that vaccines do increase risk. This answer eliminates that scenario – 50 people a day get sick the day before vaccinations, and 50 the day after. There's no obvious increased risk.
D. This doesn't tell us whether or not the vaccines *caused* the health problems.
E. If anything, this answer shows that vaccines can be dangerous. They make at least a few people sick. We're trying to prove that vaccines *don't* make people sick!

Question 5

QUESTION TYPE: Agreement

ARGUMENTS: Sharita says that there are a lot of stray cats, because people don't neuter their cats. She thinks that people *should* neuter their cats.

Chad says that stray cats cause disease, and that people shouldn't feed them.

ANALYSIS: Both Sharita and Chad agree that stray cats are a problem. Both of them would like fewer stray cats. Sharita would achieve this goal by having people neuter their pets. Chad would reduce the number of stray cats by having people not feed them.

All four wrong answers mentions thing that Sharita doesn't talk about. So we can't know whether Sharita would agree.

Notice that this is an *agreement* question. On past LSATs, most questions with two speakers were *disagreement* questions. Now the LSAC is including both agreement questions and disagreement questions fairly regularly – make sure to read the question stems carefully. I got a question wrong once because I chose a "disagree" answer on an agreement question.

_____

A. Sharita doesn't mention feeding stray cats.
B. **CORRECT.** Sharita strongly implies this – otherwise why would she recommend neutering? Neutering reduces the number of cats.

Chad lists the ways that stray cats cause problems, and he recommends not feeding them. So presumably he agrees that there are too many.

There is some small amount of doubt whether they agree – Sharita isn't explicit in saying that there ought to be fewer strays. But this is just a 'most supports' question, so doubt is allowed.
C. Sharita doesn't mention whether stray cats pose a risk to anyone.
D. Sharita doesn't mention disease.
E. Sharita doesn't mention feeding stray cats.

Question 6

QUESTION TYPE: Necessary Assumption

CONCLUSION: Most people that embezzle or commit bribery will be caught.

REASONING: The more times you commit a crime, the more likely you are to be caught.

ANALYSIS: The first two sentences are just filler. The key here is that the more times you embezzle, the more likely you are to be caught.

There's a problem though. The argument doesn't say whether embezzlers will continue embezzling. Just because someone is confident doesn't mean that they will keep committing crimes. The conclusion is that most embezzlers will be caught, but maybe most people embezzle once and then drop it.

Note: this is a rare case where a "most" answer is correct on a necessary assumption question. Negating "most" moves from 51% to 50%, which isn't normally logically significant. But the conclusion of this argument was about "most" embezzlers.

_____

A. **CORRECT.** If most people don't embezzle repeatedly, then the detective's evidence doesn't support his argument. It's still possible that most embezzlers would be caught (say, on the first try). But they would not be caught because of the reasoning in the detective's argument. That's why this is necessary to the argument.
Negation: Half or less of those who embezzle do so repeatedly.
B. Confidence was just a sideshow to the argument. The main point is that the odds of being caught go up as the criminal commits more crimes.
C. The conclusion is simply that most embezzlers will be caught. Other crimes don't matter – who care if it's even easier to catch car thieves?
D. This doesn't *have* to be true. Maybe even careful repeat offenders have patterns that make it easy to catch them if they embezzle often enough.
E. The conclusion is that most embezzlers would be caught. So the argument would be *stronger* if some embezzlers were caught the first time!

Question 7

QUESTION TYPE: Paradox

PARADOX: When grain prices rise, grain fed beef gets expensive much faster than bread does.

ANALYSIS: The first step on paradox questions is to figure out why the situation is confusing. It's odd that beef gets expensive so much *faster* than bread does. Bread is mostly made of grain, so we would expect it to get expensive faster.

Note that this question shows how you're allowed to use outside knowledge to make warranted assumptions. Everyone knows that bread is made from grains – the question doesn't need to say this explicitly.

So in fact you *must* use outside knowledge to answer this question. It's a warranted assumption to say that bread is made from grains. What you're *not* allowed to do with outside knowledge is use it to contradict the argument, or add a fact that many people would disagree with.

A. Duh. Every employer tries to reduce labor costs. Unlike the correct answer, this answer doesn't say whether labor costs are *actually* low. Employers could fail to reduce costs, despite their best efforts.
B. Everyone knows that beef is expensive and bread is cheap. The point of the stimulus was that the *change* in the price of meat was very large compared to the change in the price of bread.
C. **CORRECT.** This shows that grain prices have only a small impact on bread prices, whereas grain prices greatly affect the price of cattle feed and hence the price of cattle.
D. This explains why beef got more expensive. It doesn't explain why beef got expensive so much faster than bread.
E. So what? This just tells us a couple of interesting facts about bread and meat purchasing. We have no idea how these facts influence *prices*.

Question 8

QUESTION TYPE: Method of Reasoning

CONCLUSION: Kathy says that the two drugs probably have different side effects.

REASONING: Kathy says that the two drugs are chemically different, even though the drugs achieve their effects through the same physiological mechanisms.

ANALYSIS: Kathy doesn't disagree with Mark's facts. Instead, she points out a relevant fact that Mark ignored, and uses this to disagree with Mark's conclusion.

A. Kathy didn't mention any drug's safety record. This answer simply didn't happen.
B. This answer describes an argument by analogy, where you talk about *something else* in order to prove a point. But Kathy made no analogy – she just talked about the drugs themselves.
C. Kathy didn't mention any studies. How could this possibly be the right answer?
D. *Which* fundamental principles of medicine? Kathy didn't mention any.
E. **CORRECT.** Here we go. Mark made an analogy between Zokaz and Qualzan in order to prove that Qualzan is risky. Kathy points out that Zokaz and Qualzan are chemically different. This breaks the analogy.

Question 9

QUESTION TYPE: Flawed Reasoning

CONCLUSION: We are an environmentally responsible company.

REASONING: We pollute less than we used to, and there are no methods we could use that produce zero pollution. Environmentally responsible organizations pollute the least they can.

ANALYSIS: I'll illustrate this with numbers. Suppose 100 is the most pollution you can produce, and 0 is the least. I'll make an example that fits the CEO's facts, yet shows that his company is a horrible polluter.

The CEO says that he pollutes less than he used to, and there are no methods that let him pollute at zero. So maybe the CEO's company used to pollute at 95, and now they pollute at 93. Whoop-de-do.

An environmentally responsible organization will pollute the least that it can. If there is a method that would let the CEO's company pollute at 20, then they're not being responsible, even though they're better than they used to be.

A. The CEO didn't say this. He said that *currently* there are no zero pollution methods. So maybe the company is doing all that it can at present, even if better methods will be available later.
B. Huh? This is a completely different error. It's like saying "ice cream makes you fat, so donuts don't". The CEO didn't make this error.
C. This is a different error. It's like saying "No, I wasn't rude in the restaurant. Therefore, I am never rude". The CEO is only talking about a specific criticism: whether or not the company is environmentally responsible.
D. The final sentence didn't say that the company *attempted* to reduce pollution. The CEO says that the company *did* reduce pollution.
E. **CORRECT.** See my analysis above. It's true that the company can't produce zero pollution, but maybe they can still try harder to produce *less* pollution than they currently do. If so, they're not being responsible.

Question 10

QUESTION TYPE: Necessary Assumption

CONCLUSION: Suppression of the immune system can cause or worsen gum disease.

REASONING: You're more likely to have gum disease if you refuse to think about problems. Stress affects the immune system.

ANALYSIS: This question makes several big leaps. First of all, the first sentence doesn't talk about stress. So it's not clear that solving problems directly will reduce stress.

Secondly, the argument has, at best, established a correlation between stress/immune suppression and gum disease. It's possible that there's some other reason that those who solve problems quickly get less gum disease.

A. This is totally off base. The argument didn't even mention whether gum disease is painful.
B. **CORRECT.** If refusing to think about problems *doesn't* cause stress, then there's no link between stress and gum disease.
   Negation: Refusing to think about problems doesn't cause stress.
C. Actually, the argument implied that people who address problems quickly and directly *don't* feel stress.
   If you want to get technical, I suppose you can have a stressful life without succumbing to stress, but that's irrelevant. The argument was talking about the stress that people feel.
D. This shows an alternate reason that people who address problems get less gum disease. This *weakens* the argument if it's true.
E. It doesn't matter *why* people avoid addressing problems. It only matters that they suffer stress because they avoid problems.

Question 11

QUESTION TYPE: Flawed Reasoning

CONCLUSION: The fruits tested stay fresh better in cooler temperatures.

REASONING: The class tested three temperatures. The coolest temperature worked best.

ANALYSIS: The class tested a very limited range of temperatures. They forget that temperatures can be *much* colder than 10 degrees.

Their conclusion is that colder is always better. That's absurd – it would mean that fruits stay fresh the longest at absolute zero.

Maybe 10 degrees is the *ideal* temperature. Warmer is worse, but so is colder.

A. The conclusion was only about the fruits tested, not all fruit. If you chose this, you need to be more precise about what conclusions say.
B. The argument didn't say that coolness is the only factor that mattered. The conclusion said that cooler temperature leads to longer-lasting freshness. That kind of language *doesn't* mean that all other factors are irrelevant.
If I say "The more you study, the higher you'll score on the LSAT", it's implied that I mean "....other things equal". Obviously you'll perform worse if you don't sleep the night before the test in order to study eight extra hours.
C. CORRECT. The class only proved that, of the three temperatures, colder was better. But it's possible that very cold temperatures would be worse. The class didn't test -50 degrees.
D. The stimulus didn't mention a thermometer. And we know from outside experience that thermometers are generally reliable enough to indicate that 10 degrees is cooler than 20 degrees. We can assume that *if* the class used a thermometer, then the thermometer fine, unless we're given evidence to the contrary.
E. If I say "coolness helps preserve fruit" then that fact is my conclusion. I don't need to explain it. An explanation of why it's true could require 500 pages of plant biology.

Question 12

QUESTION TYPE: Weaken

CONCLUSION: We won't face a plague of water shortages in the near future.

REASONING: We only use a small portion of our fresh water.

ANALYSIS: Water isn't distributed evenly. Some areas are already short on water. With more population growth, they'll face more shortages. It's not that easy to share water. You can export it in bulk, but you can't make it rain in other countries.

"Plagued by" means that part of humankind faces water shortages. e.g. people say "humanity is plagued by AIDS", even though only a small portion of the global population has AIDS.

A. The conclusion says that we'll have shortages "*unless* population growth trends change". So this possibility of error is already accounted for.
B. CORRECT. This points out the possibility that we could have water shortages in some regions even if most regions have more than enough water. This new difficulty weakens the argument. You might have avoided this answer because you thought all of humanity had to face water shortages. But people say "humanity is plagued by war/AIDS/hunger" even though only portions of humanity actually face those problems.
To plague (v.) cause continual trouble or distress
C. So what? Apparently we're only using a small portion of our water, so water conservation doesn't seem like it needs to be a priority. If you thought "some regions don't have water and thus need to conserve"....well, answer B is the answer that address that concern. Answer C doesn't address differences between regions.
D. The key word in this answer is *eventually*. The argument only disagrees with the prediction that we'll face shortages in the *near future*.
E. So? The key fact in the stimulus is that we're using only a small portion of our water. This answer doesn't tell us that we'll run out of water even with massively increased agricultural usage.

Question 13

QUESTION TYPE: Paradox

PARADOX: The industrial revolution increased productivity by centralizing decision making. But recently, a bunch of already productive companies have increased their productivity by decreasing centralization.

ANALYSIS: The paradox is that centralization seems to both help and hurt productivity. We need to explain why certain companies improved productivity by decentralizing.

The industrial revolution was 200 years ago. It's possible that we've begun to reach the limits of centralization.

A. This is just a fact about most companies. This doesn't explain how some other companies managed to improve their productivity through decentralization.

B. Great – those employees must be happy! But this doesn't *explain* why decentralization worked.

C. Robots don't explain decentralization. Maybe robots require central control.

D. The stimulus was very specific. It talked about already productive companies i.e. those that *had* already learned the lessons of the industrial revolution and centralized. We need to explain why some of *those* companies improved productivity by decentralizing.
In other words, who cares about the companies mentioned in this answer choice? They're not the companies that we're talking about.

E. **CORRECT.** This explains it. The companies in question are already productive. This answer says that those productive companies can *only* become even more productive if they decentralize a bit and give employees influence.

Question 14

QUESTION TYPE: Must Be True

FACTS:

1. Epic poetry's main function is to transmit values.
2. Epic poems do this by presenting heroes as role models.
3. People get meaning in their lives from imitating these role models.

ANALYSIS: The most important thing on must be true questions is to have a clear idea of the facts. Usually the right answer will combine two or more of them.

A. The stimulus was about *epic* poetry. This answer is about all poetry. Maybe epic poetry is an unimportant part of poetry in general.

B. **CORRECT.** This combines facts 1 and 2.

C. Careful. The *transmission* of values is not done by explicit discussion, but that doesn't mean values aren't set forth explicitly. e.g. "The hero was brave, strong and noble". In my example, I didn't discuss the hero's values, but they are set forth explicitly, for you to mimic. Be brave.

D. This sounds good, but the problem is "many groups of people". The stimulus doesn't say whether many groups of people are exposed to epic poetry any more.

E. This confuses sufficient for necessary. Yes, all epic poetry presents heroes as role models. But plenty of other things present heroes as role models too....Disney movies for instance.

Question 15

QUESTION TYPE: Principle – Strengthen

CONCLUSION: The proposal is morally right.

REASONING: There's a proposal to confiscate burglars' wages. The money would go to a fund for burglary victims.

ANALYSIS: Principle – Strengthen questions are similar to sufficient assumption questions. The reasoning will be a bunch of facts about an idea. The conclusion will be that the idea is morally good.

Just look for an answer that says that one or more of the facts from the reasoning helps prove that something is morally good.

———————————

A. This tells you what to do *if* you steal money from a burglar or receive money stolen from a burglar. This answer doesn't tell you *whether* you should steal from a burglar.
Also, the money in the argument will go to a general fund for victims of burglary. So money taken from a burglar won't necessarily go to his specific victims.

B. This answer only places an obligation on burglars. That doesn't mean the Government has the right to force burglars to meet their obligations.

C. CORRECT. The government program has a good motive. This answer shows that the motive is relevant.
To be clear, this isn't a sufficient assumption, it just strengthens the argument.

D. This sounds good, but it just gives us a *necessary* condition for justifying stealing. Necessary conditions *never* help prove a point.
Suppose you're wondering if you can drive from NYC to LA, and you've got a map. If I say "you'll *only* get there if you have a map", have I helped you arrive? No! In fact, I've restricted you. Now, if you lose your map, you're lost. Before I added the condition, the map was just a nice bonus.

E. This contradicts the argument. We're trying to say that stealing from burglars *is* justified.

Question 16

QUESTION TYPE: Identify The Conclusion

CONCLUSION: It's false to think that unrelieved heartburn will probably cause esophageal cancer.

REASONING: Only those with Barrett's esophagus have a higher risk of cancer due to heartburn. Only 5% of those who get heartburn have Barrett's esophagus.

ANALYSIS: Any time an author gives their opinion about the truth, it's almost certainly the conclusion.

So when the author says "this is simply false" it means that their conclusion is that they disagree with the first sentence.

This is a good argument, by the way. You might have thought that the author admitted that heartburn can cause cancer. The author *did* admit this. But their conclusion is that heartburn isn't *likely* to cause cancer. "Likely" means "51% of the time or more" – it's a synonym for most. So 5% of the time isn't enough to make cancer risk "likely".

———————————

A. This is evidence that supports the conclusion that cancer risk isn't likely.

B. This is evidence that supports the idea that those with Barrett's esophagus *do* have an increased risk of cancer.

C. CORRECT. The first sentence made the claim that heartburn is likely to cause cancer. The second sentence shows that the author disagrees. When the author presents a claim and disagrees with it, that will be their conclusion.

D. This is just a fact that allows the author to make his argument. If advertisements weren't making this claim, the author would have nothing to talk about. But the conclusion is that the author *disagrees* with these commercials.

E. This isn't even true, necessarily. It's possible that TV advertisements are so targeted that the ads are mostly seen by those with Barrett's esophagus. So the ads would be relevant to the viewers. This targeting would be possible with ads on Hulu for example – your web browser knows a *lot* about you.

Question 17

QUESTION TYPE: Parallel Reasoning

CONCLUSION: At least some halogen lamps are well crafted.

REASONING: Anything on display at Furniture Labyrinth is well crafted. Some halogen lamps are on display at Furniture labyrinth.

- Labyrinth display → Well Crafted
- Labyrinth display SOME halogen lamps

ANALYSIS: This is a good argument. It gives one conditional statement, and then a "some" statement which connects with the sufficient condition of the conditional.

Anytime a "some" statement connects with a sufficient condition, you can make a new some statement. Here's an example:

Cat → Tail
Cat SOME Brown
Conclusion: Brown SOME Tail (i.e. some brown things have tails)

A. This answer has a *chance* of storms. In the stimulus we *knew* that lamps were displayed.
B. **CORRECT.** This is a good argument. It matches the structure of the stimulus exactly.

Written by Melissa → Disturbing
Written by Melissa SOME sonnets
Conclusion: Sonnets SOME Disturbing.
C. This is a bad argument. Gianna *can* get her car worked on, but that doesn't mean that she *will*. Also, car shops are *capable* of good work, but that doesn't mean Gianna will inevitably receive good work.
D. Maybe the lakes teem with healthy *trout,* but all the minnows are unhealthy. To be correct, this answer would have had to say that *all* fish in the nearby lakes are healthy.
E. This is a good argument, but it doesn't match the structure. The stimulus concluded that at least *some* lamps were well crafted. This answer concludes that *all* the cornmeal is healthful.

Question 18

QUESTION TYPE: Most Strongly Supported

FACTS:

1. Managers usually don't benefit from flexibility.
2. This might be because most managers already have flexibility.
3. Normal workers benefit from flexibility. They are happier and more productive.
4. The benefits diminish over time, and it's possible to make schedules too flexible.

ANALYSIS: It's hard to prephrase "most strongly supported" questions. The best approach is to get a clear idea of the facts, then look at each answer quickly in order to eliminate a few.

When you're down to 1-2 answers, check them against the stimulus to be sure they're supported by a combination of facts.

A. This is very tempting. Regular workers benefit, so shouldn't we expect managers to benefit from flexible schedules, if they didn't already have them? Maybe. But managers are different from workers. Maybe there's a *reason* these managers don't have flexible schedules – their jobs might require them to be at work during certain hours.

So we can't be sure that managers without flexibility would benefit the same way that regular workers do. E is a better answer.
B. This *contradicts* the argument. It's a warranted assumption that most workers are not managers, so we *can* expect flexibility to improve the overall morale of the workforce.
C. Hard to say. Fact 3 doesn't say how much productivity improves. And fact 4 says that the improvement is worse over the long run.
D. If you picked this, you probably misread fact 2. Managers already have flexibility. *That's* why further flexibility doesn't help them. But managers may benefit from the flexibility they already have.
E. **CORRECT.** If we assume that the typical worker is not a manager (a reasonable assumption), then managers are not a good indicator of how the typical worker will benefit from flexibility.

Question 19

QUESTION TYPE: Weaken

CONCLUSION: The respondents may have been biased in favor of Lopez.

REASONING: Most people who watched the debate said that Lopez argued better. Lopez eventually won.

ANALYSIS: First, you must understand what the argument is saying. Suppose that Lopez won the election with 60% of the votes.

In that case, it's likely that most debate viewers already liked Lopez. If 60% of people watching the debate liked Lopez, then it's hardly surprising if most people said that he won.

And that's the basis of the right answer. If we know instead that most of the audience did *not* support Lopez, then that means he must have convinced some people during the debate.

A. The question is talking about those who *did* watch the debate. We need to know how many of them supported Lopez. It's possible very few people watched the debate, maybe only 20%. That would mean that most supported of both candidates didn't watch. This answer tells us nothing.
B. This just adds confusion. If most members of the live audience liked Tanner, why did Lopez do better on television? This has no clear impact on the argument.
C. This is very, very tempting. But let's play with the numbers. Let's say only 15% of people voted for Tanner, and 20% of those watching the debate voted for Tanner. That means that those who watched the debate were more likely than the general public to vote for Tanner. Yet most of the audience would vote for Lopez.
D. **CORRECT.** This shows that a majority of the audience was against Lopez, pre-debate. But after the debate, most said that Lopez won. That's evidence that Lopez was a good debater.
E. So what? Suppose Lopez won with 51% of votes, and 51% of those who saw the debate supported Lopez. That's still a bias in favor of Lopez.

Question 20

QUESTION TYPE: Necessary Assumption

CONCLUSION: The data can't explain the origin of the prohibitions.

REASONING: Data show that certain food prohibitions were useful. But ancient peoples who made the prohibitions didn't have access to that data.

ANALYSIS: This is a tricky flaw. I'll illustrate with an example. Let's say you're with a group of people, and you come across two doors, A and B.

Some people from your group go through each door, and return. They can't remember what happened. But the people who went through door A came back with good food, fine clothing and bountiful treasure. The people who went through door B came back moaning in pain, and died shortly thereafter.

You don't know what happened beyond the doors, but wouldn't you choose to go through door A instead of door B?

Now suppose that scientists later studied the doors. They found that through door A there was a generous wizard, and that through door B there was an evil sorcerer. Obviously, the group's decision to go through door A *can* be explained in terms of this data, even though at the time the group only had access to the effects of the wizards, and not the full data.

In other words, you can repeat a good decision without knowing why it works. The original peoples might have seen that a food was causing harm. They wouldn't know why – only future data could explain the harm. But the people nonetheless banned the harmful food, and thus the later data can explain the decision.

I've made this explanation longer because I wanted to give you a full explanation of the situation. It's one of the most subtle that I've seen.

(Answers on next page)

A. CORRECT. The negation of this answer says that we don't need to worry about what the people originally knew. It completely wrecks the argument – maybe we *can* explain the prohibitions in terms of our data, even if the original people didn't have access to the data.
Negation: The origins of a food prohibition don't need to be explained with reference to the understanding that the people who adopted the prohibition had.

B. The stimulus didn't say whether any of the food prohibitions were contradictory. This is totally irrelevant.

C. Negate this and you get: there's a correlation between the social usefulness of a food prohibition and the nutritional value of that food. That has no impact on the argument. The argument didn't talk about how nutritional food was.

D. "Often" is a synonym for most. So the negation of this answer is "half or less of the time, the origins of a food prohibition are forgotten within a few generations". The change from "most" to "half" has no effect on the argument. "Most" statements tend to be useless for necessary assumption questions.
This isn't relevant in any case. The argument is about *what* the original reasons were, not *how long* they were remembered.

E. The negation is "the originators of the prohibitions generally *didn't* have a non-technical understanding of the medical impacts of the prohibitions ".
This negated version *helps* the argument, by showing that the medical function can't help explain the origins.

Question 21

QUESTION TYPE: Must Be True

FACTS:

1. Published book → literary agent submission OR manuscript request
2. Serious attention → Renowned figure OR Requested manuscript after review of proposal

Note: The first sentence has a most statement. I didn't draw it, because it doesn't link up with anything. Meanwhile, I combined the two facts in the first sentence into fact 1 above.

ANALYSIS: Imagine this as a real world situation. How does a book get published? The publisher gets interested somehow and gets a manuscript. If they like it, they publish it. So, the first step is the manuscript. The second step is publication:

1. Manuscript: Renowned, or requested
2. Published: Literary agent, or requested

So requests are an important part of the system. You can only sidestep a request by being renowned, and then by having your literary agent submit.

A. Hard to say. Maybe most unrequested manuscripts come from renowned figures.

B. The first sentence talks about publishing. We're not told if most books are fiction. The renowned author reference is just there to confuse you: renowned authors were mentioned in the *second* sentence, and not in reference to publishing.

C. The second sentence describes when a book will get careful attention. That sentence never mentions whether fiction is an important factor.

D. Literary agents are only mentioned in the *first* sentence, in reference to publishing. The stimulus doesn't say whether literary agents are a major factor in attracting careful attention. If the publishing house requested a manuscript from a writer then the publishing house might give it very serious attention even without an agent.

E. CORRECT. A manuscript needs serious consideration to be published. If the manuscript was unrequested, the the author needs renown to get attention.

Question 22

QUESTION TYPE: Sufficient Assumption

CONCLUSION: Most of the drinking water will become polluted.

REASONING:

1. No budget for inspectors → Federal standards not met in most dairies
2. We don't have a budget for inspectors

ANALYSIS: The evidence lets us prove that most large dairies won't meet federal standards. But that doesn't prove that water will become polluted. We need to connect the evidence to the conclusion.

As with all sufficient assumption questions, just look at what you already know, and look where you want to go. Then add a new statement that connects what you know to where you need to go:

No budget → standards not met → water polluted

_____

A. We're trying to conclude that the water *will* become polluted. This answer shows us a way that water *won't* become polluted.
Note that this statement can't tell us what would happen if dairies *don't* meet standards: negating the sufficient never tells you anything.
B. This is very tempting. But this answer only says that without inspectors we can't keep *all* drinking water clean. Maybe we can still keep 99.9% of it clean without more inspectors. The conclusion was that *most* water would be polluted.
C. This is close, but it gives us a *necessary* condition for water becoming polluted. Necessary conditions never prove that something will happen. We need a *sufficient* condition for water becoming polluted.
D. CORRECT. We already know that most large dairies won't meet federal standards, because we don't have the budget for new inspectors. This answer uses that information to let us prove that therefore most water will be polluted.
E. Close, but not quite. We know that inspectors won't be hired, and therefore *most* large dairies won't meet federal standards. But we don't know if *all* large dairies will fail to meet standards.

Question 23

QUESTION TYPE: Flawed Parallel Reasoning

CONCLUSION: The Vegetaste Burger will probably be very successful.

REASONING:

1. Successful product → Massive ad campaign
2. Vegetaste will have a massive ad campaign

ANALYSIS: The president gives us a single conditional statement, then tells us that Vegetaste meets the *necessary* condition of that statement.

(Technically it's not a conditional, because it says "almost all". But drawing it as a conditional simplifies the question).

A necessary condition never proves anything. It's as if I said that because something has a tail, it's a cat. So we need another argument with one conditional statement and the necessary condition as evidence. Then the argument should incorrectly conclude the sufficient condition.

_____

A. This is a silly argument. It's like saying "Barack Obama must be the president of some other country, because most people in America are not president". But this is a flaw of numbers, not the flaw made in the stimulus.
B. We can say that if you work at Coderight, you *probably* have ten years experience. Donna will probably meet this sufficient condition, but the argument concludes that she will *certainly* have the experience. So this is a bad argument. But it doesn't reverse sufficient and necessary.
C. This is actually a pretty good argument. If 95% of Acme's workers are factory workers, and 95% of them oppose the merger, then at least 90.25% of Acme's workers oppose the merger.
D. CORRECT. This mirrors the structure:
President → Ph.D
Robert has a Ph.D
We can't expect Robert to become president because he meets the necessary condition. Maybe Robert is a hobo with a Ph.D
E. This is a pretty good argument. Evidence from the past can let us make probabilistic predictions about the future.

Question 24

QUESTION TYPE: Role in Argument

CONCLUSION: Life may be able to begin under lots of difficult conditions.

REASONING: Earth is 4.6 billion years old. We found bacteria 3.5 billion years old. These bacteria had a long evolutionary history, indicating that they must have appeared during the harsh conditions following the Earth's formation.

ANALYSIS: The bacteria are 3.5 billion years old. But they had a long evolutionary history.

The question asks: why does the argument mention this fact? Well, it proves that the ancestors of the bacteria were very, very old. So old that they must have been around in the early day of Earth's history, when conditions were rough.

This lends support to the conclusion that life can arise under difficult conditions.

A. There *is* support for the claim that the bacteria had a long evolutionary history: they were complex. And this fact doesn't *illustrate* the conclusion (i.e. show an example of). Instead, this fact *supports* the conclusion.
B. There *is* support for the claim that the bacteria have a long history: they are complex.
C. **CORRECT.** The support for the claim is that the bacteria were complex. This is why we think they had a long evolutionary history. And this fact about history supports the claim that the bacteria evolved under difficult conditions. That in turn supports the conclusion that life all around the universe could evolve in difficult conditions.
D. Nope. There is some support provided to this claim. But the claim about evolution also supports another claim: life evolved under difficult conditions.
E. It's true that the claim about the bacteria's history supports a conclusion: the bacteria must have evolved during a difficult period. But this conclusion *does* support the main conclusion. The final sentence says "this suggests", referring to the previous sentence.

Question 25

QUESTION TYPE: Necessary Assumption

CONCLUSION: Astronomers thought that the stars were within a few million miles of the Earth.

REASONING: The astronomers thought that the stars moved around the Earth. If the stars were very far away, they would have to move very fast.

ANALYSIS: The flaw is *not* thinking that the stars revolve around the Earth. That's just context to set up the situation. You can reason correctly from false hypotheticals, i.e. "*If* unicorns exist, then....".

The conclusion is the second sentence ("They concluded"). The astronomers think the stars can't be far away, otherwise stars would move very fast. So what....why is it a problem for stars to move fast? The astronomers only *implied* that great speeds were a problem. If an argument implies something but doesn't state it, then that is an *assumption*.

You can use some outside knowledge on this question. Stars appear in the same position each night. Everyone agrees on this – it's why sailors could navigate by the stars. It's why astronomers thought stars would have to travel fast each night.

A. The astronomers were assuming that the stars *do* revolve around the Earth. This talks about what happens if they *don't*. It's as though you're planning for how to take the LSAT, and I make an argument about what happens if you *weren't* required to take the LSAT. Irrelevant.
B. Why would it matter if one star moved 0.00001 mph faster than another star?
C. If you negate this, you get "Earth remains motionless while the stars revolve around it". That doesn't contradict the astronomers.
D. **CORRECT.** The astronomers' *only* reason for saying the stars couldn't be far away was that the stars would move quickly if they were far away. **Negation:** Stars move at very great speeds.
E. If you negate this, you get "stars more than a million miles away could *not* reappear in the same position". This strengthens the argument: the stars have to be even closer. The astronomers were predicting a maximum, not a minimum.

Question 26

QUESTION TYPE: Method of Reasoning

CONCLUSION: People appreciate paintings for more than being exact replicas of scenes.

REASONING: If people only cared about replicating scenes, then photography would have completely eliminated paintings.

ANALYSIS: The first few lines are just context. I've summarized the reasoning above.

This is a good argument. We all know that a camera can replicate a scene more accurately and more quickly than a painter can.

Yet people still paint, and people still enjoy new paintings. So there must be some other things that people like about paintings.

A couple of the answers mention that the argument is a defense of people's taste. It isn't. The argument may perhaps defend abstract impressionism, but the argument isn't defending the fact that people like more than realism in paintings. That's just a fact that the argument wants to prove.

———————

A. The stimulus doesn't mention "what most people appreciate". This couldn't possibly be the right answer. Also, the conclusion is not about an abstract principle. The conclusion is about what people appreciate in paintings.

B. What aesthetic principle? The stimulus doesn't mention any. And the argument isn't *defending* people's tastes. It's merely describing them.

C. The stimulus is talking about the present, not about history. The stimulus uses a historical fact, but only to make a claim about what's true in the present.

D. CORRECT. The historical fact is that photography hasn't displaced painting. The claim is that people like paintings for more than their ability to reproduce scenes.

E. The argument doesn't say that people are *right* to like paintings for more than their realism. This argument is not a defense of people's tastes.

Preptest 71
Section I - Logical Reasoning

Question 1

QUESTION TYPE: Sufficient Assumption

CONCLUSION: The agency is unlikely to achieve its goal.

REASONING: The agency is selling the banks. The banking system will not be strengthened if the former owners buy them back.

ANALYSIS: Most of this argument is fluff. The argument starts after the word "but": the banking system will be weaker if the former owners buy their banks back. Pay attention to words like "but", they show the author's opinion and evidence.

So we know exactly one reason that the plan could fail: the former owners buy back the banks. You can put this into a conditional statement:

Buy Back → Fail

To prove that the plan will fail, we just need to show that the sufficient condition will happen.

_____

A. The stimulus doesn't mention whether all the banks must be sold. Maybe the plan can succeed even if some banks don't find buyers.
B. The stimulus doesn't say it's a problem for one owner to buy multiple banks. Maybe there are thousands of banks for sale. It surely wouldn't be a problem if one owner bought two small banks.
C. This answer aims to trap you because you assumed that the no one will buy banks unless the economy is stronger. The argument didn't mention the economy. We have no idea how the economy relates to the banking system.
D. The banks sold by the agency *failed*. The government had to buy take them over. The country's other banks *didn't* fail, so presumably they will be stronger. It's reasonable that the failed banks will be weaker for some time.
E. CORRECT. This shows there are two possibilities: either the banks won't sell, or the owners will buy them back. Either option means the plan failed.

Question 2

QUESTION TYPE: Method of Reasoning

CONCLUSION: Falling circulation and falling advertising are the real reasons newspapers are in trouble.

REASONING: The inflation adjusted price of newsprint is no higher than it was ten years ago.

ANALYSIS: The newspapers said newsprint prices are the cause of their troubles. The author destroys this argument by showing that newsprint is not more expensive than it used to be. The author proposes an alternate cause: falling circulation and advertising.

Note that this alternate cause is not well supported. The author hasn't proven these factors are hurting newspapers. But we only need to analyze the structure of the argument: the author disproves a claim, and proposes a rival claim.

Three wrong answers mention criticism of a practice or method. The argument doesn't mention or criticize any methods. An example of such criticism would be "The newspaper industry uses ink, but this is costly. They should use laser printers."

_____

A. What popular analogy? An analogy is a comparison between two similar situations. That doesn't happen here. If you chose this answer you should look at the Wikipedia article on analogies; the LSAT mentions them frequently.
B. It's true that this argument uses historical data. But not to raise doubts about the effectiveness of an approach. The argument uses historical data to disprove a point in an argument.
C. Similar to B. The argument doesn't mention any methods or criticize any methods.
D. CORRECT. The explanation is newsprint. The argument challenges this and introduces another explanation: advertising and circulation.
E. Same as B and C. The argument doesn't criticize any practices.

Question 3

QUESTION TYPE: Flawed Reasoning

CONCLUSION: Alcohol consumption does more good than harm.

REASONING: Moderate alcohol consumption has a few good effects.

ANALYSIS: There are two flaws with this argument.

1. The author uses evidence about "moderate" alcohol consumption, then makes a conclusion about all alcohol consumption. Watch for concept shifts.
2. The author gives evidence of alcohol's positive effects, and doesn't mention negative effects. The author then makes a conclusion about the *net* effects of alcohol. You always have to consider both benefit and harm.

This question shows that you have to be careful when you pre-phrase answers. The right answer uses the first flaw. If you only spotted the second flaw and fixated on it, you could easily miss the right answer on this otherwise easy question.

Whenever I form a pre-phrase, I am ready to abandon it if I don't see it in the answers.

A. The argument doesn't mention why people chose to drink alcohol. The argument is about alcohol's effects, not how people use it.
B. The argument doesn't mention popular belief. This answer is completely unsupported.
C. This isn't a flaw. I can truthfully say that "pens can be used to write". It doesn't matter that pencils can also be used to write, my first statement is still true. So alcohol can be beneficial even if other things are also beneficial.
D. **CORRECT.** The conclusion is about *all* alcohol consumption, including binge drinking. The evidence is only about moderate consumption.
E. Alcohol doesn't have to harm *all* bacteria. Alcohol would potentially be useful even if it killed only some types of harmful bacteria.

Question 4

QUESTION TYPE: Complete the Argument

CONCLUSION: Grodex Corporation should use the innovative new educational methods.

REASONING: Grodex Corporation generally requires creative workers. Childhood education shows that innovative methods produce creativity while traditional methods produce memorization.

ANALYSIS: You always have to watch for shifts in concepts. All of the educational evidence in the argument is about *children*. And you know from real life that children are different from adults.

The argument ends on "because". So we are not looking for a conclusion. We are looking for a reason for the conclusion.

To prove that the innovative methods will work for Grodex, we need to show that the methods that work with children will also work well with adults.

A. Nonsense. The argument doesn't even mention high school. If you chose this, you need to focus more directly on what's said in the stimulus.
B. The argument wasn't making a comparison of using educational seminars vs. not using them. Instead, the argument was about what *type* of educational seminars to use.
C. This tells us the seminars might not be effective. It doesn't tell us what type of seminar to use.
D. **CORRECT.** This shows that the evidence about children is also applicable to the adults who will take Grodex's seminars.
E. The argument doesn't say whether creativity and memorization are linked. It's not clear how this proposed linkage is relevant to adult educational seminars. If the two were linked, would that change Grodex's actions?

Question 5

QUESTION TYPE: Identify The Conclusion

CONCLUSION: Colonizing other planets would only be a temporary solution to overcrowding.

REASONING: Earth will be too crowded if our population keeps growing at a geometric rate. Even if we send half the population to Mars, population growth will soon leave Earth just as crowded.

ANALYSIS: LSAT authors usually use the phrase "some say" to indicate an opinion they will disagree with. This argument does that in the second sentence. Then this author says "however" in the third sentence to indicate that they do disagree with the opinion in the second sentence. That's the conclusion.

Note that the author's conclusion is about what would be true *IF* the population keeps growing geometrically. The author doesn't say that the population *WILL* keep growing geometrically. This is an important distinction on the LSAT, and it eliminates two answers.

———————

A. This first sentence is not the conclusion. It is just a fact that supports the conclusion and adds context to the argument. .
B. The author didn't say population *will* continue to grow geometrically. She just said what would happen *if* population grew geometrically.
C. This is just a fact that supports the author's point. Since this is true, then it's likely that in a few centuries we will have one person per square foot *if* population grows geometrically.
D. Same as B. The author didn't say that population *will* grow geometrically.
E. **CORRECT.** The word "however" in the third sentence indicates that the third sentence is the conclusion. The author disagrees with the opinion in the second sentence. Whenever an LSAT author says "some say", then their conclusion is probably disagreement with the "some say" opinion.

Question 6

QUESTION TYPE: Strengthen

CONCLUSION: The complexity of chocolate probably masks the low fat flavor.

REASONING: Studies compared regular and low fat versions of ice cream flavors. Compared to regular ice cream, people dislike low fat vanilla, but they don't mind low fat chocolate. Chocolate has a very complex flavor.

ANALYSIS: This argument makes a classic LSAT error. The author makes a comparison between chocolate and vanilla, but they don't give us any information about vanilla! A comparison must give information about both groups.

So, we don't know anything about vanilla. Maybe it's complex too! In that case, we'd need another explanation for low-fat chocolate's appeal.

———————

A. It doesn't matter whether people prefer chocolate to vanilla. The argument's comparison is between full fat and low fat versions of the *same* flavors.
B. If you picked this, you probably assumed that an experiment shouldn't be biased. But in this case, the bias would be equally present in both the chocolate and vanilla experiments. Yet the two experiments had different results. So knowledge of the fat content couldn't have caused the difference between chocolate and vanilla.
C. The argument didn't say chocolate worked because people *liked* it. The argument proposed that the complexity of chocolate's compounds *masked* the low fat flavor.
D. **CORRECT.** The author made a comparison between chocolate and vanilla, but didn't tell us anything about vanilla! This answer completes the comparison: chocolate is indeed more complex. Therefore complexity could have caused the difference.
E. Awareness isn't relevant. People *perceive* the complexity of chocolate when they eat it, whether or not they are *aware* chocolate is complex. Also note that this answer doesn't say the people *in the studies* were aware of complexity – it only says "most people" are aware of complexity.

Question 7

QUESTION TYPE: Identify The Conclusion

CONCLUSION: Gillette's argument isn't convincing.

REASONING: Gillette pointed out some benefits to knowing genetics. But Gillette ignores the fact that knowledge of the human genome might be harmful.

ANALYSIS: On "identify the conclusion" questions, you don't need to consider whether the argument is good or bad. You just need to identify what the author is saying.

The author thinks Gillette is wrong. The "however, because" indicates this conclusion. What comes before the "however" is the conclusion, and what comes after "because" is the evidence.

Note that the ethicist has not said whether she thinks genetic research is a *bad* idea. She's merely pointing out that Gillette's argument is unconvincing. You can disagree with an argument without believing in the opposite conclusion.

A. The ethicist didn't even say this. She may agree with Gillette that knowledge of the genetic code will cure genetic disorders.
B. The fact in this answer is just evidence.
The author says this knowledge is something Gillette fails to consider, and Gillette is not persuasive *because* he fails to consider it.
C. The ethicist did not say whether we shouldn't pursue genetic research. She just said Gillette's conclusion is not supported.
The ethicist thinks there is an *absence of evidence* that genetic research is good. But that doesn't mean she thinks there is definitive evidence that it is a bad thing. She may simply be undecided on its benefits.
D. Same as A. The ethicist didn't say Gillette is wrong about genetic disorders. Maybe mapping the genome will prevent 3,000 disorders, but harm us in other ways.
E. **CORRECT.** The "however, because" indicates this is the conclusion. If "however" is in the middle of a sentence, then whatever comes before the however is usually the conclusion.

Question 8

QUESTION TYPE: Most Strongly Supported

FACTS:
1. Subjects listened to music.
2. Under hypnosis, half were asked to remember the music.
3. Under hypnosis, the other half were asked to remember the movie they watched.
4. Both groups gave equally confident and detailed descriptions.

ANALYSIS: Both groups were under hypnosis, and listened to music. One group was told they heard music, the other was told they saw a movie. The second group remembered seeing a movie.

So we've got an experiment with two groups, and *one* difference between them: one group was told a lie, and they believed it.

We can't conclude that hypnosis alone is the cause of anything. *Both* groups were under hypnosis, and the first group behaved normally. All we can say is that the lie was influential while under hypnosis.

As a side note, "equally confident" could mean that both groups were equally *unconfident*.

A. The stimulus didn't give us information to evaluate most claims made about hypnosis.
B. The stimulus only told us about one situation where hypnosis hurt recall. That's not enough information. Maybe in other circumstances hypnosis can improve recall.
C. Way too strong. We know in *one* situation hypnosis led to false memories. But maybe hypnosis doesn't mislead in most situations.
D. **CORRECT** The second group remembered a movie they hadn't seen. Based on common sense, telling them that they saw a movie must have caused this. People would normally know they hadn't seen a movie.
E. In the stimulus, the movie group was given *false* visual memories: this isn't an enhancement.

Question 9

QUESTION TYPE: Method of Reasoning

CONCLUSION: A baby's health depends on how much food the mother gets while she is pregnant.

REASONING: There was a correlation between babies' birth weights and the success of crops the year before.

ANALYSIS: This argument has two flaws. First, it uses evidence from a correlation to prove causation. This never works. Second, it switches terms inappropriately. Stop – before reading this explanation, look at the reasoning and conclusion again – try to spot the shifts in terms.

Did you find it? The argument switches from birth weight to health and from crop success to food access. These shifts aren't warranted. First, birth weights. A higher birth weight doesn't necessarily mean a baby is healthier. The argument should have made this explicit.

Second, crop success. Maybe crop success doesn't lead to more food for mothers. This could be a region of farmers. When crops succeed, the mothers are richer, less stressed, etc. But perhaps they normally have enough food either way.

A. **CORRECT.** See the explanation above. The "claimed correlation" is between birth weights and crops. The causal relation is between health and food access.

B. An example of this would be "....therefore, babies' birth weights are *only* affected by crop success". The argument didn't say anything like that.

C. An example of this would be "....since there used to be a correlation between crops and birth weights, there is still such a correlation."

D. An example of this would be "....because birth weights and crop records are linked, there must be a common cause. Maybe weather explains both crop success and heavier birth weights."

E. There are two reasons this is wrong. First, the argument didn't *explain* any causal relations. Second, there *aren't* two causal relations! The relation between crop success and birth weights is just a correlation.

Question 10

QUESTION TYPE: Point at Issue

ARGUMENTS: Vincent says that science requires measurement, and happiness can't be measured because it is entirely subjective.

Yolanda points out that optometry relies on subjective reports, and optometry is scientific. Yolanda is implying that subjective reports can be used to measure things.

ANALYSIS: For point at issue questions, you must pick something that both debaters explicitly disagree about. You need the two debaters to answer a firm "yes" and "no" to the answer. For the right answer:

1. Both debaters must have a clear opinion it.
2. If you asked the debaters whether they agreed with the answer, one would answer "yes" and the other would answer "no".

This lets you eliminate some answers quickly. For instance, Vincent doesn't mention optometry. We can't know his opinion on it, so any answer that mentions optometry is out.

A. Yolanda doesn't say whether she thinks happiness is entirely subjective.

B. Vincent might agree optometry is subjective. Perhaps he thinks optometry has a non-subjective component that Yolanda is ignoring.

C. **CORRECT.** Yolanda says optometry is scientific, and relies on objective reports. Vincent says that science requires measurement, and that subjectivity cannot be measured. Therefore, Vincent would probably disagree that science can *rely* on subjective reports.
(A discipline might be able to use subjective reports if it didn't *rely* on them.)

D. Yolanda doesn't say whether happiness research is *as* scientific as optometry. Her argument is just that happiness can be scientific, despite its subjectivity. So we don't know what Yolanda thinks. Vincent has no opinion on this question.

E. This answer just gets Richard's belief backwards. He believed "Subjective → ~~Measured~~". This answer says "~~Measured~~ → Subjective". So neither author believes this answer.

Question 11

QUESTION TYPE: Role in Argument

CONCLUSION: Increasing population in cities may decrease nationwide pollution.

REASONING: City dwellers use mass transport and live in more efficient homes. Thus, people in cities produce less pollution per capita.

ANALYSIS: To find the conclusion, ask yourself "what are they trying to tell me?". Everything in this argument supports the claim that moving people to cities will reduce pollution.

Conclusion words are useful, but can be misleading. The final sentence uses the word "thus". The final sentence is *a* conclusion, but it's an intermediate conclusion. The fact that city dwellers produce less pollution per capita supports the first sentence: we might decrease pollution by moving people to cities.

Note that the first sentence also has conclusion indicators. "Although....may" indicates the author's opinion, which is usually the conclusion.

A. The LSAT draws a line between what should be and what is. This question only talks about what is. This answer talks about what "should" happen. We don't know whether people *should* move to cities. Pollution is not the only factor.
B. Reread the argument carefully. It did *not* say that cities aren't polluted. NYC is definitely more polluted than Maine. But, *per capita,* the people in cities produce less pollution.
C. The first sentence is not useless fluff. Notice that it says "although....may actually". Those words indicate the first sentence is the author's opinion, and therefore a conclusion.
D. The first sentence starts with "although". That word indicates that the second part of a sentence will be *in contrast* to the first part.
E. **CORRECT.** Ask yourself "why is the author telling us this?" Everything supports the first sentence. The words "although....may actually" indicate that the first sentence is the author's opinion. The rest of the argument supports this opinion.

Question 12

QUESTION TYPE: Strengthen

CONCLUSION: The mountain snowpack in the Rockies will probably melt earlier, which will cause greater floods and less water for summer.

REASONING: Global warming will probably increase winter temperatures in the Rockies. This will cause more precipitation to fall as rain rather than snow.

ANALYSIS: This is actually a pretty good argument. Why does it need strengthening? Because the conclusion is probabilistic. Further evidence will help prove the probability correct.

As for why the argument is pretty good, it has to do with the relevant authority of the climatologist. I've written a note on the next page about this. You do *not* need to know about the note to get 175+, but you may find the information interesting nonetheless.

A. The argument said *rain* will cause flooding. This answer says there will be more precipitation, but that could be snow. Global warming has led to more snow in some regions.
B. **CORRECT.** The situation in this answer matches the stimulus exactly. So it strengthens the conclusion. The cause is leading to the effect in other mountain regions, so we can expect the same to be true in the Rockies.
C. This could be true, but how does it strengthen the argument? The argument was talking about the entire Rocky Mountain region, and the effect global warming would have.
This answer talks about specific, milder regions within the Rockies. That doesn't necessarily tell us what global warming will do. Those mild regions have had thousands of years to adapt, while global warming is happening very fast.
D. This isn't even talking about mountains. Irrelevant. Mountain regions could diverge completely from the average.
E. The stimulus didn't talk about larger snowpacks. Global warming makes snowpacks melt faster, but they may not be larger.

Note on Relevant Authority (Q12)

The speaker is a "climatologist" instead of a "politician" or an "environmentalist". The LSAT has previously used relevant expertise to allow an author to speak from authority. The issue isn't strictly relevant to answering this question, but make sure you note who's speaking on LR questions.

This is a strengthen question, which usually indicates a flawed argument. But given the authority of the speaker, this may actually be a good argument. The fact that the speaker is a climatologist certainly makes the argument more compelling than it otherwise would be. We can assume a climatologist has relevant expertise and is correct when they say that winter temperatures will rise in the rockies, and that more precipitation will fall as rain.

We can also believe the speaker when they say this means that the mountain snowpack will probably melt earlier, and cause flooding, etc. So why does this argument need strengthening at all? Because it says "probably". Probably is a weak statement – it indicates the climatologist isn't certain in their conclusion. Supporting evidence is *always* useful for a probabilistic conclusion, no matter the authority of the speaker.

A second anecdote to demonstrate that the identity of a speaker can be relevant: I once challenged question 25, section 3 of LSAT Preptest 64. I received a thorough reply, which included this quote "In the context of journalism, it is a reasonable application of the "principle of charity" in argument interpretation to presume that the information provided by the journalist constitutes a relatively complete picture of the relevant facts." In other words, the fact that the speaker was a journalist had a small role to play in the question.

It's possible to overthink these things. I got question 25, section 3 of LSAT Preptest 64 right, very fast. The answer was obvious. It was only when a student questioned me that I noticed a potential flaw. In 99.9% of cases you'll never need to consider relevant expertise. But know that the speaker's identity is explicitly part of LSAT questions.

Question 13

QUESTION TYPE: Weaken

CONCLUSION: We shouldn't feed animals GMO plants.

REASONING: Rats that ate GMO potatoes for 30 days had two problems. A control group fed a normal diet of foods did not develop these problems.

ANALYSIS: In a scientific experiment, you should keep variables the same, except the variable you're testing. The stimulus fails to do that. One group of rats eats only GMO potatoes. The other group eats "a normal diet". I'm pretty sure rats normally eat more than potatoes.

So the intestinal deformities could have been caused by the fact that rats weren't eating their normal diet, rather than because the potatoes were GMO.

———————————

A. **CORRECT.** This shows that the first group wasn't eating normal food. Maybe they got sick because rats don't digest potatoes well, and because they were missing foods they'd normally eat. Imagine eating nothing but potatoes!
B. You must always take answer choices at their weakest on weaken questions. "Tended to eat more" has a wide range of meanings. At it's weakest, it could mean that 51% of the rats ate 2% more potatoes at the start of the month. That doesn't tell us anything. (Though even if we took a stronger version of this answer, I'm not sure how it would weaken the argument!)
C. This affects nothing. The stimulus is talking about rats that *developed* intestinal deformities. The rats in the experiment were not the ones who had intestinal deformities at birth.
D. You might think that this shows that regular potatoes would have the same effect. But food is more than its nutritional value. "Has arsenic" is not a nutritional value – but you shouldn't eat an apple laced with arsenic! Maybe GMO potatoes have similar non-nutritional, poisonous effects.
E. You don't have to be able to explain something in order to warn against it. If 100% of people who eat a certain food die, then it's valid to say "don't eat it!!", even if you don't know why people die.

Question 14

QUESTION TYPE: Parallel Reasoning

CONCLUSION: It can't be true that we perceive an object by creating a mental image of the object.

REASONING: We'd need a new self to perceive the mental image. The inner self would need its own mental image, and this would go on to infinity.

ANALYSIS: This argument describes an infinite process. It's absurd to think our mind uses infinite process to form mental images, because infinite processes never end – we'd never get anything done!

This argument is hard to think about. Let that go. It's not your job to question the truth of premises. You must instead look for structure, and match it.

1. One thing requires a second thing.
2. The second thing requires another thing.
3. This goes on forever.

In practice, you should simply look through the answers for a process that continues forever. Only the correct answer has such a process.

A. This answer doesn't describe an infinite process. Also note that this answer says "highly unlikely", while the stimulus said *cannot* be correct."
B. This answer has the word infinite, but this answer describes an infinite *number* of theories. The stimulus described an infinite *process*. Those are different. For instance, an infinite process keeps going forever, referring back to itself. An infinite *number* of wrong theories already exist.
C. **CORRECT.** This answer describes an infinite process. Since *no* theory is new, every theory must have a similar theory that preceded it. This can't happen – obviously at some point a human thought up the first theory. So this infinite process is impossible, just like in the stimulus.
D. This answer has the word absurd, just like the stimulus. But you have to look at what "absurd" refers to. There is no infinite process here – the definition of "foundation" is simply wrong.
E. There's no claim of infinity here. This is just a factual argument that shows that some libraries existed before the library at Alexandria.

Question 15

QUESTION TYPE: Most Strongly Supported

FACTS:
1. You should not greatly exceed the recommended daily intake (RDA) of vitamins A and D – they are toxic.
2. Some vitamin fortified foods have 100% of the daily intake of those vitamins per serving.
3. Many people eat 2-3x the standard servings of some vitamin fortified foods.

ANALYSIS: We know "some" vitamin fortified cereals have 100% of the RDA. It's a warranted assumption that other vitamin fortified cereals have a significant percent of the RDA, say 30-50%.

We know some people eat 2-3x the recommended serving. And it's a warranted assumption that people get vitamin A and D from other food sources – everyone knows that.

This is just a most strongly supported question. It's probable, though not certain, that at least one person, somewhere in the world, has exceeded the RDA by eating lots of vitamin fortified cereal.

A. We don't know why people overeat cereal. Maybe they are aware of the RDA, and their mistake is simply about serving size.
B. **CORRECT.** At least some vitamin fortified foods have 100% of the daily intake. Presumably other such foods at least have high quantities of vitamins. Since "many" people eat large servings, and since they likely get some vitamin A and D from the rest of their diet, it's likely at least some people exceed the daily intake.
C. The only mistaken belief in the stimulus is how big a serving is. But people may pour cereal because they want to eat enough food – they may not be considering vitamin intake.
D. People may be deficient in certain vitamins even if they eat vitamin fortified foods. People might want to supplement those vitamins.
E. Manufacturers might not realize how people eat! Also, we only know vitamins A and D are toxic in extremely high doses. It's possible 2-3x the RDA is not a concern, and thus manufacturers don't need to worry about overeating.

Question 16

QUESTION TYPE: Necessary Assumption

CONCLUSION: It's likely that most countries that say their oil reserves haven't changed are wrong.

REASONING: A few countries say their reserves haven't changed last year. But oil reserves are unlikely to stay the same, year on year.

ANALYSIS: Notice the quantity words "several" and "most" in this stimulus. You must always pay attention to quantity words.

Several is perhaps 3-7 countries. And in the whole world, perhaps 100-150 countries have oil reserves. "Likely" might mean 70% of countries will see a change in reserves. So it's perfectly possible for it to be "unlikely" that oil reserves remain unchanged, and for 3-7 countries to have oil reserves that didn't change. 3-7 is a small percentage of the total. So the argument has to assume it's unlikely for this *group* to have its reserves unchanged.

A. Who cares what happens in one country?
Negation: "One country is likely to be right that its oil reserves are unchanged."
B. CORRECT. The conclusion is about "most" countries. If we negate this answer, we no longer have information about most countries that stated their reserves didn't change.
Negation: It is likely that only *half or less* of the countries which claimed unchanged reserves had oil fields that were drained or discovered.
C. We don't care *how* reserves change (e.g. slowly or quickly). We only care if they *did* change.
Negation: In 1997, no single country experienced both a a gradual drop and also a sudden rise in oil reserves.
D. Who cares what happens in one country?
Negation: One country incorrectly stated its reserves hadn't changed, but during 1997 it didn't discover new reserves or drain old ones.
E. This answer is irrelevant. We care about whether nations *are* correct, not whether they have an *obligation* to be correct.
Negation: A nation can experience changes in its oil reserves without having the obligation to report them correctly.

Question 17

QUESTION TYPE: Must be True

FACTS:

1. Sound insulate (SI) → Quiet for home (Q)
2. Quiet for home (Q) → Fine for institutions (I)
3. Combined statement: SI → Q → I Contrapositive: I̶ → Q̶ → S̶I̶
4. EM industries not quiet enough for home: Q̶
5. Inference: EM industries not sound insulated: S̶I̶

ANALYSIS: Usually, you should draw 'must be true' questions, using letters. I kept the words in the first two statements so they're clear to you. But, the combined diagram above is how I actually draw.

After you make a diagram, the next step is to see how the fact about EM industries fits into the logical chain. Since EM is Q̶, then they must be S̶I̶. You can and *should* be 100% certain about this kind of deduction on must be true questions, before checking the answers.

A. This is an incorrect reversal of the first diagram.
B. CORRECT. This is true, according to the contrapositive diagram above.
C. We don't know. Being quiet enough for the home is a sufficient condition for being useful in institutional settings. EM fails to meet this sufficient condition. Failing to meet a sufficient condition doesn't tell you anything. It's possible some EM motors are quiet enough for institutions, or it's possible that none are.
D. This is an incorrect reversal of the first fact. Sound insulation guarantees quiet, but something could be quiet even if it's not insulated.
E. This is an incorrect negation of the second fact. Even if something is not quiet enough for use in the home, it might still be quiet enough for institutional settings.

Question 18

QUESTION TYPE: Flawed Reasoning

CONCLUSION: The factory won't cause health problems.

REASONING: The protestors complaining about health problems were sent by developers who were worried about the value of their land.

ANALYSIS: This is an ad hominem argument. The author attacks the motives of the protestors, in order to claim that their conclusion is wrong.

This is *never* correct. It's possible the factory poses a health risk – maybe that's why developers chose to highlight that issue rather than another concern!

You must always attack the evidence and reasoning of your opponent, never their identity.

A. The argument didn't do this.
Example of Flaw: The protestors claim the factory will kill everyone in town. But it won't kill anyone.
B. The argument didn't do this either. Note that this isn't really a flaw: it's perfectly valid to persuade by pointing out harmful consequences.
Example of Flaw: We must build the factory. Otherwise the local economy will fail and house prices will drop.
C. **CORRECT.** This answer choice describes an ad hominem flaw. The author didn't say the protestors were wrong, she just said they were biased.
D. It is a flaw to generalize from a small number of cases, but the argument didn't do this.
Example of Flaw: The factory will make everyone sick. These two homeless orphans developed a cough while living near a similar factory.
E. This is a flaw, but the argument didn't do it.
Example of flaw: You must admit that it's possible I'll win the lottery. Therefore it's 100% certain that I'll win the lottery.

Question 19

QUESTION TYPE: Principle

PRINCIPLE: Should Intentionally misrepresent other's view (M) → Purpose is to act in interest of other (P)

Contrapositive: P̶ → M̶

ANALYSIS: Principle questions make me angry. I'm angry at you right now for reading this. These questions are *soooo* easy, but people have trouble with them. Gah!

On principle questions, you must focus only on what you can conclude. You can only conclude necessary conditions. So on this question, you can conclude only *one* thing. If someone is misrepresenting the belief of another, then they should act in that person's interest. To violate the principle, they would *not* act in that person's interest.

So you're looking for *two* things:

1. Misrepresenting *someone else's* beliefs.
2. Purpose is not in the interest of that person.

If you get stuck, look at that list of *two* things. The wrong answer you're considering is missing one of them. Figure out what it is.

A. **CORRECT.** It's definitely against someone's interest to make them look ridiculous. This means that Ann shouldn't have misrepresented Bruce's beliefs.
B. Claude is acting in Thelma's interests: he is preventing someone from bothering her. No one likes being bothered.
C. John's purpose appears to be acting *for* Maria's interest: he wants people to respect her.
D. Harvey is misrepresenting *his own* beliefs.
E. It doesn't sound like Wanda is misrepresenting George's beliefs. He knows little about Geography, so maybe he doesn't know Egypt is in Africa. It's also not clear Wanda wants to harm George: maybe there is good reason to let people know the truth about his geographical limitations.

Question 20

QUESTION TYPE: Paradox

PARADOX: The family earned more from wool, but didn't get richer overall.

The family earned more from wool because they sold *much* more internationally, and international prices rose.

ANALYSIS: Several answers talk about low domestic wool prices. Who cares?! The family was selling *dramatically* more wool internationally. Besides, the first sentence *literally says* that the family earned more money from wool. A lot more money! There's *no* doubt about this.

So the family is poorer, *even though* they're raking in cash from wool. Use your common sense (you're allowed). If you sell wool, you have sheep. We use sheep for many things: meat, sheep's milk, cheese, etc. So it's quite likely that the family made money from these as well. Answer C says that the family lost money on non-wool sales.

A. The family wasn't selling as much wool domestically, so domestic wool prices don't matter. International wool prices sound like they were increasing faster than inflation.
B. This sounds tempting. But this family sold a *lot* more wool abroad, at higher prices. And the first sentence says that the family *earned more* from wool sales. There's zero doubt on that point.
C. **CORRECT.** This is the only answer that explains how wool sellers could lose money, even if they are making more money from wool. Maybe this family only made 30% of its money from wool, and the rest from sheepskin and mutton sales.
D. This talks about Australian wool producers in general. But the question is only about a specific family. This family is earning *lots* more from international wool sales. Presumably they're doing well even with the increased competition.
E. This answer doesn't explain why a wool farmer could lose money even though wool sales are increasing. Don't focus on whether an answer could be true – you need to pay attention to whether it explains the paradox.

Question 21

QUESTION TYPE: Flawed Reasoning

CONCLUSION: It wasn't wrong for Meyers to take the compost.

REASONING: The lawyer said Meyers didn't meet a sufficient condition for something being wrong.

ANALYSIS: This flaw question uses conditional reasoning. When a flaw questions uses conditional reasoning, there are only two possible errors. I'll use a sample sentence to demonstrate them: All cats have tails ($C \rightarrow T$)

- Incorrect negation (Not cat, so no tail $\cancel{C} \rightarrow \cancel{T}$)
- Incorrect reversal (Has a tail, so is cat $T \rightarrow C$)

If you see conditional reasoning on a flaw question, assume they've done one of these two errors. Drawing isn't necessary. You just need to see whether they reversed or negated, then look for that answer. That said, here's the drawing:

Good reason → Stealing → Wrong
The lawyer incorrectly negated good reason: $\cancel{G} \rightarrow \cancel{W}$

A. This is different. A fact is a fact. A moral judgment is an idea about a fact (e.g. it's good, it's bad, we should, we shouldn't)
   Example of flaw: You pointed out that millions of children are starving. How dare you say it is *fine* that millions of children are starving?
B. This answer describes a hypothetical situation. The lawyer was talking about what actually happened. The lawyer didn't say what would happen *if* Meyers thought the compost was someone's property.
C. **CORRECT.** This describes an incorrect negation. "A condition by itself enough...." is a sufficient condition. The argument assumed this sufficient condition was also necessary.
D. This isn't a flaw! If the compost was Meyers' property, it would have been fine for him to take it, and he wouldn't need a lawyer!
E. This is a different flaw.
   Example of flaw: Mrs. Jones said the compost was hers. This is possible. Therefore it is *certain* that the compost belongs to Mrs. Jones!

Question 22

QUESTION TYPE: Necessary Assumption

CONCLUSION: There's no problem with predatory pricing.

REASONING: The threat of competition will keep companies from raising prices, even if their competitors go out of business.

ANALYSIS: On necessary assumption questions, you must ask how the evidence could *fail* to justify the argument. What is the author assuming?

Here, they're assuming that competition would work. But if competitors *can't* enter the market, then this argument falls apart.

_____

A. The argument said the *threat* of competition is what keeps companies from raising prices. Actual competition is not necessarily required.
   Negation: Some successful companies may avoid creating competitors.
B. "Unlikely" and "Likely" are related to most. Likely = 51%, unlikely = 50% or less. Since you must negate in the slightest way possible, negating unlikely means moving from 50% to 51%, which is never a significant change.
   Negation: It is likely that multiple companies will engage in predatory pricing.
C. Company size wasn't relevant. The issue is lack of competition. In a small market a company might drive out all competitors even if it isn't that big.
   Negation: At least one company that isn't large and wealthy can engage in predatory pricing.
D. Negating this makes the argument *stronger!* Additional reasons to avoid raising prices mean we don't need to worry about predatory pricing.
   Negation: There is at least one other reason companies avoid raising prices (e.g. Compassion, legal requirements, cost of changing ads, etc.)
E. **CORRECT.** The author assumed that prices are the only reason we should worry about predatory pricing. There could be other reasons. Maybe predatory pricing is not *fair* to competitors.
   Negation: Some pricing practices are unacceptable even if they do not result in unreasonable prices.

Question 23

QUESTION TYPE: Flawed Parallel Reasoning

CONCLUSION: Frank doesn't embezzle.

REASONING: Wants to prosecute → Charged
~~Charged~~   ~~Embezzle~~

ANALYSIS: This argument gives a single conditional statement, then negates the necessary condition. We could have correctly concluded that the prosecutor doesn't want to prosecute Frank. But we don't know if Frank is an embezzler.

You could call it a concept shift. Prosecuting Frank for embezzlement doesn't mean Frank embezzles, and not prosecuting doesn't mean he is innocent.

_____

A. This is a different error. It's a mistaken reversal: Knew → 10
   Incorrect reversal: 10 → knew
B. This is a different error. It's an incorrect negation Lottery → stay home
   Incorrect negation: ~~lottery → stay home~~
C. **CORRECT.** This argument correctly negates the necessary condition of a conditional statement. And then it repeats the concept shift error in the stimulus: we could conclude that Makoto does not *believe* the oven is on, but it's very possible that the oven is *actually* on. Belief ≠ fact, just like lack of prosecution ≠ innocence.
   Believe oven on → Rush home
   Still at work. Therefore oven *actually* off.
D. This answer repeats the same concept shift error, moving from belief about getting a promotion, to *actually* getting a promotion. But, this argument makes an incorrect reversal. The stimulus correctly negated the necessary condition.
   Believed promotion → Come in early
   Incorrect reversal: Come in early → *actually* getting a promotion.
E. This repeats the belief/fact concept shift. However, the stimulus and answer C both negated the necessary condition of the conditional statement. This answer presents a flawed version of the sufficient condition.
   Believe going to be fired → ~~come in to work~~
   Flawed sufficient condition: Lucy *is* going to be fired.

279

Question 24

QUESTION TYPE: Flawed Reasoning

CONCLUSION: Removing tonsils early will prevent all sleeping problems in children.

REASONING: Tonsils can sometimes cause sleeping problems, and removing them can help.

ANALYSIS: This is an awful argument. There are *thousands* of reasons a child could have sleeping problems. Removing tonsils eliminates *one* possible cause. Tonsils are not the *only* cause of sleep problems.

Something can be a cause without being a necessary cause.

A. The pediatrician is a *relevant* authority. And the pediatrician presents evidence; they are not asking us to take their word for it.
   Example of flaw: I'm a wealthy industrialist. I feel that children should have their tonsils removed, so clearly I'm right.
B. This answer refers to circular reasoning. That's a different flaw – the evidence and the conclusion have to be *exactly* the same.
   Example of flaw: Children would have no sleep problems if they had their tonsils removed, because removing tonsils eliminates sleep problems.
C. This is a different flaw.
   Example of flaw: Removing tonsils reduces infections, and also reduces sleep problems. So clearly doctors that remove tonsils are intending to cure sleep problems and not just reduce infections.
D. This is a different flaw.
   Example of flaw: One *possible* reason for removing tonsils is to reduce sleep problems. So clearly, *this child's* tonsils were removed to reduce sleep problems, and not for any other reason.
E. **CORRECT.** Maybe sleep problems are caused by fear of monsters under the bed, or playing too many video games late at night. There are a million-and-one reasons a child could have trouble sleeping, even if they have their tonsils removed.

Question 25

QUESTION TYPE: Principle

PRINCIPLE: Knowledge not publicly available → Unethical for officials to profit from knowledge

ANALYSIS: On logical reasoning questions, you must be *rigorous*. You must focus on *exactly* what condition allows you to prove a principle.

We have *one* sufficient situation for calling something unethical. Someone must:

1. Be a *current* government official, and
2. Use knowledge not publicly available, and
3. To benefit *themselves*
4. Financially

This is very similar to criminal law, where multiple conditions must be met for a crime. You must be rigorous and discard any answers that miss one of the above conditions.

Many answers describe situations where officials *might* be profiting. No good. We need definite proof that officials profited.

A. There's no evidence the official profited from his former company's bid. We don't even know that the bid succeeded. We also don't know if the official used knowledge that wasn't public.
B. This officer is a *retired* government official. The principle only applies to current officials.
C. It's not clear the official used knowledge that isn't available. She set up the shelters *after* the new law was passed.
D. **CORRECT.** This matches all four conditions. A current official used secret knowledge to benefit himself financially by avoiding a tax.
E. The official sold her stock *after* the investigation was announced, so there is no violation.

Section II - Logic Games
Game 1 - Film Schedule
Questions 1-5

Setup

This is a straightforward pure sequencing game. Except for the final question, there's absolutely nothing tricky here.

If you found this difficult, I have good news for you. This type of game is *very* learnable. Just redo it until it makes sense, and you'll be able to do *every* sequencing game with ease. Set high standards for yourself. A skilled LSAT student should be able to solve this in 4-5 minutes.

It's best to combine all the rules into one big diagram. I don't draw them separately. It is a waste of time, and in my experience it tends to confuse students. Better just to connect everything rule by rule. Here's the first rule:

$$F <^{\displaystyle J}_{\displaystyle L}$$

The second rule connects on J:

$$\begin{matrix} K \searrow \\ & J—H \\ F \nearrow \\ & L \end{matrix}$$

The third rule attaches on to L:

$$\begin{matrix} K \searrow \\ & J—H \\ F \nearrow \\ & L—G \end{matrix}$$

That's the entire setup. No need to make things more complicated than they are. The diagram reads left to right. Kangaroos or Fiesta could be first, as they have nothing before them. Hurricanes or Glaciers could be last, as they have nothing after them.

It's important to note that, for example, Jets could be before or after Glaciers. They're not directly connected, so there's no reason we can't put Glaciers before Jets, even though Glaciers is further right on the diagram.

Main Diagram

$$\begin{matrix} K \searrow \\ & J—H \\ F \nearrow \\ & L—G \end{matrix}$$

Question 1

Unusually for a first question, this is not an "acceptable order" question. That means the LSAT was expecting you to make deductions in your setup, such as the main diagram we created.

We're looking for what must be false. The slow way to do this question would be to test each answer choice and prove that it could work (thus eliminating it).

The fast way is to look through the answers to find the ones that seem more difficult. For instance, **A** is a poor candidate, because it places Fiesta early on. On our diagram, Fiesta is early: the only restrictions on Fiesta are that it goes *before* other variables. So it's easy to place Fiesta early, and **A** is unlikely to be correct.

It should be clear that **E** is **CORRECT**, once you have practice reading this type of diagram. Kangaroos comes before Jets and Hurricanes. That means that Kangaroos can go fourth at latest.

I'm going to show the other answers are all possible, but this isn't something you should do under timed conditions.

This diagram proves that **A** and **C** are wrong:

K	F	J	H	L	G
1	2	3	4	5	6

This diagram proves that **B** and **D** are wrong.

F	L	G	K	J	H
1	2	3	4	5	6

But I'll emphasize that this is not how you should solve this type of question. Rule violations on sequencing questions tend to be obvious.

Rule violations tend to happen when something is placed too near the edge. **e.g.** 5th is one space away from last, but Kangaroos always has to be at least two spaces away from last.

Question 2

$$K \searrow J - H$$
$$F \diagup \diagdown L - G$$

I've repeated the main diagram. To solve "must be true" questions like this one, you should just look at the diagram to see what has to be true.

Fiesta is always before Hurricanes, so **A** is **CORRECT.**

None of the other answers have to be true. There are no left-to-right connections between the variables mentioned in those answers. A left-to-right connection is the only way you can prove one variable comes before another.

Question 3

The new rule on this question doesn't change much. If you find yourself hesitating, then it is best to redraw the diagram to add the new rule. This should only take 10 seconds or so. If it takes you longer, practice. Here's the diagram, with Glaciers before Hurricanes:

K
 ＼
  ＼ J ＼
F ＼   ＼ H
   ＼   ／
    L − G

The only real change is that Hurricanes now has to be last. Kangaroos and Jets could still go before Glaciers. So **A** is wrong. Glaciers could go as late as fifth.

E is **CORRECT.** Lovebird now has to have Glaciers and Hurricanes after it, so Lovebird can be fourth at latest.

Question 4

This question places Lovebird earlier than Kangaroos. I drew a new diagram showing this. I recommend trying this modification yourself. It's very quick to draw a new rule. Most students vastly overestimate how long it takes to make drawings.

     ／K — J — H
F — L — G

From this diagram, it's obvious that **A, B** and **C** are wrong. Lovebird has to go second, since Kangaroos, Jets, Hurricanes and Glaciers come after Lovebird.

D is **CORRECT.** It not only could be true, it *has* to be true.

E is obviously wrong, as the diagram shows that Jets has to come *after* L.

Drawing the new diagram adds ten seconds, but likely saves you thirty seconds on the answer choices.

Question 5

This is the only question that most students find truly difficult on this game. Fewer than half got it right. Everyone hates rule substitution questions.

There is a way to do rule substitution questions quickly however. It's very difficult for the test makers come up with a new rule that has the same effect. Usually their only option is to describe the effects of the rule in another way. Let's see how to do that. Here's the main diagram again:

K
 ⟩J—H
F⟨
  ⟍L—G

Now, let's look at the full effects of placing Fiesta before Jets and Lovebird.

- Fiesta is before J – H and L – G.
- Kangaroos is the only variable that can come before Fiesta.

I can think of two ways of phrasing this:

1. Every variable except Kangaroos has to come after F.
2. Only Kangaroos can come before F.

Answer **A** uses my second variation. **A** is **CORRECT.**

I think **B** and **D** are fairly obviously wrong. They both force something to happen that normally doesn't have to happen. Ordinarily, Kangaroos can come after Lovebird, so **B** is wrong. And normally, Kangaroos can come before Fiesta, so **D** is wrong.

C and **E** are trickier to eliminate. **C** is the most popular wrong answer. It places Fiesta first or second. It's true that Fiesta normally has to go in one of those positions. But that's not *all* that's true about Fiesta.

We also need the rule to force Fiesta to be before Lovebird, and answer **C** doesn't do that. The rule in answer **C** allows this scenario:

L	F	G	K	J	H
1	2	3	4	5	6

Fiesta is second, but Lovebird is before F!

E is the second most popular answer. It says that Fiesta or Kangaroos must be first.

E is also something that *has to be true* normally, but we're not looking for something that must be true. We're looking for something that replaces the rule. This scenario is possible if we replace the rule in question with answer **E:**

K	J	H	L	G	F
1	2	3	4	5	6

Kangaroos is first, but Fiesta is last! That violates the normal rules.

Game 2 - Applicants and Human Resources
Questions 6-11

This is a grouping game. I've set it up vertically. You can set this type of game up horizontally too. Either way is fine, depends how your brain works.

```
R  __
S  __
T  __
U  G
   ‾
```

I've added G to group U. You should always read all the rules before drawing. Often one rule is very easy to draw and you should start there.

I next placed the final rule on the diagram:

```
   R  __
 ⌐ S  __  __
 ↳ T  __
   U  G
      ‾
```

The final rule says that S has more candidates than T, so S always has at least two candidates. The arrow reminds me that S has more than T. It's important to note that Tipton could evaluate at most two candidates. If Tipton evaluated three candidates, then Smith would have to evaluate four, and there would be no candidates left for the other two officers.

This is a non-standard rule, so you're welcome to use another symbol to remind yourself that S has more than T. But it's best if you can find a way to draw the rule directly on the diagram. The fewer rules in your list of rules, the better.

Next, is my list of rules. Here are rules 2, 3, and 4:

$$\boxed{\text{FL}}$$

$$I \leftrightarrow M, H$$

$$\underline{K} \,|$$

I've drawn rules 2 and 3 slightly differently. I normally prefer a box to show that variables must be or can't be in the same group. But that doesn't work for rule 3, so I used the dual arrow to show that Inman can't go with M or H.

The final rule has a vertical line to the right of K. That symbol means that the group K is in is closed: there can be no more candidates there. This type of rule occurs frequently enough that you should adopt this symbol.

Main Diagram

```
   R  __
 ⌐ S  __  __
 ↳ T  __
   U  G
      ‾
```

1 $\boxed{\text{FL}}$

2 $I \leftrightarrow M, H$

3 $\underline{K} \,|$

Question 6

For acceptable order questions, go through the rules and use them to eliminate answers one by one.

Rule 1 eliminates **E.** Grant must be evaluated by Ullman.

Rule 2 eliminates **B.** Farrell and Lopez must be evaluated by the same officer.

Rule 3 eliminates **C.** Hong and Inman can't be evaluated by the same officer.

Rule 4 eliminates **D.** Kent must be evaluated alone.

A is **CORRECT.** It violates no rules.

Question 7

You should start local rule questions by drawing the new rule, then making a deduction. If Hong is evaluated by Rao, then Inman can't be evaluated by Rao:

```
Ɽ  R  H
      ___  ___
    S
      ___  ___
    T
         ___
  U  G
```

Then you must ask yourself which of the remaining rules are affected by this new situation. Kent's rule is very important. Kent must always be alone, and now there is only one group where Kent can be alone. Kent must be evaluated by Tipton:

```
Ɽ  R  H
      ___  ___
    S
      ___  ___
    T  K |
         ___
  U  G
```

Once a diagram gets filled up, you should ask yourself who you can still place. Only FL and I,M are left, and IM can't go together.

We need two people to be evaluated by Smith, so FL must go there:

```
Ɽ  R  H        I ⟷ M
      ___
    S  F  L
      ___ ___
    T  K |
         ___
  U  G
```

Only Inman and Madsen are left. They must go in different groups. They can go anywhere, except Inman can't go with Rao.

From this diagram, **B** is **CORRECT. B** could be true, and the diagram contradicts all the other answers.

286

Question 8

This question says that Tipton evaluates two candidates. And Rule five says that Smith must evaluate more candidates than Tipton does. So if Tipton evaluates two candidates, Smith must evaluate three candidates. That leaves one candidate for R and U:

R   __ |
S __ __ __ |
T   __ __ |
U   G |

Next, look to the rules and see what applies. Kent must be alone in a group. That means Kent must be evaluated by Rao:

R   K |
S __ __ __ |
T   __ __ |
U   G |

Just like on question 7, you must now see who's left to place. There's FL, and I, H and M. I, H and M can't go together. That means FL must be evaluated by Rao. This lets us separate I and HM.

R   K |
S   F L __ |
T   __ __ |
U   G |

I, H and M are left. Inman has to go with FL, because if Inman were evaluated by Tipton then either H or M would also be there. Next, since only Tipton has space left, both Hong and Madsen must go there:

R   K |
S   F L I |
T   H M |
U   G |

C is CORRECT. Farrell can't be evaluated by Tipton. All of the other answers have to be true.

This may seem like a lengthy process, but on the page it should take about 15 seconds. It takes a long time for me to write and for you to read because I'm going one step at a time, and I have to make sure what I'm doing is clear. But with practice, you can learn to see these steps intuitively in your head and do them quickly.

Question 9

This question says Madsen is evaluated alone. That means that there are two candidates who must be evaluated alone: Madsen and Kent.

Smith always evaluates at least two candidates, and Ullman always evaluates Grant. So that means that Rao and Tipton must evaluate Madsen and Kent.

Madsen and Kent are interchangeable on this question, I've drawn a line to show this. I use this type of line whenever an entire group is interchangeable:

```
  R  M|
 ⌐ S  ─   ─
 ⌊ T  K|
   U  G
```

The next step is logically difficult. There are four people left to place: FL, H and Inman. H and Inman can't go together.

That means that one of H/I will go with FL. So these four variables will be distributed in a group of three and a group of one.

We need at least two people to go with Smith. So the group of three, the group with FL, must be evaluated by Smith:

```
  R  M|
 ⌐ S  F   L   H/I
 ⌊ T  K|
   U  G   I/H
```

Hong and Inman are interchangeable between Smith and Ullman.

B is CORRECT. Lopez must be evaluated by Smith.

Notice that all the other answers mention Madsen, Kent, Inman and Hong. These four variables are all interchangeable with another variable on this question, so they could never be the right answer.

Question 10

Farrell is always evaluated alongside Lopez (rule 2). This question adds Inman to the group, for a total of three candidates.

There are only two officers that can evaluate these three candidates: Rao and Smith. Tipton can't evaluate three candidates, because then Smith would have to evaluate four candidates.

And Ullman can't evaluate three *additional* candidates. Then Ullman would have four candidates, and there wouldn't be enough candidates left for Rao, Smith and Tipton. You need at least four candidates for those officers, since Smith always evaluates at least two.

So only Smith and Rao can handle FL and Inman. I drew a separate scenario for each possibility. If you practice making local scenarios, you should be able to do this in 15-20 seconds and then quickly solve the question.

First let's place FLI with Rao. Kent has to go with Tipton, because Kent has to be alone:

```
   R  F   L   I
  ⌐ S  ─   ─
  ⌊ T  K|⌐
    U  G|
```

Only Hong and Madsen are left to place. They must be evaluated by Smith, since Smith must evaluate more candidates than Tipton does:

```
   R  F   L   I
  ⌐ S  H   M
  ⌊ T  K
    U  G
```

Now let's place FLI with Smith:

```
 ⌐R   __
 |S   F   L   I
 └T   __
  U   G
```

Rao and Tipton are the open groups, and they are interchangeable. Kent fills one of the groups. Now only Hong and Madsen are left to place. One of H/M goes with Rao or Tipton. The other H/M is flexible: they can go in the same group, or with Ullman:

```
 ⌐R  H/M
 |S   F    L    I        H/M
 └T   K|
  U   G
```

The line between Rao and Tipton is a reminder than H/M and Kent are interchangeable in this scenario.

In both diagrams it is impossible for Lopez to be evaluated by Ullman. **C is CORRECT.**

We have done more work than we had to. But if you practice, it shouldn't take you too long to make these scenarios, so the wasted effort doesn't matter. The scenarios will also help you prove definitively that the other answers could be true.

As with all local rule questions, you should start by drawing the new rule. FL go with Rao:

```
  R   F   L
 ⌐S   __  __
 └T   K|
  U   G
```

I've placed Kent with Tipton. Kent must always be alone, and Tipton is the only officer left who can evaluate a single candidate.

Now we only have Madsen, Hong and Inman left to place. These three can't go together (rule 3). We also need to place at least two people with Smith (rule five).

Therefore, Madsen and Hong must go with Smith. Inman can go either with Rao or Ullman. Inman can't go with smith because of rule 3:

```
     R   F   L    ⟍
  ̶I ⌐S   H   M|    |
   └T   K|          I
    U   G           ⟋
```

E is CORRECT. We know where to place L, H, M, K, and G, for a total of five. (the question asks about *other* applicants).

Game 3 - Literature Course
Questions 12-16

Setup

This is a linear/sequencing game, with a second element: the courses are either summarized or not summarized.

I don't have any special approach for this type of game. I just mark summarized or not summarized under the diagram. Keep it simple.

(There will be examples summarized/not summarized diagram on the questions)

At first I thought this was just a sequencing game. I drew rules 3 and 4. Here's rule 3:

F — O
     K
     R

I then added rule 4:

    F — O
         K
    T   R
N

Most people would stop there. In fact, I did stop there on my own setup. But when I got to question 14, I noticed that this game is very restricted. Look at O. O is stuck in the middle. FTN are always before O, and KR are always after O.

So O is always fourth! This deduction makes the game *much* simpler. I redrew the sequencing rules as this diagram:

F , N—T   K , R
___ ___ ___ ___ ___ ___
 1   2   3   4   5   6
            O

When I want to show semi-certain placement in a linear diagram, I draw some variables floating above the diagram. For instance, KR are always to the right of O. So I drew them in that position. The comma indicates that they are reversible.

I've done the same thing with " F, N – T ". N is always before T, but the comma indicates that F could be before them, after them or in the middle.

Drawing the diagram this way may seem like a small change. You might think "I could have figured all that out without the diagram!". But did you?

In any case, all logic games diagrams are just a tool to do things faster. This particular diagram let me fly through this game in six minutes. As much as possible, you should take knowledge out of your head, and put it on the page in the clearest possible form. You want to *always* know that O is fourth, without thinking about it.

There are two more rules. Courses can't go together if they're summarized. I drew it like this:

That's more of a reminder than anything else. I kept that rule in my head. Remembering it will help you go fast. You should always take 10-20 seconds at the start of a game to make sure you've memorized the rules.

The second rule says that if N is not summarized, then T and R are both summarized:

I only drew that. I've done enough logic games that the contrapositive is obvious to me. However, if it takes you time to see the contrapositive, then you should draw the contrapositive as well:

R
 ↘
  or N
 ↗
T

290

Main Diagram

F , N — T   K , R
                O
‾   ‾   ‾   ‾   ‾   ‾
1   2   3   4   5   6

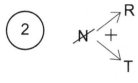

I don't draw the sequencing diagram I used in the setup. All that information is better captured in the first diagram I drew above.

Question 12

For acceptable order questions, go through the rules and use them to eliminate answers one by one.

Rule 1 eliminates **C.** T and R are summarized, so they can't go together.

Rule 2 eliminates **D.** N is not summarized, so R should have been summarized.

Rule 3 eliminates **B.** N has to be earlier than T.

Rule 4 eliminates **E.** F has to be earlier than O.

A is **CORRECT.** It violates no rules.

Question 13

If N is second, then T must go third, since N is always before T (rule 3).

$$\begin{array}{cccccc} & & & & K,R_S & \\ F & N & T & O & \_ & \_ \\ \hline 1 & 2 & 3 & 4 & 5 & 6 \\ & \cancel{S} & S & & & \end{array}$$

The question also says that N is not summarized. This means that both T and R are summarized (rule 2).

A is CORRECT. Since N is not summarized, there's no reason we can't summarize F.

B is wrong because K is beside R, and R is summarized.

C is wrong because O is beside T, and T is summarized.

D doesn't work on this question since N is second, and T must go after N.

E doesn't work because T is third, after N. And since N is not summarized, T must be summarized (rule 2).

Question 14

Not much changes on this question. O is summarized, so whoever goes 3rd and 5th can't be summarized. That's all we know:

$$\begin{array}{cccccc} F, & N-T & & K,R & \\ & & O & & \\ \hline 1 & 2 & 3 & 4 & 5 & 6 \\ & & \cancel{S} & S & \cancel{S} & \end{array}$$

A and **B** are easy to eliminate. The diagram above shows that F can be first, and K can be sixth.

There are no summarization restrictions for these variables. A key to this game is that, except for N, you can *always* make a course not summarized.

C is CORRECT. It's a little tricky to explain. Try drawing this yourself.

If F is summarized, it can only go first or second, since no summarized course can go beside O on this question. Let's try placing F first. F is summarized, so the second course can't be summarized:

$$\begin{array}{cccccc} & N-T & & K,R & \\ F & & & O & & \\ \hline 1 & 2 & 3 & 4 & 5 & 6 \\ S & \cancel{S} & \cancel{S} & & \cancel{S} & \end{array}$$

You may see the problem. We must place N and T second and third. Neither position can be summarized here. But if N isn't summarized, then T has to be summarized (rule 2). So this can't work.

The same problem happens if you place F second. N is first and T is third. Both positions can't be summarized, because they are beside F. But if N isn't summarized, then T must be summarized. We are breaking a rule:

$$\begin{array}{cccccc} N & F & T & O & \_ & \_ \\ \hline 1 & 2 & 3 & 4 & 5 & 6 \\ \cancel{S} & S & \cancel{S} & S & & \end{array}$$

This next diagram proves that **D** and **E** are both possible, and therefore wrong:

$$\begin{array}{|c|cccc|c|c} \hline N & T & F & O & K & R \\ \cancel{S} & S & \cancel{S} & S & \cancel{S} & S \\ \hline 1 & 2 & 3 & 4 & 5 & 6 \end{array}$$

Question 15

If the final two courses are not summarized, then that means that R is not summarized, because R is one of the final two courses. We know this from our setup diagram: R is always fifth or sixth.

The contrapositive of rule 2 says that if R is not summarized, then N is summarized.

$$F, N_S - T \qquad K, R$$
$$\frac{}{1} \quad \frac{}{2} \quad \frac{}{3} \quad \frac{O}{4} \quad \frac{}{5} \quad \frac{}{6}$$

There are a few ways we could place F, N and T. The most important thing is not to make two of them summarized and beside each other. Note that T could be summarized, if you place N first.

A is wrong. K is always fifth or sixth, so on this question it can't be summarized. **C** is wrong for the same reason.

B is **CORRECT.** This diagram shows that it's possible for O to be summarized:

$$\frac{F}{1} \quad \frac{N}{2} \quad \frac{T}{3} \quad \frac{O}{4} \quad \frac{K}{5} \quad \frac{R}{6}$$
$$\cancel{S} \quad S \quad \cancel{S} \quad S \quad \cancel{S} \quad \cancel{S}$$

D is wrong because if F and T are summarized, then the first three courses would all be summarized. This violates the first rule.

E is wrong because if R is not summarized, then N *must* be summarized.

Question 16

Everyone hates rule substitution questions, and this is the second on this section. Ouch.

I actually find rule substitution questions very easy. I'll try to convince you this is possible. There are two things a substituted rule must do:

1. *Allow* everything allowed by the old rule.
2. *Ban* everything not allowed by the old rule.

This gives you an easy way to eliminate answers. **A, B** and **E** add extra restrictions.

- **A:** This says T is discussed third. That doesn't normally have to be true. Wrong answer!
- **B:** This says T is discussed earlier than F. Not a normal restriction. Eliminate!
- **E:** This says F is discussed third. Normally, F can also go 1st or 2nd. Bad answer!

Have the courage of your convictions. Rule substitution answers are full of silly restrictions. If a restriction contradicts the normal rules, eliminate that answer.

Now we are left with **C** and **D.** The second part of my guidelines says that rules have to ban everything that's normally not allowed.

C doesn't do this. **C** says that K and R have to be among the last three. I'm sorry, but K and R have to among the last *two*. This answer seems too broad. Let's look at **D.**

When I did this question, I went right to **D** because it said O has to be fourth. That's the most important deduction in the game, and it's also a consequence of the rule we're replacing.

Rule substitution answers usually work by describing a consequence of the rule we're replacing. **D** does describe a consequence of the rule (O is fourth), so this is very promising. Now let's see where this leaves us. O is fourth, and we know from rule 3 that N and T have to be before O.

(question continued on next page)

This diagram shows what we've deduced so far.

F, KR

N — T

O

1 2 3 4 5 6

We still have to place F and KR. This answer says that KR are beside each other and reversible. So they need two spaces.

The only two spaces open are 5 and 6. That means KR goes there, and F has to go before O. So this exactly matches our original setup. **D** is **CORRECT.**

I didn't prove this answer with this degree of certainty on the test. I just eliminated **A, B** and **E** like I showed you.

Then I discarded **C** because it said "last three", and I picked **D** because it placed O fourth. I did do a quick mental check that the rest of the rule worked, but those were the main elements I used to quickly arrive at the answer.

Game 4 - Seven Paintings
Questions 17-23

Setup

This is a linear game. I normally find linear games very easy, but this one was difficult. I even made a mistake on question 21, because I read the local rule wrong.

The setup diagram is pretty standard however. There are seven spaces, which we can draw horizontally. Since the Vuillard can only be third or fourth, I draw two diagrams. This only takes a few extra seconds, and it helps with visualization.

$$\begin{array}{ccccccc} & & V & & & & \\ \underline{} & \underline{} & \underline{} & \underline{} & \underline{} & \underline{} & \underline{} \\ 1 & 2 & 3 & 4 & 5 & 6 & 7 \end{array}$$

$$\begin{array}{ccccccc} & & & V & & & \\ \underline{} & \underline{} & \underline{} & \underline{} & \underline{} & \underline{} & \underline{} \\ 1 & 2 & 3 & 4 & 5 & 6 & 7 \end{array}$$

This dual setup isn't especially useful on this game, but on about 50% of games, dual diagrams produce incredible deductions. So I draw them out of habit, in case they produce something. Even if they don't, it only takes a moment, and I can visualize better by looking at them.

Next I drew rules 1-3, which are pretty standard.

Rule 1 says that the Turner is before the Whistler:

T—W

Rule 2 says that the Renoir is before the Morisot, with one painting in between:

Rule 3 says that the Pissarro and the Sisley are beside each other:

There are no major additional deductions from the setup. However, you should take some time to think about how the rules work together.

There are seven variables. The most restricted set of variables is R_M. Exactly one painting is in between them. Who can it be?

Not Pissarro or Sisley, because they are a block of two paintings. So only the Turner, the Whistler and the Vuillard can go in between the Renoir and the Morisot.

Games often present limited options, and it's important for you to think about the most restricted points in advance. The fact that only Turner, the Whistler and the Vuillard can go between R_M is very important.

Main Diagram

$$\begin{array}{ccccccc} & & V & & & & \\ \underline{} & \underline{} & \underline{} & \underline{} & \underline{} & \underline{} & \underline{} \\ 1 & 2 & 3 & 4 & 5 & 6 & 7 \end{array}$$

$$\begin{array}{ccccccc} & & & V & & & \\ \underline{} & \underline{} & \underline{} & \underline{} & \underline{} & \underline{} & \underline{} \\ 1 & 2 & 3 & 4 & 5 & 6 & 7 \end{array}$$

(1) T—W

(2) R_M

(3) PS

You could equally draw one diagram, and add a fourth rule that says V = 3 or 4. Whether or not you do this is personal preference. I do like having one fewer rule in my rule list.

Question 17

For acceptable order questions, go through the rules and use them to eliminate answers one by one.

Rule 1 eliminates **B.** The Turner must be closer to the entrance than the Whistler.

Rule 2 eliminates **A.** The Renoir must be closer to the entrance than the Morisot.

Rule 3 eliminates **D.** The Pissarro and the Sisley must be next to each other.

Rule 4 eliminates **E.** The Vuillard must be third or fourth, not second.

C is **CORRECT.** It violates no rules.

Question 18

This question places the Sisley in the seventh position. Whenever a question gives you a new rule, you can make an additional deduction.

Ask yourself which rules affect the Sisley. Rule 3 does: the Pissarro must be beside the Sisley. So the Pissarro must be in sixth on this question.

The Vuillard is the next variable I placed, since it can go third or fourth. I first tried putting the Vuillard third:

		V			P	S
1	2	3	4	5	6	7

We needs three spaces for the Renoir and the Morisot, so they can only fit around the Vuillard:

	R	V	M		P	S
1	2	3	4	5	6	7

In this diagram, the Turner could only go first, since the Turner has to go before the Whistler (rule 1). This doesn't help us, since "first" is not one of the answers.

So instead we can try putting Vuillard fourth:

			V		P	S
1	2	3	4	5	6	7

R_M are the next hardest to place. They can only go first and third, or third and fifth (around the Vuillard).

It doesn't make sense to put them around the Vuillard, because then only spaces 1 and 2 would be open for the Turner and the Whistler. We already know the Turner can be in first place, and that's not the answer.

So let's place R_M first and third:

R		M	V		P	S
1	2	3	4	5	6	7

Here we can see that the Turner and the Whistler can go second and fifth:

R	T	M	V	W	P	S
1	2	3	4	5	6	7

So **A** is **CORRECT.** The Turner can go second.

Question 19

This is the last of the "easy" questions on this game. After this, people start making lots of mistakes.

If you got this wrong, it's worth sketching some diagrams on your own page to see how the rules work together. This question is testing whether you can visualize restrictions and interactions between rules. I'll walk you through how I did it. Bear in mind that this takes a lot of text to *explain,* but the process of drawing it on your page should only take 10-30 seconds.

If the Pissarro is fifth, then the Sisley can be fourth or sixth. I first tried fourth:

$$\frac{}{1} \quad \frac{}{2} \quad \frac{}{3} \quad \frac{S}{4} \quad \frac{P}{5} \quad \frac{}{6} \quad \frac{}{7}$$

Since the Vuillard can only be third or fourth, this means the Vuillard must go third:

$$\frac{}{1} \quad \frac{}{2} \quad \frac{V}{3} \quad \frac{S}{4} \quad \frac{P}{5} \quad \frac{}{6} \quad \frac{}{7}$$

This diagram doesn't work. We need three spaces for R_M, but in the diagram above there are only two consecutive spaces open.

So since the Sisley can't go fourth, it must go sixth. And that's the answer: **C is CORRECT.**

Whenever you're working on a question like this, you should always glance over the answers whenever you make a deduction. Often the first deduction you make will be the right answer.

Question 20

This is where the questions start to get hard. I think question 20, in particular, has the potential to slow you down, unnecessarily.

I have a secret. I skip questions like this. Then I keep them in the back of my mind. As I draw scenarios for other questions, I eliminate answers. By doing this you can often eliminate all but two answers, and you only have to draw a couple of diagrams to prove which answer is right.

The correct answer to question 17 proves that Morisot can go third, so **A** is wrong. Unfortunately, none of the other questions produced scenarios that disproved answers here. Still, eliminating one answer is a good way to start.

I recommend making very rapid sketches to disprove the other answers. Do this before reading the rest of my explanation – this is a good review exercise. It shouldn't take long, and you often don't need to complete a sketch on the page to see that a scenario would work.

For instance, here's **B,** in two steps:

Step 1:

$$\frac{}{1} \quad \frac{}{2} \quad \frac{R}{3} \quad \frac{V}{4} \quad \frac{M}{5} \quad \frac{}{6} \quad \frac{}{7}$$

Step 2:

$$\frac{P}{1} \quad \frac{S}{2} \quad \frac{R}{3} \quad \frac{V}{4} \quad \frac{M}{5} \quad \frac{T}{6} \quad \frac{W}{7}$$

Remember, these diagrams only have to prove that something *could* be true. In the diagram above, PS could be reversed, but who cares? Either way, the diagram proves the Renoir can be third.

(question continued on next page)

Here's **C,** in two steps:

Step 1:

_	P	S	V	_	_	_
1	2	3	4	5	6	7

Step 2:

T	P	S	V	R	W	M
1	2	3	4	5	6	7

Here's **D,** in three steps.

Step 1:

_	_	T	V	_	_	_
1	2	3	4	5	6	7

Step 2:

_	_	T	V	R	_	M
1	2	3	4	5	6	7

Step 3:

P	S	T	V	R	W	M
1	2	3	4	5	6	7

Note that these don't take long at all. I just try putting T third, then see what else has to be true, and then finally what can be true. Here are the steps to prove that T can be third:

- T third
- V must be fourth
- R_M must be 5 and 7
- PS must be 1 and 2 (or vice-versa)
- W must be 6

Since the diagram works, you can eliminate that answer. I'll emphasize that if you *practice* doing this, and you know the rules, it should take 5-10 seconds to go through the steps above.

By process of elimination, **E is CORRECT.** Here's why, there's no space for PS:

Step 1:

_	_	W	V	_	_	_
1	2	3	4	5	6	7

Step 2:

T	_	W	V	R	_	M
1	2	3	4	5	6	7

PS ?

Now, you're probably saying to yourself "I don't have time to make all those drawings!". Actually, you do. There are three problems:

1. You overestimate how long it actually takes you to draw.
2. You haven't practiced drawing quickly.
3. You don't know the rules well enough.

I did those sequences of drawings on paper first. Each one took me about five seconds. Here's the steps:

1. Place the variable in the answer choice third.
2. Place Vuillard fourth.
3. Place R_M, the next most restricted element.
4. Place PS.
5. Place W after T.

None of that should take long. It should be automatic. Step 1, step 2, step 3, step 4, step 5, bam!

Improving is simple. On review, practice making these drawings until you are blazing fast at it. This skill will transfer over to new games.

Question 21

In the setup I said that only the Turner, the Whistler and the Vuillard can go between R_M. This question restricts R_M further. Since Turner must go before R_M and Whistler must go after, only Vuillard is left to go between.

There are two scenarios, since Vuillard can go third or fourth. Let's build both at once. This is how I sketched it on my page:

```
__  R   V   M   __  __  __
 1   2   3   4   5   6   7

__  __  R   V   M   __  __
 1   2   3   4   5   6   7
```

RVM are a block. The question says that we have to place Turner and Whistler before and after this block. In the first diagram, Turner must go first, and Whistler goes after, along with PS:

```
                W, [PS]
 T   R   V   M   __  __  __
 1   2   3   4   5   6   7
```

The other diagram, with Vuillard fourth, doesn't work. Once we place Turner and Whistler, there is no place to put the PS block:

```
                        [PS] ?
 __  T   R   V   M   W   __
  1   2   3   4   5   6   7
```

(Turner doesn't have to go second, I just placed it there to illustrate that this doesn't work)

So only the other scenario works. We can use this to eliminate answers.

```
                W, [PS]
 T   R   V   M   __  __  __
 1   2   3   4   5   6   7
```

The diagram contradicts **B** through **E**. **E** is wrong because if Whistler were sixth then there'd be no way for PS to be beside each other.

A is **CORRECT.** Pissarro could go fifth. This scenario proves it:

```
 T   R   V   M  [P   S]  W
 1   2   3   4   5   6   7
```

Question 22

Less than half of students get this question right. To do this question well, you have to be comfortable with making quick drawings to see what's possible.

Let's look at who we have to place for this question:

1. V, which goes third or fourth
2. PS, which go together
3. R_M, which form a block of three
4. T_W, which form a block of three

Apart from V, there is no variable that just takes up one space! That's very restrictive.

Once you see these are the restrictions, you must draw it. This is not the time for hesitation. I've seen students waste 40-60 seconds trying to work things out in their heads. This does not work! You will learn more in five seconds of drawing than ninety seconds of thinking. Watch this progression of drawings where I try to make a correct scenario with Vuillard fourth:

$$\frac{}{1} \ \frac{}{2} \ \frac{}{3} \ \frac{V}{4} \ \frac{}{5} \ \frac{}{6} \ \frac{}{7}$$

$$\frac{R}{1} \ \frac{}{2} \ \frac{M}{3} \ \frac{V}{4} \ \frac{T}{5} \ \frac{}{6} \ \frac{W}{7}$$

$$\boxed{PS}\ ?$$

$$\frac{R}{1} \ \frac{}{2} \ \frac{M}{3} \ \frac{V}{4} \ \frac{T}{5} \ \frac{}{6} \ \frac{W}{7}$$

I put Vuillard fourth, and I placed the three remaining blocks. You can switch the order of R_M and T_W, but the result is the same: we're missing the two open spaces required for PS.

So let's try putting Vuillard third. Again, I'll show the progression of my sketch:

$$\frac{}{1} \ \frac{}{2} \ \frac{V}{3} \ \frac{}{4} \ \frac{}{5} \ \frac{}{6} \ \frac{}{7}$$

$$\frac{P}{1} \ \frac{S}{2} \ \frac{V}{3} \ \frac{}{4} \ \frac{}{5} \ \frac{}{6} \ \frac{}{7}$$

$$\frac{P}{1} \ \frac{S}{2} \ \frac{V}{3} \ \frac{R}{4} \ \frac{T}{5} \ \frac{M}{6} \ \frac{W}{7}$$

I made this to prove that Vuillard can go third: it's a way of confirming that we were right to think that Vuillard can't go fourth.

This is just a could be true scenario. I know that PS can reverse positions, and R_M and T_W can also reverse positions. You don't need to draw every possible scenario for a diagram to be useful.

Since PS, R_W and T_W can all switch positions, none of those letters are possible candidates for something that must be true. That leaves Vuillard. We saw that Vuillard can't go fourth, so Vuillard must go third. **E is CORRECT.**

Question 23

Remember in the setup I said that only the Turner, the Vuillard, and the Whistler can go between the Renoir and the Morisot?

This restriction is rather central. In this question, the Turner is beside the Vuillard. That means that neither the Turner nor the Vuillard can go in between R_M. So only Whistler can.

Once you make a deduction like that, it usually answers the question. **B** is **CORRECT.** The Renoir must always come before the Whistler, because they go in this order: RWM

This may not be a satisfactory explanation for this question. That's the trouble with questions like this. Either they take forever, and you solve them with brute force, or you solve them quickly.

I personally didn't figure out the solution in advance. I make one scenario with the Turner next to the Vuillard. In the process of drawing, I noticed that the Renoir had to be before the Whistler, and *at that point* I realized there was no other way.

Making drawings is a revelation. You see things you could never possibly realize if you just try to think a question through. If I can teach you one thing, it's this: practice drawing, rather than thinking.

I'll repeat that, because it's important. Instead of thinking: draw, and draw quickly. In the process of drawing, you will figure things out.

To draw well, and fast, you need to know the rules. There's no substitute for this.

Section III - Logical Reasoning

Question 1

QUESTION TYPE: Flawed Reasoning

CONCLUSION: TekBank is more expensive than GreenBank.

REASONING: GreenBank has free ATMs. TekBank charges for its ATMs.

ANALYSIS: You're allowed to use common sense to form hypotheses on the LSAT. You *know* from your everyday life that banks have many fees. ATM fees are just a small part of the costs of having an account.

So TekBank could be cheaper than GreenBank if TekBank has no monthly fees, no overdraft fees, etc.

———————

A. This is not a flaw (in this case)! The conclusion is only about an economic factor (cost), so it's appropriate for the evidence to only involve economic factors.
Example of flaw: GreenBank will make you happy, because GreenBank is inexpensive.
B. This didn't happen.
Example of flaw: GreenBank is better. A teller at a Chicago branch of TekBank insulted me once, three years ago!
C. **CORRECT.** Here we go. To make a proper comparison, we'd have to know that GreenBank was at least as affordable as TekBank in other respects as well, such as monthly fees.
D. This is a different flaw.
Example of flaw: Overall, GreenBank is a friendly bank to deal with. So this particular GreenBank teller, Grumpy Bob, is surely friendly.
E. This is a different flaw.
Example of flaw: There is no evidence that TekBank offers better interest rates than GreenBank. So it must not be true that TekBank offers better interest rates.

Question 2

QUESTION TYPE: Point At Issue

ARGUMENTS: Klein argues that Einstein's theory is wrong. We have only found 1/10th of the matter predicted by the theory.

Brown argues that the theory has been successful in other areas, so it's more sensible to conclude that the theory is correct, and that we simply haven't found the remaining 9/10ths of matter.

ANALYSIS: For point at issue questions, the right answer must meet two criteria:

1. Both people have an opinion about the answer.
2. The opinions are different.

Most answers fail the first test, because only one author has an opinion about the answer.

———————

A. Both Klein and Brown *agree* this is true.
B. Klein doesn't mention whether Einstein's theory has had successes.
C. Neither Klein nor Brown says whether an acceptable alternate theory exists at present.
D. **CORRECT.** Klein agrees. Brown thinks instead that we simply haven't found all the matter.
E. Both Klein and Brown seem to accept that current estimates of matter found are accurate.

Question 3

QUESTION TYPE: Paradox

PARADOX: Chimpanzee anger can lead to both threat gestures and attacks. But threat gestures are rarely followed by attacks, and attacks rarely are preceded by threat gestures.

ANALYSIS: You might wonder why the stimulus says *both* of these things:

- Attacks rarely come after threat gestures.
- Attacks are rarely preceded by threat gestures.

These sound similar, but they are *very* different. The first refers to the odds of an attack, *if* you have a threat gesture. The second refers to the odds that a threat gesture occurred, *if* there was an attack.

Let's imagine two situations:

- 1,000 threat gesture incidents, 10 attacks, all attacks preceded by threat gestures
- 1,000 threat gesture incidents, 500 attacks, only 30 attacks preceded by threat gestures

In the first situation, it's true that attacks rarely come after threat gestures. But attacks are *always* preceded by threat gestures. So the first situation contradicts the second fact.

The second situation is consistent with both facts. Attacks rarely come after threat gestures. And threat gestures rarely come before attacks.

A. This explains why chimps make threat gestures, but it doesn't explain why chimps don't attack.
B. **CORRECT.** Threat gestures prevent chimps from having to make attacks. This explains why attacks rarely are preceded by threat gestures – if the chimps *had* made threat gestures then they wouldn't have felt angry enough to attack.
C. Suppose chimpanzees also display aggression by making funny faces. How does that explain anything about attacks and threat gestures?
D. This doesn't explain why chimpanzees don't attack after making threat gestures.
E. Tempting, but this statement doesn't *explain* why threat gestures don't lead to attacks. This is just a fact about chimpanzees.

Question 4

QUESTION TYPE: Strengthen

CONCLUSION: The Magno-Blanket can probably reduce pain in arthritic dogs.

REASONING: A study showed that patients reported reduced pain after being treated with Magno-Blankets. Dogs are similar to humans with respect to how close the blankets will be to their joints.

ANALYSIS: The LSAT expects you do know the basics of the scientific method. Every study should have a control group. Otherwise, your treatment method may be a placebo, or your results may be due to another factor.

For example, people might have felt reduced pain because they received human contact and attention from the doctors conducting the study. Or maybe the belief that they were being treated made the patients less stressed, and therefore better able to heal their pain.

Notice the study only says patients *reported* reduced pain. This level of detail is important. If the study *showed* that patients had a reduction in pain, then the argument would be stronger, as presumably a study has a control group if it *shows* a result.

A. Who cares about cats? We're trying to strengthen the idea that the blanket will help dogs. It doesn't matter what the blanket does to other animals.
B. This sounds pretty good, but it doesn't tell you that magnets reduce pain. In fact, *pain* is a signal transmitted from nerve cells to brains. So this answer could mean that magnets *increase* pain.
C. This answer suggests that it is *important* that we find a solution for dog pain. But this answer doesn't tell us that magno-blankets will *work*.
D. This is just a fact about who experienced the biggest benefit. We don't care who gets the most out of magnets. We only care if the magnets work, period.
E. **CORRECT.** This shows that the study followed the scientific method. Studies need control groups to be valid.

Question 5

QUESTION TYPE: Complete the Argument

CONCLUSION: The argument will likely say that there we haven't proven advertising is bad.

REASONING: Art and music changes people's preferences, and we think they are fine. Advertising also changes people's preferences.

ANALYSIS: This is a "complete the argument" question; you do not need to be critical or find flaws.

Instead, you need to understand how the author makes their case. This is an argument by analogy. The author mentions art and music classes because they are similar to advertising. So the author will conclude that advertising is fine, just like those classes.

The author agrees that advertising can change preferences. Their point is that this is not necessarily bad, since music and art classes do the same thing, and those classes are ok.

Notice the word "however". This means the author disagrees with the first sentence.

———————

A. This answer is a factual statement about how much advertising changes preferences. The author isn't concerned with the degree of preference shift. Her point is that the preference shift doesn't matter.
B. Nonsense. The author *doesn't* think advertising is pernicious (bad). She mentions art and music classes to prove that advertising is acceptable.
C. **CORRECT.** Art and music classes change preferences, and we don't think they are bad. So if advertising is bad, it's not simply because it changes preferences.
D. This goes too far. The author didn't say advertising is good. She just pointed out that we can't say it is bad merely because it changes preferences, since art and music classes also change preferences.
E. The stimulus contradicts this answer. Music and art classes *do* change people's preferences. The author appears to agree that advertising changes preferences.

Question 6

QUESTION TYPE: Principle

CONCLUSION: High school counsellors should tell students what life is like for local newspaper reporters.

REASONING: Most journalists work for local newspapers. High school students interested in journalism imagine a life of glamour.

ANALYSIS: Notice that the conclusion says what counselors "should" do. On the LSAT, you can *never* assume anyone "should" do anything. For example, this is *not* a good argument, even though everyone would agree with it: "We can save these kittens from a burning building at no risk to ourselves. So we should save those kittens".

We need to add the principle "you should save kittens, if you can do so without risking your health". Making that underlying principle *explicit* supports the argument. We must find a similar principle for this question. The argument says we should tell these kids the truth. Why would someone think that is a good idea? They must believe something like "if you can correct a mistaken impression, you should".

———————

A. The most tempting wrong answer. The conclusion is only that we should tell students what journalism is like. The argument didn't say we should *discourage* students.
B. The conclusion was about telling the truth, not about encouraging people to seek goals. And where did maximizing the chance of a happy life come from?
C. This doesn't match the stimulus. The conclusion wasn't that we should encourage people to be international reporters. It was that we should let them know most reporters aren't international.
D. **CORRECT.** This is the most complex answer. Never ignore an answer because it uses big words! "disabuse of unrealistic conceptions" = make sure the students know the truth.
E. Tempting, but we have no idea if local journalists regret their choice. It's true that high school students want to be international journalists. But maybe once they become local journalists they'll realize it's actually quite fun.

Question 7

QUESTION TYPE: Flawed Reasoning

CONCLUSION: The "safety" features are useless.

REASONING: Most pedestrian injuries happen at cross-walks with "safety" features.

ANALYSIS: This argument mixes up relative and absolute. Safety features improve *relative* safety. That means they make you safer.

Meanwhile, the safety of the crosswalks is absolute. They are either "safe" or "unsafe". So, the crosswalks in question could be *extremely* dangerous (an absolute measure). That's why they have safety features. The features make them *safer,* but not *safe*.

My explanation may seem rather abstract, but once you grasp this relative/absolute difference, you'll see it *everywhere*. Think deeply about this one. Here are some examples.

"You are *safer* with a fire extinguisher in a burning building, but you are not *safe.*"

"You are *less* healthy if you skip the gym one week, but you are probably not *unhealthy.*"

_____

A. **CORRECT.** If the safety features are placed only at the most dangerous intersections, then maybe those intersections would be even more dangerous without the features.
B. This isn't a flaw! If a safety feature really did fail to prevent injuries, why would we want it?
C. The argument didn't say this! No other safety features were mentioned. For a flaw answer to be correct, it has to happen.
D. Think about what this answer *really* means. It's insane. If the sidewalks in question have *no* other safety features, that means that every sidewalk in the country with stripes and flashing lights literally has *no* other features, such as a crosswalk sign.
The author didn't assume this, and I don't know why they would. You have to take answers literally. This one is rather extreme.
E. Totally irrelevant. The author doesn't say anything about injuries to drivers.

Question 8

QUESTION TYPE: Strengthen

CONCLUSION: The Korean aurora borealis helps confirm that John of Worcester saw sunspots.

REASONING: Sunspots typically produce an aurora borealis, after five days. Koreans observed an aurora borealis five days after John of Worcester claimed he saw sunspots.

ANALYSIS: This seems like a good argument. There is no horrendous flaw. The conclusion is appropriately mild: it just says the Korean sighting *helps* confirm John's claim.

To strengthen the argument, we can simply make the confirmation stronger. As things stand, it's possible that some other element caused the aurora borealis. The right answer shows that *only* sunspots could have caused the aurora.

_____

A. This *weakens* the claim by showing the aurora borealis might have occurred even if John's sighting was false.
B. Nonsense. The argument didn't claim John was the first person to see sun spots. The author just said John *did* see sunspots, so it doesn't matter who else saw them on a previous occasion.
C. **CORRECT.** This virtually guarantees the conclusion. It eliminates the possibility that the aurora borealis had another cause. Therefore there was heavy sunspot activity on the day that John of Worcester claimed to have seen sunspots.
D. This weakens the argument, by adding necessary conditions to John of Worcester's claim. We don't know if John met these necessary conditions.
E. This is just a neat fact. We're trying to prove that John did see sunspots. These illustrations don't prove anything. In fact, if John *didn't* see sunspots, then these illustrations are false.

Question 9

QUESTION TYPE: Principle

CONCLUSION: If you want to improve society, then you shouldn't believe that individuals can't affect it.

REASONING: If you don't think individuals can affect society, you will feel too helpless to change it.

ANALYSIS: On LSAT principle-justify questions, you must first of all figure out what the argument is saying. Let's look at the logic. It boils down to this:

"If you think individuals are powerless, then you'll turn into a helpless loser and you won't accomplish anything. Therefore you *shouldn't* believe that individuals are powerless."

Notice the word "should" in the conclusion. On the LSAT, you can *never* prove that something "should" happen unless you have a premise that says what you "should" do. So we need a "should" statement that links the premise and the conclusion. Like this:

"If something makes you a helpless loser, then you *shouldn't* believe it."

A. This doesn't match the conclusion, which was about what you should *believe*.
B. We're trying to prove that individuals *should* reject the belief that historical forces determine the future. This answer tells us what people should do *if* they reject this belief.
   So this refers to the wrong term. This is an *extremely* common technique for tricky answers.
C. Like answer B, this refers to the wrong thing. This answer talks about what you should do *if* you already feel helpless. We must prove that you *should avoid* beliefs that make you feel helpless.
D. **CORRECT.** If this is true, then you shouldn't accept the belief that society is determined by vast historical forces. We know that would make you feel too helpless to improve society.
E. Rubbish. The stimulus was about what we should *believe,* not how we should *act.*

Question 10

QUESTION TYPE: Must Be True

FACTS:

1. Subcontract → Lose control
2. **Contrapositive:** ~~Lose control~~ → ~~Subcontract~~
3. The company only subcontracts with companies that maintain control

ANALYSIS: We have a conditional statement (facts 1 and 2) and a fact (fact 3). You can combine them. The stimulus says that the companies the president uses for outsourcing don't lose control. According to the contrapositive above, those companies therefore don't subcontract.

Several wrong answers bring in outside assumptions about outsourcing being poor quality. The stimulus doesn't support this. If you outsource, you lose *control* over quality, but that doesn't necessarily mean the quality is lower. It just means you don't *control* whether or not quality is high.

A. **CORRECT.** This must be true. If the subcontractors were allowed to subcontract, then they would lose some control. Since the subcontractors *don't* lose control, we know they don't subcontract.
B. The stimulus never talks about disappointment. This answer is trying to make you bring in outside assumptions about outsourcing and poor quality.
C. This has to be *false.* If the company's president wanted full control, then they wouldn't outsource. You always lose control when you outsource.
D. This is similar to B. This might be true in real life, but nothing in the stimulus tells us that subcontracting leads to poor quality. We only know it leads to loss of control, which is not the same thing.
E. Careful. Loss of control doesn't necessarily mean loss of quality. We only know subcontracting leads to less control.
   Also note that this says *uniformly* better quality. That's a strong statement – it means every single in house product is better (i.e. there are zero duds).

Question 11

QUESTION TYPE: Sufficient Assumption

CONCLUSION: If students don't achieve broad mastery, they aren't being taught using appropriate methods.

REASONING: Students achieve broad mastery if they are taught with appropriate methods and they devote significant effort to their studies.

ANALYSIS: This is an unusually tricky sufficient assumption question. To get this right, you really need to draw it and see the flaw first. In fact I'm going to draw it like a logic game.

This is a *long* explanation. However, when I did this question myself, I did it rather quickly. The reason is that this process takes a long time to *explain,* but this process does not take a long time to *do.*

You should use this explanation to understand, but then practice the diagramming process on your own so that you learn it and can apply it quickly.

First let's look at the conclusion. We need to get from lack of broad mastery to lack of appropriate methods:

$$\cancel{B} \longrightarrow \cancel{M}$$

Now let's look at the evidence. If you have appropriate methods AND significant effort, you have broad mastery:

The contrapositive is that if you don't have broad mastery, you're missing appropriate methods or significant effort:

And this is where the flaw is. If we lack broad mastery, it's possible we have appropriate methods, and the problem is that we lack significant efforts. Not good. We need to make it 100% certain that lack of broad mastery means no appropriate methods.

There are two possibilities when you lack broad mastery: M̶ or E̶. We can guarantee the conclusion by showing that either possibility leads to M̶.

If we say that all appropriate methods lead to effort (M → E), then this attaches on to the diagram as the contrapositive (E̶ → M̶):

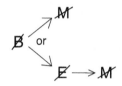

Now this matches the conclusion. If we don't have broad mastery, then we don't have adequate methods, no matter which path we choose.

Note: My diagrams are just one letter. If you make long, confusing acronyms, your own diagrams will destroy you. I've seen this happen time and time again. Diagrams are just a tool. The real knowledge should be in your head. Pick one useful letter, and *remember* what the letters refer to.

Note: I didn't do this diagram the first time I did this question. I solved this question with intuition. But following these steps will help improve your conditional logic, and there will be easier questions that you *can* solve up front.

(Discussion of answer choices on next page)

A. CORRECT. See the explanation above. This answer matches the addition statement I added to the diagram, and proves the conclusion. If this is true, then lack of broad mastery inevitably leads to lack of adequate methods.

B. This is a reversal of part of the evidence: broad mastery → significant efforts.

We're looking for something that tells us what happens if we *don't* have broad mastery. The "even if" part of this answer choice is meaningless fluff, it means that appropriate methods are neither sufficient nor necessary.

C. This tells us: broad mastery → appropriate methods. That's a reversal of the evidence from the argument, where appropriate methods were part of a sufficient condition for broad mastery. Contrapositive of the answer: ~~appropriate methods → broad mastery.~~

Not helpful. We need an answer that tells us what happens if we *don't* have broad mastery. It needs to b the sufficient condition: e.g. ~~broad mastery~~ → [something useful].

D. So? This was already implied by the stimulus. We only know that appropriate methods are a sufficient condition if they are accompanied by effort.

E. This is the same as D. We already know this is true. Efforts are only sufficient if accompanied by appropriate methods.

QUESTION TYPE: Identify The Conclusion

CONCLUSION: The heavier can doesn't necessarily have more food.

REASONING: The heavier can could simply have more water.

ANALYSIS: The conclusion is the first sentence: the heavier can may not have more food. There are at least three ways to identify the conclusion here:

1. It's the first sentence. If there are no conclusion indicators, the first sentence is usually the conclusion.
2. "Not necessarily". Any statement of probability, or showing that something might not be the case, is often the conclusion.
3. What receives support? The second and third sentences support the idea that the heavier can may not contain more food.

A. CORRECT. This is the first sentence, which receives support from the other two sentences.
B. This is evidence that supports the idea that a can might be heavier because of water and not because of food.
C. This is evidence that suggests that some cans may be heavier simply because of water weight.
D. Technically, the argument doesn't even say this is true. The final sentence merely says it's *possible* to include more water. The argument doesn't say companies actually *do* include more water. Maybe all companies are scrupulous.
E. The real conclusion is that a heavier can may not have more food. Having more water merely *supports* the idea that a can has less food.

Question 13

QUESTION TYPE: Principle

FACTS:

1. Some three years olds who could count could not remember their own phone numbers.
2. The children did manage to remember their phone numbers once they were taught a song containing their phone numbers.

ANALYSIS: Remember, you are looking for a principle illustrated by the situation. So the stimulus is an example, and the right answer has a principle that matches.

You are not trying to support the stimulus, and you're not trying to figure out what could be true based on the stimulus. You want the stimulus to be an example illustrating the right answer.

All we know here is that songs seem to be useful.

A. Tempting, but there might have been *other* ways the children could have learned. For instance, a nursery rhyme.
B. The children knew the words to express numbers. They just couldn't *remember* their phone numbers.
C. This goes too far. The situation doesn't show that the songs were the *best* method; the children didn't try any other methods beyond those they came up with on their own. We just know songs were useful.
D. We have no idea how the children learned to count. And we have no indication that the children don't know the meaning of numbers.
E. **CORRECT.** This is all we can say. Songs appear to have helped. We don't know if songs are the best method, or the only method, but they helped.

Question 14

QUESTION TYPE: Sufficient Assumption

CONCLUSION: The theorists are wrong, critics shouldn't strive to be value neutral.

REASONING: Critics can never achieve the goal of being value neutral.

ANALYSIS: Here's a quote I read once:

"Why not aim for the stars? You may not reach them, but you probably won't come up with a handful of mud either."

Many of the goals we pursue are unattainable, yet it still makes sense to pursue them, because we move in the right direction.

For instance, you want a 180. Frankly, I doubt you'll get a 180 (*I* didn't get 180). So according to these theorists, you should just give up, it's pointless.

Fuck those guys, right? Who cares that you won't attain the goal of 180. If you improve 10-20 points in the attempt, then the attempt was very worthwhile!

In other words, it may be useful to *attempt* to be value neutral, even if we can never become 100% value neutral. Since we want to prove the theorists correct, we should eliminate this possibility and say that goals are worthless if they can't be achieved.

A. We're trying to prove that critics *shouldn't* try to produce value neutral criticism.
B. **CORRECT.** It *is* impossible to be 100% value neutral, so this answer tells us not to try.
C. This shows a way that critics might fail to be neutral. But this doesn't prove that critics shouldn't *try* to be neutral.
D. The stimulus is talking about what *critics* should do. Readers are only mentioned to describe a benefit of being value neutral. The argument is not about readers!
   Also, it's not clear how readers will be affected if critics don't attempt to be value neutral.
E. This weakens the argument by showing that it can be useful to try to avoid value judgments.

Question 15

QUESTION TYPE: Flawed Parallel Reasoning

CONCLUSION: All microscopic organisms must be able to feel pain.

REASONING: Amoeba withdraw from harmful stimuli. Humans do this, and we feel pain.

ANALYSIS: There are two errors here:

1. Humans withdraw because we feel pain. But amoeba might withdraw for a different reason. (Maybe they have an instinct to avoid harm)
2. The conclusion generalizes from amoebas to all microscopic organisms.

Drawings would be distracting and wouldn't make the question any clearer. Do not draw diagrams unless there's a reason. I've seen people get so focussed on unhelpful drawings that they forget to look for the flaws. The two flaws are **1.** forgetting that reasons can differ, and **2.** overgeneralization.

A. **CORRECT.** This generalizes from poets to artists. And it ignores the possibility that there are many reasons for using odd language. People under hypnosis may do so because they have low inhibitions, but poets might have other reasons.

B. This answer doesn't overgeneralize (e.g. from corporations to all businesses), and it doesn't say that corporations *definitely* act the same as non-profits. (The conclusion says "probably").

C. This doesn't overgeneralize from one type of athlete to all athletes. And the rest of the argument isn't terrible. We know "most" athletes have the same reason for practice. Since all boxers practice to excel, it does seem "probable" skaters have the same reason. Probable = most.

D. This is a good argument. The second sentence is completely irrelevant. But the first sentence does prove the third sentence. Generally and probably are both synonyms for "most". So if predatory birds "generally" hunt alone, then it does seem "probable" that a given type of predatory bird (hawks) hunts alone.

E. This answer is part right because it says that the reason for something is similar (though not the same) in two different cases. But it doesn't overgeneralize to *all* mountains.

Question 16

QUESTION TYPE: Strengthen - Exception

CONCLUSION: Sunspots probably help cause changes in hare populations.

REASONING: Sunspots are correlated with changes in hare populations.

ANALYSIS: This is an open ended argument. There are a million reasons why sunspots could affect hare populations. You're trying to prove that correlation = causation in this case, so you just have to eliminate answers that provide a link.

A. The stimulus says increases in predator populations drive hares to forests and thus lead to shrinking hare populations. And this answer shows that sunspots affect predator populations.

B. **CORRECT.** This says that weather affects hare populations, and sunspots *don't* have anything to do with it. So this doesn't strengthen the idea that sunspots are a cause.

C. Hare populations are linked to changes in predators. If predators get more effective due to sunspots, then this will affect hares.

D. You might think this repeats the stimulus, but the LSAT never does that. A correlation just means that when one thing goes up, the other thing also goes up. This answer adds new information: the *amount* of the increase in sunspots and hare populations is also highly correlated. e.g. A 16% increase in sunspots leads not just to an increase in hares, but a ~16% increase.

E. The stimulus says hare populations depend on availability of food – there is less food in forests, and hare populations decline. So if sunspots decrease grass, then it makes sense that hare populations would also decline.

Question 17

QUESTION TYPE: Most Strongly Supported

FACTS:

Successful Economy → Flourishing Science → young people excited about science → good communication

Contrapositive:

~~Good Communication~~ → ~~Young people excited about science~~ → ~~flourishing science~~ → ~~successful economy~~

ANALYSIS: I normally don't draw "most strongly supported" questions, but this one is conditional. All the statements in the stimulus can be connected.

It's important to remember what your diagram means. There is a time element to these statements. A successful economy requires an *active* flourishing community. An active flourishing community requires that *past* young people were once excited. A community might continue to flourish for a while even if current youth are bored with science.

A. This is a mistaken reversal of the final sentence.
B. "Depends principally"? We know excited young people are a necessary condition, but they may not be the main one.
Something can be a necessary condition without being the *principal* necessary condition.
C. CORRECT. This follows from the logical chain I drew in the "Facts" section. A successful economy leads to good communication. That means there was good communication at some point in the past, since that led to past young people getting interested in science and forming the current scientific community.
D. The stimulus only says that "many" youth must *resolve* to become scientists. This answer says "most" youth must *actually* become scientists. That's far stronger. Resolving to do something doesn't mean you'll do it, and many is not most.
E. Nonsense. Good communication was only mentioned as a factor necessary for encouraging youth to want to become scientists. It's possible that an individual scientific *project* can succeed without good communication.

Question 18

QUESTION TYPE: Flawed Reasoning

CONCLUSION: Most businesses that currently don't have videoconferencing would benefit by buying it.

REASONING: Most companies that have bought videoconferencing equipment have benefitted.

ANALYSIS: This argument has a sample bias. It's possible that the businesses that bought videoconferencing equipment *knew* they would benefit from it.

Meanwhile, the businesses that haven't bought it have no use for videoconferencing, so they know they wouldn't benefit.

A. Not quite. The argument said that many businesses actually did benefit from the equipment, so the argument is stronger than this answer choice implies.
Example of flaw: Many businesses pay for expensive lunches for their managers. So clearly these lunches are worth the cost.
B. This describes a mistaken reversal of a conditional statement. The argument didn't do this. You should *never* pick this type of answer unless you've found a conditional reasoning error in the argument.
Example of flaw: Video conferencing will help businesses. So anything that isn't video conferencing won't help businesses.
C. This is a different flaw.
Example of flaw: Johnson said the free money making machine will be useful because he likes the color of the machine. Johnson has made a stupid argument. Therefore it's not a good idea to take the free money making machine.
D. CORRECT. See the explanation above. Businesses that bought the equipment probably knew they had a use for it. Meanwhile, businesses that haven't bought it probably realize they *don't* have a use for it.
E. This is a different flaw. The argument didn't compare cost or value.
Example of flaw: Pizza costs more than water, which is free. So pizza is more useful than water.

Question 19

QUESTION TYPE: Necessary Assumption

CONCLUSION: None of the trucks purchased 3 years ago were diesel powered.

REASONING: The company purchased 20 trucks 3 years ago. They sold none of those trucks this year, but they did sell all of their diesel trucks this year.

ANALYSIS: I found this question very difficult, and had to read it three times then come back to it. If the company sold all its diesel trucks last year, how could it not have sold any of the 20 trucks 3-year old if they were diesel powered?

It turns out I made a simple oversight. What if the company sold some of the 20 trucks *last* year, or *two* years ago?

I'll give a numerical example. Let's say the company owned five diesel trucks of type X. Three years ago, they bought four diesel trucks of type D. They also own two regular trucks, type T.

Two years ago, they sell all D trucks. And last year year they sell all their remaining diesel trucks, the X's. Here's the stock of trucks at the end of each year:

Four years ago: XXXXX TT
Three years ago: XXXXX DDD TT
Two years ago: XXXXX DDD TT
Last year: XXXXX TT
This year: TT

So in this example, the company did buy diesel trucks three years ago (DDD). It didn't sell them last year, but only because it already sold them two years ago.

A. Not required.
   Negation: One truck sold last year was gasoline powered, the rest were diesel.
B. Who cares what used trucks the company bought? The stimulus is about the 20 *new* trucks.
   Negation: The company also bought a used truck 3 years ago.
C. It doesn't matter whether the company bought other trucks. We only care about the 20 trucks bought three years ago.
   Negation: Two years ago, the company bought a new gasoline powered truck.
D. **CORRECT.** If some trucks were sold two years ago, then they could have been diesel trucks even though they weren't sold last year.
   Negation: The company sold some of the 20 trucks earlier than last year.
E. We don't care about trucks purchased *more* than 3 years ago. The question is about trucks purchased *exactly* 3 years ago.
   Negation: The company still has a truck it bought 18 years ago. Wowza!

Question 20

QUESTION TYPE: Flawed Reasoning

CONCLUSION: Telepathy is possible between people who are psychologically close, such as between friends or family.

REASONING: A good friend or family member often knows what you are thinking.

ANALYSIS: This is a tricky question, because it uses the word "psychic" in an uncommon sense. Most people think psychic means "telepathic" or "paranormal". That's definition number one in most dictionaries. But look at definition two from my Oxford dictionary:

Psychic 2. of or relating to the soul or mind: he dulled his psychic pain with gin.

This is really the only sensible definition of "psychic" in the context of the question. If you read "psychic" as meaning paranormal, then the first sentence would mean: "It is indeed possible that psychic people are psychic". That's not just circular reasoning – it's bloody stupid. No one would make such an argument, and the LSAC would never print it. So E, one of the most popular answer choices, is wrong. If there are two possible meanings in an argument, you should avoid the totally ridiculous meaning.

You should ask yourself: why are they telling me this? The author is saying close family members know each other's thoughts, and therefore they must be telepathic. The author's error is ignoring an obvious alternate explanation: family members have experience with each other. They know common reactions and body language.

A. Sample size is not well understood. You can have reliable results from just a few hundred people. And the bigger the effect, the smaller the sample size required. The "amazing" frequency here is presumably so remarkable that only a small sample is needed.

You do not need a large sample size to determine that arsenic is often fatal if ingested. You *do* need a large sample to conclude that a green button will lead to more website sales than a blue button.

B. CORRECT. You're allowed to use common sense on the LSAT (yes, really!). You know from experience that you can often guess what close friends and family are thinking. You're not telepathic – you just know them pretty well.

C. What emotion? This answer didn't happen. **Example of flaw:** You've *got* to work on this business with me! Don't you care about me at all? I'd be so sad if you didn't help.

D. The author didn't say this. They said family members have an "amazing" ability to know what we're thinking. Presumably family knows far more than the norm. But regular people could still sometimes get things right.

E. Very tempting, but this answer depends on a misunderstanding of the full meaning of "psychic". See the explanation above.

Question 21

QUESTION TYPE: Weaken - Exception

CONCLUSION: Sulfur fumes permanently damage your sense of smell.

REASONING: Workers from a sulfur factory identified fewer scents than a control group did.

ANALYSIS: There are a million and one ways to weaken an argument like this. I didn't bother pre-phrasing anything. I just opened my mind to possibilities, eliminated the easy answers, and focussed more narrowly on what was left.

———————————

A. **CORRECT.** This would have been a factor for both the factory workers and the control group, so this couldn't really have affected anything. Don't let the term "not perfectly" throw you – this answer is useless. It sounds like the smells were close enough for the study to be useful.

B. This means the sulfur workers were tested in a smelly factory. Maybe they couldn't identify the smells because of the overpowering smells in the factory. It's very reasonable to assume that the sulfur smell could overpower scents. Sulfur smells like rotten egg farts. You can use this kind of knowledge – true facts about the world are warranted assumptions.

C. This shows the control group was experienced at identifying scents. That experience could explain why they identified more scents.

D. Maybe the other noxious fumes cause loss of one's sense of smell.

E. This is like answer C. The factory workers don't know as many smells, so it's unreasonable to expect them to identify as many smells as the control group did.

Question 22

QUESTION TYPE: Principle

PRINCIPLE:

2+ Overdue AND Children's Books AND Previous Fine → Fine

APPLICATION: Kessler has more than one book overdue.

ANALYSIS: This is a straightforward conditional reasoning question. There are *three* sufficient conditions to establish that we must fine someone:

1. At least one of the overdue books is not a children's book
2. The person has a previous fine
3. More than one book overdue

Kessler meets the third condition. The stimulus says we must "justify" the application of the principle. So we need all three conditions. The right answer must show that Kessler meets the other two.

———————————

A. I almost chose this. But, the second condition is that one of the *overdue books* is not a children's book. This answer just says that Kessler has *some* books out that aren't children's books. Maybe all his *overdue* books are children's books.

B. **CORRECT.** This meets both missing conditions.
   1. One of the overdue books isn't for children
   2. Kessler has been fined before.
   Since the application contained the other sufficient condition, this answer proves the necessary condition.

C. The first condition works. Since Kessler does have some books out on loan that are overdue, this answer proves they must be non-children's. But the second condition doesn't work. We need to know that Kessler was fined previously, not just that he previously had overdue books.

D. This meets the second condition: Kessler was fined before. But this fails the first condition. We need to know that Kessler has some overdue books that aren't children's books.
   The final bit is fluff that adds nothing ("none of the fines were for children's books")

E. We need to know that Kessler *was* fined, but this answer says that he wasn't.

314

Question 23

QUESTION TYPE: Most Strongly Supported

FACTS:

1. Most medical lawsuits happen because people think their doctors are negligent or careless.
2. Doctors are less compassionate than they used to be, and more rude and patronizing.
3. This is because doctors view medicine as a science, and because certain economic incentives encourage doctors to treat patients rudely.

ANALYSIS: On most strongly supported questions you need to see how the facts fit together. I've rearranged the facts from the stimulus into three key groupings. I prephrased the answer as "economic incentives and the view of medicine as a science contribute to lawsuits", but the right answer didn't do this.

Instead the right answer just rephrased the second sentence of the stimulus (note: not the second fact above.)

A. We know that economic incentives are a factor. But that doesn't mean they are the main cause. For instance, we also know that the view that medicine is a science encourages lawsuits.
B. We know that both economic incentives and the view of medicine as a science encourage doctors to treat patients rudely. But we don't know why doctors view medicine as a science – the stimulus didn't say. You can't say that two things are linked just because they produce the same effect.
C. Careful. We know that most lawsuits arise due to patients' perceptions. But perceptions can be accurate! So perceived negligence could be actual negligence, and the lawsuits could be justified.
D. This is way too strong. The scientific outlook certainly has some downsides (rudeness, etc.), but it may have advantages as well.
E. **CORRECT.** This is just a restatement of the second sentence. Doctors view medicine as a science, and this makes them less compassionate. The way you view something is an action, and being less compassionate is the same as not caring.

Question 24

QUESTION TYPE: Parallel Reasoning

CONCLUSION: Even settling → poured while ground was dry OR crack

REASONING: Wet → ~~Solid Foundation~~ → ~~Settle Evenly~~ or Crack

ANALYSIS: I solved this question in 20 seconds. I just looked at the structure of the conclusion, which said "either A or B will be true". Only one answer, A, matched that structure.

That's the easy way, and probably how you should solve a question like this under timed conditions. But, if you're really interested in the structure of arguments, you can follow along with the rest of this explanation to see how this is a good argument, and why the conclusion is true.

Get a pencil and paper and draw it yourself, this is easily the least intuitive argument I've found in logical reasoning, ever. What follows is only for advanced students.

Let's review the logic. The stimulus gives two conditional statements. They join on "not having a settled foundation." I'm drawing the diagram with acronyms, look at the reasoning section above if you're not sure what they refer to:

W → ~~SF~~ → SE or C

SE and ~~C~~ → SF → ~~W~~

I've drawn the contrapositive as well.

Now, the question does something with logic that I've never seen any other LSAT question do. The conclusion is a correct deduction, but if you read the diagram left to right, you won't see it. Let's take a look at why the deduction is nonetheless true.

Look at the contrapositive diagram. There are two sufficient conditions: settling evenly, and not cracking. We need both to prove the necessary.

(question continued on next page)

If the concrete settles evenly, there are two possibilities: either the concrete cracks, or it doesn't:

SE and ~~C~~ → SF → ~~W~~

If the concrete doesn't crack, then we can conclude SF and ~~W~~. (Not wet is the same as dry. There's no in between with wet and dry.)

If the concrete does crack....well, that was the conclusion, right? Either the foundation is dry or it will crack. Voila.

So the two possibilities in the conclusion just describe the concrete either cracking or not cracking.

A. CORRECT. This conclusion matches the "either/or" structure from the stimulus. That's really all you need to know, since every other answer fails this test.
That said, here is the diagram that shows this really matches the structure of the stimulus:

~~B~~ and ~~D~~ → PE → WP

Not Blurred is the same as poured evenly in the stimulus, and the two exclusive possibilities are either dark or not dark, which proves the conclusion "dark or working properly". See the analysis above for the full explanation.
B. This says "*both* properly exposed and properly developed". We're looking for something that says either/or.
C. This says "the camera *is* working properly". We're looking for something that says either/or.
D. This says "the photograph *will not be* dark." We're looking for something that says either/or.
E. This says "A or B → Will not work properly". We're looking for something that says "A → either B or C".

Author's note: Here's how I really approach parallel answers: I look to see if the conclusion matches the structure of the conclusion in the stimulus. The harder the argument, the more likely LSAC left you a shortcut by allowing you to quickly eliminate wrong answers for structural reasons. If I still have two answers after looking at structure, then I focus more narrowly, but often only one answer is left.

Question 25

QUESTION TYPE: Strengthen

CONCLUSION: Evidence indicates that a certain property development hasn't hurt wildlife.

REASONING: Wildlife numbers have increased, and the park can support them.

ANALYSIS: This argument sound pretty good, so you have to ask yourself: "How could this evidence not lead to this conclusion?" Imagining an actual wildlife reserve. What would you look for in a successful reserve? You'd probably want to see lots of animals, and *many different types of species*.

The stimulus only mentions the number of animals increased. What if the development has killed off some species? Maybe the park is now only full of animals that thrive near humans, such as raccoons, squirrels and pigeons. Eww. You can strengthen the argument by eliminating this possibility.

It's perfectly ok to use outside knowledge this way. We're just using it to form guesses. The wrong way to use outside knowledge is to assume something *has* to be true. But thinking something *might* be true lets you answer many questions quickly.

A. CORRECT. This shows that species diversity hasn't declined. If all the animals were raccoons, then the argument would not be persuasive. This answer eliminates that possibility.
B. It's not clear how this affects the argument. If the previous survey was also taken in summer, then this has no effect. If the previous survey was taken in another season, then the argument is slightly *weaker* since the recent survey was biased. (Though the survey measured species numbers. The impact of diversity isn't clear.)
C. The stimulus says the park currently *is* capable of supporting the wildlife it contains, so it doesn't matter that it couldn't have done so a decade ago.
D. This *weakens* the argument. Maybe the old techniques found 10% of animals, and now we found 90%. The "increase" is just a mirage. There could even be fewer animals.
E. The conclusion is only about how animal life is doing. Plants are nice, but they don't matter here.

Question 26

QUESTION TYPE: Paradox

PARADOX: Life spans have increased, and we are healthier. Yet we have a higher rate of serious infections.

ANALYSIS: We need something that explains why infections are up even though health in general has improved. Answer E does this by showing that our health treatments only work because they expose people to infections. (e.g. chemotherapy)

Most people get this question wrong. It's a very good question, because it tests your ability to spot detail. The stimulus says that the *rate* of infections has increased. An example of rate is "37 infections per thousand people". Answer choice D is the most popular answer, but it says *number* of infections. An example of a number is "37".

People confuse number and rate all the time. Take crime statistics. Cities tend to be *safer* than rural regions. New York city has a high *number* of murders, because millions of people live there. But the murder *rate* in NYC is actually quite low.

A. You must take "some" at its weakest on answer choices. This answer could mean that 0.00001% of doctors prescribe the wrong medicine. That doesn't affect anything.
B. This doesn't explain anything about infections.
C. This doesn't explain why infections have increased, even though health is better.
D. This is incredibly tempting. It is warranted to assume that population has increased – everyone knows this is true. So based on this answer, we can say that there is a higher *number* of serious infections.
   But the stimulus is talking about *rate,* not number! Rate = amount of infections per capita. So the total population has nothing to do with the rate.
E. **CORRECT.** This shows that the treatments that improve our health also increase the infection rate.

Section IV - Reading Comprehension
Passage 1 - The Washington Color School
Questions 1-6

Paragraph Summaries

1. Sam Gilliam was part of the Washington Color School, a group of abstract African-American painters.
2. Gilliam thought African-American art was too conservative and too overtly political. He wanted art that abstractly expressed the African-American experience.
3. Gilliam captured the African-American experience with folded drapes.

Analysis

I normally don't teach LSAT vocabulary words, but this passage uses one that crops up often enough that you should know it: representational.

Representational art is the opposite of abstract art. And the word itself contains the key to its definition: representation.

You've been to art galleries. You've seen abstract art, and representational art, you just didn't necessarily know the word for the latter. Any picture you saw that painted a real object from the world is "representational", meaning that a painting of a fruit bowl "represents" the fruit bowl.

Rene Magritte played with this idea in 1928, when he painted "The Treachery Of Images". It shows a pipe, with the text "this is not a pipe". The painting is, in fact, not a pipe. It is merely a representation of a pipe.

A purely abstract painting, on the other hand, does *not* represent anything. Think of Jackson Pollack's work, or google "Voice of Fire", a work whose purchase caused no little controversy in Canada.

If you're clear on representational vs. abstract, then you will find some reading comprehension passages and logical reasoning questions easier to understand.

This passage is a good example. The first paragraph confuses many students. But all it's really saying is that the Washington Color School was more abstract than preceding groups.

Likewise, look at the start of the second paragraph. Gilliam rejected the strictly representational and explicitly political art of his African-American contemporaries.

It's easy to read over that sentence and not understand what it's talking about. But the passage will make more sense if you think of what such a painting would look like.

"The Problem We All Live With" by Norman Rockwell is an example of such a piece. Rockwell was not African-American (as a Canadian, I confess ignorance of African-American political art of the 1960s), but his painting is both strictly a representation of a scene, and explicitly political in that Rockwell criticized the crowds who taunted the young girl as she was escorted to school.

Gilliam thought paintings like that were too conservative. He wanted to represent the African-American experience through purely abstract works. Now, I'm not enough of an art connoisseur to understand how abstract works can represent an experience, but you don't need to know that. If you understand everything I've written so far than you know more than most students do when they read this passage.

The final paragraph describes how Gilliam aimed to achieve his effects. I still frankly don't know enough to say how draped canvasses represented the African-American experience, but that's not something you need to know. For a paragraph like the third one, you just need to be able to quote details if a question asks about them.

Question 1

DISCUSSION: Main point and primary purpose questions are much the same: use your paragraph summaries, and ask yourself "why is the author telling me this?"

This passage is a description of Gilliam's work, of its context within the African-American abstract art movement, and of what Gilliam was trying to achieve.

A. **CORRECT.** This is the best fit. This passage is above all a description of Gilliam's work.

B. Gilliam's work was far more than political. See lines 30-34. Gilliam wanted to describe the whole of human experience.

C. The passage mentions Gilliam's style, but not the *evolution* of Gilliam's style.

D. The passage does say that Gilliam's views were rare (line 35). But that's not the *point* of the passage, and the passage doesn't do much to *prove* that Gilliam's views were rare. This answer choice describes an argument devoted to *proving* that few others held Gilliam's views.

E. The passage didn't describe any technical limitations.

Question 2

DISCUSSION: Gilliam's work was abstract, yet also represented the human experience.

Representational art is any art that shows recognizable objects, such as people, animals, photographs, etc. Gilliam's art was abstract, not representational.

See the analysis section for a longer description of what representational art is.

A. This painting is representational, because it shows a man. Gilliam's work was abstract.

B. This art is still somewhat representational, because it shows photographs. Gilliam's work was abstract and represented no forms.

C. Same as A and B: this answer describes representational art. Gilliam's art was abstract.

D. This has canvas, like Gilliam's work, but this art is representational, because it shows the sea and clouds.

E. **CORRECT.** This is the only answer that describes abstract art. There are no recognizable forms in this piece. Also, this answer matches lines 39-41: Gilliam folded canvases onto each other.

Question 3

DISCUSSION: Lines 27 explains why the author mentioned the collage artist. Gilliam did not much like that type of art. "Though" is a logical word that indicates opinion; it's important to note any lines that start with though, but, however, etc.

So the collage art was an example of the popular art that Gilliam rejected as overly conventional.

A. Gilliam was *part of* the Washington Color School. The Color School made abstract art. The collage art was representational, not abstract.
B. We don't even know if there *was* animosity between abstract and representational artists, in general. We only know Gilliam didn't think much of abstract art.
C. This might be true, but it's not the point. The only reason the author mentions a collage is to give us an idea of what Gilliam objected to. The passage does not focus on the popularity of art, only line 27 mentions it, in passing.
D. **CORRECT.** Lines 27-35 make this clear. Lines 21-27 explain the collage, lines 27-29 explain Gilliam's reasoning for disliking it, and lines 29-35 show Gilliam's alternate approach.
There's nothing particularly special about the collage. The passage mentioned it because it's always nice to have an example for clarity.
E. Gilliam's art was *not* concerned primarily with political issues. Gilliam wanted to represent all of human experience. See lines 29-35.

Question 4

DISCUSSION: We can see Gilliam's opinions in two places: lines 16-21 and 28-30. Gilliam clearly is dissatisfied with representational art, but he is not too harsh about it.

A. This is exceptionally strong answer. If Gilliam felt this way, he would basically spit on the art of those who made representational art.
Gilliam clearly dislikes representational art, but he hasn't expressed open hatred.
B. **CORRECT.** The passage is clear about this. See lines 16-21, and 28-30.
C. "Whimsical" means means playfully or fancifully. Gilliam seems deadly serious about art.
If you don't know a word, see if it reminds you of similar words, such as "whimsy" or "whim".
Acting on a whim is probably a phrase you know.
D. Lines 16-21 and 28-30 clearly show that Gilliam disapproves of representational art.
E. Lines 16-21 and 28-30 contradict this answer.

Question 5

DISCUSSION: There's no fast way to answer this type of question. Either you remember the details mentioned in the answer choices, or you don't.

I personally check each answer against the passage. Because I have a good method for retaining where information is located, this takes me 2-10 seconds per answer, and is much faster than staring at the answers and going "hmm....." while trying to think my way to disproving them.

A. Lines 45-49 say this.
B. Lines 35-39 say this.
C. Lines 34-35 say this.
D. Lines 12-21 show this. You don't need to find the specific lines to disprove it. If you know that Gilliam was part of the Washington Color School, then you should know that the Color School was different from Gilliam's contemporaries. Gilliam rejected the style of his contemporaries.
E. **CORRECT.** The passage never mentions inspiration in general. Lines 43-45 mention that laundry "partially" inspired Gilliam, but we have no evidence that ordinary images are always the most inspirational images.

Question 6

DISCUSSION: A is the most common wrong answer on this question. I think it's tempting because it feels similar to Gilliam's attitude of defiance towards representational art.

But the similarities end there. On "author agrees" questions, you must interpret the statements literally. Interpreted literally, A is insane. Completely bonkers. I've seen few more insane statements on the LSAT.

No one would *ever* believe A. Not even that guy that made "Artist's Shit".

A. This statement is crazy.
   You must take LSAT statements literally. Interpreted literally, this statement is batshit insane. For example, it would include "You should not worry if your painting is so aesthetically ugly that it literally frightens people to death". No one believes that, including Gilliam.
B. Gilliam's art is abstract, so it's unlikely he believes this.
C. Lines 36-39 contradict this.
D. **CORRECT.** Lines 30-34 show that Gilliam was concerned with showing the complexity of human experience. And the first paragraph shows that Gilliam was part of the Washington Color Field school, so presumably he liked their philosophy.
E. Lines 36-39 show that Gilliam cared little for public expectations.

Passage 2 - Multiplayer Online Games (Comparative)
Questions 7-13

Paragraph Summaries

Passage A
1. Description of online multiplayer games.
2. Edward Castronova notices that games have economies.
3. Castronova realized that players auction video game goods on online auction sites.
4. Video game players are creating real world wealth.

Passage B
1. Most games ban players from trading game items for money.
2. Questions about taxation of video game goods.
3. In-game only wealth should be treated like gathering fish: taxed only upon sale.
4. We should tax the sale of items earned in game. This prevents virtual tax shelters and is in line with tax policy.

Analysis

These two passages are completely different in tone, yet many students do not notice the difference. If you struggle with tone and author's opinion questions, you should go over these passages with a fine toothed comb. Look for every word that indicates emotion or value judgement.

The first passage has a tone of excited discovery. Wow, look! There's an economy here. This is so cool guys! Oh my god, they're selling things! For money! Woooooo, economics!!

I'm exaggerating, but this passage is about as enthusiastic as LSAT reading comprehension passages will get. Take a look at lines 17-20: "....Castronova *stared*.....he realized with a *shock* what he was looking at."

Emphasis mine. I've never seen the LSAT describe someone as shocked, or experiencing any extreme emotion. This passage is astonishingly high on the LSAT emotional scale.

Notice that Castronova's article was published in 2004. I was at university in 2004. We had desktop computers, and no one had cellphones. I think I had gotten a high speed internet connection six years prior.

So, massive online games were *very* new. This article reflects that newness. An economist was only just noticing that these games have economies, and he wasn't looking for economies within the games. It was a surprise discovery.

The tone of passage B is very different. This article was published in 2007. The world has had three years to catch up to the fact that games have economies. Now the legal system has taken notice of online games. This paper discusses how to tax online game assets.

Tax policy? Bleh, so dull. In 2004 players would have been shocked that the government would take an interest in their games. But now (2014 at the time of writing) it's obvious that game earnings have real value, and passage B reflects an early version of this understanding.

As for the content of passage B, the argument seems rather sensible. The author argues for a clean division between games as entertainment and games as centers of e-commerce.

This passage is interesting in that five out of seven questions are entirely based on the main point of each passage and the relationship between them. One question (number 8) is partially based on this, and only question 13 is based on specific details.

On every passage, you should ask yourself "why are they telling me this". It's a useful question everywhere. But on these passages, it's essential.

Question 7

DISCUSSION: The first passage is about Edward Castronova's excited discovery of real economies in online games. The second passage is about how we should *not* tax online games, for the most part.

_____

A. The first passage is about Edward Castronova's *discovery*, not about the economist himself. And the second passage is about taxation, not intellectual property.

B. **CORRECT.** This matches both passages. Read my analysis section on the previous page if you're not sure why this is the answer.

C. The first passage doesn't mention the *growth* of online games. And the second title is too broad: the second passage is only about taxation, not all law.

D. The first passage is definitely not a guide to making money by playing games. And the second passage is about how to tax *video games,* not how to deal with online tax shelters in general.

E. These titles are too strong. *Communism* was a new economic paradigm. Online games are just a small niche in the economy. And passage B is mainly about *not* collecting revenue from video games.

Question 8

DISCUSSION: Virtual players skin animals to create valuable items. This generates wealth (lines 23-25). Real life fisherman gather fish, which produces a good which can be eaten or sold.

So both activities generate wealth using labour. One is virtual, one is real. The second passage suggests that such activities should not be taxed unless and until the good is sold. (lines 45-51)

_____

A. "The latter" is fishing. Lines 45-51 say that fish is "property". By any normal definition of the word, property is a form of wealth.

B. **CORRECT.** Read lines 45-51 for the full picture. The author only mentions fishing because it is similar to generating wealth online. (Lines 23-25 say that skinning animals online creates wealth.)

C. Lines 50-51 say that creating wealth online should *not* be taxed.

D. The author thinks *neither* gathering fish nor generating wealth online should be taxed. (lines 45-51)

E. The fishing in line 49 is real world fishing.

Question 9

DISCUSSION: See the passage analysis section for a full overview of the two passages. The author of passage A is very excited about the discovery of the new online video game economy. Lines 17-18 describe Edward Castronova's shock at finding an economy. This is strong language for the LSAT. The author of passage A is excited.

Passage B has a scholarly tone. See lines 44-45: "This article will argue that....policy support that result."

A. Neither passage is critical or apprehensive (afraid of) the online video game economy.

B. The *second* passage is academic. This question asks about the style of the first passage. And neither passage is dismissive.

C. **CORRECT.** See lines 7-8 "curious", or 13 "even more interesting" or 17-18 "stared....with a shock". The author of passage A is extremely excited about this new discovery.

D. Passage A is definitely curious about this new phenomenon. Undecided is not the right word however. Here's an example of an undecided but curious article:

"I don't know about these online games. They seem difficult. Can you really make money in them? That's so different from anything I know. Is it really possible? I bet there's some mistake here. I definitely want to know more though."

E. Passage A is definitely enthusiastic. They are not skeptical however. No part of the passage questions whether Castronova is correct.

Question 10

DISCUSSION: This question tests the same thing as question 7: did you understand the differences in tone between the two passages?

Passage A is excited about a new phenomenon. Passage B is a scholarly discussion of how to apply the law to this somewhat less new phenomenon.

You can use the scholarly element in passage B to eliminate wrong answers. Only answers A and D have a scholarly second title.

A. This answer's title for the first article sounds scholarly. The tone of passage A is more like "woah, there's artificial intelligence here!".

B. Both of these titles describe newspaper stories. But the second passage was scholarly. Also, the first title should be "Retailers discover e-commerce" and the second should be "how the law applies to e-commerce"

C. The first part is pretty good. The second title is not good however. It describes a newspaper article about a debate between scientists.

D. **CORRECT.** The first title has the same tone of discovery. The second title has the same tone of scholarly discussion of how to apply the law to a new area.

E. Edward Castronova is notable because he noticed the new online economy. He isn't a renegade. And the second title describes a newspaper article, not a scholarly article.

Question 11

DISCUSSION: The first passage seems general. You don't need to understand any economics or video game concepts to follow along.

The second passage is scholarly, and probably came from a journal.

Some of the wrong answers are goofy. Clearly, neither passage was from a science fiction novel or a speech before a legislature.

A. CORRECT. If you don't see that this is correct, reread my analysis section and then reread the passage. Look for any words that indicate tone or style.

B. I studied economics. A technical journal for economists would probably sound like this: "Does the marginal utility of online video games justify the opportunity cost of playing them? And can rents created within the game provide an alternate and complementary incentive for participation?"

C. Science fiction novel? Passage A is talking about the real world.

D. Passage *B* is from a law journal. Passage A is probably from a generalist magazine. And neither article is from a speech to a legislature.

E. If you chose this, I'm not even sure you read the passage. This answer is just silly: who would read a science-fiction novel that discussed video game tax policy at length?

Question 12

DISCUSSION: Another question about the relationship between the passages. Knowing the main point of each passage would answer at least three questions on this passage.

Passage A describes a new phenomenon. Passage B describes how to deal with the taxation issues that arise from that new phenomenon.

A. CORRECT. The first part is obviously correct. You may have hesitated about the second part. Are online game economies really a problem? Yes. See lines 56-58. If we don't tax online economies to some extent, they will be a tax shelter.

To be clear: "A problem raised" is not really a negative term. The author of passage B could think "online economies are excellent. There's just one small problem (issue) we have to address".

B. Passage A isn't describing an economic theory. The passage just describes Edward Castronova's discovery of online economies, in an article addressed at the general public. A theory would be like "online economies behave exactly like real world economies. This paper will show...."

C. Passage B didn't say it would be *difficult* to tax online games. Passage B was debating *whether* and *how* we should tax online games.

D. Hogwash. Before Passage A, there wasn't even a common interpretation of online economies. Edward Castronova discovered them. So there's no common interpretation for Passage B to affirm.

E. Passage B isn't theoretical. An article is not theoretical just because it is scholarly. Passage B is discussing the very *practical* issue of whether we ought to tax online economies.

Question 13

DISCUSSION: This is the trickiest question. Lines 52-55 make a distinction between games that are intentionally commodified, and those that aren't.

The first paragraph of Passage B also makes this distinction, though it's less clear. Paragraph one says "but some actually encourage *it*."

"It" is real world trade in virtual items. It's reasonable to say that those games have been commodified. In game transactions are explicitly viewed as economic transactions by the games' creators.

The creators economize the games by giving intellectual property rights, which is answer D.

A. Lines 52-54 talk about selling *virtual* items for real currency. This answer talks about selling a *real* item for virtual currency. E.g. "I'll sell you my house for $10,000 elf-dollars".
This answer would have been correct if it had used the right words, but it used the wrong words instead.

B. The word "avatar" doesn't appear in passage B. This answer has no support.

C. Passage B doesn't mention whether all players gain wealth simply by playing longer. Some games may have high costs that reduce wealth.

D. **CORRECT.** Lines 26-29 support this. The games that grant intellectual property rights are encouraging real world commerce. This amounts to "intentional commodification".

E. Passage B never mentions whether you can trade elf-dollars for orc-dollars (for example). In fact, passage B doesn't even mention whether you can trade virtual currency for real currency. Passage B only mentions virtual *items* for real currency.

Passage 3 - Success and Talent
Questions 14-19

Paragraph Summaries

1. Opposing view: Some people think that talent is innate.
2. Recent studies suggest that talent only occurs within specific fields of expertise. E.g. Athletes have good reaction time in their sports, but not necessarily in general.
3. Most high performers only became good through training. Even anatomical characteristics can be trained.
4. Motivation is more likely than talent to be a predictor of great ability.

Analysis

This passage is an argument. It's important for you to understand why the author says the things they say.

Their overall point is this: talent is acquired, not innate. The paragraph summaries above show how each section fits into the argument.

The particular details used to support the argument are not that important. You should know where to find details, but you don't need to memorize them. These are the important facts you should retain:

- Talent can be learned
- Top performers largely don't rely on genetic talent
- Motivation and time are required for success
- Some innate talent is required (lines 55-56)

The passage is nuanced. The author does not say their theory is definitely right. Lines 62-64 just say that motivation is "more likely" to be important than innate talent.

And talent is a factor. Height, for example (45-47) definitely matters and can't be changed. And lines 41-45 imply that some innate skills are useful for chess. They're just not essential. If you lack certain innate talents, you can overcome them by training other skills.

Question 14

DISCUSSION: The passage is nuanced. Research suggests that motivation is more likely to be important than innate talent. (lines 62-64)

The author does *not* say that innate talent is useless. For instance, lines 41-45 show that superior innate capacities can help chess players, *but* chess players can overcome these limits with training.

And lines 55-56 show that you need *some* talent to succeed. The author's point is merely that it's not as important as we think.

―――――――――――

A. The passage said many traits, such as perception, are *not* inborn. They can be altered by training. The passage did not say that inborn traits (such as height) can be altered by training.
B. The author didn't say that anyone can achieve exceptional levels of performance. Exceptional performance is, by definition, rare. You don't need innate talent for exceptional performance, but there may be other necessary conditions.
C. This goes too far. Lines 41-45 show that superior traits can be useful. Chess players can *circumvent* innate limits with training, but not having innate skill is still somewhat of a disadvantage.
D. **CORRECT.** This is the best summary of the passage. It is appropriately nuanced. The author did not say that their argument is conclusively correct. Lines 62-64 just say that superior performance is "more likely" due to motivation than innate talent.
E. This isn't necessarily true. The psychologists are only mentioned in the first paragraph. The author has presented good evidence that the psychologists are wrong. But that doesn't mean the psychologists will change their beliefs: people often hold onto wrong beliefs.

Question 15

DISCUSSION: The final paragraph is the conclusion – line 51 says "therefore". This paragraphs sums up the argument that learned skills are more important than innate talent.

The paragraphs ends by saying that since motivation is required for skills, then motivation is likely more important than talent.

———————————

A. What? The final paragraph doesn't even mention education. You can learn skills outside of the education system.
B. There's no contradiction in the final paragraph. I have no idea what this answer choice might refer to.
C. There are two problems here. Recapitulating evidence would mean listing everything that was said in paragraphs two and three. The fourth paragraph simply didn't do this. The fourth paragraph restated the conclusion, but it did not restate the evidence. Restating the evidence would be: "Because studies show that talent is specific to the field of expertise (paragraph 2) and because adult performers were not exceptional as children (paragraph 3)" etc.
The second half of this answer is also false. The fourth paragraph does not discuss future research. Look all you want, you won't find it. Instead, the second paragraph makes a conclusion about the importance of motivation.
D. What possible objection? I have no idea how to disprove this answer. It simply has no basis in paragraph 4.
E. **CORRECT.** The two inferences are:
1. Extended training + a common level of talent may account for outstanding performance.
2. Motivation may be more important than talent.

"Suggests instead" (line 54) is what shows that these *are* inferences. This answer is very abstract. If you see an abstract answer, don't glaze over. There are good odds it's actually the answer. Take the time to figure out what it refers to.

Question 16

DISCUSSION: You must take LSAT answers literally. If a statements says "talent plays no role" then this means talent has *zero* impact. That's a silly idea, and the authors don't agree. Lines 55-57 show that some talent is required.

Yet answer E is the most common answer chosen: it says talent plays *no* role. That's insane.

———————————

A. **CORRECT.** I had a bit of difficulty choosing this answer. It feels right, but there's no line in the passage that proves it. Nonetheless, I believe it's well supported.
Consider an adult chess player. They have exceptional memory and perception. Lines 51-55 show that extensive training + reasonable talent is enough for exceptional skill. But the argument doesn't rule out exceptional talent + moderate practice as a way to gain skills.
So does this chess player have exceptional innate talent? We don't know. How would we know? We can see the chess player is skilled. It would be difficult to reconstruct the past and see if these skills were innate or learned.
B. Lines 55-57 contradict this. You don't need the highest level of talent to succeed. You just need the level of talent common to reasonably competent performers.
C. The passage didn't say whether any fields actually do require exceptional talent. And the whole point of the argument is that exceptional talent tends not to be required.
D. This isn't supported. Lines 62-64 say motivation is required, but the passage doesn't say what affects motivation.
E. This answer directly contradicts the passage. Lines 51-57 say that "that level of talent common to all reasonably competent performers" is necessary for exceptional performance. The passage says talent is not as important as we think, but the passage definitely says some talent is necessary.

Question 17

DISCUSSION: This question stem is very clear: it tells you that the passage *literally* says the answer. If you can find the right line, you can be 100% certain of your answer. This type of question tests your recall, and how well you can skim to find information.

Keeping up intense practice is only mentioned in the final paragraph, so you just have to look there. Note that the question is not asking what's necessary for success. The question is asking what's necessary to keep up practice.

It's hard to know what to say about the wrong answers except that they're not mentioned in the passage, or not mentioned as being necessary for practice. The question asks about what's required for practice, not for being skilled.

A. CORRECT. Lines 57-59 say this.
B. Emotional support is never mentioned.
C. The passage never mentions whether instruction at a particular level helps people practice. You might have picked this because lines 36-39 say that early practice is crucial for the vast majority of performers. But the question asks about what is necessary for *practice* itself, not for talent.
D. The passage never mentions leisure.
E. The passage never mentions self-discipline or control.

Question 18

DISCUSSION: Lines 21-27 are the key lines for sifting through these answers. The author uses *new* evidence to argue against an old theory.

That one sentence I wrote above disproves all four wrong answers.

A. The author didn't "revise" a theoretical model. The old model was that talent was innate. The author completely rejects this model.
B. Lines 17-27 show that the author's argument is based on *new* research.
C. CORRECT. Lines 17-27 show that the author's argument is based on new research. The "certain views" is the opposing viewpoint in paragraph 1. The particular class of cases can refer to one of two things: exceptional performers, or, perhaps, those exceptional performers that do not depend on innate talent. (Some cases of exceptional performance may depend on innate talent, because some traits are indeed innate, see lines 45-47)
D. The author mentioned the old viewpoints in paragraph 1, but the author didn't mention any "probable objections" to his new theory. Any new objections would have to take into account the evidence the author refers to paragraphs 2-4.
E. The author's theory is not abstract, and the evidence is not old. Lines 21-27 show that the author uses *new* research. And the author's theory of talent is practical: it's based on elite performance in the real world.

329

LSAT 71 - SECTION IV, RC

Question 19

DISCUSSION: This question refers to lines 32-35. These lines are precise, and they say two things:

- Chess players have good memory for arrangements of chess pieces in typical chess arrangements.
- Chess players do not have good memory for chess pieces in non-typical arrangements.

The passage doesn't say whether chess players have good memories for other things or for other games.

A. This is the most popular wrong answer. Read lines 32-35 carefully: the passage doesn't say anything about other games. We have no idea how well chess players remember things that don't involve chess pieces.
(In case that doesn't convince you: it's possible that these sequences of moves in other games are *also* typical of chess, in which case chess players would remember them)

B. The passage doesn't mention sequences without spatial elements.

C. Lines 32-35 say that chess player can remember chess configurations. It does sound like remembering a whole game is more challenging than remembering a configuration. But this answer is only talking about easy games. We have no evidence that chess masters are incapable of remembering whole games.

D. **CORRECT.** Specifically, lines 32-35 say that chess players do not have a good memory for *non-typical* configurations of chess pieces.

E. Logical analysis simply isn't mentioned in the passage. There is no evidence to support this answer choice.

Passage 4 - The Physics of Mirrors
Questions 20-27

Paragraph Summaries

1. Description of the field-of-sight explanation for mirrors.
2. Some physicists offer a persuasive, but flawed, front-to-back reversal explanation.
3. This front-to-back explanation is persuasive because it seems natural, but we can't trust our senses with mirrors. They are 2-d, but simulate 3-d.
4. Scientists like the front-to-back explanation because they can separate the observer from the event. But in this case there is no event (reflection) without an observer.

Analysis

You don't necessarily need to know details in this passage. For example, I forgot all the details in paragraph 1. I just know that's where the field-of-sight explanation is.

In fact, as I write this explanation, I don't remember any of the details from paragraphs two and three. So what do I know? I took note of the structural elements of the argument. I remember everything I wrote in the paragraph summaries above, and I know what the author is saying. If a question asks about the details, I know where to find them, because I know the organization of the passage.

The author's main point is that mirrors are deceiving. We should explain them in terms of what actually happens (field-of-sight explanation) rather than what makes intuitive sense (front-to-back explanation).

When we look at a mirror, we imagine 3-d objects. In fact, our eyes focus on mirrors as if we were looking at a 3-d scene, rather than a 2-d object (lines 38-41).

But mirrors are not 3-d. They are flat sheets of glass. There is no object inside them which is the reverse of real world objects. Instead, something happens with light (spare me the details, they're in paragraph 1!) which reverses our vision left-to-right, making the image reversed.

Paragraphs 2-4 are devoted to showing that the front-to-back theory of mirrors is wrong. The front-to-back theory is based on our intuitions. When we look into a mirror, it looks like the objects are reversed from front-to-back.

This theory makes sense in terms of how we imagine mirror objects in our heads (our "mental constructs" of mirror objects). But this theory gives a false impression of what happens in the real world. Lines 34-36 say that we take what we see in mirrors and imagine it wrong in our heads.

Many answers talk about mental constructs, so the test-makers assume you will find them confusing. It's a fancy term for "stuff you imagine". We don't see the real world. Light hits our eyes, and our brains turn that into mental images. These images aren't real, and what you see may not be what someone else sees.

However, in most cases, our mental images of the world give us a good idea of what the world is actually like. But in the case of mirrors, our mental constructs are inaccurate. A mirror is just a flat piece of glass. But we see it as a 3-d scene.

The final paragraph explains another reason why the front-to-back theory is popular. Scientists like to separate objects and observers.

This doesn't work with mirrors. If no one looks into a mirror, there is nothing to see. The phenomenon of a reflected object is only there if an observer can see the object.

(continued on next page)

Analysis Continued

Structural words are extremely important on reading comprehension. They let you skip over the details and focus on a few key points. When you review RC passages, highlight structural words to train yourself to process them automatically. Here are some examples:

- however (line 14)
- it is clearly (line 22)
- yet (line 23)
- however (line 27)
- note (line 38)
- In addition to (line 42)
- However (line 48)

This passage has an unusually high number of structural words. That means the questions will test whether you understand the author's purpose. I'm this paragraph after having written explanations for all the questions on this passage, and almost all of the questions test overall comprehension, not details.

Frankly, these questions are easy if you understand the passage, but almost impossible if you don't. In fact, if you still don't understand the passage, then I fear my explanations may be rather difficult to follow, because I have to use words such as "front-to-back explanation", as that is what this passage is about.

I recommend two steps if you found this passage difficult:

1. Reread the passage, and other hard science passages, until they start to make some sense.
2. Go to your local library, and get 20-30 back issues of the economist. Start reading the science sections.

The Economist science section is about three pages long. It's well written, yet not dumbed down, so it matches the style of LSAT reading comprehension science passages.

Question 20

DISCUSSION: Lines 48-51 contain the answer to this question. In the analysis section I mentioned the importance of structural words such as "however". This question is a perfect example: you should take special notice of lines that follow "however", such as lines 48-51.

A. **CORRECT.** See lines 48-51. The two elements are "what mirrors do" and "what happens when we look into mirrors"
B. The author appears to agree with the field-of-sight explanation in paragraph 1. Whether or not this is true, the main point of the passage is to argue against the front-to-back theory.
C. Nonsense. The author didn't say that no other expert could give an explanation of mirrors.
D. It's true that the explanation of mirrors is still subject to debate. But the author's main point is that one side of the debate is wrong.
E. This answer made me laugh. LSAT authors tend to know everything. They have the truth, and they're here to give it to us. The only time an LSAT author would argue an issue is complicated is if some other person argued the issue was simple.

Question 21

DISCUSSION: This question tests two things:

1. Do you remember that the left-to-right explanation is discussed only in the first paragraph.
2. Can you reread the first paragraph and retain the details long enough to spot the right answer?

Don't make this question more complicated than it needs to be. The right answer is directly in the paragraph. The wrong answers are calculated to confuse you. It should only take about 15 seconds to reread the first paragraph – rereading is far faster than reading the first time.

(left-to-right reversal is part of the field-of-sight explanation, in the first paragraph)

_____

A. Front-to-back is the alternate explanation, it is described in paragraphs 2-4. This question asks about the left-to-right explanation, which is only mentioned in paragraph 1.
B. **CORRECT.** Lines 10-12 say this.
C. Lines 7-10 say that mirrors images depend on the position of the *observer,* but the position of the object isn't mentioned. Size makes no sense: small objects reverse, and big objects don't? You know from experience that size doesn't affect whether a mirror image reverses.
D. There are no two-dimensional objects. There are two dimensional *images,* but not objects. If you ever come across a perfectly two-dimensional object, call a mathematician.
E. Lines 28-31 mention mental constructs. These are only mentioned to explain why the front-to-back theory is persuasive. Mental constructs have nothing to do with the first paragraph and the field-of-sight theory.

Question 22

DISCUSSION: Lines 28-32 mention mental constructs. That sentence starts with "It seems natural because....mental constructs".

To answer this question, you need to read the previous line, to see what "*it* seems natural because" refers to. "It" is a pronoun. Whenever you see one, you must refer to earlier lines so that you know what "it" is. The LSAT uses this pronoun trick time and again.

The previous sentence says that the front-to-back explanation appeals strongly to people. This is because we deal with mental constructs of objects.

So mental constructs help us to understand and accept the front-to-back explanation of mirrors. By the way, "mental construct" just means images you make in your head. Like when you imagine your dog – it's not a real dog, it's just your imagination. But usually it bears some resemblance to your dog.

This question is extraordinarily confusing, and highlights the importance of going back to the passage. If you understand lines 28-32, then this question is easy. If you don't, then you'll waste time bouncing between nonsensical answers. None of the wrong answers make any sense. All of them refer to things that were never mentioned in the passage.

_____

A. There is no top-to-bottom explanation. This answer is total nonsense designed to confuse you.
B. **CORRECT.** Read lines 26-32 in full and you'll see that mental constructs help us understand the front-to-back explanation.
C. This is a nonsense answer. "Complex perceptual observations" does not appear in the passage.
D. I don't even know what this means. I'm assuming you only picked this because you had no idea what any of the answers meant.
    The passage didn't talk about rejecting associations between constructs and perceptions. In fact, the passage says that mirrors are confusing *because* we assume our mental constructs and objects/perceptions are the same.
E. The passage doesn't talk about overemphasizing senses. This is another nonsense answer.

Question 23

DISCUSSION: The front-to-back explanation is the opposing explanation mentioned in paragraphs 2-4.

The author does not accept this theory. Lines 26-28 say that it is successful "to a point". Right away we can narrow things down to D or E.

In the passage analysis section I highlighted words that indicated the author's opinion, such as "however". Those words are crucial to the argument, and to answering this question.

A. The author only thinks the front-to-back explanation is successful "to a point". See the analysis above.
B. Same as A.
C. Same as A and B.
D. It is not a bad thing to be consistent with previous theories. You may know that from common sense. In any case the author does not say consistency is a bad thing.
E. **CORRECT.** The front-to-back theory does not offer an explanation of mirrors based on the observer. It treats the objects in mirrors as real, which is false (21-25). Lines 48-54 say that any good theory of mirrors must consider what happens when an observer looks in.

Question 24

DISCUSSION: You might think that the point of the passage is to compare two theories of mirrors. But the field-of-sight theory is only mentioned to establish that we have a pretty good explanation of mirrors. After the first paragraph, the field-of-sight theory is not mentioned again.

Instead, the rest of the passage discussed the front-to-back theory. The main point of the passage is that the front-to-back theory is not satisfactory. This is because it doesn't consider what happens when we look into mirrors (lines 48-54).

A. The passage doesn't give any evidence against the field-of-sight theory. It appears the author agrees that this theory is correct.
B. This is a tempting answer, but the front-to-back theory is *not* based on empirical evidence. We use our mental constructs to imagine the front-to-back theory (lines 28-32), but these constructs are contrary to fact (lines 34-36). The front-to-back explanation is based on a false idea.
C. Lines 48-51 did mention two necessary conditions for an explanation of mirrors, but this is not the same as listing difficulties that need to be overcome. A difficulty is a specific obstacle that needs to be removed, for instance "we need to construct a physically perfect mirror" or "we need to figure out a way to measure light entering a mirror".
D. **CORRECT.** Paragraphs 2-4 are dedicated to showing why the front-to-back theory is inadequate. See the passage analysis section and the discussion above for more details.
E. The passage does explain why the front-to-back theory is accepted. But it is not because of theoretical support. Instead, the front-to-back theory receives support for two reasons:

1. The front-to-back explanation seems natural to us, due to the way we imagine mirrors (lines 26-32)
2. Scientists like to separate the observer from the phenomenon (lines 42-45)

Question 25

DISCUSSION: Author agreement questions are heavily based on the passage. You can usually find a specific line that proves the right answer.

Questions like this show that it's worthwhile to take extra time reading and understanding the passage. This will improve your recall of the details, and help you spot the right answer on this type of question.

———————

A. The author actually never mentions optical equipment or mirror quality. Presumably an explanation for mirrors should make sense even for poorly constructed mirrors, and even if we don't have fancy equipment to confirm the theory.

B. The author only mentioned two theories of mirrors, and they only argued one of them was wrong (the front-to-back) theory. So the author doesn't say why mirrors explanations fail *in general*.

C. **CORRECT.** Lines 42-45 support this. They say that the observer/phenomenon separation is part of the reason why some scientists support the front-to-back theory.

D. Lines 28-30 say "we" think in terms of mental constructs. Mental constructs seem natural. The passage doesn't say any of us avoid mental constructs. And even some scientists like the front-to-back theory, so they must be thinking in terms of mental constructs.

E. This is almost right. If it had ended by saying "mental constructs interfere....with an accurate understanding of how mirrors work" then this answer would have been right.
But the answer doesn't say that. You need to read every word on the LSAT. The passage doesn't say that mental constructs interfere with our understanding of perceptions.

Question 26

DISCUSSION: The author appears to think that the field-of-sight theory is correct. It's discussed in the first paragraph. If you reread that paragraph, you'll find not one criticism of the theory.

The field-of-sight theory is only mentioned in order to provide a contrast to the front-to-back theory. The author argues that the front-to-back theory is wrong. Presumably the field-of-sight theory does not share any of those errors. Otherwise the author would have said so. From the descriptions of the two theories, they seem very different.

———————

A. The only traditional desire is the one mentioned in lines 42-45: scientists want to separate observer and phenomenon. There's no mention of a traditional desire to simplify explanations.

B. **CORRECT.** Lines 21-25 show that the front-to-back theory is based on the false idea that mirror objects are 3-d. Since the author does *not* say the same thing about the field-of-sight theory, we can assume the field-of-sight theory does not make such an assumption. From the description in paragraph one, the left-to-right reversal in the field-of-sight theory doesn't depend on the belief that the mirror image is 3-d.

C. The *front-to-back* theory does not take into account what an observer sees (see the final paragraph). But this question is talking about the field-of-sight theory.

D. The field-of-sight theory is only mentioned in the first paragraph, and the first paragraph doesn't say that people fail to understand the reality of mirrors.

E. The field-of-sight theory is only mentioned in the first paragraph. The author appears to approve of it. They never say it is incorrect or unsuccessful.

Question 27

DISCUSSION: Read lines 34-41 to get the full picture. We look *at* objects. If you see an apple, you focus on it. But you look *into* landscapes. Think about what you see when you're on top of a hill, overlooking the land below. You look off into the distance, you are not focussed.

A mirror is an object. It's a flat surface. Yet we look *into* it, like we would any landscape. That's pretty amazing. I can't think of any other object that has this affect on us.

So lines 39-40 help illustrate what it means for mirrors to show us 3-d reality.

A. Lines 39-40 are talking about *seeing* objects in a mirror. They don't mention *imagining* objects.

B. Lines 39-40 don't mention mental constructs. This answer is designed to confuse you by mentioning an irrelevant concept from earlier in the passage.

C. **CORRECT.** See the explanation above. Knowing that we focus *into* mirrors helps us understand how they are like landscapes, not objects.

D. Mental constructs are mentioned in lines 28-30. They aren't relevant here. We when focus our eyes on the distance, that's a physical act in the real world, and not an image that we're constructing in our heads.

E. This is an oddly hallucinogenic answer. "If you are on drugs, then the chair will have a rounder shape than normal". Normally, our psychological states don't affect the shape of objects.

Appendix: LR Questions By Type

Strengthen

Preptest 67

Section II, #3
Section IV, #4

Preptest 68

Section II, #13
Section III, #7
Section III, #17

Preptest 69

Section I, #1
Section I, #13
Section IV, #23

Preptest 70

Section I, #3
Section I, #25
Section IV, #1
Section IV, #4

Preptest 71

Section I, #6
Section I, #12
Section III, #4
Section III, #8
Section III, #16
Section III, #25

Weaken

Preptest 67

Section II, #1
Section II, #17
Section IV, #6
Section IV, #10
Section IV, #24

Preptest 68

Section II, #4
Section III, #9

Preptest 69

Section I, #17
Section I, #22
Section IV, #7
Section IV, #19

Preptest 70

Section I, #16
Section IV, #12
Section IV, #19

Preptest 71

Section I, #13
Section III, #21

Sufficient Assumption

Preptest 67

Section IV, #13

Preptest 68

Section II, #23
Section III, #15

Preptest 69

Section I, #25
Section IV, #13
Section IV, #21

Preptest 70

Section I, #1
Section I, #7
Section IV, #22

Preptest 71

Section I, #1
Section III, #11
Section III, #14

Parallel Reasoning

Preptest 67

Section II, #19
Section IV, #19

Preptest 68

Section II, #9
Section III, #22

Preptest 69

Section IV, #10

Preptest 70

Section I, #19
Section IV, #17
Preptest 71

Section I, #14
Section III, #24

Flawed Parallel Reasoning

Preptest 67

Section II, #23
Section IV, #25

Preptest 68

Section II, #25
Section III, #24

Preptest 69

Section I, #14
Section IV, #14

Preptest 70

Section I, #10
Section IV, #23

Preptest 71

Section I, #23
Section III, #15

Necessary Assumption

Preptest 67

Section II, #6
Section II, #14
Section IV, #2
Section IV, #11
Section IV, #16
Section IV, #18

Preptest 68

Section II, #15
Section III, #18
Section III, #23

Preptest 69

Section I, #4
Section I, #7
Section I, #19
Section IV, #8

Preptest 70

Section I, #13
Section I, #21
Section IV, #6
Section IV, #10
Section IV, #20
Section IV, #25

Preptest 71

Section I, #16
Section I, #22
Section III, #19

Method Of Reasoning

Preptest 67

Section II, #12
Section IV, #12

Preptest 68

Section II, #26
Section III, #20

Preptest 69

Section I, #23
Section IV, #4

Preptest 70

Section IV, #8
Section IV, #26

Preptest 71

Section I, #2
Section I, #9

Must Be True

Preptest 67

Section IV, #17

Preptest 68

Section II, #1
Section II, #18
Section III, #4

Preptest 69

Section I, #21
Section IV, #20

Preptest 70

Section I, #8
Section I, #22
Section I, #24
Section IV, #14
Section IV, #21

Preptest 71

Section I, #17
Section III, #10

Most Strongly Supported

Preptest 67

Section II, #7
Section II, #11
Section IV, #5
Section IV, #15

Preptest 68

Section II, #8
Section II, #10
Section III, #2
Section III, #10
Section III, #13

Preptest 69

Section I, #10
Section I, #12
Section IV, #2
Section IV, #9

Preptest 70

Section IV, #2
Section IV, #18

Preptest 71

Section I, #8
Section I, #15
Section III, #17
Section III, #23

Paradox

Preptest 67

Section II, #2
Section II, #4
Section IV, #3
Section IV, #23

Preptest 68

Section II, #3
Section II, #6
Section III, #6
Section III, #14

Preptest 69

Section I, #15
Section IV, #5

Preptest 70

Section I, #5
Section I, #12
Section IV, #7
Section IV, #13

Preptest 71

Section I, #20
Section III, #3
Section III, #26

Principle

Preptest 67

Section II, #8
Section II, #15
Section II, #18
Section II, #25
Section IV, #7
Section IV, #8

Preptest 68

Section II, #5
Section II, #16
Section III, #1
Section III, #12

Preptest 69

Section I, #6
Section I, #8
Section I, #18
Section IV, #6
Section IV, #17

Preptest 70

Section I, #6
Section I, #14
Section I, #23
Section IV, #15

Preptest 71

Section I, #19
Section I, #25
Section III, #6
Section III, #9
Section III, #13
Section III, #22

Identify The Conclusion

Preptest 67

Section IV, #1

Preptest 68

Section II, #17
Section II, #19
Section III, #8
Section III, #11

Preptest 69

Section I, #9
Section IV, #1
Section IV, #24

Preptest 70

Section I, #18
Section IV, #16

Preptest 71

Section I, #5
Section I, #7
Section III, #12

Point At Issue

Preptest 67

Section II, #10
Section II, #16

Preptest 68

Section II, #21
Section III, #25

Preptest 70

Section I, #4

Preptest 71

Section I, #10
Section III, #2

Agreement

Preptest 69

Section I, #2
Section IV, #25

Preptest 70

Section IV, #5

Complete The Argument

Preptest 67

Section II, #5
Section II, #24
Section IV, #20

Preptest 68

Section III, #19

Preptest 69

Section I, #16

Preptest 71

Section I, #4
Section III, #5

Role in Argument

Preptest 67

Section II, #20
Section II, #22
Section IV, #22

Preptest 68

Section II, #11
Section II, #22

Preptest 69

Section I, #11
Section IV, #12

Preptest 70

Section I, #17
Section IV, #24

Preptest 71

Section I, #11

Argument Evaluation

Preptest 68

Section II, #2
Section II, #14

Preptest 69

Section I, #5

Preptest 70

Section I, #11

Flawed Reasoning

Preptest 67

Section II, #9
Section II, #13
Section II, #21
Section IV, #9
Section IV, #14
Section IV, #21

Preptest 68

Section II, #7
Section II, #12
Section II, #20
Section II, #24
Section III, #3
Section III, #5
Section III, #16
Section III, #21

Preptest 69

Section I, #3
Section I, #20
Section I, #24
Section IV, #3
Section IV, #11
Section IV, #15
Section IV, #16
Section IV, #18
Section IV, #22

Preptest 70

Section I, #2
Section I, #9
Section I, #15
Section I, #20
Section IV, #3
Section IV, #9
Section IV, #11

Preptest 71

Section I, #3
Section I, #18
Section I, #21
Section I, #24
Section III, #1
Section III, #7
Section III, #18
Section III, #20

Thank You

First of all, thank you for buying this book. Writing these explanations has been the most satisfying work I have ever done. I sincerely hope they have been helpful to you, and I wish you success on the LSAT and as a lawyer.

If you left an Amazon review, you get an extra special thank you! I truly appreciate it. You're helping others discover LSAT Hacks.

Thanks also to Anu Panil, who drew the diagrams for the logic games. Anu, thank you for making sense of the scribbles and scans I sent you. You are surely ready to master logic games after all the work you did.

Thanks to Alison Rayner, who helped me with the layout and designed the cover. If this book looks nice, she deserves credit. Alison caught many mistakes I would never have found by myself (any that remain are my own, of course).

Thanks to Ludovic Glorieux, who put up with me constantly asking him if a design change looked good or bad.

Finally, thanks to my parents, who remained broadly supportive despite me being crazy enough to leave law school to teach the LSAT. I love you guys.

About The Author

Graeme Blake lives in Montreal Canada. He first took the LSAT in June 2007, and scored a 177. It was love at first sight. He taught the LSAT for Testmasters for a couple of years before going to the University of Toronto for law school.

Upon discovering that law was not for him, Graeme began working as an independent LSAT tutor. He teaches LSAT courses in Montreal for Ivy Global and tutors students from all around the world using Skype.

He publishes a series of LSAT guides and explanations under the title LSAT Hacks. Versions of these explanations can be found at LSAT Blog, Cambridge LSAT, as well as amazon.com.

Graeme is also the moderator of www.reddit.com/r/LSAT, Reddit's LSAT forum. He worked for a time with 7Sage LSAT.

Graeme finds it unusual to write in the third person to describe himself, but he recognizes the importance of upholding publishing traditions. He wonders if many people read about the author pages.

You can find him at http://lsathacks.com and www.reddit.com/r/LSAT.

Graeme encourages you to get in touch by email, his address is graeme@lsathacks.com. Or you can call 514-612-1526. He's happy to hear feedback or give advice.

Further Reading

I hope you liked this book. If you did, I'd be very grateful if you took two minutes to review it on amazon. People judge a book by its reviews, and if you review this book you'll help other LSAT students discover it.

Ok, so you've written a review and want to know what to do next.

The most important LSAT books are the preptests themselves. Many students think they have to read every strategy guide under the sun, but you'll learn the most simply from doing real LSAT questions and analyzing your mistakes.

At the time of writing, there are 72 official LSATs. The most recent ones are best, but if you've got a while to study I recommend doing every test from 19 or from 29 onwards.

This series (LSAT Hacks) is a bit different from other LSAT prep books. This book is not a strategy guide.

Instead, my goal is to let you do what my own students get to do when they take lessons with me: review their work with the help of an expert.

These explanations show you a better way to approach questions, and exactly why answers are right or wrong.

If you found this book useful, here's the list of other books in the series:

(Note – the series was formerly titled "Hacking the LSAT" so the older books still have that title until I update them)

- Hacking The LSAT: Full Explanations For LSATs 29-38, Volume I
- Hacking The LSAT: Full Explanations For LSATs 29-38, Volume II
- LSAT 62 Explanations (Hacking the LSAT Series)
- LSAT 63 Explanations (Hacking the LSAT Series)
- LSAT 64 Explanations (Hacking The LSAT Series)
- LSAT 65 Explanations (Hacking The LSAT Series)
- LSAT 66 Explanations (Hacking The LSAT Series)
- LSAT 67 Explanations (Hacking The LSAT Series)
- LSAT 68 Explanations (Hacking The LSAT Series)
- LSAT 69 Explanations (Hacking The LSAT Series)
- LSAT 70 Explanations (Hacking The LSAT Series)
- LSAT 71 Explanations (Hacking The LSAT Series)
- LSAT 72 Explanations (LSAT Hacks)
- Explanations for 10 Actual, Official LSAT Preptests, Volume I: Preptests 62-66 (LSAT Hacks Series)
- Explanations for 10 Actual, Official LSAT Preptests, Volume II: Preptests 67-71 (LSAT Hacks Series)

Except for LSAT 72, the single volume books cover the same preptests that are covered in this book.

If you *are* looking for strategy guides, try Manhattan LSAT or Powerscore. Unlike other companies, they use real LSAT questions in their books.

I've written a longer piece on LSAT books on Reddit. It includes links to the best LSAT books and preptests. If you're serious about the LSAT and want the best materials, I strongly recommend you read it:

http://redd.it/uf4uh

(this is a shortlink that takes you to the correct page)

Free LSAT Email Course

This book is just the beginning. It teaches you how to solve individual questions, but it's not designed to give you overall strategies for each section.

There's so much to learn about the LSAT. As a start, I've made a free, five day email course. Each day I'll send you an email teaching you what I know about a subject.

LSAT Email Course Overview

- Intro to the LSAT
- Logical Reasoning
- Logic Games
- Reading Comprehension
- How to study

What people say about the free LSAT course

These have been awesome. More please!!! - **Cailie**

Your emails are tremendously helpful. - **Matt**

Thanks for the tips! They were very helpful, and even make you feel like you studied a bit. Great insight and would love more! - **Haj**

Sign up for the free LSAT email course here

http://lsathacks.com/email-course/

p.s. I've had people say this free email course is more useful than an entire Kaplan course they took. It's 100% free. Good luck - Graeme

CPSIA information can be obtained at www.ICGtesting.com
Printed in the USA
BVOW10s2152111115

426814BV00008B/33/P